THE GREAT WALL

In this 1667 engraving, the Jesuit priests Adam Schall (left) and Matteo Ricci (right) hold between them a map of East Asia, featuring an unbroken, uniformly crenellated Great Wall running across north China. It was during the late seventeenth century that, thanks to Jesuit accounts sent back from China to Europe, the myth of a single, ancient Great Wall began to take shape in the West.

THE GREAT WALL

China Against the World

1000 BC–AD 2000

Julia Lovell

VIKING
CANADA

VIKING CANADA

Published by the Penguin Group

Penguin Group (Canada), 90 Eglinton Avenue East, Suite 700, Toronto, Ontario,
    Canada M4P 2Y3 (a division of Pearson Penguin Canada Inc.)

Penguin Group (USA) Inc., 375 Hudson Street, New York, New York 10014, U.S.A.
Penguin Books Ltd, 80 Strand, London WC2R 0RL, England
Penguin Ireland, 25 St Stephen's Green, Dublin 2, Ireland (a division of Penguin Books
    Ltd)
Penguin Group (Australia), 250 Camberwell Road, Camberwell, Victoria 3124,
    Australia (a division of Pearson Australia Group Pty Ltd)
Penguin Books India Pvt Ltd, 11 Community Centre, Panchsheel Park, New Delhi –
    110 017, India
Penguin Group (NZ), cnr Airborne and Rosedale Roads, Albany, Auckland 1310, New
    Zealand (a division of Pearson New Zealand Ltd)
Penguin Books (South Africa) (Pty) Ltd, 24 Sturdee Avenue, Rosebank, Johannesburg
    2196, South Africa

Penguin Books Ltd, Registered Offices: 80 Strand, London WC2R 0RL, England

First published in Canada by Penguin Group (Canada), a division of Pearson Penguin
    Canada Inc., 2006
Simultaneously published in Great Britain by Atlantic Books, an imprint of Grove Atlantic
    Ltd., Ormond House, 26-27 Boswell Street, London WC1N 3JZ, 2006; and in the
    United States by Grove/Atlantic, Inc., 841 Broadway, New York, NY 10003, 2006

1 2 3 4 5 6 7 8 9 10

Copyright © Julia Lovell, 2006

Typeset by Avon DataSet Ltd, Bidford on Avon, Warwickshire B5O 4JH
Cartography by Jeff Edwards

Page xi constitutes the extension of this copyright page.

Manufactured in the U.S.A.

ISBN 0-670-06376-2

Library and Archives Canada Cataloguing in Publication data available upon request
British Library Cataloguing in Publication data available
American Library of Congress Cataloging in Publication data available

Visit the Penguin Group (Canada) website at **www.penguin.ca**

Special and corporate bulk purchase rates available; please see
    www.penguin.ca/corporatesales or call 1-800-399-6858, ext. 477 or 474.

To my parents

CONTENTS

CONTENTS

LIST OF MAPS AND
ILLUSTRATIONS

MAPS

ILLUSTRATIONS

Endpapers: an eighteenth-century Chinese depiction of the late Ming border wall in northeast China. *Lin yu xian zhi*, Vol. I (1929).

Frontispiece: Adam Schall and Matteo Ricci holding a map of East Asia. Athanasius Kircher, *China monumentis* (Amsterdam: 1667).

LIST OF MAPS AND ILLUSTRATIONS

First picture section

1. Ming border wall as depicted by Lieutenant Henry William Parish during the Macartney embassy of 1793. Sir George Staunton, *An authentic account of an embassy from the King of Great Britain to the Emperor of China...* (London: G. Nicol, 1797).
2. The wall built by the state of Zhao in Inner Mongolia, *c.*300 BC. Daniel Schwartz/Lookatonline.
3. A herder and his flock on the Mongolian grasslands. Roy Chapman Andrews, *Across Mongolian Plains* (London: D. Appleton & Co., 1921).
4. Ming Chinese sketch of Xiongnu barbarians. Wang Qi, *San cai tu hui*.
5. Qin Shihuang, the First Emperor and builder of the first Long Wall across north China. Qi, *San cai tu hui*.
6. Tamping work in Chinese wall-building. Guo Po, *Er ya yin tu* (1801).
7. Section of Han wall. M. Aurel Stein, *Ruins of Desert Cathay*, Vol. II (London: Macmillan, 1912).
8. Jin wall in Mongolia. Daniel Schwartz/Lookatonline.
9. Mongol soldiers in training. From the fourteenth-century Persian manuscript, *Jami al-Tawarikh* by Rashid ad-Din.
10. The Cloud Terrace. William Edgar Geil, *The Great Wall of China* (New York: Sturgis & Walton Company, 1909).

Second picture section

11. Ming sketch of kiln and carrying pole. Qi, *San cai tu hui*.
12. Partially restored Ming wall at Jinshanling, near Beijing.
13. Ming map of Border Garrisons. Qi, *San cai tu hui*.
14. Wall in Ordos country, northwest China. Geil, *The Great Wall of China*.
15. Section of Ming wall built across a village in northeast China. John Hedley, *Tramps in Dark Mongolia* (London: T. Fisher Unwin Ltd., 1910).
16. The First Pass Under Heaven at Shanhaiguan. Geil, *The Great Wall of China*.

17. Jiayuguan, northwest China. Stein, *Ruins of Desert Cathay*, Vol. II.
18. Li Yongfang surrenders. *Manzhou shilu*, Vol. I (Liaoning: 1930).

Third picture section

19. An impression of the imperial Chinese throne. Louis D. Le Comte, *Memoirs and Observations…* (London: Benj. Tooke, 1697).
20. Lord Macartney's audience with the Chinese emperor as depicted by Parish. Staunton, *An authentic account of an embassy from the King of Great Britain to the Emperor of China.…* .
21. Nineteenth-century German cartoon of imperialist Western armies gathering to storm the Chinese giant. Collection Claude Estier, *Histoire de la Chine en 1000 Images* (Paris: Cercle Européen du Livre, 1966).
22. The loess hills of northwest China. Harry Franck, *Wandering in China* (London: T. Fisher Unwin Ltd., 1924).
23. Chinese soldiers marching along the Great Wall, early 1937.
24. Richard Nixon at the restored Great Wall, Badaling, February 1972.
25. Ming wall near Beijing undergoing Communist restoration. Daniel Schwartz/Lookatonline.

The author and publishers are grateful to the following for permission to reproduce illustrations: endpapers, frontispiece, 1, 3, 4, 5, 6, 10, 11, 13, 14, 15, 16, 18, 19, 20, 22 by permission of the Syndics of Cambridge University Library; 2, 8, 25, courtesy Daniel Schwartz/Lookatonline, first published in *The Great Wall of China* (London: Thames and Hudson, 1990, rev. edn 2001); 7, 17, The British Library and the Clarendon Press; 9, Bibliothèque nationale de France; 12, Rosamund Macfarlane; 23, Getty Images; 24, © Bettmann/CORBIS.

ACKNOWLEDGEMENTS

Enormous thanks are due to the editorial team at Atlantic Books. First of all, to Toby Mundy and Angus Mackinnon, for giving me the idea for the book in the first place and for their patient encouragement as I meandered through the writing process; then, once more, to Angus for his exceptionally acute, scrupulous editing of the manuscript. I'm also extremely grateful to Clara Farmer and Bonnie Chiang, for their expert managing of the production process, and for the care and attention they have poured into the book; and to Lesley Levene, the book's extremely sharp-eyed copy editor. I owe profound thanks as well to my agents, Toby Eady and Jessica Woollard, for their help and encouragement throughout.

I was generously assisted at key moments by a number of scholars and academics: first and foremost, by Sally Church, who solved so many of my classical Chinese traumas, suggested maps and sources, and provided fantastically detailed and constructive criticism of the completed manuscript, thereby saving it from any number of errors. Frances Wood also gave the book an astonishingly precise and close reading, for which I am deeply grateful. Joe McDermott, Roel Sterckx and Hans van de Ven all patiently fielded a stream of inquiries from me about facts and sources, while Charles Aylmer, the exceptional librarian of the Chinese department at the Cambridge University Library, amazed me time and again with his encyclopaedic bibliographical knowledge of any area of Chinese history I asked him about. Ruth Scurr and Hannah Dawson gave me invaluable help and advice on the Enlightenment. Many thanks also to Chee Lay Tan, for help with poetry translations. All errors and short-comings that remain are of course my own.

The book was completed during a research fellowship held at Queens' College, Cambridge. Over the past two and a half years, I have benefited greatly from the relaxed, supportive research atmosphere of this college community.

But my largest debt is undoubtedly to my family: to my husband, Robert Macfarlane, for his meticulous readings and patient ruthlessness in hunting down faulty syntax and mixed metaphors (those that are left are exclusively my own doing); and to my mother, Thelma Lovell, for her own painstaking editing of the manuscript. Both my parents and parents-in-law generously provided invaluable hours of childcare to make time for writing. And in a broader sense, this book would never have been fin-ished without the endless support and encouragement – given in ways that are too numerous to mention – of my husband, parents, brother, sis-ter and parents-in-law; I am more grateful than I can say.

J. L.

NOTE ON ROMANIZATION
AND PRONUNCIATION

I have used the Pinyin system of Romanization throughout, except for a few spellings best known outside China in another form, such as Chiang Kai-shek (Jiang Jieshi in Pinyin).

In the Pinyin system, transliterated Chinese is pronounced as in English, apart from the following sounds:

VOWELS

a (when the only letter following most single consonants, except for t): *a* as in after

ai: *eye*

ao: *ow* as in cow

e: *uh*

ei: *ay* as in may

en: *en* as in happen

eng: *ung* as in lung

i (as the only letter following most consonants): *e* as in she

i (when following c, ch, s, sh, zh, z): *er* as in writer

ia: *yah*

ian: *yen*

ie: *yeah*

iu: *yo* as in yo-yo

o: *o* as in stork

ong: *oong*

ou: *o* as in so

u (when following most consonants): *oo* as in loot

u (when following j, q, x, y): *ü* as the German ü

ua: *wah*

uai: *why*

uan: *wu-an*

uang: *wu-ang*

ui: *way*

uo: *u-woah*

yan: *yen*

yi: *ee* as in feed

CONSONANTS

c: *ts* as in bits

g: *g* as in give

q: a slightly more aspirated version of *ch* as in choose

x: a slightly more sibilant version of *sh* as in sheep

z: *ds* as in woods

zh: *j* as in jump

NOTE ON NAMES

Chinese emperors generally made their way through at least three names within and after a single lifetime: the name they were given at birth; the name by which their reign period was known when they ascended the throne; and their posthumous temple name. Thus, before he became emperor, the founder of the Ming dynasty was called Zhu Yuanzhang; his reign period was known as Hongwu ('overwhelming military force'); after his death, he was referred to as Taizu ('great ancestor').

In general, as Chinese names can be complicated to remember, and to avoid confusing the reader, I have tried to minimize the number of names used to refer to each single individual. Where an individual is discussed after he comes to the throne, I have chosen to use the name by which he is known as emperor, for example Emperor Wu (the 'martial' emperor) of the Han. In the chapters about the Sui, Tang and Ming dynasties, as several of the rulers are discussed before they become emperor, I have initially used their personal names, then changed to use the names by which they or their reign periods were referred to after they became emperor.

In the chapters about the Ming dynasty, when discussing a particular emperor, in the interests of simplicity I have chosen to refer directly to the person by the name of his reign period. For example, after he becomes emperor, Zhu Yuanzhang should in all correctness be referred to as 'the Hongwu emperor' rather than simply as 'Hongwu'. In most cases, I have shortened his name to 'Hongwu' in order to avoid this longer, slightly more unwieldy usage.

When referring to the three most famous Qing emperors, I have, again for the sake of simplicity, directly used the names by which they are best known in Western scholarship, even though these are the names of their reign periods and not their personal names: Kangxi, Yongzheng and Qianlong.

Finally, in Chinese names, the surname is given first, followed by the given name. Therefore, in the case of Zhu Yuanzhang, Zhu is the surname and Yuanzhang the given name.

Although Chinggis is considered a more correct Romanization than Genghis Khan, I have used the latter in this book, as it is still the name by which the individual is most widely known.

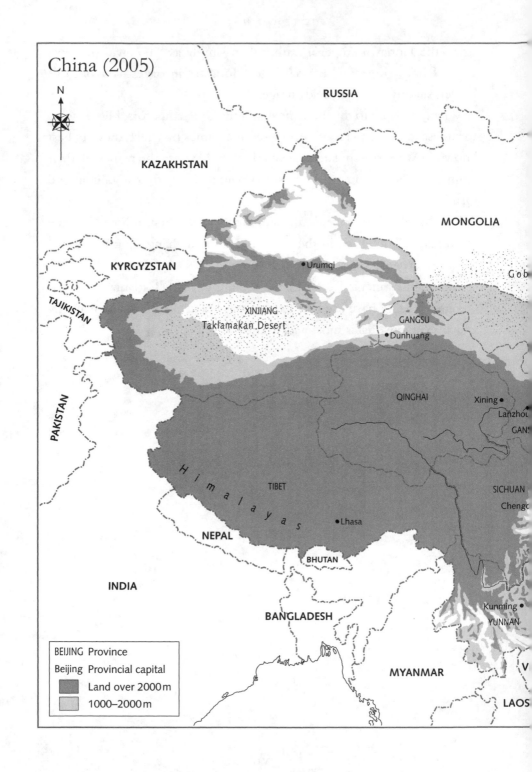

China (2005)

INTRODUCTION

Who Made the Great Wall of China?

On 26 September 1792, King George III dispatched the first British trade mission to China, a 700-strong party that included diplomats, businessmen, soldiers, scientists, painters, a watchmaker, a gardener, five German musicians, two Neapolitan Chinese priests and a hot-air-balloon pilot. Packed into three substantial ships, they brought with them the most impressive fruits of recent Western scientific progress – telescopes, clocks, barometers, airguns and, naturally, a hot-air balloon – all intended to dazzle the Chinese emperor, Qianlong, into opening trade with the West, by convincing him that he and his 313 million people needed Britain's technological marvels.

For the past decade, Britain had been running up a serious trade deficit with China: while the Chinese were quite happy to service the growing British tea addiction, they wanted nothing, except copious amounts of silver, in return. The few British merchants – employees of the East India Company – allowed to operate in China were contained in the city of Canton, as far away as possible from the political capital, Beijing. There, they were restricted to rat-infested warehouses and residences, denied all contact with the Chinese or instruction in their language, and forced to trade through local officials, who entertained themselves by extracting large customs duties from their foreign guests. Every level of the economic hierarchy, it seemed, was dedicated to cheating Westerners, from the provincial Superintendent of Maritime Customs down to local shop-keepers, who filled foreign sailors with perniciously strong liquor in order to 'rob them of what money they have about them'.[1] With East India Company profits in China failing to offset the costs of rule in India and British tea-drinkers pushing trade figures further into the red, Asia was rapidly becoming a British money sink.

It was in this potentially ruinous context that Henry Dundas, Home Secretary and former president of the East India Company, approached Lord Macartney, an experienced and canny diplomat, and asked him to lead the embassy to China. Macartney stated his terms for accepting the mission: £15,000 for every year he was out of Britain and an earldom. In exchange, Dundas stipulated, Macartney would spread the gospel of free trade, open new ports and new markets for Britain in China, establish a permanent embassy in Beijing and conduct industrial and military espionage. The deal was struck.

In June 1793, after nine months at sea and pauses in Rio de Janeiro and Madeira, where the ships' wine stocks were replenished, the British mission reached Macao, the Portuguese enclave off the southern coast of China whose tropical humidity daubed the island's buildings with green mould. For the next four months, the British and their extensive cargo crawled up the coast towards an audience with the emperor in his northern capital, Beijing. They were observed at all times by a suspicious imperial bureaucracy, which deluged the British party with hospitality – on one day alone, the British were provided with 200 items of poultry – while managing to avoid helping further the cause of the embassy in any material way. On finally completing their pilgrimage to Beijing, the British were told the emperor would only receive them even further north, at his summer retreat in cool, mountainous Jehol.

When the British – almost a year after leaving Portsmouth and with their accompanying band wearing loaned green and gold fancy dress already used at least once previously by a French embassy – were at last ushered into the celestial imperial presence on the occasion of His birthday and presented George III's written requests in a jewel-encrusted box, the emperor received them with no more than reserved cordiality. Perhaps because he had read too many excitable rumours about the British presents in the Chinese press, which speculated that the British had brought foot-high dwarfs and an elephant the size of a cat, the emperor was underwhelmed by the reality of telescopes, planetariums and carriages. The presents assembled by Dinwiddie, the embassy's astronomer, in the summer palace at Beijing, Qianlong commented, were useful merely for the amusement of children.[2] The only reaction provoked by a Parker lens was hilarity when a playful eunuch received a scorch after sticking out a finger under it. The spring-suspension coach the British brought, hoping to open the door to exports, was immediately deemed impossible for the emperor to use, on the grounds that Qianlong could never 'suffer any man to sit higher than himself, and to turn his back towards him'.[3]

Qianlong made his formal reply to British requests in a special edict presented to Macartney on 3 October but actually composed on 30 July, more than six weeks before the British had met the emperor and handed over their gifts. The mission, in other words, had been doomed long before it neared its destination. 'We have never valued ingenious articles,' Qianlong made clear, 'nor do we have the slightest need of your country's manufactures.'[4] He was true to his words: seventy years later, when British and French soldiers destroyed the imperial Summer Palace just outside Beijing, Macartney's presents were discovered, untouched, in a stable. It was, it would seem, members of the embassy who made most use of their technological wonders while in China: Macartney travelled to Jehol in a British coach, while Dinwiddie tested the range and precision of a telescope by focusing it on the pleasure boats and scantily clad sing-song girls of Suzhou, a canal city on China's east coast.

For all the trials the British tolerated to ingratiate themselves with the Chinese – suffering hours of Chinese theatre, being laughed at during public banquets for their ineptitude with chopsticks – the embassy failed in every single one of its objectives. Language was a substantial barrier. After the Neapolitan Chinese priests originally brought along as inter- preters had jumped ship at Macao, terrified of political retribution from the imperial court for having left China without authorization, the only member of the party who could speak a little Chinese – picked up from the escaped priests – was Thomas Staunton, the twelve-year-old son of Macartney's second-in-command, George Staunton. This left the embassy largely dependent on the translating efforts of Portuguese and French missionaries stationed at the Chinese court, whom Macartney respectively found 'false and crafty' and 'restless and intriguing'.[5] The impressive list of presents submitted to the emperor was rendered into gibberish: the planetarium, for example, was merely phonetically tran- scribed, then described for the emperor in flowery classical Chinese by court interpreters as a 'geographical and astronomical musical clock'.[6]

But the greatest stumbling block was that of diplomatic etiquette. Late Qing China was locked into the traditional Chinese vision of interna- tional relations, in which all foreigners were backward barbarians with little or nothing to offer Chinese civilization and whose rightful relation- ship with the imperial court was one of respectful subordination. According to idealized Chinese diplomatic conventions over one and a half millennia old, foreigners were (theoretically at least) allowed to visit China only as inferior vassals bringing tribute, not as political equals and certainly not as representatives of 'the most powerful nation of the globe' – as Macartney and the British confidently saw themselves.[7] Instead of a ministry of foreign affairs, Qing China possessed a (Tribute) Reception Department, fully equipped with a complex range of regula- tions governing the frequency, length, size and number of prostrations required of tributary envoys. The Chinese and the British would never be able to agree on terms for trade while they couldn't even agree on terms for each other's existence. To call the Sino-British encounter of 1793 a clash of civilizations is an overstatement: neither side found enough common diplomatic ground even to get within a whiff of a collision.

As a pragmatic envoy but also a proud Briton, Macartney spent weeks wrangling over diplomatic protocol. A particular sticking point was his refusal to perform the kowtow, the obligatory gesture of deference to the emperor: a set of three genuflections, each containing three full prostrations with the head touching the ground. Macartney was prepared to tip his hat, go down on one knee and even kiss the emperor's hand (this third option, horrified Chinese officials quickly made clear, was quite out of the question), but he would not kowtow unless a Chinese official of equal rank to him kneeled before a portrait of George III. This last proposal was even more inappropriate than hand-kissing: Qianlong was the ruler of 'all under heaven' (*tianxia*, a traditional Chinese usage for China) – his subjects could never admit the equal authority of another sovereign. The idea of China as the centre of the civilized world, to whom all other peoples owe allegiance, is one of the most resilient threads running through Chinese history. Even today, 160 years after the Opium Wars began forcing China out of the tributary system and into modern international trade and diplomacy, some Chinese historians still cannot believe that Macartney never kowtowed to the emperor.[8]

Chinese pressure on Macartney to submit to the kowtow started in August, a full six weeks before the British audience with Qianlong, and steadily intensified. The strategies of persuasion employed by the Chinese ranged from the ingeniously roundabout to the viscerally direct. In mid-August, officials conversationally observed to the ambassador that Chinese clothing was better than Western, 'on account of its not impeding or obstructing … genuflexions and prostrations … They therefore apprehended much inconvenience to us from our knee-buckles and garters, and hinted to us that it would be better to disencumber ourselves of them before we should go to Court.'[9] By the beginning of September, with no solution to British intransigence in sight, the emperor himself ordered a reduction in the rations offered to the British to 'persuade' them to comply with imperial ritual.[10] When Macartney and the mandarins were not arguing about the major issue of whether the British would kowtow to the emperor, they nitpicked over whether Macartney's offerings to Qianlong were 'presents' or 'tribute'. Macartney insisted they were presents from the ambassador of a diplomatic equal; just as firmly, Qianlong maintained that Macartney was no more than a subordinate 'conveyor of tribute'.[11]

Even if the British had submitted to Chinese protocol, however, it is far from certain they would have obtained anything more from Qianlong than they did (namely, a few auspiciously shaped lumps of jade, boxes of china and lengths of cloth, some of which appeared to be recycled items of tribute from Korean, Muslim and Burmese vassals). Two years later, a far more tractable Dutch embassy visited China whose members kow-towed at the drop of a hat, or rather a wig (the Dutch ambassador van Braam elicited hoots of Chinese laughter when his wig fell off as he kow-towed to the emperor on a frosty roadside). Although the truculently unbending British were, according to the mission's comptroller, John Barrow, given accommodation in Beijing 'fitter for hogs than for human creatures', the complaisant Dutch fared little better, housed in a stable, with carthorses for company.[12] True, the British embassy had their rations cut after the kowtow row heightened, but they at least were never insulted with meat on bones that looked to have been already gnawed, as were the Dutch, who speculated that they were perhaps the emperor's leftovers. The Dutch kowtowed on thirty separate occasions, often at unseasonable hours in freezing temperatures, without, a gloating Barrow noted, 'gain-ing ... one earthly thing' except for some 'little purses, flimsey silks, and a coarse stuff somewhat similar to that known by seamen under the name of bunting'.[13] Worse still, bored Chinese officials appear to have taken cynical advantage of Dutch willingness to kowtow to the imperial presence, making their visitors prostrate themselves in turn to some pas-try, a few raisins and a premasticated sheep's leg, on the grounds that they were gifts sent by the emperor himself.

After this spectacular diplomatic failure, it should come as no surprise that the travel memoirs of members of the British embassy were less

6

than complimentary towards China. *Travels in China* by Barrow, later founder of the Royal Geographical Society, strikes the typically peevish tone of the discontented Briton abroad. Chinese dramas were 'gross and vulgar', Chinese music 'an aggregation of harsh sounds', Chinese acrobatics disappointing: 'A boy climbed up a pole or bamboo 30 or 40 feet high, played several gambols, and balanced himself on the top of it in various attitudes,' he reported a curmudgeonly Macartney as commenting, 'but his performance fell far short of what I have often met with in India of the same kind.'[14] And as for sanitary facilities, 'There is not a water closet, nor a decent place of retirement in all China.'[15] Only one thing met with universal British approval: the Great Wall.

Macartney and his company made use of their lengthy waiting time in China to undertake a little tourism. En route in his neat English post-chaise to meet the emperor in Jehol, Macartney stopped at the Gubeikou pass north-east of Beijing to have a closer look at the wall. This is exhibition Great Wall country, providing the kind of vistas that had even the haughty British filling their journals with superlatives: walls and towers snaking over the spines of cloud-dappled mountains, brushed with green scrub in summer (as Macartney would have witnessed), dusted with snow in winter. Arriving at a breach in the construction, Macartney observed it to be of 'blueish coloured brick', twenty-six feet high, about five feet thick and strengthened by square towers built at 150- to 200-foot intervals. Altogether, he used up two whole pages of his journal (as it now stands in modern published form) precisely recording the depth of its foundations, the number of rows of bricks counted, the thickness of the mortar, and so on. 'It is carried on in a curvilinear direction often over the steepest highest and craggiest mountains as I observed in several places, and measures upwards of one thousand five hundred miles in length.' Staggered by what he saw, Macartney proclaimed the whole thing 'the most stupendous work of human hands'.[16] His fellow visitor Barrow, who clearly had too little to keep him otherwise occupied, racked his brains for spurious and unverified comparisons to evoke the grandiosity of the construction. The amount of stone in the wall, Barrow asserted, was equivalent to 'all the dwelling-houses of England and Scotland':

Nor are the projecting massy towers of stone and brick included in this calculation. These alone, supposing them to continue throughout at bow-shot distance, were calculated to contain as much masonry and brickwork as all London. To give another idea of the mass of matter in this stupendous fabric, it may be observed, that it is more than sufficient to surround the circumference of the earth on two of its great circles, with two walls, each six feet high and two feet thick![17]

Another member of the party, Lieutenant Henry William Parish, busied himself producing equally fanciful and romantic paintings of the wall festooning bosomy hills as far as the horizon stretched, interrupted by artistically ruined towers, their square stone edges becomingly frayed.[18] All the British tourists were unhesitatingly unanimous in dating the wall they saw as 2,000 years old; given the presence of small holes apparently designed for wall-mounted firearms, they marvelled at the early Chinese use of gunpowder, 'for all their writing agree that this wall was built above two hundred years before the Christian era'.[19] 'At the remote period of its building,' gushed Macartney in conclusion, 'China must have been not only a very powerful empire, but a very wise and virtuous nation, or at least to have had such foresight and such regard for posterity as to establish at once what was then thought a perpetual security for them against future invasion...'[20]

Macartney's visit marks a crucial episode in the modern history of both China and the Great Wall, his experiences and reactions helping to construct the view of the wall that is still widely, if erroneously, held today. Macartney encountered and identified two Great Walls: the physical, bricks-and-mortar version now familiar to millions of appreciative tourists, built in the sixteenth and seventeenth centuries AD, and the mental wall that the Chinese state had built around itself to repel foreign influences and to control and encircle the Chinese people within. His admiration for China's physical wall, together with his frustration at the mental wall, were to become typical of nineteenth-century Western politicians, merchants and adventurers eager to trade with China. Macartney and his fellow tourists helped begin the construction of the Great Wall of China as we now see it.

When the Chinese empire's disdain for trading with the West underwent very little change of its own accord in the half-century following Macartney's visit, Western resentment of the invisible wall erupted into gunboat diplomacy: the Opium Wars of 1840–42. By 1800, the British thought they had found a perfect solution to their tea-trade deficit, the ideal product to give China something to do with all its British silver: Indian opium. The Chinese government thought otherwise, banning opium in 1829 and, when drug-smuggling increased, dispatching a commissioner, Lin Zexu, to Canton to stop the illegal trade. After neither Chinese nor British merchants took any notice of his order to destroy opium stocks, he took action himself and flushed a year's supply of opium into the sea. The British retaliated by shelling Canton; war was declared. Forty-seven years after Macartney's failed approach, Sir Thomas Staunton, the son of his second-in-command – in 1793 a twelve-year-old whose fluency in Chinese had charmed the emperor into personally presenting him with a yellow silk purse from his own belt, in 1840 MP for Portsmouth – stood up in Parliament and argued for blowing open the gates to trade with China by force. The Opium War, he argued, 'is absolutely just and necessary under existing conditions'.[21]

The Chinese emperor was hubristically underprepared for the conflict, firmly believing that if Westerners were 'deprived of China's tea and rhubarb for a few days, they would suffer constipation and a loss of vision that would endanger their lives'.[22] In the event, despite the war's interruption of three years' tea-trading, the British remained sufficiently robust in health to bombard south China into submission, and to negotiate the Chinese out of 27 million silver dollars and Hong Kong. The Opium War was the prelude to further nineteenth-century acts of aggression against China in the name of free trade and openness: the sack of Beijing by French and English soldiers, the annexation of north China by the Russians, the cessation of the New Territories to Hong Kong.

Britain's gunboat diplomacy forcibly opened China's invisible Great Wall to a steady stream of visitors; they in turn produced a steady stream of travelogues with dewy-eyed paeans to the physical wall. By the turn of the century, the wall had been definitively labelled by Western observers as 'Great', as the 'most wonderful wonder of the world', built (extrapolating from a sketchy reference in a Chinese history of the second century BC) around 210 BC by China's First Emperor, and responsible for protecting China from the Huns and redirecting them instead towards the sacking of Rome.[23] Western enthusiasm made verifiable historical facts about the wall unnecessary: it was enough to assume, as Macartney and his fellow travellers did, that the wall as it presently stood was thousands of years old, a symbol of Chinese civilization, power and precocious technological accomplishment, overwhelmingly successful in intimidating unwanted intruders, uniform in its bricks-and-mortar course across the thousands of kilometres of China's fixed northern border, and so on and so forth. At the same time, the invisible Great Wall encircling the Chinese, and determined to exclude Macartney and his barometers, was identified as the cause of the empire's isolationist stagnation, emblematic of autocratic, landlocked China's lack of interest in maritime trade and conquest, of its failure to keep step with historical progress as defined by the Western colonial powers. Between the eighteenth and twentieth centuries, the colossal physical reality of the wall combined with its powerful visual symbolism to transform the Great Wall into the all-defining emblem of China in the Western imagination.

The mythology of the Great Wall continued to grow ever more extravagantly throughout the twentieth century. In 1932, decades before the era of rocket science, the millionaire cartoonist, writer and sinophile Robert Ripley popularized the claim – first non-empirically advanced in 1893 – that the wall was the only man-made structure visible from the moon.[24]

Although this conjecture was confirmed by Neil Armstrong, his observation was later shown by *Geographical Magazine* to be just a cloud formation.[25] Nevertheless, the notion survived into the twenty-first century, endlessly cited by Chinese patriots, copy-hungry journalists and guidebook and school textbook writers. Joseph Needham, in his monumental history of Chinese science and engineering, *Science and Civilisation in China* (begun in the 1950s), took the whole idea one hyperbolic step further when he remarked that the wall 'has been considered the only work of man which could be picked out by Martian astronomers' – whoever they might be.[26]

Great Wall propaganda was given a further boost by Mao Zedong's 1935 rallying cry to his Communist revolutionaries (at the time harried into an isolated corner of north-west China by the right-wing government), 'You're not a real man if you've not got to the Great Wall,' now to be found on T-shirts, sunhats and other souvenir paraphernalia sold at the wall's tourist hot-spots. Mind-boggling and often unverifiable statistics bewilder contemporary wall-watchers and walkers at every turn: how it stretches over 6,000 kilometres, how the sections surviving today would link New York and Los Angeles, how the bricks used to build it could more than encircle the earth if reassembled into a wall five metres high and one metre thick, and on they go. In 1972, on an excursion to the wall during his breakthrough diplomatic mission to the People's Republic of China, Richard Nixon proclaimed, to Western audiences fascinated by the spectacle of America's staunchly anti-Communist president fraternizing behind the Bamboo Curtain, 'This is a great wall and it had to be built by a great people.'[27] (Dissatisfied Communist journalists later took the liberty of embroidering his enthusiasm into: 'This is a Great Wall and only a great people with a great past could have a great wall and such a great people with such a great wall will surely have a great future.'[28]) In the wall's post-Mao tourist heyday, millions have followed in Nixon's footsteps, also finding unanimously for the greatness of China's pre-eminent architectural attraction. (Virtually the only foreigners in recent history to prove impervious to the wall's charms were members of the West Bromwich Albion football team, who in 1978, as the first professional English team to visit China after its opening up to the West, declined the offer of a sightseeing trip up north: 'When you've seen one wall,' they explained, 'you've seen them all.'[29])

For centuries, impressionable Western visitors were so busy charging up the wall, breathlessly calculating how many of their own capital cities they could build out of it, or debating its visibility to extraterrestrials, that they failed to reflect on one anomalous fact: that until recent decades the Chinese themselves had been largely uninterested in their great work. Macartney noted in passing that, while he and his party diligently counted the bricks in the wall, their mandarin guides 'appeared rather uneasy and impatient at the length of our stay upon it. They were astonished at our curiosity ... Wang and Chou, though they had passed it twenty times before, had never visited it but once and few of the other attending Mandarins had ever visited it at all.'[30]

Chinese indifference only started to warm into increasingly ardent enthusiasm some seventy years ago, in the strictly instrumental interests of satisfying a clearly perceived need in modern China: to provide an emblem of China's past historical greatness to carry its sense of national self-esteem through the lean years of the twentieth century, through its failed revolutions, civil wars, foreign invasions, famines and crushingly widespread poverty. Taking its cue, predominantly, from Western wall-worship, the modern Chinese view of the Great Wall has adopted a similar, joyfully careless approach to historical precision. Modern and contemporary Chinese, menaced at most stages of the past hundred years by violent political upheaval and/or foreign aggression, have unthinkingly embraced the potent visual symbolism of the Great Wall in north-east China, seeing, in its overbearing physical presence near China's old frontier, an embodiment of ancient China's precocious sense of itself as an advanced civilization, and of the indomitable, enduring Chinese will to define and protect, with a hard-and-fast frontier, that same culture from alien incursions. 'The Great Wall,' a 1994 Chinese encyclopedia sets out in a brief, introductory English blurb, 'magnificent and solid as it is in both body and soul, symbolizes the great strength of the Chinese nation. Any invaders from outside will be defeated completely when confronting with this great force [sic].'[31]

To most Chinese, the wall's antiquity and efficacy are not historical hypotheses to be tested and investigated, but rather truths to be accepted and venerated. Visiting the parts of the Great Wall accessible at tourist sites north and north-east of Beijing can be a dispiritingly ahistorical experience. On being asked when or how, exactly, one of these stretches of perfectly restored brick wall, flawless apart from the occasional splotch of Communist cement, came to be built, the average ticket-checker will eye the questioner with a combination of pity and distrust – imagining, perhaps, that he or she is trying to be funny – before listlessly reciting the familiar, two-millennia-old story about the First Emperor. Until the first Chinese space flight in 2003, Chinese school textbooks ran happily with the myth that the wall was one of two man-made structures – the other being a Dutch sea embankment – visible from the moon. Only when Yang Liwei, the astronaut of the 2003 expedition, returned, embarrassingly announcing that he had been unable to spot a single crenellation, was the Chinese Ministry of Education sheepishly moved to excise the fallacy as 'a disadvantage to the real knowledge acquired by our elementary school students'.[32]

This brief concession to factual investigation notwithstanding, the wall – in its modern guise as national symbol – has in general become so detached from its verifiable historical reality that it now serves as a free-floating symbol for whichever trait of the Chinese nation, or even of humanity in general, requires illustration at any one moment. 'The Great Wall possesses the character of the Chinese nation,' one scholar has hypothesized. 'It also possesses the general nature of all human beings.' 'The Great Wall,' another wall theorist has projected, 'is not only to be understood as a barrier, but also as a river uniting people of various ethnic background and providing them with a common haven and meeting place.' Luo Zhewen, vice-president of the Chinese Great Wall Society, has transformed the wall into the ultimate multipurpose historical mascot, declaring that it is simultaneously a product of feudal society and an inspiration for 'the Chinese people to forge ahead on the road of constructing socialism with Chinese characteristics'; that it created the first unified, centralized Chinese nation *and* helped build a multinational China. To contemporary China's agile thinkers, the wall is both uniquely national and straightforwardly global; promotes both self-sufficiency and internationalism; propped up feudalism and currently fosters its arch-enemy, socialism; repelled invaders and built friendship across the steppe; defined a single, monolithic China and made it multicultural. Forget Great: Super Wall seems nearer the mark. The Great Wall, one commentator – abandoning any pretence at historical sophistry altogether – states plainly, 'is a world miracle. I'm not blowing my own trumpet, just because I'm Chinese. Reasoning and common sense will tell anybody in any country that this is the fact of the matter.'[33]

Up to a certain point, this light-headedly rhapsodic acclaim is perfectly understandable: the wall is, undeniably, an impressive achievement, particularly given its builders' lack of modern construction technology, extending several thousand kilometres, east to west, across difficult, at times shatteringly bleak terrain: over the scrubby mountains, raw brown plains, friable, fudge-coloured hills, sandy oases and extreme climatic zones of northern China and Inner Mongolia. The historical notoriety of the attackers it was built to repel – in particular, the Mongol hordes under Genghis Khan – has further intensified the sense of drama in which evocative images of Great Wall topography are draped. But the wall fever of the last one or two centuries has also swallowed rather too much propaganda, and obliterated from view huge swathes of a less than glorious past. The generally rapturous attention paid to the wall by tourists, politicians, patriots and Martian astronomers is no more than a recent, unrepresentative, mythologizing blip in millennia of Chinese history. For much of the 2,000 years that it has existed in some form across the north of China, the wall has been in turn irrelevant, ignored, criticized, scorned and abandoned, both physically, as a defensive construction, and figuratively, as an idea.

The first great myth of the Great Wall is its singularity, that the term meaningfully refers to one ancient structure with a coherently chronicled past. In contrast to the popular prestige and renown the wall has recently enjoyed, references to the Chinese term now universally translated as 'Great Wall', *Changcheng,* in pre-modern sources are scattered and inconclusive. Originally used in the first century BC to refer to walls built in the previous two centuries, the term rarely crops up between the end of the Han (206 BC–AD 220) and beginning of the Ming (1368–1644) dynasties. Frontier walls are instead referred to by a confusing variety of terms: *yuan* (rampart), *sai* (frontier), *zhang* (barrier), *bian zhen* or *bian qiang* (border garrison or border wall). The impressive stone Great Wall north of Beijing now visited by millions of tourists every year is not thousands of years old; it dates back about 500 years, to the building efforts of the Ming dynasty. And even the major part of this relatively youthful rampart is now derelict and distinctly uninviting to casual hikers. Its handful of tidy, showcase passes – for example, Badaling, two hours' bus ride north of the capital – were only restored and manicured in the second half of the twentieth century by Communist labour. Although from as far back as the first millennium BC many kingdoms and dynasties built walls in various parts of north China and Mongolia, most of these have now disappeared, leaving no more than sandcastle-like remains cut out of the powdery loess terrain of north-western China, or mossy, mounded seams bulging out of the ground like hairy scar tissue. At points, in its northernmost stretches, where the pebbly, patchily grassed desert is frosted in winter, the wall is now so low as to become practically imperceptible without the help of a little light underscoring from dusty snow drifted up against one side. Over the millennia of recorded Chinese history, these barriers were seldom identified as *Changcheng.*

There is, thus, no single Great Wall, but instead many lesser walls.

A second modern misconception about the Chinese wall, and about walls in general, is that they mark a hard and fast boundary between nations and cultures, and often between civilization and barbarism. The fondness of the Romans and ancient Chinese for building fixed frontiers tends to encourage the misapprehension that the past was a mass of foreign countries, all with precisely demarcated borders. But the history of Chinese wall-building gives no clear sense of a bricks-and-mortar frontier maintaining Chinese within and barbarian northerners without. While vast differences existed between, for example, the Chinese and the Mongolian nomads north of the Great Wall line, it was not the case that border walls absolutely and immovably separated a culture of rice, silk and poetry on the one side from a culture of horse milk, pelts and war on the other. The Chinese empire is often seen as arrogantly exclusive and excluding, strong on a sense of its own self-sufficient superiority, weak on openness and external influences. This view entirely overlooks the importance of the foreign factor in Chinese history: through great stretches of its past, China has been ruled either by emperors and generals in love with the culture of the northern steppe – cavalry, yurts, tunics, polo – or by northern tribes and their descendants. The frontier, and the wall-building line, fluctuated with every dynasty: many of China's non-Chinese rulers themselves built fortifications as protection against other northerners, once they had established control over China and become sinicized in the process.

A third contemporary, and quite natural, misapprehension about the Great Wall is that it is, and has always been, Great. This springs, as much as anything, from a linguistic inaccuracy. Chinese frontier walls very definitely gained something in translation: *Changcheng,* the Chinese term (only sporadically used before the twentieth century) that has been rendered into English as 'Great Wall' literally means only 'Long Wall' – not too shabby, admittedly, but lacking in the bombastic overtones of 'Great'. This has fuelled entirely unsubstantiated, Nixon-esque assumptions that a Great Wall must have a Great Past, along with a Great People, Future and the rest. Quite the contrary: over its 2,000-year history, Chinese wall-building was not invariably a symbol of national strength and prestige. It was often adopted as a defensive frontier strategy after all other options for dealing with the barbarians – diplomacy, trade, punitive military expeditions – had been exhausted or discarded. It was a sign of military weakness, diplomatic failure and political paralysis, and a bankrupting policy that led to the downfall of several once robust dynasties. (The Chinese expression for 'sitting on the fence' translates literally as 'riding the wall'.) Wall-building was in general an unpopular choice because it was associated with defeat and political collapse, with short-lived imperial houses such as the brutal Qin (221–206 BC) – the first regime to erect a more or less continuous barrier across northern China – or the Sui (581–618). And the Great Wall simply hasn't worked that well as a barrier to protect China from marauding barbarians. Ever since walls were first built across Chinese frontiers, they have provided no more than a temporary advantage over determined raiders and pillagers.

When Genghis Khan and his Mongol hordes conquered China in the thirteenth century AD, frontier walls proved little obstacle. The Great Wall offered no protection to the greatest wall-builders of all, the Ming dynasty, from their most threatening adversaries, the Manchus of the north-east, who ruled China as the Qing dynasty from 1644. Invaders could make detours around strong defences until they found weaknesses and gaps or, less effortfully, simply bribe Chinese officials to open the Great Wall forts. When the Manchus decided to make their final move on Beijing in 1644, they were let through a Great Wall pass by a disaffected Chinese general. As Genghis Khan apocryphally put it, 'The strength of walls depends on the courage of those who guard them.'

In order to go beyond the contemporary Great Wall myth and to uncover something approaching its historical reality, to avoid the anachronistic imprecision of the single, awestruck term 'Great Wall' that was blankly imposed on China's frontier defences by Western observers from the seventeenth century onwards, use of this expression here will be suspended until it is coined in a later chapter by early modern foreign visitors. Until this point in the book, in describing and differentiating the border fortifications built by successive dynasties, I have tried to use the names employed by contemporary or near-contemporary Chinese sources. Where *Changcheng,* the contemporary Chinese phrase for 'Great Wall', appears in a pre-modern context, without the later overtones of Western wall-worship, I have used the literal, matter-of-fact translation 'Long Wall'.

That the Chinese wall's less than glorious past has been obscured by later historical romantics is no great cause for surprise. Perhaps because frontier walls originally cost so much time and money to build, those subsequently left responsible for their upkeep have often found it painful to denounce them as a strategically useless waste (provided, of course, that they weren't associated with a broadly hated ideology and regime, as the Berlin Wall was). Apologists for the Maginot Line – the hugely elaborate system of reinforced underground bunkers and tunnels along the Belgian border which created one of the twentieth century's greatest defensive fiascos – proudly point out that even though over-concentration of resources on the Line exposed France to invasion elsewhere, even though the Germans easily circumvented the Line, entering France through Belgium, Holland and the Ardennes Massif, even though France was defeated and occupied as a result, the Line itself was never taken by force and the troops manning it only surrendered voluntarily (albeit under duress from a Nazi encirclement). Even if it didn't manage to defend France, even if it utterly missed the point of its own existence, the rehabilitating logic goes, the Maginot Line managed to defend *something* – itself – perfectly well. Similarly, memory of the Great Wall's historical failings – its bribable gatekeepers, its gaps that simply let the nomads through, the fact that parts of it were still being built even as Beijing was falling to the Manchus in 1644 – has been thoroughly suppressed by contemporary panegyrics to its length, breadth and general Greatness. Appearances, it would seem, count for more than performance.

Our readiness to swallow Great Wall propaganda springs also from our own historical context. In the contemporary West, where occupation and invasion are, at present, happily the stuff of millennia past, wall-building seems a quaintly old-fashioned idea, suitable for private and domestic use – excluding draughts and holding up skirting boards, say – but not much else. Ours, we like to think, is an age of globalization, defined not by obstacles or barriers, but by free-flows – of transport, trade, finance and information – through porous national boundaries. Our battles are now rarely fought on anything as archaic as the ground, or on fortifications. Wars, our governments seem to think, are best conducted from the air or at a distance: remotely controlled laser-guided bombs or cruise missiles are the weapons of choice. With the recent notable exception of the invasion of Iraq, for Western powers, committing ground troops in the long term to zones of conflict is a potentially vote-losing last resort. Walls and barriers are monuments of a lost, pre-1989 world, when life was sufficiently slow-moving and ground-based to make static walls useful, when there were enough institutionalized super-ideologies (capitalism, Communism, German expansionism) to require the erection of clear-cut barriers. History, in any case, has made a mockery of any government or individual foolish enough to erect defensive walls in the twentieth century: think again of Germany's humiliating bypass of the Maginot Line in 1940, or the joyful destruction of the Berlin Wall fifty years later.

And now that virtually no national frontier – barring anomalies such as North Korea – is impervious to the universal spread of global culture, of Coca-Cola and Nike (or Mike, as the name is spelt by its Chinese pirates), a clear dividing line between barbarism and civilization no longer seems to exist, and it is no longer necessary to build walls to divide those who can behave from those who can't. The soft-focus indulgence towards the Great Wall of China and willingness to ignore its serious failures stem, at least partly, from a sense that defensive walls are little more than relics of the past, souvenir-generating tourist spectacles devoid of any contemporary relevance. Walls make us think of an olde worlde divided by castles, moats, gatehouses, drawbridges; no one, the unspoken assumption goes, could possibly be so naïve as to waste money on building anything as concrete as walled frontiers now.

Humans, however, never tire of fighting over land, and wherever there are territorial disputes, walls tend to follow. The Chinese through history may have been rather more wall-conscious than most peoples, but the wall-building impulse is a fairly universal human one, shared by all the ancient civilizations – Rome, Egypt, Assyria. And it is an impulse that has, in fact, survived the twentieth century, the close of the Cold War and the apparent End of History. In 1980, Morocco began building and maintaining more than 2,000 kilometres of sandy wall in the middle of the Western Sahara, in an effort to police formerly Spanish territory it had seized and occupied in the decolonializing meltdown that followed the death of Franco in 1975. Since 2002, Israel has been constructing a 'defensive' wall 'designed to block the passage of terrorists, weapons and explosives into the state of Israel' between the Occupied Territories and the main area of Israeli territory. Simply calling this a wall makes it sound more benign than it is. This is not a wall in the common-or-garden stone or brick sense, but a barrier that stretches for several hundred kilometres, averages 70 metres in width, is constructed mainly out of concrete and incorporates barbed wire, electric fencing, ditches, trace paths, tank patrol lanes and buffer and no-go zones on either side.

Apart from reminding us that walls remain a favoured recourse of empire-builders everywhere, these two contemporary barriers illuminate an often forgotten aim of wall-building: offence, rather than defence. Walls are generally viewed as an inward, protective measure, as opposed to the outward, aggressive strategy of campaigns and raids. To a significant degree, Chinese pride in the Great Wall is based on the assumption that, as a military strategy, it occupies the moral high ground by being protective rather than aggressive in intent; that it expresses China's fundamentally peace-loving, non-confrontational, non-imperialist, non-acquisitive nature. (Still today, the Chinese self-image is overwhelmingly preoccupied with the idea that China's foreign policy has been exclusively defensive, fighting against and not initiating foreign invasion; its occupation of an independent Tibet in 1950 is but one notable blind-spot among many.) 'Because the Chinese people are peaceful by temperament,' one Chinese scholar has reasoned, 'for thousands of years one dynasty after another gave the world the miracle that is the Great Wall.'[34]

The purpose of walls, however, depends entirely on where you build them. Walling off permanently settled territory, such as cities or farming land, from, say, pastoral nomad raiders, is incontrovertibly defensive in intent. But neither Morocco nor Israel has built their walls anywhere near enough their own states to make them remotely meaningful as defences: the Moroccan wall is in the middle of the Sahara, and 90 per cent of the Israeli fence veers acquisitively off the Green Line border between Israel and the Occupied Territories, and into Palestine territory. The finished wall is expected to cut off 15 per cent of the West Bank and 200,000 Palestinians from the main bloc of Palestinian West Bank settlements. Small wonder, then, that both walls have been denounced by inhabitants of the areas they encroach upon and by international human rights organizations as walls of 'occupation', of 'shame and torture'. The rationale of ancient Chinese border walls can also be reviewed in this light: recent interpretations of the Great Wall's purpose hold that it was designed to protect peace-loving Chinese farmers and their civilized cities from wicked, marauding barbarians. But walls built as early as the first millennium BC swing far out into the Mongolian steppe and into the salty deserts of north-western China, hundreds of kilometres from farmable land. These walls look less land-protecting than land-grabbing, designed to enable the Chinese to police peoples whose way of life differed from their own, and to control lucrative trade routes.

The frontier zone between north China and what lay beyond – Manchuria, Mongolia, the deserts of Xinjiang – has often served as the theatre for aggressive Chinese imperialism, and a glance across millennia of Chinese frontier policy decisively undermines the grand theory of the

Great Wall as a monument to China's peaceful, live-and-let-live spirit. Throughout most dynasties and most periods in Chinese history, the language of Chinese frontier policy and command asserts an unsubtly belligerent xenophobia and sense of cultural superiority: frontier officers are given titles such as the 'General Who Smashes the Caitiffs', and their fortified strongholds dubbed the 'Tower for Suppressing the North' or the 'Fort for Suppressing the Border'. The original title of one pass in the north-west, the 'Fort Where Barbarians Are Killed' *(Shahubao),* was eventually, even by imperial Chinese standards, considered politically incorrect and the ideogram for barbarian, *hu,* replaced by a homophone meaning 'tiger'.[35] Even roof tiles found in sites near China's northern frontier stridently informed passers-by that 'All aliens submit'.[36]

Nonetheless, although China's frontier walls have not historically been everything that is now ascribed to the Great Wall, and although the generally adulatory modern fiction of a Great Wall obscures much of the complexity of the Chinese past, the wall and the thinking that lies behind it should not be thrown out like a piece of ahistorical jetsam. As a strategy that has survived for more than two millennia, China's frontier wall is a monumental metaphor for reading China and its history, for defining a culture and a worldview that has succeeded in fascinating and absorbing almost all of its neighbours and conquerors. In the opening pages of *Bad Elements,* his odyssey through the Chinese pro-democracy movement, Ian Buruma immediately seizes upon the Great Wall to illustrate the 'problem of China': its rulers' enduring preoccupation with controlling 'an enclosed, secretive, autarchic universe, a walled kingdom in the middle of the world'. To Buruma, the Great Wall, with its double implication of protection and oppression, stands for the political culture of secrecy and proud cultural isolationism that has propped up millennia of Chinese autocracy, and that continues to sustain the present Communist government and to resist the idea of democracy on the grounds that an open, democratic system would bring chaos and disunity to the rigidity of Chinese tradition. Most countries, he points out, have their modern national architectural emblems that project outwards the image with which they wish to be associated in the international imagination: France has its modernist icon, the Eiffel Tower; Great Britain the Houses of Parliament, a monument to democracy. China, not coincidentally, has the Great Wall, a ruinously expensive encirclement built to exclude and to oppress – and currently acclaimed as a wonder of national heritage.[37]

But the Great Wall sums up a worldview that is both more complex and fluid, and less swaggeringly triumphant than the strident visual symbolism of the structure now identified as the Great Wall suggests: one that reveals the hinges and shifts within the long continuities of Chinese history, the importance of foreign influences despite periodic attempts by China to exclude them, and that also proffers a window on to China's sense of itself and of the outside world (and vice versa). Once the layers of myth have been peeled away, the wall is, in fact, a perfectly serviceable emblem by which to read China; the devil, inevitably, is in the historical detail.

This book will look behind the modern mythology of the Great Wall and of Chinese wall-building, uncovering a 3,000-year history far more fragmented and less straightforwardly illustrious than its crowds of visitors imagine today. The story of the wall winds through that of the Chinese state and of the frontier policy that defined it, through the lives of the millions of individuals who supported, criticized, built and attacked it. Now acclaimed as a symbol of Chinese self-definition, of cultural greatness, of the technical genius and fortitude required to build it, the wall has also carried a range of far more negative connotations: of the bleakness of the frontier, thousands of kilometres from the centre of Chinese civilization; of the suffering and sacrifice of its builders; of costly colonial expansionism and of suffocating cultural conservatism; of the control and repression of those kept within. It is time to see the wall less as it is now – a great tourist attraction, an impressive piece of construction engineering on a now meaningless frontier – and more as it has been throughout its history.

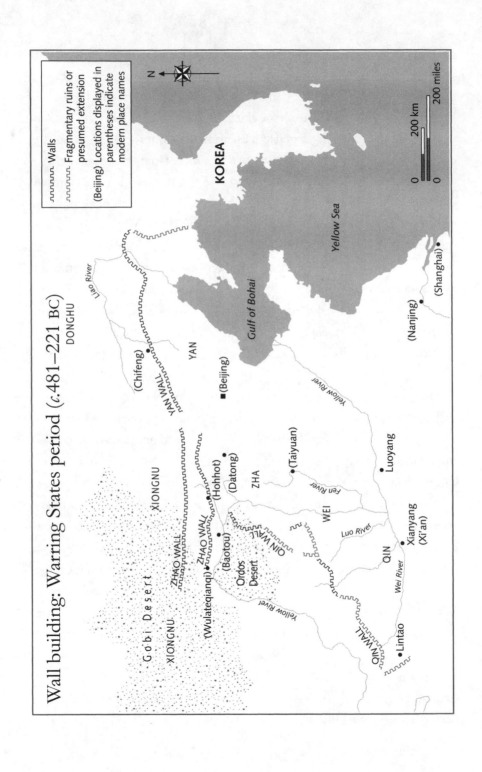

Wall building: Warring States period (c.481–221 BC)

CHAPTER ONE

Why Walls?

'Walls, walls, and yet again walls, form the framework of every Chinese city,' wrote the Swedish art historian Osvald Sirèn in the 1930s.

They surround it, they divide it into lots and compounds, they mark more than any other structures the basic features of the Chinese communities ... there is no such thing as a city without a wall. It would be just as inconceivable as a house without a roof ... There is hardly a village of any age or size in northern China which has not at least a mud wall, or remnants of a wall.[1]

The Chinese love of enclosing walls is written deep into the language itself. The earliest versions (roughly 1200 BC) of the ideograms for 'settlement' and 'defence' represent walled compounds; both concepts were clearly unthinkable without four-sided enclosures. Later classical Chinese used the same word for city and city wall: *cheng*. The character meaning 'capital city' (pronounced *jing*) was originally a picture of a guardhouse over a city gate.[2]

Wall-building and the written language have intertwined to define Chinese civilization both physically and figuratively ever since it came into existence, dividing and distinguishing China's peoples and settlements from their less settled, less literate neighbours to the north. To understand the millennia-old Chinese impulse to wall-building, to understand the conflict that created the wall, we need to trace the origins of these two incompatibly different, geographically adjoining cultures: that of agrarian, self-confidently literate, walled China and that of the pastoral nomadic tribes of the Mongolian steppe.

~

Some fifteen years ago, as soon as the Chinese Communist Party had attended to its most pressing tasks in the aftermath of its crackdown on the Tiananmen pro-democracy protesters – clearing civilian bodies from the streets, issuing a most-wanted list and rounding up those activists who had not managed to smuggle themselves out of the country – it turned its thoughts to political re-education. Once, Party leaders correctly surmised, the guns of the People's Liberation Army had been turned on the People themselves, Communist principles alone would not suffice to persuade the Chinese of the legitimacy of autocratic socialist rule. Searching for a new, state-sponsored religion around which the country could rally, the Party hit upon a fairly old-fashioned version of an old-fashioned idea: anti-foreign nationalism fuelled by angry suspicion of a West determined, as the Chinese masses were persistently lectured, to contain a rising China.

In order to convince their subjects – who, between 1989 and 1991, had seen Communist states expire across Europe – that open, Western-style democracy was fundamentally unsuited to one-party socialist China, the Communists set about proving, through an energetic countrywide campaign of patriotic education, that China possessed a unique 'national condition' (*guoqing*) as yet unready for democracy. Chinese history, or a particular view of that history, quickly became one of the most important weapons in the Party's armoury of patriotic propaganda: the proposition that the Communists were simply the inheritors of a tried and tested model of the unified, authoritarian Chinese nation supposedly established 5,000 years ago – a date that coincides roughly with the period attributed to the reign of the Yellow Emperor, China's mythical founding ancestor, said to have ruled early in the third millennium BC. (In 1994, a

26

member of the Politburo demonstrated his respectful belief in his legendary precursor by laying flowers and planting a tree at a memorial ceremony in his honour.) Capitalizing on a long-held, though hazy, Chinese public pride in the antiquity of their state, the Communist patriotic education campaign transformed the idea that the Chinese nation leapt, fully formed, into existence thousands of years ago into a cliché spouted tirelessly by agents of the Chinese Politburo, by a number of opportunistic academics and by lazy tour guides, to bludgeon anyone listening – Chinese or foreign – into believing that this is how China always was; and evermore shall be (until the Communists say differently).[3]

And, in the way of all great propaganda, it isn't true; not least because the Yellow Emperor was quite possibly the invention of a collection of power-hungry aristocrats in 450 BC. There are, in fact, strong grounds for arguing that the Chinese nation was born as recently as 100 years ago when, cast violently into the modern system of international relations that the West had constructed in its own image, seeing their country invaded by foreign powers, torn apart by internal rebellion, stymied by a reactionary, decadent dynasty and hidebound by a two-millennia-old educational and ethical system that wanted little to do with Western science and the modern world, Chinese thinkers and politicians embraced the idea of nationalist revival to rescue their country from the threat of imminent collapse. Before then, the Chinese did not even possess a single, universal term for 'China'; at any one time, the country was generally referred to by the name of the dynasty in power.[4] Although indisputably powerful and enduring across millennia, the idea of the Chinese empire was much looser and vaguer than the rigidities of modern nationalism – with its textbooks, museums and store-cupboard ancestors – allow, a concept broadly defined by slow processes of social, economic, political and cultural evolution that began some 10,000 years ago. The fixity of a single, unified, 5,000-year-old China is a twentieth-century fiction.

But thanks to archaeological discoveries of the last century, we can at least draw up an approximate timeline for the prehistoric cultural developments and innovations from which a recognizably Chinese empire would eventually arise. Farming – the crucial underpinning of the Chinese way of life – began in the northern provinces of the country around 8000 BC. Visitors today might not imagine the crumbly yellow plains of Shanxi and Shaanxi a particularly hospitable environment for novice farmers, but the lightly forested and easily worked loess soils of north China, irrigated by the lower Yellow River, encouraged the pursuit of a primitive agriculture as early as 10,000 years ago, a time when southern China remained an unmanageable jungle.

The shift towards agriculture directed Chinese society along a more fixed evolutionary path. Long-term security in farming depended on large-scale water control, which in turn required ever more sophisticated forms of social and political organization. Not surprisingly, then, one of China's favourite ancient legendary heroes – all of whom are venerated for contributing to prehistoric China a key technical, political or cultural innovation (fire, writing, medicine and so on) – is Yu, a self-taught hydraulic engineer and builder of flood channels thought to have lived near the start of the second millennium BC. By 2000 BC, farmers in northern China were leaving behind relics of an increasingly complex civilization: ambitious and extravagant bronze vessels, bells and weapons, bones used for divination, traces of large-scale building works and burial pits. This already was a highly ritualized society capable of organizing labour for massive public projects, such as construction and mining.

Chinese civilization emerges into the written record only in the thirteenth century BC, thanks to Wang Yirong, a nineteenth-century epigraphist and civil servant whose sharp eyes made one of the most sensational discoveries of modern Chinese archaeology. In 1899, as a malaria epidemic raged through Beijing, one of the reputedly more effective and more popular cures peddled to panicked, sickening residents was soup made of ground-up dragon bones. Given the scarcity of the medicine's chief ingredient in *fin-de-siècle* Beijing, pharmacists anxious to make supply meet demand passed cattle scapulas and turtle shells off as dismantled dragons, ready for pulverization. When a relative brought one of these bones home, Wang Yirong spotted mysterious scratches on its surface, looked closer and identified them as ancient Chinese characters. He lost no time in buying up the pharmacist's entire supply, thereby saving the earliest-known versions of Chinese writing from destruction. The inscribed bones were next traced back to their source in Anyang, a town in central China, where commercially minded peasants had dug them out of the ground and sold them to city apothecaries. The farmers, too, had spotted the scratches on them but, afraid they would lower their value as medicine, had rubbed many of them off; the bones that Wang chanced upon were a lucky exception.

The Anyang scapulas and shells – the oldest of which were dated back to around 1200 BC – became known as 'oracle bones', used for divination by the Shang, the first historically verifiable dynasty to rule parts of China (between approximately 1700 and 1025 BC). The Shang king would formulate a positive or negative hypothesis to which he wanted a yes-or-no confirmation (such as 'Today it will not rain'), the bones would be heated and the cracks caused by the heat examined and interpreted by shamans, with the original hypothesis, and sometimes the prognosis and answer, inscribed alongside on the bone.[5] Together with other discoveries from Anyang – ornate bronzes, burial pits, jade artefacts – the oracle bones afford insights into a society three and a half millennia old whose fundamental concerns and beliefs have shaped Chinese society ever since.

Although the Shang kingdom bore little geographical resemblance to the country now known as China (the political core of the Shang was located in Henan and Shandong – central and north-eastern China), the cultural, political and social similarities are remarkable. Shang society was centralized, stratified and agricultural, ruled by a single king who, through his administrative staff, extracted agricultural surpluses from his subject peasants and set them to work on vast public projects, such as royal tombs and military campaigns. It was a highly ritualized culture, which constantly sought the approval of ancestors and heavenly powers through sacrifice and divination. Describing the outcome of a consort's pregnancy, one oracle bone also tells us that, like many Chinese today, the Shang preferred boys to girls: 'She gave birth. It really was not good. It was a girl.'[6] The Shang even ate like modern Chinese, serving their rice separately from their meat and vegetables.[7]

But most importantly of all, the Shang used the same script as later Chinese. The awkwardness of scratching ideograms on to bones dictated an elliptical conciseness of expression that defined literary Chinese until 1921, when the wordy vernacular replaced spare classical Chinese as the official written language. It is hard to overestimate the importance of a shared writing system in forging Chinese identity through the millennia: although hundreds of mutually incomprehensible dialects are spoken across China and the global Chinese diaspora, all use the same written characters. Give literate Chinese from opposite ends of the country or globe a pen or brush, and they can communicate. Still today, Chinese across a broad range of social strata – academics, barmen, janitors and taxi drivers – unite in taking a fierce pride in their three-millennia-old literary tradition that has no contemporary analogue in most Western countries, comparing unfavourably the 'simple, superficial languages of the West' with the infinite subtlety and complexity of written Chinese.

Much, of course, was to change in China over the next 3,000 years – not least dynasties and frontiers. In 1025 BC, less than two centuries after the first extant inscribed oracle bone, the Shang were conquered by the Zhou dynasty, the royal house that would nominally claim to command the loyalty, until 256 BC, of the handful of kingdoms north of the Yangtze River whose culture could be recognizably identified as Chinese. But the basic elements of Chinese civilization – elements that Confucius, China's pre-eminent philosopher, would make the foundation of his own political and social worldview more than 500 years later – were already in place: a nexus of patriarchal custom and political organization held together by the tremendous ritual power of the written Chinese language.

And as soon as there was a coherent Chinese culture and society, there was wall-building: within and without villages, towns and cities. Today, the Chinese love of walls is no longer as immediately visible to the casual observer as it once was. A twentieth century of revolutions, wars and Communism has turned hundreds of miles of Chinese walls into just so much rubble, one of the most egregious instances of wilful destruction being Mao Zedong's replacement of the old Beijing city wall in the 1950s with a ringroad. But earlier Chinese settlements were a mass of walls, and the very earliest have been unearthed in excavations around the Longshan district of Shandong, north-east China, dating from the third millennium BC. The most impressive surviving wall from the second millennium BC (c. 1500 BC) encircles the Shang city of Ao, north of modern Zhengzhou in Henan for about seven kilometres, and is still more than nine metres high in places. It was during these two millennia that the fundamental technique of Chinese wall construction – still in use in the Ming heyday of wall-building – was learned: tamping. Planks of wood or courses of bricks were erected to create the outer shell, between which common-or-garden earth was pounded down to form the core of the wall. As they were constructed mainly from materials already on site, tamped-earth walls had the great advantage of being fast and cheap to erect – crucial considerations for a civilization that would come to build as many walls as the Chinese empire.[8]

~

While people living in northern China were gradually becoming Chinese, writing characters, worshipping ancestors and building walls, the north of their kingdom remained immovably bordered by land – present-day Central Asia, Mongolia and northern Manchuria – whose ecology did not encourage intensive farming or rigid social organization. It was these areas that produced the nomadic tribesmen – identified variously in China and the West as the Rong, the Di, the Xiongnu, the Mongols, the

Manchus and the Huns – who would worry at the Chinese frontier and motivate wall-building for the next two and a half millennia.

But until the end of the second millennium BC, the contrast in way of life between northern China and the areas further north was probably not all that dramatic, as the land often morphed only slowly from farmable loess plain into steppe and desert. Until then, the Chinese frontier regions were host not to terrifying hordes of nomadic warriors but to peaceable, relatively settled tribes, who lived off a combination of scratch farming and animal husbandry. To the north-west, via occasionally fertile Turkestan (now Gansu and Xinjiang), over the tall, thickly glaciated Tianshan mountains, China merged into the deserts and steppes of the Jungaria and Tarim basins, around whose oases primitive but sedentary herders domesticated animals. To the north-east, the rivers of lower Manchuria supported a Chinese-style agriculture, before arable land faded out further north into steppe territory more favourable to hunting and fishing. Directly north of contemporary Beijing, a range of forested mountains drew a clearer line between China proper and the Gobi desert and Mongolia, with the ecology of these latter regions far less mixed than that of the frontier zones to the far east and west. But on the western side of central northern China, the landscape blurred into steppe through the Ordos, a region delineated and irrigated by the northern loop of the Yellow River that lent itself to both agrarian and pastoral nomadic ways of life.

Around 1500 BC, however, climate change dried out the vast Mongolian plateau (2.7 million square kilometres) into the grassy steppes of the Gobi desert. This, together with a general tendency towards increased specialization in means of livelihood, decisively shifted the focus of life there from the sedentary and agricultural to the pastoral and nomadic – a world apart from tightly governed and densely populated and farmed north China. Unable themselves to feed directly off badly irrigated grasslands, Mongolians turned them over to pasturing herds (in particular, horses and sheep) and hunting. This change required extra mobility, as feeding grounds became seasonally depleted, and exceptional horse-handling skills, to control animals set loose to pasture. The nomadic inhabitants of the steppe rode the stocky, enduring Przhevalski pony, armed themselves with a small, light bow that was ideal for use on horseback and lived mostly off their herds. They recycled their animals ingeniously, into food, clothing and other daily essentials, but there were some things – principally grain, metal and desirable luxury goods such as silk – that could be obtained only from their southern, Chinese neigh-bours, either through mutual agreement (trade) or force (raiding and pillaging).

At the start of the first millennium BC, peaceful coexistence between these two ways of life – the settled agrarian and nomadic pastoral – began to appear increasingly untenable. The key theatre of conflict (and, in centuries to come, of wall-building) between settled and nomadic peoples was the Ordos, sandwiched between the steppe proper and the plains of China. The region was explored by an American geographer called George B. Cressey in the 1920s, a decade of profound internal disorder in China. His visits coincided with the heyday of the regional warlord, a period in which local power and loyalties changed course as easily as the desert sands he was charting. More than once Cressey found himself beaten back in his investigations by disorganized soldiers, at one point being forced into retreat by an approaching gang of 200 bandits (this despite his own thirty-six-strong cavalry escort). During more peaceful interludes, however, Cressey had the leisure to find the greater part of the area 'an arid desolate plain … an inhospitable waste' of climatic extremes (reaching 100 degrees Fahrenheit in summer, minus 40 in winter) covered in '[s]hifting sands held here and there by low scrub or wiry grass … where nature offers but little to man, and yields that little grudgingly'.[9] Almost everywhere, Cressey found, 'the surface of the Ordos is … composed of shifting sands … brownish ochre in color … From the mulling over of the shifting sands, quantities of finer particles are lifted into the air', thus filling the air with a characteristic 'yellow haze' carried out of the Ordos and scattered over adjoining regions 'as though dropped from a giant flour sifter'.[10] Out of fifty-eight summer days spent in the Ordos, Cressey experienced rain on only five, reporting that, in any case, the 'air can be so thirsty any rain evaporates before reaching the ground'.[11] But in other parts, particularly in low basins or where ground water lurks close to the surface, Cressey noted, 'natural vegetation ... nearly carpets the ground. Short grasses afford some feed for animals and make this area better for nomad and farmer.'[12] The Ordos was strategically all-important precisely because of its frontier position between two types of society, and because it contained both pastoral and farming land; it thus offered an economic base for domination of the steppe by either nomads or Chinese.

The first major clashes mentioned in the Chinese sources date from the ninth century BC, when poems record that a northern tribe, the Xianyun, attacked the very heart of the Zhou dominion, the capital in north-west China (just east of present-day Xi'an):

> In the sixth month all was bustle and excitement.
> The war-chariots had been made ready...
> The Xianyun were in blazing force,
> There was no time to lose.
> The king had ordered the expedition
> To deliver the royal kingdom.[13]

On one campaign, the Zhou forces emphatically 'smote the Xianyun / And achieved great merit / ... We smote the Xianyun / As far as the Great Plain.'[14] But neither was there any long-term safety in numbers: 'We shall have no leisure to rest / Because of the Xianyun ... Yes, we must be always on our guard,' the poem warns, 'the Xianyun are furious in attack.'[15] The speed attributed to the enemy assault suggests that this may be the first historical appearance of the fleet, horse-mounted nomad warriors who would harass the Chinese frontier for millennia to come. What had suddenly gone so badly wrong in a relationship that, theoretically at least, could have been peacefully regulated for the next

3,000 years by trade and diplomacy, rather than by bankrupting wars and walls?

Because the Chinese have always been better at writing things down than the nomads, it is their version of events that has dominated views of the conflict between the settled and nomadic populations. In the Chinese sources, the nomads are always portrayed as the greedy, aggressive hordes who descended in terrifying raids on the peace-loving Chinese. Chinese sources are full of hostile descriptions of rapacious barbarian nomads from the north as 'birds and beasts', 'wolves to whom no indulgence should be given'.[16] These inhuman specimens were 'covetous for gain, human-faced but animal-hearted', living in 'swamps and saline wastes, unfit for human habitation'.[17] The Chinese belief that their non-Chinese neighbours were no better than animals seeped deep into the written language: the characters for the tribes north (the Di) and south (the Man) of the central loess plain contain ideogram radicals depicting dogs and worms respectively. The northern tribes, sniffed one Chinese commentary of the seventh century BC, were tone-deaf, colourblind, treacherous fiends – in other words, deeply uncivilized.[18]

The Chinese are far from alone in their horror of nomads. Ever since the Scythians, the horse-mounted destroyers of the Assyrian empire, rocked the classical world early in the first millennium BC, Western Europe has worked every bit as hard as the Chinese to demonize the horseback 'barbarians' at its borders: the Huns ('they could easily be called the most terrible of all warriors' – Ammianus Marcellinus, c. AD 390); the Avars (their 'life is war' – Theodoros Synkellus, c. 626); the Hungarian Tatars ('who live like wild beasts rather than like human beings' – Abbott Regino, c. 889).[19] True, the burning and pillaging unleashed throughout thirteenth-century Asia and Europe by Genghis Khan, the most famous nomad in world history, has hardly been a good advertisement for the peace-loving qualities of the Mongolian steppe-dwellers. Equally, a certain tendency towards aggression is inseparable from nomadism and its unsettled, peripatetic way of life. Indeed, over the centuries, warfare and military discipline became such an integral part of existence for nomadic tribes in Inner Asia that neither Turkic nor Mongolian languages developed separate, native terms for soldier, war or peace.[20] (Pre-modern Chinese records, by contrast, had at their disposal seven different terms for border raids.[21])

All the same, we should not accept at face value the Chinese characterization of their northern neighbours as insatiably violent, barbarian invaders. Chinese prejudices against the northerners sprang directly from a stridently Sino-centric worldview that, like the idea of China itself, came into being during the second and first millennia BC. As Chinese geographical orthodoxy had it, China – the full extent of the world as it was then known to its inhabitants – was divided into concentric zones: the inner were ruled directly by the Chinese king, the outer were occupied by subordinate barbarians. Although the belief that China occupied the centre of the civilized world was not fully refined and institutionalized until the Han dynasty (206 BC–AD 220), as early as the Shang the Chinese state began devising the diplomatic protocol that dominated Chinese foreign relations until the nineteenth century: the tribute system, which defined all outer zones as subject vassals owing homage to the Chinese ruler. The idea that the world revolves around China persists today in the Chinese language, whose word for China, *Zhongguo,* literally translates as 'the middle kingdom'.

China's high cultural self-esteem resulted in a knee-jerk tendency to view the non-Chinese northern tribes as politically and socially inferior, as barely human and certainly not as worthy trade partners or targets of diplomacy. And if Chinese rulers were too contemptuous of the nomads to consider dealing or trading with them, the nomads were left little choice but to extract the goods they needed through raiding.

There is also much evidence to suggest that, until the first millennium BC, Chinese states did more than just snub their northern neighbours; that the inhabitants of the frontier territories were more often targets of Chinese aggression than aggressors themselves. Until about 1000 BC, the archaeological remains of the peoples living around the Great Wall zone do not appear particularly warlike. Archaeologists have uncovered traces of a pastoral, sheep-rearing culture, quite civilized enough to leave behind painted pottery, ritual vessels and jade. Graves unearthed in Central Asia contain no weapons: life was clearly not so violently uncertain that it was considered necessary to give the dead man weapons for his passage to the next world.[22] Under the Shang, the northern barbarians seem to have suffered far more at the hands of the Chinese than vice versa. The Shang were constantly at war with the frontier, non-Chinese people they called the Qiang, hunting, capturing and disposing of them as human sacrifices (up to 500 at a time) and slaves.[23]

China, in fact, has a far more impressive record of conquest and expansion than its nomadic neighbours. From its original heartland in present-day north China, the Chinese imperium spread to colonize the jungle-covered south of the country. The history of much of the area south of the Yangtze River between the first millennia BC and AD is one of an aboriginal land being colonized by Han Chinese from the northern provinces of the country. Nomadic tribes, by contrast, have less often had ambitions of conquest; those nomadic warriors who came to rule substantial parts of China were the exception rather than the rule. The annexation of China by the most notorious of them, the Mongols under Genghis Khan and his descendants, was more the consequence of an over-extended plundering expedition than of a calculated imperialist schema.

But whichever side was the primary aggressor – northern tribes greedy for Chinese goods or Chinese greedy for foreign vassals – it was clear that China's rulers and armies were unable either to defeat the northerners militarily or to contemplate compromise or negotiation. And so, in the ninth century BC, according to a poem of two centuries later, the Chinese first turned to a policy that would remain a comforting, albeit counter-productive, last resort for the next 2,000 years: wall-building.

The King charged [his general] Nan Zhong

To go and build a wall in the region.

How numerous were his chariots!

How splendid his dragon, his tortoise and serpent flags!

The Son of Heaven had charged us

To build a wall in that northern region,

Awe-inspiring was Nan Zhong;

The Xianyun were sure to be swept away![24]

Fighting talk, but also famous last words: although the kingdom of Zhou nominally survived until 256 BC, continued depredations from the north (by the Xianyun, the Rong and the Di tribes) drove the Zhou out of their north-western capital in 771 BC and effectively brought about the collapse of Zhou as an effective ruling house around this time. The invaders were helped by the fecklessness of the Zhou king, who sometimes entertained himself and his favourite queen by lighting the capital's beacon towers – built to summon the barons to the capital in the event of barbarian attack – and enjoying the look on their panicked faces when they rushed to the palace and found not a barbarian in sight. When the barbarians finally did come, of course, the barons took no notice of the beacons, thinking they were just another practical joke, and stayed at home, no doubt grumbling about their monarch's sense of humour, while the capital was sacked. The lesson of this first failed set of fortifications was, however, entirely lost on the Chinese, who continued to build bigger, more expensive but ultimately futile walls for the next 2,000 years.

After the decline of Zhou, the Chinese empire was split into a collection of smaller states, the largest of which – Qin to the west, Wei, Zhao and Yan to the north and north-east, and Chu to the south – jostled among each other for supremacy all the way up to and throughout the Warring States period (c. 481–221 BC), so called for the condition of almost permanent war existing between kingdoms. When the Chinese states were not fighting each other, they were contending with escalating attacks by their northern neighbours. The most serious of these was the near-destruction of Wei in 660 BC by the Di tribe, in which the Wei army was almost totally wiped out and the capital devastated, leaving only 730 survivors. The Chinese fought back vigorously and brutally – in one instance, a force of non-Chinese northerners was bludgeoned to death with copper ladles – weakening the Di and Rong by a combination of means both fair and foul: false surrenders, intriguing between non-Chinese ministers and rulers, and breaking treaties whenever convenient.[25]

But the Chinese were in the end victims of their own success. Although troublesome, the Di and the Rong – now thought to have been predominantly farming shepherds or mountain-dwellers – had provided a usefully inhabited barrier (in contemporary Shanxi, Shaanxi and Hebei) between northern China and Mongolia, insulating China from purely nomadic tribes further north. The Chinese destruction of the Di and the Rong around the middle of the millennium erased this buffer zone and brought the Chinese into direct contact with horse-riding warriors of the Mongolian steppe proper, at a time when the tenor of life on the steppe was becoming ever more nomadic and warlike. In the seventh century BC, Central Asian warriors began to be buried with their horses and weapons; in one grave, archaeologists found the bronze tip of an arrow still buried in the knee of a skeleton.[26]

The strategic imperatives that came with the new proximity of the nomads – for whom a new term, *Hu,* was coined in the Chinese sources in 457 BC – had two major consequences for the Chinese way of life: the introduction of nomadic fighting techniques (and nomadic fighters themselves) into the Chinese repertoire of warfare and the construction of the greatest walls that China had thus far seen.

In 307 BC – in the middle of the Warring States period – King Wuling of the northern state of Zhao started a court debate about fashion: should upper garments be buttoned to the left or down the middle?

Behind this seemingly frivolous and innocuous question of style lay a strategic issue of huge political and cultural significance. King Wuling planned to swap the traditional Chinese gown for the side-buttoning tunic of the nomads, and the aristocratic Chinese chariot for their mounted archers. Contained within this mooted change of dress was a revolution in worldview: an acceptance of the military superiority of the nomads and of the need to fight them on their own terms. 'I propose,' proclaimed King Wuling, 'to adopt the horseman's clothing of the Hu nomads and will teach my people their mounted archery – and how the world will talk!'

The king's culturally conservative advisers were vehemently opposed to abandoning the high ground of Chinese culture: 'I have heard the Middle Kingdoms described as the home of all wisdom and learning,' the king's uncle preached, 'the place where all things needful to life are found, where saints and sages taught, where humanity and justice prevail ... But now the king would discard all this and wear the habit of foreign regions. Let him think carefully, for he is changing the teachings of our ancients, turning from the ways of former times, going counter to the desires of his people, offending scholars, and ceasing to be part of the Middle Kingdoms.' Nonetheless, pragmatism and political and military necessity won out: as Fei Yi, the king's wily adviser pointed out, 'who scruples much achieves little'. Zhao was surrounded by dangerous enemies: by the state of Yan and the Hu barbarians to the north, by Qin to the west. Mounted archers, Wuling chided his relative, were essential to warding off invasion and defeat: 'My uncle strains so at the gnat of departure from custom in clothing, yet he is swallowing the elephant of his country's disgraces.' Thus swatting aside his critics, the king 'thereafter, in barbarian garments, led his horsemen against the Hu ... reached the midst of the Hu and opened a thousand *li* of territory.'[27]

However distasteful and humiliating it felt, acknowledging and adapting to the cultural and military reality of the northern frontier had become crucial to the survival of Chinese states. Despite opposition from traditionalists, swift, mounted archers soon outmoded the chariot-based warfare of the old Zhou aristocracy. And it was the states that adapted fastest to the new methods which emerged victorious in the inter-state wars that racked the second half of the millennium. Zhao's innovation was copied so successfully by the north-western state of Qin that it in fact managed to crush Zhao around 260 BC. The elimination of Zhao, Qin's most threatening political rival, cleared the way for the conquest of the rest of China in 221 BC, a reunification that established the model of Chinese political unity that lasts up to the present day.

King Wuling's cultural pragmatism did not stop the individual states from continuing to favour a more traditionally Chinese solution to frontier problems: wall-building. From the middle of the seventh century BC, the states of Qin, Wei, Zhao, Yan, Chu and Qi began building up a lattice of walls all over China, some in the very heart of the mainland, to counter external threats – both from other states and from the steppe. Wall-building became so popular that even the non-Chinese northerners themselves began to follow this quaintly Chinese vogue: some time after 453 BC, the Yiju barbarians of the Ordos area built a double wall in self-defence against the northernmost Chinese states, and against Qin in particular.[28]

But the walls that most concern us here are those built to protect the northern frontier: the Qin, Zhao and Yan walls, all undertaken at approximately the same historical moment – the close of the fourth century BC. The Qin wall went up in the north-west amidst a frenzy of sexual diplomacy and double-crossing. During the reign of King Zhaoxiang (306–251 BC), the dowager queen Xuan seduced and had two sons by the king of the Yiju barbarians. Unencumbered by sentiment, she later 'deceived and murdered him at the Palace of Sweet Springs and eventually raised an army and sent it to attack and ravage the lands of the Yiju'.[29] This bout of Qin conquest seized land spanning from Gansu in the far north-west to the east of the Ordos region in the Yellow River loop; to protect its new gains, Qin 'built long walls to act as a defence against the barbarians'.[30]

During the reign of King Zhao (311–279 BC), the state of Yan expanded to the north-east, towards the area that came to be known later as Manchuria, drove the Eastern Hu back 'a thousand *li*' and 'built a long wall ... in order to resist the nomads'.[31] The kingdom of Zhao, under the direction of the cavalry-loving King Wuling (325–299 BC), also built a double, roughly parallel set of walls: a shorter rampart north-west of Beijing, then a slightly longer wall driving further north into Mongolia.

The engineering technology for the building of these early walls had not changed much since the tamped-earth method developed in the second and third millennia BC. Although not as durable as brick constructions, some of these walls survive in fragmentary form today: in Henan, low-lying ramparts of closely packed stone and earth mark the frontier line that divided the great southern state of Chu from its northern neighbours; in Shandong, a dotted line of rubble snakes across a stubbly hillside; in Shaanxi, only overgrown earthy mounds bristling with scrubby trees and grass, six metres high and eight metres wide in places, remain of the wall erected futilely by the Wei to defend themselves from the aggressive Qin. Ruins of the Zhao wall rising up alongside a road in Inner Mongolia are at first glance barely distinguishable from local contours, until closer inspection reveals their tightly packed man-made layers. Differentiating the Yan wall, in contemporary Hebei, from the grassy ground that lies either side and has long since reclaimed the surface of the heaped earth ramparts can be a similarly challenging task.

These walls made use of natural resources wherever possible, following the defensive contours of the land – precipices, ravines and narrow gullies. One possible reason why the remains of, say, the Qin wall, which meander 1,755 kilometres across north-west China up to Inner Mongolia, are so fragmentary is that they never formed a continuous line: across mountainous areas, which offered natural defensive advantages, all that was needed by way of man-made structures may have been the occasional lookout post or short stretch of wall to block a pass. The Qin wall's path follows the relief lines of the region, its twists and turns dictated by the need to keep to more easily defended, higher ground. Where the land was flatter, lacking natural obstacles, and artifice was required to impede invaders, ramparts were constructed of pounded earth and stones, wherever possible on sloping terrain, to raise the inner side above the outer. Both regularly and irregularly spaced mounds – three to four every kilometre – have been discovered scattered along surviving walls: perhaps platforms, towers and lookout posts. Inside the wall, archaeologists have found stone enclosures sometimes ten thousand metres square, presumably citadels and forts, and traces of nearby roads, hinting at the huge military presence and logistical effort required to man and supply the thousands of kilometers of Warring States walls.[32]

Given that the sources claim the main motive for wall-building was to 'guard against' or 'resist the barbarians', the curious thing about these northern walls is how remote most of them are from farmable land, and how close to the steppe proper – in some cases, far inside present-day Mongolia. (South of the boundary marked by the Yan walls, for example, archaeologists have turned up assuredly non-Chinese artefacts – horse fittings, animal-style ornamental plaques – that belong to the earliest pastoral nomadic cultures found in northern China and Mongolia.) Indeed, the position of these walls gives the sense that they were designed not to defend China but to occupy foreign territory, to drive the nomadic inhabitants out of their land and to facilitate the setting up of military posts that would police the movement of people across these areas.[33] King Wuling's pioneering use of cavalry had made the Chinese reluctantly dependent on the nomads for horses. The only way of escaping this humiliating reliance on trade with the despised northerners was, presumably, to invade and control their areas of production.

None of this elevates the nomads to the status of innocent victims in the millennia-old conflict between China and the steppe, but it does at least suggest we should slightly rethink the way in which they have been demonized for thousands of years in both China and the West. Traditionally, the Chinese are always the wronged parties, terrorized by the evil Huns north of the Great Wall line. But if the first frontier walls, the precursors to 2,000 more years of hostility and wall-building between China and the steppe, were designed to expand, not defend, China, they illuminate a previously ignored factor in wall history: aggressive, acquisitive Chinese imperialism. This does not, of course, mean we should excuse the subsequent 2,000 years of nomad raids as an exercise in working through colonial trauma. Nor does it make Genghis Khan any more historically sympathetic or desirable as a neighbour. But it does reconfigure the simplistic Chinese propaganda picture – first drawn in the first millennium BC – of innocent Chinese farmers defending themselves against greedy nomad raiders. It also shows that walls do not always have to be defensive: build them in the middle of newly invaded and occupied territory and they become a prop to expansionist colonialism.

Whatever the true political and military reasons for Warring States wall-building, it soon proved strategically counterproductive for almost every state that undertook it. If, on the one hand, wall-building was driven by Chinese imperialism rather than by purely defensive concerns, the net diplomatic result was to produce out of the fractured nomadic tribes a unified opposition force – the Xiongnu – that would plague China's northern borders for the next five or six centuries. If, on the other hand, the walls *were* purely defensive in purpose, their failure was even more serious. As future centuries would repeatedly demonstrate, frontier walls proved little obstacle to conquering, semi-barbarian hordes from the north – and specifically, at this historical juncture, to the armies of the north-western state of Qin, which stormed over, round or through every single one of the inter-state defences on their progress towards unifying China in 221 BC under the rule of Qin Shihuang, the First Emperor (259–210 BC). But the border these barriers established defined the zone of conflict over which walls would be built and frontier battles fought for the next two millennia.

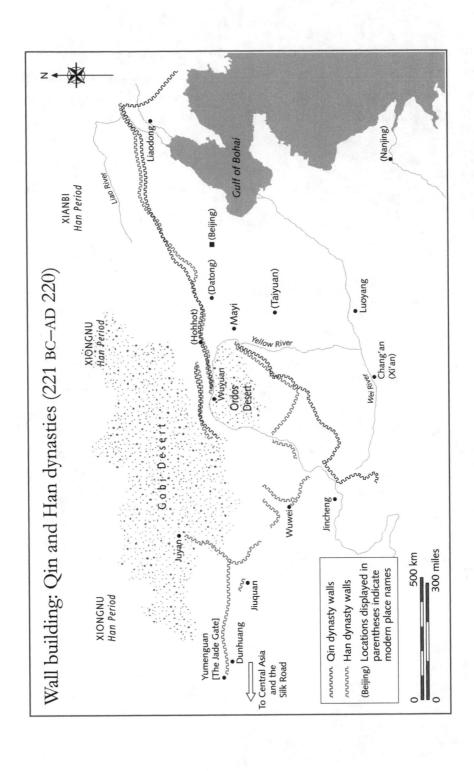

Wall building: Qin and Han dynasties (221 BC–AD 220)

CHAPTER TWO

The Long Wall

In his canonical history of China, the *Historical Records,* Sima Qian (*c.* 145–86 BC) summarized the First Emperor for posterity as a savage cross-breed: 'a man with a prominent nose, large eyes, a chest like a bird of prey and the voice of a jackal; a man of little kindness, with a heart of a tiger, of that of a wolf'.[1] A historian writing during the Han dynasty, Sima Qian was, admittedly, biased. As successor dynasty to the Qin, the Han had a strong interest in blackening the reputation of their predecessor, the first Qin emperor. And Sima Qian – a vulnerable court official who had already suffered castration for falling foul of his ruler, the Han emperor Wu – had an equally strong interest in complying with this wish.

Such historical bias notwithstanding, the First Emperor – former king of Qin and architect of the political system that would serve as the organizing model for China to the twentieth century and beyond – undoubtedly deserves a place in any roll-call of China's greatest despots. Ever since his dynasty fell in 206 BC, only four years after his death and fifteen years after he unified China, the Chinese have tended to treat him like an embarrassing parent, inheriting from him all the key features of their political and cultural landscape – including the first Long Wall – while denouncing his tyrannical excesses.

Although the idea of China as a cultural unity defined by shared custom and ritual had come into approximate existence some time around 1000 BC, thanks to the Zhou empire's claim to command the allegiances of the kingdoms clustered around contemporary central China, for the next 800 years or so it remained more of a theoretical ideal than a geographical and political reality. Even before the collapse of its real authority in 771 BC, the Zhou empire spanned only the northern half of the country now known as China, reaching no further south than the Yangtze River. And this relatively circumscribed area was itself far from culturally homogeneous. The fantastical art and literature of the southernmost Chinese polity, Chu – with its glamorous cast of gods, goddesses and bizarre mythological creatures – reveal a civilization far more exotic and shamanistic than that of the comparatively earthbound Zhou heartland further north. The areas beyond Chu – contemporary Yunnan, Guizhou and the other southernmost provinces of Mainland China – were inhabited by aboriginal tribes existing outside the cultural sway of any loosely bound Chinese empire. After Zhou power waned, the concept of unity became more tenuous still, as the country remained violently divided during the Warring States period: individual states intrigued and fought for supremacy, while advisers and generals abandoned their native areas in search of powerful, foreign patrons, playing rulers off against each other and angling for the best promotions.

Confucius (551–479 BC) – later enshrined by the Han as imperial China's pre-eminent philosopher – was very much a man of his (early Warring States) age. Although his philosophy preached political unification, his career – a succession of peregrinations between states in search of the political post he felt he deserved – faithfully reproduced the divisions of his era. Nostalgic for a long-lost mythical ideal of Chinese unity and virtue nurtured by the Zhou dynasty, Confucius hoped to end the conflict and fragmentation of his own era through a moral revival. If everyone conducted himself (Confucianism barely acknowledges the existence of women as social beings) with humane benevolence, he believed, the country would be peacefully reunified. The social code that held together Confucius's injunctions to be good was the correct performance of ritual, loosely understood as encompassing all forms of public and private behaviour: bowing, mourning parents, wearing the correct colour of lapels, playing the correct kind of music, worshipping the correct mountain, hiring the correct number of dancing girls, and so on and so forth. Confucius's great, popularizing innovation was to break his political philosophy down into the manageable, bite-sized analogy of family relationships. Confucius equated the bond between father and son with that between ruler and subject. Good fathers and sons, his logic went, make good rulers and subjects; good rulers and subjects will bring China back to its rightful state of peaceful, prosperous unity. Tend to your own family garden, he preached, and the country will prosper; perform your own social role properly and everything else will slot harmoniously into place.

Within his own lifetime, Confucius's scheme to unite Warring States China – a world of opportunistic rulers, ambitious arrivistes, ruthless generals and plotting ministers – by training sons to be obedient, regulating lapel colour and moderating dancing girls, came to nothing. Having failed all his life to persuade a king to appoint him to the powerful ministerial post that would permit him to put his ideas into practice, he died poor, unemployed and ignored beyond his circle of disciples. Instead, it took the relentless efforts of a jackal-hawk-tiger-wolf from the 'barbarian' north-western frontier – the first Qin emperor – to drag the fragments of the Chinese polity together: someone unafraid of obliterating hundreds of thousands of lives on his path to the imperial throne. And once he had reached his goal, China was largely defined, both inside and out. The Qin emperor unified China's political institutions, joined the country through a network of roads, provided the etymological root from which Western names for his empire (China, Chine, etc.) were later derived, and assembled the first single Long Wall.

~

Before it took over the Chinese world, the state of Qin approximated to the present-day north-western province of Shaanxi. Bordered by the Rong and Di tribes to the west and north, it was heavily influenced by its non-Chinese neighbours. Late Qin rulers tried to give their antecedents rigorously Chinese credentials, claiming the founder of the state was born to the granddaughter of a remote descendant of the Yellow Emperor after she swallowed a black bird's egg. A less romantic but more plausible version of early Qin history has it that the dynasty's founder was a chieftain expert in the barbarian art of horse-breeding, to whom the Zhou king in 897 BC granted a tiny appanage in which to raise horses for him. By 256 BC, this gift had swollen into a historical mistake of vast proportions, when it defeated and subsumed the ailing house of Zhou.

Throughout its pre-unification history, the state of Qin honed its military and political machine through wars and intrigues with the Rong and Di, and as a result came to be seen by the less successful of the Warring States as decidedly barbarian and 'un-Chinese'. 'Qin has the same customs as the Rong and Di,' pronounced a noble of Wei to his king in 266 BC. 'It knows nothing about traditional manners, proper relationships and virtuous conduct.' Worse still, its people did not even play civilized music – according to Confucius, a crucial ingredient of basic moral decency. 'Now the beating of earthen jugs, knocking on jars ... and striking on thigh bones, the while singing and crying "Woo! Woo!"' carped Li Si, the future chancellor of the Qin empire, 'such indeed was the music of Qin.'[2] Rather than improve themselves in the refined arts of the Chinese, the Qin preferred to specialize in feats of military brutishness. King Wu, who ruled a few generations before the First Emperor, died in 307 BC from injuries sustained while competitively lifting bronze tripod vessels. Sima Qian laconically relates that in the twenty-five years preceding the First Emperor's accession to the Qin throne in 247 BC, Qin armies caused the deaths of up to 756,000 foreign soldiers or civilians in war. His casualty figures for 364–234 BC – currently disputed by historians – are an astounding 1.5 million.

Throughout his lifetime, the First Emperor demonstrated an inclination towards barbarism that more than did justice to his savage antecedents. In addition to the massive loss of life caused by his pre-unification military campaigns, he press-ganged hundreds of thousands of Chinese into his monumental public projects: roads, canals, palace complexes, walls. Some 700,000 convict labourers were set to work on his mausoleum and tomb alone (which he began when he first became King of Qin at the age of thirteen and which took almost forty years to complete). Many of these unfortunates were killed as soon as the work was finished, in order to protect the secret location and contents of the tomb. Indeed, the liquidating of its builders was so thoroughly done that knowledge of the mausoleum's extent disappeared from the historical record until a handful of Chinese farmers digging wells thirty kilometres east of present-day Xi'an in 1974 brought up to the surface a few terracotta arms and legs. Further investigations unearthed three huge pits, the largest being 12,500 square metres, each containing thousands of broken figurines of soldiers, horses and chariots: the now world-famous terracotta warriors.

Since the earliest times, the Chinese have imagined that the afterlife will be similar in all important ways to earthly life and therefore have always arranged, if possible, to be buried together with the items (in either original or model form) that they found useful in their lifetime and that they would therefore expect to need in the next life. The sheer number of soldiers (an estimated 8,000; not all the fragments have yet been pieced together) that the First Emperor desired to take with him thus speaks eloquently of the huge personal guard that he attached to himself while he lived, and of the vast scale of his imperial building projects. The pits containing the terracotta warriors, moreover, were only the external, buffer-zone chambers of the mausoleum; the tomb itself – which promises to contain fabulous riches – has never been fully opened. (Archaeologists are waiting until they feel confident that their technologies of preservation will be sufficient to protect what lies inside; on being dug up and exposed to the air, the original brightly painted colours of the terracotta warriors faded in minutes.) Our main guide to its contents is Sima Qian, who describes it as an ingeniously booby-trapped Aladdin's cave, sealed with bronze walls and filled with rare and precious exotica. 'With mercury the various waterways of the empire, the Yangzi and Yellow Rivers, and even the great ocean itself were created and made to flow and circulate mechanically ... Lamps were fuelled with whale oil so that they might burn forever without being extinguished.' Finally, as a security measure, artisans 'were ordered to install mechanically triggered crossbows set to shoot any intruder'.[3]

When the First Emperor wasn't building, he was obliterating, and on an equally grand scale. After his conquest, he disarmed the entire empire and melted down all confiscated weapons into bronze bells and statues. But the destructive act that truly sealed his future reputation for infamy was his burning of books and massacre of scholars. In furious response to a request by a Confucian scholar for the emperor to re-create kings and fiefs, and thereby to dismantle the newly unified, centralized Qin empire, the emperor gave orders to burn all extant copies of the Confucian classics (history, poetry, philosophy) and to 'execute in the marketplace' anyone who discussed these works. The only books to survive his intellectual purge were utilitarian manuals of 'medicine, divination, and horticulture'.[4]

The political tool that enabled the First Emperor to give full rein to his mania for control was Legalism, a rationalist, utilitarian school of philosophy which introduced the basic features of subsequent Chinese statecraft: a centralized bureaucracy and uniform legal system. Unlike Confucius, who believed that people were basically good and merely needed their innate benevolence to be coaxed out of them, Legalists held that humans were essentially evil by nature and could only be kept in check by laws. The mastermind of Legalism was a fourth-century prime minister of Qin called Shang Yang, who ensured that every Qin household was registered – making it easier to extract taxes, military service and corvée labour – and placed under the jurisdiction of a centrally appointed magistrate. The entire population was divided into groups of tens and fives, with each member of each group made responsible for reporting criminal activity by another member. Wrongdoing was, in turn, dealt with by harsh punishments 'applied equally to the great and the powerful'.[5] Anyone who failed to report a crime committed by another member of his or her group 'would be chopped in two at the waist'.[6] Shang Yang himself came to a bad end, a victim of his own success: after evenhand-edly applying the law to a tutor of the heir apparent, the vengeful heir, once in power, subjected his zealous prime minister to the most brutal of Shang Yang's own punishments: being torn to pieces by chariots.[7] But the profits – tax revenue and conscripted labour – from Shang Yang's ration-alizing reforms supplied an army that enabled Qin to crush its rival Warring States.

Once he had unified the Chinese world, the first Qin emperor extended Shang Yang's bureaucratic formula throughout his empire. Despite the bad press that the first Qin emperor has received from later historians (his public image has not been well served by his few famous admirers, who include Mao Zedong, probably the most destructive dicta-tor to rule China), he did lay the foundations of the modern, unified, bureaucratic Chinese state: standardizing currency, weights, measures, laws and script, installing ruthless police controls and subordinating the peasantry to the government. If contemporary Chinese politicians were to compare the Qin system with theirs, the similarities would probably be easier to spot than the differences. And, of course, contemporary Chinese are perfectly happy to rejoice in one other Qin contribution to China: a *changcheng,* a long frontier wall, the construction of which was directed by Qin's great general, Meng Tian.

Meng Tian and his male relatives were archetypal success stories of their time. Meng Tian's grandfather was one of many able soldiers and advisers who, like Confucius, left their native state to better themselves in the service of another (in his case, departing Qi for Qin). A family of highly competent and ruthless military men, the Meng clan became the Rottweilers of Qin, biting whoever they were ordered to bite – the states of Zhao, Han, Wei and Chu – until, apparently untroubled by any untoward pangs of loyalty towards his ancestors' state, Meng Tian crushed Qi in 221 BC, the year of Qin unification. Once Meng Tian had more than proved himself in this last test of loyalty, the Qin emperor decided to entrust to him his toughest mission yet: building his frontier wall.

But before the First Emperor could give free rein to his great passion – diverting the Chinese masses into enormous imperial building projects – he indulged in his second-favourite pursuit: destruction. According to an inscription of 215 BC, he began by pulling the old state walls down:

> He has demolished the inner and outer walls of cities.
>
> He has cut through the embankments of rivers.
>
> He has levelled the bulwarks at mountain defiles.[8]

And with that accomplished, the Qin emperor set about organizing the construction of his own wall. In the entry corresponding to the year 214 BC, Sima Qian writes:

After Qin had unified the world Meng Tian was sent to command a host of three hundred thousand to drive out the Rong and Di along the north. He took from them the territory to the south of the [Yellow] River, and built a Long Wall constructing its defiles and passes in accordance with the configuration of the terrain. It started at Lintao, and extended to Liaodong, reaching a distance of more than ten thousand *li*.*[9]

This was clearly a serious business: a huge military expedition, followed by well over 4,000 kilometres of wall-building in extreme climates and on frequently inaccessible terrain, from the bumpy sands of far north-west China at Lintao (present-day Gansu), over and above the loop of the Yellow River around the Ordos, crossing into the dry, cold,

* One *li* is roughly half a kilometre.

unfarmable steppes of Inner Mongolia, and ending in the north-eastern region of Liaodong, near Manchuria, whose long, bitter winters are hardly differentiated from the climate of the Mongolian steppe that borders it to the west. To make the building process even more challenging, Inner Mongolia and the northernmost parts of China's northern provinces, Shanxi and Shaanxi, which nestle inside the loop of the Yellow River, undulate across mountainous terrain between 2,000 and 3,000 metres above sea level. Joining the whole massive edifice to the emperor's power centre further south was the 'Straight Road', which ran some 800 kilometres from Inner Mongolia, over the Yellow River, almost as far south as the Qin capital in Xianyang, near contemporary Xi'an. This was the most impressive branch of the extensive network of roads built for the Qin emperor by his gangs of corvée labourers, which in total covered about 6,800 kilometres – more than rivalling the 6,000 kilometres of roads which Gibbon estimates the Romans built.[10]

What relation, however, does this astonishing feat of engineering bear to the structure now known as the Great Wall? When Macartney and his mission arrived at the (Ming) wall in the late eighteenth century, they automatically assumed that the wall they were viewing in its present form was the legendary 2,000-year-old work of the Qin emperor. During the wall's long heyday of the nineteenth and twentieth centuries, Chinese and Western, serious and popular historians alike have continued to parrot this version of history. 'The Wall is the product of Chin [sic],' pronounced William Geil, the author in 1909 of an eccentric account of an odyssey along the Great Wall.[11] In his 1932 cartoon panel, Robert Ripley – the illustrator-journalist who told the world that the Great Wall was visible from the moon – exuberantly peddled a similar line: 'The One and Only! First Emperor of China – Who Built the Great Wall!'[12] Modern Chinese, who, in the face of severe material poverty, have comforted themselves by turning their country's long history into a source of spiritual riches, have been delighted to go along with the idea that their ancestors built the longest, oldest, greatest wall – ever. In 1986, the *China Daily*

– the Communist Party's English-language broadsheet – trumpeted that 'The 6,000-kilometre-long wall was built more than 2,500 years ago, running from the coastal town of Shanhaiguan pass in northeastern China to Jiayuguan pass in northwestern China.'[13] We know that the stone-and-brick façade of what is now acclaimed as the Great Wall was erected during the Ming dynasty; could the Ming simply have restored or maintained a wall that had already existed for almost 2,000 years?

There are a number of points in Sima Qian's account of the Qin emperor's work which do not quite square with this tidily continuous view of history. The biggest difficulty is geographical. The arc of the wall that Sima Qian describes runs much further north than the line taken by the currently extant Great Wall, which skirts the bottom rather than the top of the Yellow River loop. Jiayuguan (the Pass of the Pleasant Valley), the westernmost pass mentioned by the *China Daily,* is irrefutably a Ming construction begun in 1372, on the edge of Chinese Turkestan, amid the fine dull-yellow sands near the western border between Gansu and Xinjiang. According to Sima Qian, however, the western terminus of the Qin wall was at Lintao, near present-day Lanzhou, safely within the confines of eastern Gansu. Chinese builders did not make their way as far west as Jiayuguan for at least another hundred years.

A second problem with Sima Qian's account is how casually straightforward it makes the whole building of the Qin Long Wall seem. Visit the Great Wall today and a passing glance at its stone-and-brick corridors hugging the tops of high, arching peaks immediately begs a few rudimentary logistical questions: how were the materials – earth, stone, brick – obtained and transported? How did the workmen then manage to lodge them into position on the scrub-filled mountain spines? Of these fundamental wall-building matters, Sima Qian says nothing.

These inconsistencies suggest two conclusions. First, given the bad geographical fit between the Qin and Ming walls, and the lack of descriptions of hammering stone and heaving building blocks, it is probable that the Qin wall bore little resemblance to the brick-and-stone version restored north of Beijing today. It was far more likely made of tamped earth, similar to the walls separating the Warring States, most of the materials for which were available on site. A Chinese folk name for ancient northern walls – 'earth dragon' – evokes the materials originally used in their construction.[14] The few hundred kilometres of Inner Mongolian wall ruins – sometimes three metres at their base, rarely as much as 3.5 metres high – that archaeologists have confidently dated back to the Qin are a pragmatic combination of tamped earth and stones, presumably a reflection of whatever came to hand over 2,000 years ago.[15] A surviving section further south, in Ningxia, now looks barely artificial, a mossy ridge rising up out of the land like a bulging vein.[16]

Second, despite the Qin emperor's love of razing the old in order to raise the new, the wall along the northern frontier was unlikely to have been entirely his own work. Instead, in places, it was quite possibly built on earlier fortifications: parts of the Yan wall stretching north-east from Mongolia to Manchuria, and perhaps the Qin wall in the west, south of the Yellow River. Recent archaeological work suggests that although Meng Tian's wall pushed beyond the old Zhao rampart, further north over the top of the Yellow River loop, the line of the Qin imperial wall coincided with the starting point of the older Qin rampart in Gansu, and with a zone in eastern Mongolia and north-east China along which Yan archaeological relics have been found.[17] These walls were only patchily man-made, as they made use of the land's topographical defences wherever possible. Wall-building was more a case of joining ravines and precipices with stretches of wall or with fortresses than of erecting a brand-new, continuous line of defence. Another passage from Sima Qian makes this point:

[Meng Tian] seized control of all the lands south of the Yellow River and established border defences along the river, constructing forty-four walled district cities overlooking the river and manning them with convict labourers transported to the border for garrison duty ... Thus he utilised the natural mountain barriers to establish the border defences, scooping out the valleys and constructing ramparts and building installations at other points where they were needed.[18]

If these explanations for the speed and ease with which the wall went up fail to satisfy, we have to fall back on the fantastical legends that have for millennia surrounded the building of the Qin wall: that the emperor had either a magic whip, shovel or horse before which the Long Wall simply sprang up within twenty-four hours. Any puzzling detours taken by the wall are explained by the historical surmise that the emperor and his horse took a wrong turning during a dust storm. Another persuasive, frequently cited explanation for how the emperor circumvented the engineering problems of wall-building is that an exceptionally large dragon happened to be flying over that part of China, grew tired, bellyflopped to the ground and turned into the Long Wall.[19]

But if we don't accept mythical explanations for the location of the wall, then it is worth pondering why the First Emperor settled on the areas he selected for wall-building. The northern parts of the Ordos region are, after all, a long way from the arable land of China proper. The later, Ming version of the Great Wall line has a far more obvious strategic importance, cutting across the agrarian base of the Yellow River loop and hovering to the north of the capital, Beijing. The Qin wall, by comparison, is in many places too distant from arable land and major cities to have much immediate defensive significance for Chinese farmers.

Superstition is one explanation for the emperor's choice. For all the legalistic rationalism of his regime, the First Emperor was a great believer in the occult. Obsessed by the thought of death, he expended vast amounts of money on dispatching alchemists to search for elixirs of life and magic mushrooms – and, of course, executed them when they inevitably failed to return with the hoped-for longevity potions. He also listened religiously to the voice of prophecy and in 215 BC was terrified by an oracle inscription that forecast 'he who will destroy Qin is a Hu'.[20]

Taking 'Hu' to mean the Hu nomadic barbarians, the emperor promptly dispatched his general, Meng Tian, and troops northward to expel the northern tribes from the Ordos and build walls.

Another plausible explanation is that the Qin wall shared the same strategic rationale as Warring States walls built in the region: rather than defending the Chinese against nomad attack, the Qin wanted to stay on the offensive against the non-Chinese northerners, maintaining outposts from which further, even more expansionist campaigns could be fought. Between the fourth and third centuries BC, the northern tribes were getting decidedly the worst of things on the frontier, beaten out of the Ordos and far back into Mongolia and Manchuria by armies of the individual states. It seems unlikely that, after these repeated pummellings, the Hu barbarians would have been in any position to recover so quickly to become a threat to the new Qin empire.

One final possible reason for the remoteness of Qin walls – credible given what we know about the First Emperor – was pure totalitarianism: the Wall was the Qin gulag, a huge, arbitrary building project designed to swallow up soldiers demobilized after the big push to unify China, and the thousands of convicts who had fallen foul of the Qin regime. In 213 BC, for example, the emperor exiled 'those law officers who presided in criminal courts but did not uphold justice and had them build the Great Wall'.[21] A year later, his unfortunate eldest son, Fusu, was himself banished to guard the northern frontier, after remonstrating with his father about the harshness of his rule.

Although it bore little physical relation to the contemporary Great Wall, the Qin wall generated the earliest stories of suffering and sacrifice involved in wall-building. Until desperate twentieth-century patriots adopted the Great Wall as a nationalist symbol, these legends dominated and shaped popular sentiment about the wall, fuelling traditions that demonized walls in the mass imagination as the oppressive recourse of tyrants and that transformed the frontier into a bleak, lonely graveyard of ordinary Chinese. Even if the speed at which the Qin wall went up indicates it was not quite the elaborate logistical and engineering challenge that the stone wall now visited by tourists north of Beijing looks to have been, songs and myths, such as this Qin-period ode, evoke its unrelenting consumption of corvée labour, and commemorate the numbers who died in its construction:

> If you have a son, don't raise him.
> If you have a girl, feed her dried meat.
> Can't you see, the Long Wall
> Is propped up on skeletons.[22]

Springing from a culture as son-worshipping as China's, these four short lines speak powerfully of the sense of hopeless desperation generated by the wall's bottomless appetite for conscript workers: why nurture a son, simply to have him die building the wall? Another myth surrounding the wall's construction tells how the emperor created nine suns, interminably stretching out his labourers' working day in order to speed construction. (Happily for the builders in this story, a friendly spirit came to their rescue, blocking out eight of the suns with as many magic mountains, which were then joined up to form the Long Wall.)

Perhaps the best-known of the wall's legendary casualties is Mengjiang, a devoted wife who travelled to the north-eastern terminus of the wall, Shanhaiguan, to which her husband had been assigned as a forced labourer, in order to bring him warm winter clothes. (One version of the story recounts that Mengjiang's husband was wrested from her by Qin conscriptors on their wedding night.) When she arrived, however, she discovered that he had already died of cold and exhaustion. Her sobs caused the wall to open up and reveal his bones, along with those of thousands of other workmen, which she reburied before hurling herself – a chaste and virtuous Chinese widow – into the sea. Another account has it that the lecherous Qin emperor, who happened to be passing by on a tour of inspection, was so taken by her that he tried to make her his concubine, before she escaped his advances by suicide. Four rocks that loom out of the sea at Shanhaiguan, the easternmost point of the Great Wall today, are said to be her tomb.

One of the earliest tourists to visit the Wall, Sima Qian did not mince his words in denouncing the sacrifices Meng Tian forced out of his builders:

I went to the north border and returned by way of the Straight Road. In my travels I saw the Long Wall and fortifications that Meng Tian built for Qin, cutting through mountains and filling up valleys to open up the Straight Road. He was indeed careless with the populace's labour. When Qin first destroyed the feudal lords, the hearts and minds of the world were not yet settled and the injured not yet recovered, yet Meng Tian, as a famous general, did not vigorously admonish, did not relieve the plight of the populace, did not nourish the aged, did not pity the orphaned, or labour at renewing harmony among the common people, but instead bent to the Emperor's whims and embarked on construction.[23]

Widespread resentment at the ruthless mobilization of slave labour – of which Mengjiang's legend has spoken so potently for millennia – required for state projects such as the wall eventually proved to be the downfall of Qin, along with three other classic ingredients of Chinese dynastic decline: feckless usurpers, conspiring eunuchs and the loss of capable and loyal generals along the walled northern frontier.

In 210 BC, the First Emperor set off on what turned out to be the last of his many imperial tours of inspection. As his health was now deteriorating, his obsession with finding an elixir of life intensified. In 219 BC, he had commissioned an erudite called Xu Fu to set out to sea with several thousand young boys and girls in search of fabled islands of immortals. When the emperor finally caught up with Xu Fu on the east coast of China in 210, the quick-thinking alchemist somehow managed to convince his emperor that his party would have fetched back the elixir from the island of immortals without any difficulty at all, if only they hadn't been constantly harassed by large sharks. Completely taken in, the emperor himself stood guard on the coast for a time, taking pot-shots at the troublesome creatures with an automatic crossbow. Not long after, and while still on his travels, he died.

The Hu that would prove the Qin's downfall was not a northern Hu barbarian but one who was much closer to home: the emperor's weak and mentally unbalanced second-born son, Huhai, who, as bad luck would have it, was accompanying him on tour at the time of his death, together with his tutor, the ambitious and scheming eunuch Zhao Gao. Fusu, the heir apparent and the emperor's former favourite, was still guarding the northern frontier with Meng Tian. Taking full advantage of being in the right place at the right time, Zhao Gao and Huhai kept news of the emperor's death secret while, one by one, they picked off all their political opponents. They first destroyed the late emperor's summons to Fusu to return and succeed him, and replaced it with a forged command that Fusu and Meng Tian should kill themselves for having slandered his rule. Fusu immediately complied; Meng Tian, unable to believe that the master he had served so loyally should demand his death, paused for deliberation, until an uncharacteristic anxiety about the feng shui of his Long Wall finally pushed him towards suicide. 'My offence does indeed merit death,' he ruminated. 'Beginning at Lintao and reaching to Liaodong, I built walls and dug moats for more than ten-thousand *li*; was it not inevitable that I broke the earth's veins along the way? This then is my offence.'[24] The last, and perhaps most deserving, of the Qin wall's casualties, he then swallowed poison.

Once in power, Zhao Gao and Huhai vigorously pursued the First Emperor's most exploitative policies, squeezing taxes and corvée labour out of the populace in order to complete the huge royal palace begun at Xianyang and the vast system of roads. On Zhao Gao's recommendation, after gleefully murdering members of the nobility, Huhai retreated into the inner palace, wallowing in feasts, concubines and theatricals, leaving the business of ruling (or, more accurately perhaps, venting grievances against enemies) to his eunuch tutor. Having succeeded in thoroughly isolating the Second Emperor, Zhao Gao drove his former master to madness and suicide, before himself being stabbed by Ziying, Huhai's eldest son.

But the decisive Ziying ruled only for forty-six days. While the Qin leadership tore itself apart, the pressures of conscription, taxes and harsh punishments – the basis of the Qin legalist state – turned increasing numbers to banditry. Some hundred years later, a Han official pointed directly to frontier policies as the trigger for revolt, describing the sufferings of not only the frontline soldiers but also civilians, struggling to satisfy an insatiably corrupt supply trail:

The troops were in the wilderness without shelter more than ten years, and countless men died … Starting out from the coast, food supplies dwindled from 192,000 pecks [decalitres] to ten on their journey to the Yellow River. Men hastened to plant but could not meet the army's demands for food; the women weaved but could not meet the demands for tents. The people were tired and poor and unable to nourish … the weak, whose corpses dotted the roadsides. Because of all this, the realm under Heaven began to rebel.[25]

One year after the First Emperor's death, Chen She, a former hired labourer, was prevented by heavy rain from transporting his charge of 900 convicts to a penitentiary settlement on time, the harshly Legalist penalty for which was death. 'At present,' he ruminated, 'flight means death and plotting also means death. Comparing these two deaths, it would be better to die for founding a state.'[26] Thus preferring to be hanged for a sheep rather than for a lamb, he initiated a rebellion that drew in Liu Bang, the later founder of the Han dynasty, and crushed the Qin.

One legend about these dynasty-destroying revolts tells how the rebels armed themselves by breaking into the First Emperor's mausoleum and snatching the weapons from the hands of the terracotta warriors, before vandalizing the burial pit. The story is plausible: when the terracotta figures were first uncovered in the 1970s, they looked to have been smashed to fragments by intruders. If it is true, it must count as one of history's great ironies that the army fashioned by the First Emperor – at such cost to his people – to protect him on his uncertain journey to another life armed the rebellion that destroyed his dynasty.

And so the Qin empire collapsed, and with it Chinese control of the areas north of the Yellow River. In the disorder that accompanied the fall of the Qin, the Chinese conscripts abandoned the frontier and the northern barbarians reoccupied their lost territories, rendering the Qin wall meaningless as a defensive barrier. As Sima Qian chronicles,

After Meng Tian died, and the feudal lords revolted against the Qin, plunging China into a period of strife and turmoil, the convicts whom the Qin had sent to the northern border to garrison the area all returned to their homes. Now the pressure against them had relaxed, the Xiongnu once again began to infiltrate south of the bend of the Yellow river until they had established themselves along the old border of China.[27]

It is at this point in the history of Chinese frontier walls that a new kind of frontier power emerges in the Ordos and Inner Mongolia: the Xiongnu, a politically united and effectively led force of nomadic warriors who were able to terrorize China more successfully than had any of the fragmented northern tribes of the steppe in the preceding millennium.

Almost immediately after the Qin fell, when moralistic Confucianism replaced utilitarian Legalism as imperial Chinese orthodoxy, the dynasty became a byword for tyranny, its history – and its wall – an object lesson in how not to govern China. In a scolding essay entitled 'The Faults of Qin', the Han scholar Jia Yi (201–160 BC) preached that the Qin disintegrated because 'it failed to display humanity and righteousness or to realise that there is a difference between the power to attack and the power to consolidate'.[28] The Qin emperor 'believed in his heart that with the strength of his capital within the Pass and his walls of metal extending a thousand miles, he had established a rule that would be enjoyed by his descendants for ten thousand generations'.[29] To later Chinese political philosophers and historians, the Qin collapse perfectly illustrated the supreme misapprehension of the absolutist ruler: that force – huge armies, terrifying laws and long walls – without virtue could secure an empire.

Not that any of this stopped the sanctimonious Han, and virtually every dynasty that succeeded it, from pursuing the same frontier policy whenever they could afford it, and often when they could not: building long, expensive and, in the end, similarly unreliable walls.

CHAPTER THREE

Han Walls: *Plus ça change*

A round 209 BC, Touman, the Shanyu or supratribal leader of the Mongolian Xiongnu, faced a succession dilemma. Preferring a younger son to the heir apparent, Maodun, he needed to get rid of the elder to install his favourite as heir. Clearly unwilling to contemplate anything as obviously unpaternal as assassination, he decided instead to send Maodun off to a neighbouring tribe, the Yuezhi, as a hostage, then lead an attack on his neighbours, in the hope that they would retaliate by killing him. Unfortunately, as it turned out for Touman, Maodun stole one of their fastest horses and managed to escape, eventually finding his way home. Impressed by his bravery and daring, his father gave him a force of 10,000 cavalry to command.[1]

As soon as Maodun was back among the Xiongnu, Touman realized he had made a deeply unwise choice of enemy. As insurance against a repetition of recent events, Maodun immediately set about building up his own power base by turning his troops into an unshakeably loyal personal guard. Part of his programme of military discipline involved training his soldiers to aim at whatever target he did: 'Shoot wherever you see my whistling arrow strike!' he ordered, 'and anyone who fails to shoot will be cut down!' Maodun shot, in turn, at his best horse, his favourite wife and his father's best horse, executing all those who had failed to follow his example. Finally, 'he shot a whistling arrow at his father'; 'every one of his followers aimed their arrows in the same direction and shot the Shanyu dead.'[2]

Before Maodun took over the tribe, the Xiongnu had looked rather beleaguered. To the south, the Chinese had driven them from their ancestral land, the Ordos; to the west, the Yuezhi, in present-day Gansu, had extracted hostages from them; and to the east, the Donghu (literally, the 'eastern barbarians') treated them with obvious contempt, demanding from them at will their finest horses and women. But in the few years following his usurpation in 209 BC, Maodun had retaken the lands lost to General Meng Tian, invalidating the northernmost Qin Long Wall as a frontier. He had also defeated both the Donghu and the Yuezhi, through a combination of strategic cunning and ruthless violence. After his victory over the former, Maodun made an emphatic diplomatic example of the Donghu leader – who had tried to seize a piece of Xiongnu land – by using his skull as a drinking cup. Following their defeat by Maodun, the Yuezhi moved from Gansu in north-west China to much further west, to present-day Kyrgystan and Tajikistan – a migration that would have important consequences for Han wall-building.

~

Until the fall of the Qin dynasty, the Chinese had dominated the northern frontier, especially after they negated the nomads' single greatest advantage by themselves adopting steppe-style cavalry. What gave Chinese states the upper hand in frontier offensives was political unity: their ability to find efficient ways of organizing and exploiting the population for political and military ends. The steppe tribes, by contrast, were too fragmented to make any significant inroads against the Chinese, too politically disorganized to conquer or control new territory. United, the Chinese stood in the Ordos; divided, the Xiongnu fell back to northern Mongolia. All this changed after Maodun succeeded in imposing an unprecedented cohesion over the fractious nomads. By creating a three-tiered ruling hierarchy throughout his dominions – the Shanyu at the top, with imperial governors and local tribal leaders below – Maodun man-

aged to conquer and hold on to a steppe empire. In the process, he transformed the Xiongnu into one of the most feared and renowned raiding
powers in Chinese frontier history. 'On the attack,' Sima Qian described,

the man who kills the main enemy figure is rewarded with a cup of wine. The captured war booty is dispersed among the warriors; if they capture people, they make
them slaves. Therefore, in their war each person struggles for his personal gain.
They cleverly draw the enemy out, then attack. When they see the enemy, they
swarm like birds upon their profits. Upon defeat, they scatter like the clouds.[3]

In China, centuries after their fall from supremacy, the Xiongnu remained
a byword for the terrifying northern barbarian enemy. Their notoriety
even spread west, where over-excitable historians – beginning with the
eighteenth-century scholar Joseph DeGuignes – identified them as the
Huns, deflected on to Rome by the obstruction of the Great Wall.

Although the Chinese were, naturally, not best pleased that the
Xiongnu had been so effectively unified, they were unable to do much
about the steppe while regional leaders were still battling to fill the power
vacuum created by the Qin collapse. Not that this prevented Liu Bang (d.
195), the future founder of the Han dynasty, from attempting to repair
and man the old Qin wall north of the Yellow River, while civil war still
raged.[4] But by 202 BC, Liu had dragged China out of the chaos of civil
war and declared himself first emperor Gaozu of the Han. With China
nominally pacified and reunited, he immediately tried to recover the military initiative on the steppe.

In order to defeat his rivals at the close of the civil war, Gaozu had
been forced to reward his allies with autonomous kingdoms, abandoning
the absolute centralization favoured by the Qin. In 201 BC, following a
Xiongnu attack on the northern border town of Mayi (not far from
Taiyuan, the present capital of Shanxi province), one of these kings, Han
Xin, defected to Maodun. Since Han Xin's disloyalty set a dangerous
precedent, the emperor gathered together a Han army and led it up further north to Pingcheng. There, amid the freezing, raw, crevassed brown

expanses of the northernmost tip of Shanxi, the campaign ended in catastrophe: after 30 per cent of the Chinese soldiers lost their fingers to frostbite, Maodun lured them into the attack with a feint of weakness, then swooped down in an ambush. The emperor found himself surrounded by some 400,000 Xiongnu cavalry until he negotiated his way out of the siege, allegedly by bringing his full powers of moral suasion to bear on Maodun's family. According to one story, Gaozu threatened the Shanyu's wife that he would bombard Maodun with Chinese beauties if she did not intervene on his behalf to break the encirclement.[5]

The diplomatic outcome of this chastening defeat was the 'Peace and Friendship' (*heqin*) policy. The Chinese offered friendship, in the form of brides and bribes – imperial princesses, silk and grain; the Xiongnu offered peace – when it suited them. This material and marital blackmail was not an overwhelming success from the Chinese point of view: Xiongnu raids continued and Maodun's demands became ever more outrageous. In 192 BC, he even asked for the hand of Empress Lü, Gaozu's widow and de facto ruler between 188 and 180 BC. 'I am a lonely widowed ruler,' reads his letter of proposal. 'Your majesty is also a widowed ruler living in a life of solitude. Both of us are without pleasures and lack any way to amuse ourselves. It is my hope that we can exchange that which we have for that which we are lacking.'[6] The furious empress's first instinct was to respond by launching an attack on the presumptuous barbarian, but her generals tactfully reminded her that 'even Emperor Gaozu, with all his wisdom and bravery, encountered great difficulty at Pingcheng'.[7] Slowly thinking better of the idea, she instead composed a polite thank you, but no: 'My age is advanced and my vitality is weakening. Both my hair and teeth are falling out, and I cannot even walk steadily … I am not worthy of [Maodun] lowering himself. But my country has done nothing wrong, and I hope he will spare it.' (There is an unmistakably supplicatory note to the empress's plea that Maodun should not invade China in revenge for her refusal.)[8]

The humiliating aspects of Peace and Friendship notwithstanding, within a few decades its trade and gift diplomacy smoothed relations between Chinese and Xiongnu far more successfully than walls ever had. By the mid-second century BC, the northern border was fairly peaceful, with the communities on it suffering only minor raids. The old frontier walls seem to have lost their military significance as, Sima Qian tells us, 'from the Shanyu downwards, all the Xiongnu grew friendly with the Han, coming and going along the Long Wall'.[9]

~

Peace and Friendship went severely against the grain of Sino-centric self-importance, however. Chinese appeasement of the Xiongnu, wrote the outraged Confucian official Jia Yi, was as unbalanced as 'a person hanging upside down'.

The Son of Heaven [emperor] is the head of the empire. Why? Because he should remain on the top. The barbarians are the feet of the empire. Why? Because they should be placed at the bottom. Now, the Xiongnu are arrogant and insolent on the one hand, and invade and plunder us on the other ... Yet each year Han provides them with money, silk floss and fabrics. To command the barbarian is the power vested in the Emperor on the top, and to present tribute to the Son of Heaven is a ritual to be performed by the vassals at the bottom. Hanging upside down like this beggars understanding.[10]

Yet the Chinese at least had the sense to realize that, unless they wanted a repeat of the defeat of 200 BC, nothing could be done until they had properly recovered – economically and organizationally – from civil war. By 141 BC, the year that the reign of the emperor Wu began, austerity policies pursued by the first six Han emperors looked to have set the Han back on their feet. The imperial treasuries had been stuffed with cash for so long that 'the strings holding the coins together had fallen apart'; a surplus of grain overflowed from the granaries, left rotting and exposed to the elements.[11] Emperor Wu ('the martial emperor') ploughed these funds straight into the military, which enjoyed a dramatic renaissance during his fifty-four-year rule. One of the reasons for Gaozu's embarrassing failure at Pingcheng had been his unfamiliarity with the conventions of steppe warfare, his inability to fight the Xiongnu on their own terms. By Wu's reign, these tactical lessons had been learned and, led by some of the greatest military geniuses in Chinese history – Wei Qing, the 'General of Carriage and Cavalry'; Huo Qubing, the 'Swift Cavalry General'; Zhao Ponu, the 'Hawklike Attacking Marshal'; and Zhang Qian, the 'Marquis of Broad Vision' – a new series of Chinese offensives against the barbarians began.[12] The most enduring legacy of these campaigns, apart from the rate at which they emptied the imperial coffers, was walls.

Emperor Wu's first target was that old bugbear of relations between China and the steppe: the Ordos. After a few years of inconclusive skirmishes, in 127 BC Wei Qing rode out north and reconquered the old Qin territory south of the Yellow River, seizing more than a million cattle and sheep in the process. Uncowed by this Han resurgence, the Xiongnu kept up their raids, each time provoking Chinese campaigns deeper and deeper into the steppe, the furthest almost 440 kilometres north of Beijing. One of the greatest Chinese triumphs was Wei Qing's ambush and near-capture in 124 BC of a Xiongnu king who had over-confidently drunk himself into a stupor before the arrival of the Han forces.

The Han lost no time in rebuilding walls, 'repairing the old system of defences that had been set up by Meng Tian during the Qin dynasty and strengthening the frontier along the Yellow River'.[13] Archaeologists now think that the Han went a good deal further than repairing old walls; that they erected thousands of kilometres of their own across the northern frontier. Fifteen kilometres of assuredly Han wall have been excavated in Hebei, north-east China, still eight metres wide at its base, but only a squat 1.5 metres high.[14] Remains found of the Inner Mongolian wall built up during Emperor Wu's reign include embankments, beacon stations and forts, all a combination of a tamped-earth core and stone frontage, pragmatically drawn from their immediate surroundings. Set hundreds of kilometres beyond the Han frontier at Wuyuan, the ruins of a fortified town in Inner Mongolia roughly 125 metres square – its original walls now resembling elongated dry stone heaps, sometimes 2.8 metres high – enclose clusters of stone buildings and scattered relics left by past occupants: tiles, ceramics, farming implements and arrowheads.[15]

The second arm of Emperor Wu's assault on the Xiongnu stretched far out west, to east of the Taklamakan desert in present-day Xinjiang. If the ancient Chinese viewed the northern steppe lands ('swamps and saline wastes, not fit for habitation') with a combination of terror and contempt, they regarded the mysterious far west with even greater trepidation. Early imperial China might have been expansionist, but it still believed there was no place like home: civilization ended some 200 kilometres from the capital. Han China would have drawn some of its 'knowledge' about the west from a third-century-BC piece of imaginative geography, the *Classic of Mountains and Seas,* which informed its nervous readers that out west, in the land of Mount Scorched and River Coldhot, reptiles looked like hares, men grew arms back-to-front and an avian breed known as the Mad Birds went about in officials' caps.[16] A slightly more earthbound Chinese source – the official *History of the Han* – gave prospective travellers visceral warning of the perils of going west: the risk of starvation and robbery, the dizzying heights of 'the Greater and the Lesser Headache' mountain ranges, the slopes of 'the Fever of the Body' which 'cause a man to suffer fever; he has no colour, his head aches and he vomits'.[17]

But for Han China, political needs overruled the terrors of altitude sickness. After 209 BC, the Xiongnu had conquered the tribes bordering western China. This not only constructed a Xiongnu power bloc on the western border; it also created the very real possibility of a dangerous alliance between the Xiongnu and the Qiang tribe, which occupied present-day Tibet. Emperor Wu's grand strategy was to cut off the right arm of the Xiongnu by colonizing the Gansu corridor, a stretch of relatively farmable and governable land between the mountains, steppes and deserts lying due north and south, fortifying it against further

Xiongnu assault with a wall and cultivating anti-Xiongnu alliances with the western peoples: a ragbag of tribes, mini-states and walled cities, the smallest of which had a population of 1,000, the largest one of over 600,000.

In 139 BC, Emperor Wu's envoy and general, Zhang Qian, set out on a pioneering diplomatic mission to the west. Zhang's final destination would be the new resting place of the Yuezhi tribe – then in the process of migrating towards Bactria, in contemporary northern Afghanistan about 6,500 kilometres west of the Han capital at Chang'an (near present-day Xi'an) – and his mission would be to persuade them, as a personal favour to the Chinese, to return to the site of their ignominious and bloody defeat at the hands of the Xiongnu in Gansu and expel the invaders. Unwisely taking a short cut through Xiongnu territory, Zhang was promptly captured and detained for over ten years, gaining a Xiongnu wife and children in the process, until he managed to escape and, slave to imperial duty that he was, continue his journey westwards, over the Pamir mountains to Bactria. When he finally tracked down the Yuezhi, they did not prove amenable to the idea of confronting the Xiongnu to suit the political ends of the Chinese. They were, they informed him politely but firmly, perfectly happy where they were. Zhang Qian then began his weary trudge home, only to be captured yet again by the Xiongnu before finally escaping back to Chang'an, after another year's detention.

Overlooking the obviously abortive outcome of Zhang Qian's mission, Wu was enraptured by his envoy's tales of the western oasis states, whose inhabitants farmed and lived in walled towns (both reassuringly familiar to the Chinese), and of their many 'unusual products': jade, wine, pearls, monkeys, peacocks, coral, amber, lions, rhinoceroses, eggs as big as water jars.[18] Most exciting of all were Zhang Qian's stories of the exceptionally hardy 'heavenly' blood-sweating horses of Ferghana, east of Bactria, which Wu determined to possess for his cavalry forces. Zhang Qian suggested a means of doing so. The way of life in these states, he reported, was 'not unlike that of China ... their forces were weak, and they prized Han wealth and goods ... If they were really won over and made into subjects by the exercise of moral pressure it would be possible to extend [Han] territory for ten thousand *li*.'[19] Zhang Qian's reports suggested a second excellent reason – economics – for Chinese expansion and wall-building westwards, and trailblazed one of the most famous trade routes in the world: the Silk Road. The idea was to establish a route which could be defended from Mongolian and Tibetan marauders, and thus to provide protection for (and extract customs duties from) merchants and their valuable caravans on their way to and from Central Asia and northern India.

During the 120s and 110s BC, it became clear that 'moral pressure' – diplomatic overtures that included marriage between an extremely unwilling Han princess and the king of a tribe settled around the Ili River, around present-day Krygyzstan – alone would not work its magic on the western states, and the Chinese ended up resorting to brute force. Around 120 BC, fresh from chasing the Xiongnu far into northern Mongolia, Wu's generals – leading hundreds of thousands of cavalry and infantry – annihilated a force of perhaps 40,000 of the Xiongnu in the west. Some two years later, the Shanyu was himself briskly chased back out north.[20] Another few years later, after the king of the western state closest to China – a Xiongnu sympathizer – had been captured by Zhao Ponu, the 'Hawk-like Attacking Marshal', and 700 light cavalry, the Han felt that the north-west had been swept sufficiently clear of troublesome barbarians to permit the building of a string of forts, garrisons and walls stretching out beyond the Gansu corridor as far as Yumenguan, the 'Jade Gate' pass, about seventy-five kilometres north-west of Dunhuang and on the edge of the saline swamps of the Lop Nor lake.

The strategic reasons for choosing Dunhuang and Yumenguan as the last outposts of Chinese civilization in the north-west are obvious from a glance at the region's topography. Both are located at the end of the Gansu corridor, the furthest logical point of extension for China before the land became utterly inimical to Chinese patterns of life and organization: desert, mountain or a hostile combination of the two. For those braving the Silk Road from the east, Dunhuang was the final agricultural stop-off at which supplies for the desert journey ahead could be bought, its oasis-fed peach and pear orchards supplying the markets that traded briskly with the town's steady stream of travellers. Beyond Yumenguan, the land became dramatically less welcoming. A salty, swampy river valley merging into desert prevented easy passage further west, while the north and south were blocked by mountains. If Dunhuang and Yumenguan could be held, they would prevent the Xiongnu or their allies from rampaging eastwards along the Gansu corridor into central China and Wu's extravagant capital, Chang'an – a conglomeration of scarlet and white palaces, of imperial pleasure gardens and lakes, devotional halls and pavilions, vibrant markets and clustered civilian dwellings packed 'as closely as the teeth of a comb'[21] – and they would guarantee safe passage for outward- and inward-bound trade caravans along this same corridor. Hundreds of years after the Han, Dunhuang remained the axis of communication between China and the West. When Buddhism drifted into China via Indian monks, Dunhuang – as the first point of contact between travellers from the West and China – became a religious centre, a repository of Buddhist art and learning, its rocky cliff hollowed out into a honeycomb of cave shrines decorated by wealthy, devout travellers either praying or offering grateful thanks for a safe passage across the perilous desert.

~

Some 2,000 years later, in the second week of March 1907, centuries after the old trade routes of the Silk Road had been submerged by the Central Asian desert, a barbarian-laden caravan of wind-blasted camels and donkeys approached Dunhuang from the west, in search of plunder. Almost a year previously, its leader, an Anglo-Hungarian explorer-archaeologist called Aurel Stein had set off from India for China's westernmost frontier, travelling over frozen, avalanche-ridden passes, up snow walls, then into the glaring, blistering, dusty heat of the Taklamakan desert. By

December 1906, the smooth, sandy, parched expanses of the Takla-makan – its skies perilously prone to erupting suddenly into *kara-buran,* 'black hurricanes' that for hours on end scoured the desert and any unlucky passers-by with an abrasive whirlwind of sand and pebbles – had given way to the hard-frozen clay banks, Gobi gales and sandstorms of the Lop Nor desert in winter. Chinese travelogues traditionally mapped the ashen, lunar landscapes surrounding the salty Lop Nor lake as a spectral no man's land, where pilgrims, travellers and merchants were waylaid by ghosts and spirits, then led astray to their deaths. The only navigating marks on the whole desolate landscape, remarked the Chinese Buddhist pilgrim Faxian at the end of the fourth century AD, were 'the dry bones of the dead left upon the sand'.[22] Passing through some thousand years later, Marco Polo described its near-absolute emptiness, barren of everything but ghostly voices that made solitary, nocturnal wayfarers 'stray from the path ... in this way many travellers have been lost and have perished'.[23] In the winter of 1906, the desert threatened to defeat even the expedition's camels: Stein fell asleep at night to the sound of their moans of pain, as their driver stitched ox-hide on to their feet, to reinforce soles cracked by the unyielding, saline clay.[24]

Driving Stein on through this almost unfathomably difficult journey was the prospect of treasure troves of archaeological booty, traces of once flourishing oasis cities strung out along and enriched by the old Silk Road, but abandoned centuries ago, after the Ming dynasty shut the doors on caravan traffic between China and the far west, and in time swallowed up by the shifting sands of the Taklamakan (literally, in Turki, 'go in and you won't come out').[25] To those who survived it, the Silk Road in its heyday brought the profits of a vigorous two-way trade between China and India (and, eventually, Europe) in gold, ivory, jade, coral, glass, cinnamon, rhubarb and, of course, silk. But the Silk Road did not merely transport luxury commodities into the hands of those hungry for material exotica; it was also the highway along which Buddhism travelled from India to China. As monks set off into Chinese

Central Asia along the same paths taken by laden caravans, monasteries, grottoes, pagodas and stupas – their interiors bright with devotional art – sprang up in their wake, throughout the settlements where they paused for rest.

Stein had learned of the existence of these oases of early Buddhism from a rather less spiritual source: from spies and surveyors playing the Great Game, the nineteenth-century Anglo-Russian imperial tussle for alliances, influences and intelligence across the diplomatic no man's land of Central Asia. In the 1860s, as part of British India's continuing campaign to gather clandestine geographical and political information from Great Game country, an Indian clerk was dispatched to the then unknown Taklamakan and charged with mapping and observing everything he saw. Buried amid his copious jottings on topography and Russian activities, there glimmered vague stories of ancient houses and objects dug out of the desert; within forty years, these reports would fuel a seven-nation race across the desert to retrieve the remnants of Serindian (Stein's term for the hybrid Indian-Chinese style of art nurtured by Silk Road traffic) Buddhist civilization, to uncover thousands of buried manuscripts, sculptures and wall paintings. As the rumours gathered pace, and foreign travellers began to bring back reports of ancient items on sale in desert bazaars – musty black bricks of tea, four-pound gold coins, Buddhist figurines – the lost Silk Road trail drew in some of the most remarkable European explorer-archaeologists of their age: the Swedish Sven Hedin, the first European to penetrate deep into the Taklamakan and uncover the principal sites of these extraordinary finds; the French Paul Pelliot, an arrogantly brilliant sinologist fluent in thirteen languages; and Aurel Stein, later knighted by the King of England for services rendered to the archaeological collection of the British Museum, excoriated in China as an imperialist cave robber.[26]

In the winter of 1900–1901, Stein had made his first raid into the Taklamakan, travelling for weeks to reach Khotan, the now submerged capital of the province, often waking to find his tidily luxuriant moustache frozen hard to his top lip. Drawing warmth from fires fuelled by wood from ancient orchards that had once flourished near the former oasis, Stein and his labourers dug to uncover Buddhist frescoes, stucco reliefs, scraps of manuscript in both Brahmi and Chinese, enormous sculpted figures from the first millennium AD. His appetite whetted, Stein's aims for his second trip were more ambitious yet: to pursue, with competitors from Germany and France snapping at his heels, reports of the 'Caves of the Thousand Buddhas', hundreds of Buddhist grottoes lined with wall paintings, sheltered inside a cliffside twenty-five kilometres from Dunhuang, looming over a green valley at the close of the Gansu corridor, the last gasp of fertile, irrigable land before the walls of sand dune either side closed in to the Lop Nor desert.

Approaching again from the west in 1906–7, Stein spent months on the last stage of his journey, across the pitted, saline clay around Lop Nor, pausing several times en route at semi-buried ruins to unearth yet more Silk Road manuscripts and bright Buddhist frescoes, and to rummage through an ancient Chinese rubbish dump. But finally, only a few dozen kilometres from Dunhuang, he found his progress interrupted 'by an unmistakable and relatively well preserved watch-tower', some 4.5 metres square and seven metres high.[27] Rising up before him amidst gravel flats, belts of sand dunes and 'a maze of strange, towering clay terraces', from 'hopeless desert in which one might for weeks search in vain even for a salty spring', were the porous ruins of a frontier defence system,

remains of old Chinese road towers, and ... the line of an ancient 'Chinese wall' which traversed the desert for a great distance ... In many places it had almost been completely covered by drift sand; but the tamarisk layers which had been used to strengthen the *agger* cropped up so persistently that the eye caught the straight line as it stretched away for miles on the coarse sand.[28]

With the shadows of night descending, 'the desolation about this first relic of human agency in the desert was intense'.[29]

Following the wall along for almost five kilometres to the east, Stein began to stumble across millennia-old detritus: scraps of silk and hemp, and a wedge of wood that announced 'the clothes bag of one Lu Dingshi'. In places 2.5 metres thick and almost two metres high, its true elevation obscured by 'drift sand', several metres deep, 'which the winds had heaped up against it', the wall was bolstered every few kilometres by watchtowers set behind it, sometimes eleven metres square and almost seven metres high. As darkness fell, after some sixteen kilometres hiking along the wall line, Stein bagged his last ruin of the day, a large tamped-earth tower, a little eroded on its top layers to present 'the effect of a small truncated pyramid. Heavy impregnation with salt made the structure shimmer in the darkness.' Stein had found the westernmost extent of Han China's walls: the 2,000-year-old ramparts – built in the two decades either side of 100 BC – supporting the Jade Gate pass, their tamped-earth-and-twig layers sometimes several metres high, sometimes only betrayed by 'a slight swelling of the gravel soil ... and half-petrified reeds cropping out from its side and top'.[30]

For the time being, Stein delayed no more than a day or two on the wall, anxious to press on to Dunhuang itself. Once there, he came to hear of a rumour as astonishing as the story of the caves themselves: that the Daoist priest who guarded the caves had, a few years ago, chanced upon an enormous, secret cache of ancient manuscripts in one of the cave temples. Setting out immediately for the caves to investigate, Stein was frustrated to discover that the priest had gone begging in the town of Dunhuang, presumably to raise money for crude restoration work already begun. With the recess containing the manuscripts firmly locked and bolted, and the holder of the key absent, Stein had no choice but to return at a more propitious moment. He decided, then, to kick his heels for a month or two in the sands around the old Han wall before returning, in late May, to persuade the priest to part with thousands of books, manuscripts and silk paintings dating from the first millennium AD, in exchange for the equivalent of £130.

The blowy dust-filled desert landscapes of far north-west China are, in many respects, a preservationist's worst nightmare. Winds reshape sands into mounds that swamp former walls and ditches, or hammer exposed earthworks: by Stein's time, the surviving fragments of Han fortifications around Dunhuang had been eroded to resemble termite-ridden sandcastles. But sandstorms could also be randomly forgiving to man-made efforts: sand deposits and local desiccation had protected many of the remains uncovered by Stein. With the help of a torpid team of opium-addict workers – 'the craziest crew I had ever led digging' and in regular need of drug breaks – Stein found not just fragments of wall up to eight kilometres long in continuous stretches, sometimes almost two metres high and studded with ruined watchtowers, forts and storehouses, but also relics and artefacts that enabled him to date his findings, and to imagine the kind of life that was led around them.[31] Rootling around in long-abandoned ancient Chinese rubbish heaps near the watchtowers, he turned up bowls, ladles, chopsticks, combs, dice, ornaments, weapons and, as would befit a military post along the Silk Road, fragments of Shantung silk.[32] Most historically illuminating of all, he unearthed a number of bamboo slips on which were etched or written dated details of how the Han administration made these far-flung outposts of Chinese authority workable: supplying granaries and clothing stores, managing the postal system (kept moving by conscript runners), policing the borders, exacting customs duties, posting ambassadors out to Central Asian states, establishing military agricultural colonies to ease provisioning problems. 'There are reports of troop movements, rapid changes at headquarters – & urgent reminders about starving detachments,' Stein wrote to a friend.

I feel at times as I ride along the wall to examine new towers, as if I were going to inspect posts still held by the living ... Two thousand years seems so brief a span when the sweepings from the soldiers' huts still lie practically on the surface in front of the door, or ... the track within the wall trodden by the patrols of so many years ... and weak points along the marsh-edge where prowling Hun freebooters might have lurked for a rush.[33]

The earliest of these slips went back to the start of the first century BC, linking the garrisons with Han-period accounts of wall-building under Emperor Wu. Further inscriptions on tablets, letters and silk in Indian and Aramaic script hinted at the cosmopolitan nature of the traffic passing back and forth through China's most remote garrison. Altogether, Stein traced the wall for ninety-six kilometres, ending at its westernmost point, where it prudently stopped just short of a 'huge depression ... an impassable bog in most places' which 'with its glittering salt efflorescence looked at times as if it were still one big lake'. Southwards lay a chain of formidably high dunes; beyond them, snowy mountains signposting the way to the Tibetan plateau.[34]

The extent of these westernmost defences suggests a force of at least several thousand soldiers was required to man them – the users of the everyday objects Stein found. The ruins of one guardhouse – last occupied, Stein deduced, in 57 BC – evoked the enforced simplicity of frontier life, its interior divided into three bare rooms, decorated by hooks for weapons, and once warmed by a fire in one corner, its floor littered with coarse rope shoes and rags of worn, much-mended silk. Beyond the artefacts that told of how the soldiers were kept busy on garrison duties – wood gathered for the beacon fires that transmitted warnings of imminent attack, and tools for farming – and how their basic needs were met, a few tablets, slips and relics offered clues about their social and professional lives. Leave seems to have been short – one soldier, surnamed Wang, worked 355 days in a year. But Stein also found evidence of socializing: a note scratched on wood by three friends come to call on the garrison commandant, for example, or a tablet announcing the imminent celebration of a family feast.[35] Cultural diversions ranged from high to low, from calligraphy practice to gambling with dice. Fragments of literary texts – books of divination and astrology, and the moralizing textbook *Biographies of Eminent Women* – show that choices of comfort reading (self-help and slushy, popular classics) don't change much across continents and millennia. Sometimes, however, soldiers posted out to the western end of the Chinese earth could still their discontent no longer, grumbling in private letters about the last five years spent in this 'miserable country', about the emperor's failure to respond to petitions for promotion away from the desert, about how rotten the spring weather was.[36]

Like the remains of the Qin wall, none of these extensive and elaborate Han constructions bore much physical resemblance or historical relation to the stone fortifications restored around Beijing today. The written sources seldom identify the westward extension of the Han wall as one stretch of a single 'Long Wall' but instead provide scattered references to *ting* (military posts), *zhang* (barriers) or *sai* (frontiers, implying border walls). A more historically rigorous chronicler of Chinese walls than most of his fellow Western wall-explorers, Stein himself only occasionally referred to his discoveries as forming part of the 'Great Wall', preferring instead the term 'Chinese *limes*', making use of the Roman word for an ancient defensive system. True, the general westward defence line sketched out by the Han more or less followed the strategic route taken by wall-builders all the way up to the sixteenth and seventeenth centuries. But the Han defences outstretched even those of the Ming, the most assiduously wall-building dynasty of all, which reached no further than Jiayuguan, about 220 kilometres east of Dunhuang. The basic building principle for these fortifications was the same as that used for all the early Chinese walls so far encountered: the relatively cheap and easy tamping technique, compressing layers of the local terrain, in this case, clay or gravel, between fascines of whatever natural substance came to hand (generally tamarisk twigs or reeds, occasionally sun-dried bricks). Where fibrous, layered twigs were used, the overall effect, as it survives in discrete, ruined blocks today, resembles a massive, sandy millefeuilles, served up on the yellow-grey scree of the desert. Erected quickly in a season or two, these walls also steadily deteriorated: although some were lucky enough to be protected by shifting dunes, fortifications left exposed were hammered by steppe winds and sand particles. Struck 'by the skill with which the old Chinese engineers had improvised their rampart' using materials 'particularly well adapted to local conditions', Stein estimated that 'it could hold its own against ... all forces, in fact, but that of slow-grinding but almost incessant wind erosion'.[37]

~

Wherever possible, the Han tried to take the moral high ground over the Qin, as the more humane, virtuous, friendly face of Chinese empire. Not for the Han were the tyrannical Qin excesses of taxation, conscription and gigantic public works. But in wall construction, the Han far outbuilt their illustrious predecessors. Archaeologists have estimated that the Han restored or built over 10,000 kilometres of wall, to the Qin's 5,000, and their walls generated as much popular suffering and melancholic legend as their Qin forerunners.[38] The official record – such as this Emperor Wu-period propaganda ode – was, of course, triumphantly bombastic about the fruits of frontier toil:

> When the emperor makes his imperial tour, all is resplendent.
> As the summer arrives, he goes north, to Sweet Spring Palace.
> Both winter and summer being mild, he travels to Stone Pass Palace,
> and receives the northwestern states.
> The Yuezhi are humbled, the Xiongnu submit.
> ...boundless joy reigns for ten thousand years.[39]

Social history tells a different story. The Han government had constant difficulties persuading civilians to settle the bleak frontier zone, and bamboo slips and wedges of wood made up as passports found near Dunhuang suggest that the walls were designed as much to keep the unfortunate Chinese border people in as they were to keep unruly barbarians out. An important part of garrison work – particularly in the northwest – was policing ingoers and outgoers, preventing Chinese civilians from fleeing to the Xiongnu, and evading their tax and corvée obligations. The Han faced similar problems persuading farmers to settle in the inhospitable far north. Between AD 2 and 140, for example, the population of the northern provinces shrank from 3,000,000 to 500,000.[40] Aurel Stein inferred that a subsidiary rampart he discovered built perpendicular to the main north-westerly thrust of wall might have been designed to prevent Chinese fugitives from escaping too easily into the salty flats beyond the Jade Gate Pass.[41] Considering what the humans and camels of Stein's party suffered on their journey from the west, life further east must have been unbearable in the extreme to make the Taklamakan desert look inviting. Stein's tentative hypothesis certainly makes a mockery of the clichéd view of the wall as a benignly protective cordon defending paradisaical China from its covetous barbarian neighbours. The exhausting desolation of border garrison life, hundreds of kilometres from the comforting security of civilization, is evoked by plaintive poetic voices:

> We fight south of the wall, we die north of the wall;
> If we die, unburied, in the wilds, our corpses will feed the crows.
> ...
> The waters run deep and turbulent, the reeds grow dark and murky;
> The cavalry fight to the death, their exhausted steeds pace up and down,
>   whinnying.
> Near the bridge a house used to stand, whether to north or south, no-one
>   can know.
> If the rice isn't harvested, how will you eat?
> Although we are willing to serve loyally, how can we live this way?
> You will be remembered, worthy, honest soldiers.
> We sally forth at dawn, but do not return at dusk.[42]

Another poet laments the lonely separations enforced by frontier service:

> Green grow the grasses on the bank;
> I think endlessly about how far away your path has taken you,

So unimaginably far.

I dreamt that I saw you again,

That you were by my side,

But woke to remember you are in foreign lands;

Foreign lands and different regions,

Always on the move, separated from me.

The withered mulberry trees know the sharpness of the wind,

The oceans know the bite of the cold.

But those who return think only of themselves,

No-one will speak of you to me.

A guest has arrived from distant parts,

He brings me an envelope.

I call to my son to open it:

Inside there is a letter on white cloth.

I kneel to read it,

what will it say?

You start by telling me to eat more,

You end, saying how much you miss me.[43]

For garrison officers and commanders, too, frontier life was harsh. Considering the hardships the job entailed, Wu received remarkably committed service from his generals. There were, of course, attractions to the career: for a natural and exceptionally skilful horseman and archer such as Huo Qubing, steppe warfare must have offered a uniquely exhilarating combination of speed, risk and opportunity. Huo's speciality was breaking off with a few hundred of his best cavalry from the main body of the army to strike deep into enemy territory, emulating the strategies of the nomads themselves.

Nonetheless, battling the Xiongnu hordes was undoubtedly the toughest, riskiest and most exhausting military job in the empire. Generals such as Huo Qubing and Zhang Qian were faced with the fiercest nomad fighters in Central Asia: defeat in battle probably meant death or, worse still, spending the afterlife as the Shanyu's drinking cup. The physical and climatic conditions were hostile in the extreme, lurching between mountain and desert, between freezing winters and burning summers. During one battle against the Xiongnu, a dust storm arose of such severity that both armies were obscured to each other. With very limited means of communication across huge, unwelcoming swathes of land (running battles could last for six days on end), the margins for error, such as delays in arrival of reinforcements, were large. And the task never seemed to end: one year, Huo Qubing could defeat 100,000 Xiongnu and resettle the surrendered south of the Yellow River; the next year, the Xiongnu would raid again.

Huo Qubing's exceptional successes, in any case, came at a huge human cost. A workaholic, he could be mercilessly insensitive to his soldiers' needs for food and rest. Sima Qian portrays him as a tyrannical hedonist, forcing his soldiers to dig out a sports field for his own recreational entertainment when they were so lacking in food they could barely stand up. For both generals and soldiers, however, the rewards for victories were considerable: titles and land for the supreme commander, riches for his men. But the penalties for defeat were also severe: with the exception of the apparently infallible Huo Qubing, almost every other general under Wu at some point found himself in trouble with the emperor over mistakes made on the battlefield. Failure on campaign, whether it entailed arriving late for a rendezvous or losing soldiers, merited the death penalty. Commanders were occasionally permitted to save themselves by paying large fines – a useful source of loose change for the imperial purse. Civilians protested this harsh treatment at their peril: Sima Qian, Emperor Wu's grand historian, was offered an unappealing choice between death and castration after speaking out in defence of Li Ling, a failed general. (He chose the latter and completed his history.) One of the most heartless stories of Wu's handling of his generals concerns Li Guang, a renowned strategist who, after being badly injured and captured by the Xiongnu, played dead until he spotted a sturdy horse, on to which he leapt and galloped fifteen or so kilometres to rejoin his men and lead them back into Chinese territory, dispatching several Xiongnu pursuers with bow and arrow as he went. After his return to the capital, however, Wu's law officers recommended he be executed for being captured alive; he only escaped death by ransoming his own life. Unsurprisingly, even the most loyal generals, those whose job it was to stiffen the upper lip of their subordinates, came to view postings north as something to be avoided at all costs: one officer, a native of Dunhuang, pleaded not to be sent back there, comparing such a fate to ruin and death.[44] Some 2,000 years later, as Stein sat in one of the watchtowers, 'with my eyes wandering over this vast expanse of equally desolate marsh and gravel ... it seemed easy to call back the dreary lives which had once been lived here ... everything bore the impress of death-like torpor'.[45]

~

The net result of all these campaigns and walls was inevitable: exhaustion and bankruptcy. Hundreds of thousands of soldiers had been involved – 180,000 cavalrymen in a victory parade led by Emperor Wu in 111 BC alone – all of whom needed feeding, clothing, arming and, when appropriate, rewarding. The campaigns of 125–124 BC yielded 19,000 Xiongnu and a million sheep to the Chinese, but also cost 200,000 *jin** of gold in rewards and the loss of 100,000 horses.[46] And on the steppe, nomadic surrender did not come cheap: the Chinese once persuaded one of the Xiongnu kings to submit only through spending ten billion cash – the total government revenue for that year – on gifts for him and his people. If the victories left the Chinese government out of pocket, the defeats were devastatingly wasteful: 80 per cent of Chinese forces were lost in a single attack in 104 BC.[47] It was not even the case that all this effort produced long-lasting, tangible successes over the Xiongnu. The Chinese could never defeat the Xiongnu emphatically by campaigns or fortifications: since they did not occupy a fixed territory in the same way as the

* One *jin* is 244g.

87

Chinese, they could not be permanently colonized. Instead, they either fled to the northern edge of the Mongolian steppe, implicitly challenging the Chinese to undertake a wearying and futile pursuit, or waited to attack a weak point in the border defences. The Han invariably performed better against the more settled states of Central Asia, eventually managing to conquer Dayuan (Ferghana, home of the heavenly, blood-sweating horses) in 102–101 BC.

All this expenditure had to be financed, though, and taxation and conscription were the obvious answers. But both these solutions invited unfortunate comparisons between Emperor Wu and a certain earlier, catastrophically unpopular emperor of China, also renowned for his wall-building and bottomless demand for conscript labour. '[T]he burden of military service is apt to lead to disaffection,' warned one court minister, 'for the people along the border are subject to great strain and hardship until they think only of breaking away, while generals and officers grow suspicious of each other and begin to bargain with the enemy.'[48]

The vast financial costs of Emperor Wu's tactics of aggression dictated a retreat from expensive expansion and wall-building in the eighty years following his reign, and a return to the policy of Peace and Friendship. The Chinese court circumvented the loss of face that this represented by giving it a new, more congenial name: the tribute system. Han tribute relations involved much the same bribery of the non-Chinese (with money, goods and princesses) as Peace and Friendship; the only qualitative difference was that the Xiongnu accepted nominal vassal status by sending a high-born hostage to China, paying homage to the emperor and offering 'tribute' (which could include objects of no particular value or use to the Chinese). When the Chinese first attempted to institute this diplomatic relationship, the Shanyu went into a tremendous sulk. 'This is not the way things were done under the old alliance,' he objected peevishly. 'Under the old alliance the Han always sent us an imperial princess, as well as allotments of silks, foodstuffs, and other goods … Now you want to go against old ways and make me send my son as hostage.'[49]

But the Xiongnu soon realized just how cosmetic was this offering of subservience to the Chinese. In 53 BC, with the Xiongnu leadership split between two warring brothers, the weaker brother, Huhanye, who had fled south to the Han border, dispatched a hostage to China and restored himself to a position of supremacy among the Xiongnu – attracting and rewarding followers – through the profits of the tribute system. Yet provided the Chinese could swallow their gall at subsidizing the barbarian lifestyle, a peace won by tribute was cheaper than walls and war.

In 33 BC, the Chinese supplemented their Xiongnu subventions with a Chinese princess. According to Chinese legend, the beautiful palace lady Wang Zhaojun refused to bribe the court painter Mao Yenshou when he painted her portrait for the emperor's reference catalogue of concubines. In revenge, Mao added a fictitious but deeply inauspicious black mole under her right eye. When Emperor Yuandi was deciding which concubine to give up to the Xiongnu leader, this disfigurement made Wang Zhaojun – whom Yuandi had never seen in the flesh – the obvious candidate. The moment the emperor finally laid eyes on Wang Zhaojun as she was presented to the Xiongnu ambassador, he realized he had been tricked. Reneging on his agreement, however, would run an intolerable risk of renewed warfare with the Xiongnu, and Wang Zhaojun was led beyond the wall to become Queen of the Xiongnu and an important player in steppe diplomacy. Instead, the emperor vented his rage on Mao, who was promptly hacked to pieces. In later centuries, Wang became a favourite subject for melancholic Chinese poets, who toyed endlessly with her legend, sometimes letting her drown herself in a frontier river, at other times condemning her to die slowly of sorrow, pining away her years at the Xiongnu court, 'forced to haunt the outer halls, to watch the singing and dancing / Waiting with her attendants for the Shanyu to return from his night hunt'.[50]

~

By the birth of Christ, Han frontier policy had already run full circle, moving from the collapse of frontier defences amid the chaos of civil war, on to economic and military consolidation, sabre-rattling expansion and wall-building, and ending in over-extension and retreat. When, following a fourteen-year usurpation by a former regent of the Han, China disintegrated in AD 23 into two years of intensely regionalized civil war, the cycle looked set to recommence. The principal postures of frontier relations had also been thoroughly rehearsed: aggression, alliance, blackmail and compromise. Within this diplomatic framework, frontier walls marked an idealized border between Chinese and non-Chinese, sometimes but by no means constantly manned, maintained and upheld, and rarely static. While some form of diplomatic bribery approximating to the Peace and Friendship policy – the only effective, long-term way of keeping peace – remained in place, the walled borders served as either a mutually respected or unnecessary and therefore demobilized frontier. But when the Chinese unwisely went on the offensive, which they frequently did, disturbing the fragile balance of relations, devastating violence almost always ensued, against which frontier walls offered little protection.

After its restoration in AD 25, the Han dynasty would last another 200 years, but make no new wall-building mistakes. The nearest that the Chinese came to a frontier innovation in the second half of the Han was when Emperor Guangwu (AD 25–57) tried to get round the inherent strategic limitations of static walls – the fact that horse-mounted invaders could simply gallop until they reached the walls' end – by making the walls mobile, building turrets on to oxen-pulled vehicles. Chinese histories maintain a rather embarrassed silence about the success of his venture; it is certainly an experiment that no other ruler chose to repeat.[51]

Towards the end of the second century AD, the Han were displaying the unmistakable symptoms of dynastic decline: talentless emperors, domineering eunuchs, over-taxation and official corruption. As early as AD 132, in response to Han weakness, regional opposition groups (the so-called 'magic rebels') began arguing – by means of signs, miracles, prophecies or impenetrable metaphysical calculations – that the Han's cosmological energy was on the wane, that power should be transferred to a dynasty whose element was in the ascendant. The Han's inability to suppress these local rebellions forced it to appoint powerful regional commanders who inevitably, when the time seemed right, made their own bid for imperial power. The most successful of these was Cao Cao, a former Han general, who in AD 196 managed to place the fugitive last Han emperor under permanent palace arrest and found his own kingdom in the north.

Cao Cao's defeat of his rivals was contingent on a confusing series of shifting alliances between northern tribes, who seemed happy both to capitalize on China's disarray, by indulging in raiding and pillaging, and to sell their military services to the highest-paying passing Chinese faction. The distractions of the civil war prevented China's new warlord rulers from safeguarding the northern frontier from these rampaging tribes, and in AD 215 Cao Cao formally abandoned the Ordos frontier region. Not long after, China ceased to exist as a unified empire.

For 400 years, the Han dynasty had tirelessly forged alliances, presented gifts and brides, led campaigns and repaired or built perhaps 10,000 kilometres of walls across the entire span of its northern frontiers, from the north-east coast to the edge of the north-western desert. None of this effort was any defence against opportunistic tribesmen who, after the fall of the Han in AD 220, were no longer content simply with goods and grain from south of the wall. They now wanted a piece of China for themselves, and no walls were going to stop them.

Wall building: Northern Wei, Northern Qi and Sui dynasties (AD 386–618)

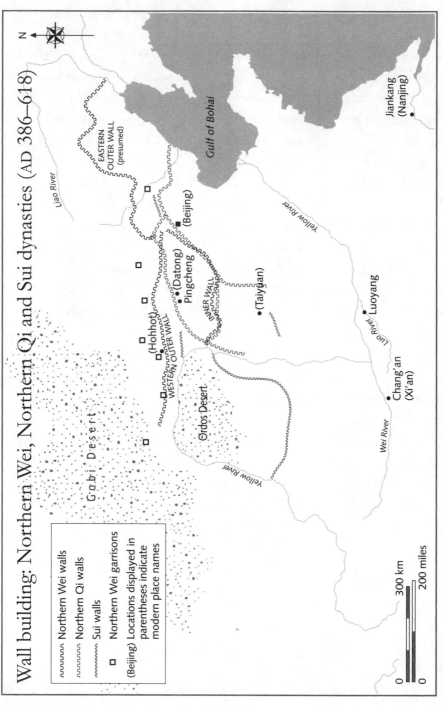

Note: locations of Northern Wei and Sui walls described in *Changcheng baike quashu* and *Changcheng guoji xueshu yantaohui lunwenji*.

CHAPTER FOUR

Shifting Frontiers and Decadent Barbarians

In 547, a Chinese civil servant paid a visit to Luoyang, ancient capital to Chinese dynasties both legendary and real since the third millennium BC. Set in the centre of the northern half of the country, the city lay amid the rivers that had carved out the plain on which it rested and between the mountains that made it defensively strong but not impregnable. There, however, he surveyed not a flourishing imperial conglomeration of temples and pagodas, a metropolis that could hope to match or even better the glorious parks and palaces of dynasties past, but a scene of charred desolation. The passer-by, Yang Xuanzhi, who years before had been a low-ranking courtier at this very city, the former capital of the recently defunct Northern Wei dynasty, would have been greeted everywhere not by the bustle of busy officials, extravagant aristocratic retinues, Buddhist processions, exotic diplomatic embassies and sharp traders going about their business, but by near-deserted vistas of destruction and dereliction. Although the blood of some 3,000 courtiers massacred twenty or so years earlier would by then have been washed away from a nearby hillside, the ground would still have been littered with the burned ruins of palaces and houses, with the rubble of a city wall once over twelve kilometres long.

Only two decades previously, Luoyang had been a very different place. Overwhelmed with nostalgia for the demolished capital that had once employed him, Yang Xuanzhi painstakingly resurrected its past glory in the wistful eulogy that his visit inspired him to compose. In his 'Record of the Monasteries of Luoyang', Yang remembered a dazzling metropolis of ostentatious Buddhist piety, studded with towering pagodas, extravagant monasteries and convents lush with orchids, irises, pine and emerald bamboo, with golden religious statues dozens of feet high, with laden orchards of heavenly carmine peaches, six-pound pears and five-inch jujubes, with parks and pleasure pools filled with exotic aquatic creatures, a city where the merchants were as rich as princes and where the princes spent tens of thousands of cash on a single meal, were accompanied at all times of day and night by flutes, gongs, trumpets and lutes, and whose horses drank from silver troughs and wore golden harnesses, a capital that drew to it, magnet-like, the allegiance of barbarians from a hundred different countries. It was in 528 that one tribe of these supposedly submissive barbarians marched on Luoyang, drowned the empress dowager and the child-emperor, butchered their officials, and sealed the doom of the capital and its ruling dynasty.[1]

Little more than half a century before Yang Xuanzhi's nostalgia trip, things had looked different again for the Northern Wei and their capital. Their Luoyang, for one thing, did not exist, but stood little more than a fortress encircled by the rubble of former city walls tenaciously overrun with brush vegetation, a derelict monument to a sacking by barbarians in 311. At the close of the fifth century, the Northern Wei were perched in a capital much further north, on the tip of Shanxi province, and recognizably remained the potent political and military force they had been another hundred years earlier: the most successful of the tough, warlike frontier tribes that had seized a piece of China after the collapse of the Han around 220, and that had triumphantly reinvented themselves as rulers of semi-nomadic, semi-Chinese states in the northern half of the country.

What, in the fifty years leading up to Yang's regretful return to the ashy ruins of this former capital, had brought this cataclysm down on

Luoyang's rulers? What had reduced the once vigorous Northern Wei to helpless hostages of the nomadic tribes among whom they had formerly ranked supreme? China, is the short, simple answer. Once in power, the nomads-turned-emperors of the fourth, fifth and sixth centuries – and the Northern Wei above all – were the first to experience the archetypal dilemma that conquest of slices of the Chinese empire created for successful steppe barbarians: whether to remain tough nomadic warriors or submit pleasurably to the civilized creature comforts of the settled Chinese culture they could dominate militarily and risk adulterating the muscular steppe traditions that had won them China in the first place.

To the new non-Chinese dynasties, the lure of China sprang partly from necessity, partly from reality and partly from propaganda. The first reason for sinicizing was practical: settled Chinese farmers could not be governed in the same way as pastoral nomads. Chinese-style government – with its focus on efficient tax administration and mass mobilization of labour for public works – had not evolved by chance, but to suit the needs of densely populated, intensive farming settlements. Secondly, China naturally attracted imitators and acolytes, as a civilization remarkably advanced in comparison to most of its contemporaries. (This remained the case as late as the eighteenth century. Contrary to popular impressions that China ruled the world until about 1500, when its insularity and backwardness had led it to be overtaken by the West, China remained a global superpower until around 1800, when the Industrial Revolution finally propelled the West ahead.) Early in the first millennium AD, China possessed technical innovations, such as paper and the wheelbarrow, a thousand years before Europe, and, thanks to its long-standing preoccupation with ceremony and ritual, a society at least theoretically more decorous than that of its neighbours. To many Asian onlookers, China and its erudite, ceremonious civilization represented a glittering example to be imitated and borrowed from. Finally, China's aura of superiority derived from its efficient and highly literate propaganda machine, from a sense of cultural self-confidence – fuelled by the reality of its own achievements – that it truly occupied the centre of the civilized world.

But as soon as one conquering horde began to abandon their steppe heritage – illiterate nomadism, animal hides, fermented mare's milk, tents – in favour of farming, poetry, silk, wine and houses with roofs, they became the sitting target for other steppe tribes that China had once been for them. Soon, they too needed to be looking anxiously over their shoulders to the west and the north, bracing themselves for raids by less decadent, still genuinely nomadic forces. For once a former steppe people had cast aside the intensely martial culture that had originally enabled them to vanquish the Chinese, within a couple of decades it became effectively incapable of successfully launching nomad-style punitive campaigns against insurgents.

This led the Northern Wei, one of the most powerful and long-lasting of the barbarian states to rule north China between the third and sixth centuries AD, to take a deeply Chinese recourse against incursions from the steppe: building walls. At the time, this seemed an excellent idea: what better physical statement was there to make about the gulf between the newly civilized, Confucian rulers of China and the still-benighted, illiterate tribes they had left behind on the steppe? But for the Wei, their walls eventually proved to be little more than that: a physical statement, not an effective defence.

~

The Northern Wei's tribal ancestors, the Xianbi, had not always been keen on Chinese culture. At about the time of their rise, during the second century AD, they were based around the Xingan mountains – a long, thin range of smoothly eroded, forested granite peaks on the border of present-day Mongolia and Manchuria – to which they had fled from Maodun's conquering Xiongnu hordes at the turn of the third century BC. Three and a half centuries after Maodun, however, the Xiongnu were a shadow of their former selves. Around AD 50, under concerted attack from neighbouring tribes, the new Xiongnu leader had been forced, humiliatingly, to kowtow to the Chinese, and obey the Han emperor's order that he move his capital to Meiji, within the north-east corner of the Yellow River loop. In AD 89, a Chinese force passed out of the walled frontier at Shuofang, in the north-west of the Yellow River loop, and effectively destroyed, for the time being, the remnants of northern Xiongnu power.

The Xianbi star went into the ascendant as a direct result of Xiongnu decline. 'During the reigns of Emperor Ming and Zhang (58–88), the Xianbi kept to the line of the Wall and there was no trouble,' recorded a late Han chronicle. 'During the time of the Emperor He (89–105) ... the Xiongnu were routed. The northern Shanyu took flight and the Xianbi moved in and occupied his land. The remainder of the Xiongnu who did not go with him still numbered over 100,000 tents and all styled themselves Xianbi. The Xianbi gradually grew in power from this time.'[2]

By the 140s AD, as the Xianbi moved to take over Mongolia and occupy the Ordos, inside the northern Yellow River loop, the Chinese responded to the rise of this new steppe power with distinctly poor judgement. Mindful of a traditional and well-loved Chinese frontier strategy, 'to make use of barbarians to control barbarians',[3] they persisted in trying to woo them as allies against the Xiongnu with money and trade – Xianbi 'tribute' in the form of sables and horses was reciprocated by Chinese gifts twice as valuable – while failing to register that the Xiongnu threat was as nothing compared to that of the Xianbi, who were busily expanding all over former Xiongnu territory. The Chinese were even generous, or careless, enough to arm the Xianbi, after failing to control the frontier wall passes sufficiently to prevent contraband sales of Chinese iron. The Han emperor of the time, Ling, clearly underestimated the nature of the Xianbi threat, sponsoring a high-society fashion for the barbarian tent, which he used in his palace. Far from flattered by the Chinese court's imitative cult of barbarianoiserie, the Xianbi remained an uncontrollable frontier menace, quite unawed by the prestige of Chinese civilization.

To the Chinese, the tribal laws and customs of the Xianbi made the Xiongnu look almost civilized. Although the Xiongnu were, in Chinese eyes, assuredly barbarians, their organization and administration struck a few chords in the ordered, bureaucratic Chinese mindset: there was hierarchy and hereditary succession – descendants of Maodun asserted their claim to the Xiongnu leadership quite effectively for 500 years, a century longer than the most enduring of Chinese dynasties, the Han. The Xianbi, by contrast, took an altogether more anarchically meritocratic approach to succession. Allegiance went to the leader who could demonstrate greatest prowess in battle. Instead of continuous family names, only 'the personal names of their most valiant chieftains were used'. Thus the weak or pacific were forgotten, while the belligerent were commemorated. The result was a tribal society even more endemically violent than that of the Xiongnu. The Xiongnu at least acknowledged the possible existence of peace, rather than war: any Xiongnu who unsheathed his sword at a time of peace would be punished by death. Among the Xianbi, however, 'if there were murders, the tribes were told to avenge themselves'; only 'if vengeance went on indefinitely' would they apply to the head chief 'to arrange matters'.[4] Entente with the Chinese and adherence to a boundary marked by a frontier wall were not in the best interests of a powerful Xianbi chieftain. Provided that they were successful generals, the personal prestige and power of Xianbi leaders thrived during times of war. Little surprise, then, that they proved more interested in extermination than negotiation.

~

Although the premature death of the first great Xianbi leader, Tanshihuai, in the 180s AD brought temporary respite to the Middle Kingdom's northern frontier, by this point Han China was disintegrating of its own accord into the hands of Chinese warlords more aggressive, opportunistic and risk-taking even than the nomads themselves. With the former cultural and military distinctions between Chinese and barbarians thus confused, the old frontier marked by walls also blurred, and for three and a half centuries, between the collapse of the Han in AD 220 and the reunification of China under the Sui dynasty in 581, political regimes and boundaries changed constantly, with anarchy and civil war never far away. The 'Three Kingdoms' – Wei in the north, Shu-han in the west and Wu in the south and south-east – were succeeded first by the Western Jin dynasty, which briefly reunited China between 280 and 316, then by the Eastern Jin, then by the Song, the Qi, the Liang and the Chen, toppled in turn by a series of rebellions by aristocrats, armies and magicians.[5]

The northern tribes remained happy to offer themselves to the Chinese as swords for hire until 304, when, tired of this circus of warlord allegiances, they started, for the first time, to found their own states across north China. The decision was partly driven by financial consider-ations: during times of civil war in China, the profits of tributary alle-giance were deeply unsatisfactory; indeed, in the aftermath of Han collapse, far from being able to keep the nomads in silk and tea, north China was so impoverished that the Xiongnu had traded its own sub-sidies back over the frontier. This new development was also influenced by the success of the Chinese civilizing process on the Xiongnu. Ever since some of the Xiongnu tribes had been resettled within the Yellow River loop in AD 50, they had been increasingly exposed to Chinese ways of life and government. In an additional effort to keep the frontier under control, Chinese warlord rulers since the fall of the Han had kept the Shanyu hostage at court. The net result of this policy was a fully and confidently sinicized Xiongnu leader: the first Xiongnu emperor, Liu Yuan, was a descendant of Maodun, had a classical Chinese education and – more practically – commanded 50,000 Xiongnu troops. After founding their state in 304, the Xiongnu proceeded to destroy Chinese control of the north, capturing both capital cities – Luoyang in 311, Chang'an in 316 – and executing emperors, entirely uninhibited by a recent wave of Chinese frontier wall-building.

One year after nominally reuniting China in 280, the Chinese Jin dynasty began to build walls against northern raiders, in the north-east, over the modern provinces of Hebei and Liaodong, nearing the eastern coast of Bohai. In 281, the dynastic history relates that a defence official 'reopened the old frontier and took 1,000 *li* of territory. The old Qin wall was rebuilt, extending over 3,000 *li* of mountains and ravines ... He divided the army into defence garrisons, building beacon towers to watch over the area. After this, peace was obtained on the national borders, and not even a dog barked in alarm.'[6] Almost nothing is now left of this sketchily described wall, which, despite the sense of security it gave the dynasty's dogs, failed to safeguard the Jin state from either within or without. After the Jin tried disbanding its armies following reunification, demobilized soldiers generated income by selling weapons over the northern borders, while the dynasty was destroyed by the Xiongnu barbarians already cosily ensconced within its borders. After the Xiongnu coup, China was carved up between barbarian states north of the Yangtze River and the Chinese Eastern Jin dynasty south of the river. Up to 70 per cent of the Chinese upper classes fled south, to the southern capital in Nanjing, their flight exposing them to a severe spiritual crisis that led many to find comfort in a new, foreign faith: Buddhism.

There was, however, more to ruling China than possessing a Confucian education and a large army, as the Xiongnu and the fifteen other barbarian groupings who founded states in north China between 304 and 439 soon discovered. Some lasting as few as ten years, none more than sixty-two, all faced the problem of how to rule two types of land – fields and steppe; of how to reconcile the Chinese habit of settled farming and government with the pastoral nomadic way of life, one which was ideal for waging war but less suited to post-conquest territorial administration. Chinese governing principles concentrated on fostering long-term agricultural development and boosting tax yields, to fund ever larger, denser, more sophisticated settlements. Nomadic tribes – including even the sinicized Xiongnu – were far more interested in short-term exploitation of land (for pasture or raiding), moving on to new pastures every few months. Another difficulty was the age-old hostility between nomads and Chinese: the Chinese viewed the northern tribes as raiding barbarians, while the nomads viewed the Chinese as raiding targets. The two societies, moreover, had very different ideas of rulership. Chinese political tradition asserted the emperor's authority over, and concern for, 'all under heaven', while the political interests of a tribal leader were far more narrowly limited to the welfare of his own people. A Shanyu with pretensions to the universal concerns of a Chinese emperor was bound to create discontent among his tribesmen.

In states across the whole breadth of the northern Chinese landmass – from the plateaux and valleys of Tibet in the west to the steppe and forests of Manchuria in the north-east – these same conflicts surfaced and resurfaced. If the tribal way of life dominated, the Chinese felt exploited and terrorized; if the Chinese way of government dominated, and bureaucrats began to dominate over soldiers, the nomad armies on whom the state's military strength depended felt alienated, and rebelled against the imperial court. As Fan Shi, a high-ranking nomad of a north-western kingdom, complained to the smart-talking Chinese minister hired by his state: 'In earlier times, my group participated with past leaders in launching this undertaking, but now we have no powers. You never even had to make your horse sweat, how dare you take control? It's as if we do the ploughing and sowing, and you eat the product!' 'Then,' the unfazed minister quipped back, 'we should make you chef, too. Why should you just have to plough and sow?' 'If it's the last thing I do,' the infuriated nomad snapped, 'I will hang your head on Chang'an's city gate!'[7] (The fashions of the time were against the disgruntled Fan, who was executed by his king shortly afterwards.)

Tribes from only one region – the Xianbi of Manchuria – managed to rule both China and steppe with much success, largely because geographically and economically the area naturally combined steppe and farming ways of life. In lower Manchuria, the Liao River plain permitted Chinese-style agriculture; further north lay steppe and forest, which supported pastoralism and stock-raising. The region was also well placed strategically, adjoining but geographically isolated from the plains of north China by mountains and a single coastal pass which, in the Ming dynasty, became the key border wall fort that gave access from Manchuria to the rest of China. In a retreat, Manchuria could be a defensive stronghold; in an attack, it offered speedy access to the rest of China. Its relative isolation from China and its political chaos gave Manchuria time and space to develop its own form of dual government, splitting the administration into a Chinese-style bureaucracy for agricultural areas and a tribal leadership for the military.

As early as 294, a Xianbi tribe was successfully introducing Chinese forms of organization to their Manchurian territory: building a walled capital, encouraging farming, producing silk, employing Chinese bureaucrats and naming their state after Yan, the old Warring States Chinese kingdom of the north-east. But it wasn't until 352, when his officials petitioned him to become emperor, that the Xianbi leader Murong Jun demonstrated the depth of his assimilation of Chinese ways. He responded with a wholly convincing fluency in the unctuously self-abasing language of Confucian rulership: 'Our home was originally the desert and steppe, and we were barbarians. With such a background how could I dare place myself in the distinguished line of Chinese emperors?'[8]

Early the next year, he declared himself emperor.

~

The Yan dynasty – which fell only eighteen years after its founding – didn't last any longer than most of its competitors, but it did show other frontier tribes how, in principle, a government might be organized to rule both nomads and Chinese. When the Tibetan tribe that had destroyed the Yan itself collapsed into strife over the succession, the stage was clear for the emergence of another tribe of Xianbi origin, the Tuoba, who founded a state – the Northern Wei – more sizeable, more enduring and, ultimately, more Chinese than any of its barbarian predecessors.

Forced into retreat after backing the wrong (Chinese) side in the 311 struggle for Luoyang, the hunting, herding, yurt-dwelling Tuoba, led by their chieftain Tuoba Gui, fought their way from a makeshift stockade headquarters in western Manchuria to rule an empire that spanned the northern half of China. Between 396, when Tuoba Gui declared himself emperor of the Northern Wei, and 410, the Tuoba took over north-east China. By 439, they had made the north-west their own too.

The more territory the Tuoba took over, the more they needed the settled, bureaucratic Chinese way of life to control their new acquisitions. Fabulously wealthy from his war profits (at least in livestock terms – one campaign before 396 alone brought in over 4 million cattle, sheep and goats), Tuoba Gui set about behaving increasingly like a respectable Chinese ruler: writing down laws, prohibiting nomadism and reorganizing his tribesmen into state garrisons, with fixed land allocations. But the Tuoba's most emblematic overture towards Chinese permanency was to build: first capitals – complete with palaces, roads and temples – and second frontier walls to protect their new dominions from covetous nomads further north.

For the first eleven years of his reign of conquest, Tuoba Gui established capitals nomad-style. He had, in other words, only temporary capitals, moving his court between the towns to which his battles took him, mainly in the Yinshan region of central Inner Mongolia. But the capture in 398 of a rival state's capital filled Gui with a longing for his own city and he promptly selected Pingcheng, in northern Shanxi – not far from the probable border line of the Qin and Former Han. The historical site of numerous border battles, raids and defences (including Gaozu's humiliation at the hands of Maodun in 200 BC), Pingcheng was a good strategic choice for an empire that encompassed both steppe and farmland, sandwiched as it was between the Tuoba's old stronghold, the Yinshan mountain range, to the north, the Ordos to the west, and Shanxi and Hebei to the south. With its immoderate climate (winter temperatures sink as low as minus 15 degrees centigrade) and inhospitable topography (Shanxi reaches up to an average height of 1,000 metres above sea level) the region retains its frontier bleakness even today. Further south, diligent irrigation has turned Shanxi's soft, yellow terraces of loess soil into fertile growing ground for crops such as wheat and millet. In the colder, drier north of the province, however, the earth fissures into empty, barren crevasses, varied only by mud-walled villages of the same harsh brown, some of which still have their old frontier beacon stations. If the settlement on Pingcheng was old, however, the Tuoba capital itself was newly manufactured. Gui's capital was built on immigration: 360,000-odd officials, commoners, tribesmen and other 'assorted barbarians' dragged up north from campaigns in Hebei. One thousand square kilometres of northern Shanxi were transformed into an imperial domain, some of which was turned over to Gui's forced immigrants to farm, in order to supply the new city.[9]

By nomad standards, Gui's Pingcheng was imposing, complete with suburbs, canals, several palaces and a huge deer-park built by prisoners of war. The Chinese, however, were not impressed, scornfully likening the city not to a settled capital but to a nomadic encampment which 'moved around following water and pasture and had no city walls'.[10] Pingcheng also posed logistical problems; being so far north, it was vulnerable to famines caused by frost and drought. Taking the capital further south, however, would leave the northern steppe area dangerously exposed to attack by nomadic tribes less softened by Chinese creature comforts. More worryingly, one Chinese official warned, familiarity could breed contempt. If the Tuoba relocated south to live among the bulk of the Chinese, they would lose the terrifying mystique which was still useful for overawing their new subjects.[11] For a few decades, the question was put aside.

As the Tuoba settled down in the north, a space opened up on the steppe for a new wave of predators to emerge: the Rouran, a tribe sometimes insultingly written *Ruru* in Chinese (literally, the 'squirming worms').[12] If the Rouran fondly imagined that the Tuoba had so rapidly turned decadent, however, they were badly mistaken. For most of the fifth century, the Tuoba army enjoyed the best of the Chinese and nomadic worlds, building a wall across the length of the northern frontier, from which punitive campaigns were launched against the Rouran. In 423, irritated by border raids on key farming colonies set up north of Pingcheng, a Tuoba prince 'built a Long Wall … Starting in Chicheng, extending as far west as Wuyuan, it ran for more than two thousand *li*, with defence garrisons stationed along its length.' Chicheng is in modern Hebei province, a little over one hundred kilometres north of Beijing, while Wuyuan was a frontier fortress town founded by the Former Han general Huo Qubing, about halfway along the northern edge of the Yellow River loop. The new wall skirted the old stronghold of the Tuoba Wei, the area they had occupied before moving further south to Pingcheng, roughly reiterating the line into the deserts of Inner Mongolia followed by the old Zhao wall of the Warring States era.[13]

A year later, in 424, some 60,000 Rouran broke through the wall and stormed Shengle, a former Tuoba capital north-east of the eastern corner of the Yellow River loop, about forty kilometres south of Hohhot in Inner Mongolia. Two years of Wei campaigning followed, in which the Rouran were driven far back into the desert. In 429, the Wei armies again went north, defeated the Rouran and resettled them on the grassy plains south of the Mongolian desert, but north of the wall. At the same time, Wei emperors began maintaining a string of key garrisons to regulate the nomads on the steppe, from the Yellow River loop in the west to Chicheng, the eastern terminus of the Wei wall. More offensive than defensive, the early Northern Wei Long Wall was clearly succeeding in its purpose: safeguarding and even expanding the northern reaches of an empire.[14] In 429, an elated Wei emperor Shizu embarked on final campaigns to take the Yellow River basin, feeling invincible with respect to enemies south and north:

The Chinese are foot soldiers and we are horsemen. What can a herd of colts and heifers do against tigers or a pack of wolves? And as for the Rouran, they graze in the north during the summer, while in autumn they come south and in winter raid our frontiers. We have only to attack them in summer in their pasture lands. At that time their horses are useless: the stallions guarding their herds, the mares chasing their foals. In a few days, they will be unable to find grass or water, and will collapse.[15]

Unlike Chinese dynasties, many of whom were obsessed with rhetorically asserting their cultural superiority over the 'human-faced but animal-hearted' nomads, the non-Chinese Northern Wei pragmatically concentrated on analysing and exploiting the strengths and weaknesses of their steppe antagonists.

For most of his reign, Shizu resisted the idea of more luxurious, less functional building. Walls were admissible when designed to support further extension of a hard-won military empire. When diverted into capitals and palaces, by contrast, they became an emblem of futile decadence, the frivolous recourse of history's failures (uppermost in Shizu's mind was the 431 collapse of the north-western state of Xia at the hands of Wei only fourteen years after a splendid, triple-walled capital had been built). But finally, from 450 onwards, Shizu – in the last two years of his reign – and his successors gave in to aspirations of grandeur and began sprucing up Pingcheng. The capital soon became an enormous, garrisoned palace complex, a mass of imperial buildings – three for the emperor alone, one for the heir apparent, with separate buildings for palace women – and military barracks. The city, in effect, was a bizarre and supposedly harmonious marriage between the military culture that had won China for the Tuoba and the settled, ceremonious Chinese way of life for which the Wei were beginning to yearn. Though Pingcheng probably seemed deeply civilized to the Tuoba Wei, Chinese observers were less than admiring, singling out for especial disdain the persistence of Xianbi religious cults: 'Every year, on the fourth day of the fourth month, they sacrifice oxen and horses, with minstrels galloping around the altars on horseback.'[16]

Chinese visitors may have been underwhelmed by Pingcheng, but the Northern Wei themselves thought their capital worth protecting by a new band of wall. In 446, Shizu set about building a 'barrier around the capital ... sending 100,000 men from the provinces of Si, You, Ding and Dai [in modern Shanxi, Greater Beijing and Hebei] ... It started in Shanggu, and extended westward for thousands of *li* until it met the Yellow river ... Building work finished in the second month of [448].'[17] A speculative arc for this wall has been traced from the forested mountains of Shanggu – now Yanqing, north-west of Beijing – passing south-west into brown Shanxi, dipping perhaps as many as 125 kilometres south of Pingcheng before picking up to end near the yellow loess hillsides near Pianguan on the eastern bank of the Yellow River. Together with the outer wall built in Inner Mongolia in the 420s, the Wei wall around Pingcheng strategically prefigured the later double-layered Ming Long Wall defences protecting Beijing, the inner wall designed to safeguard the capital in case of the outer wall's collapse.

~

The Northern Wei's delicate equilibrium between tribal and Chinese influences was tipped by the rise to power of Empress Feng after the death of her husband in 465. A Chinese aristocrat by birth – her father served as a provincial governor – Feng had been driven into the Xianbi imperial harem after his execution. Bearing, from this time on, a serious grudge against Xianbi custom, she waged full-scale war on it as soon as her emperor husband's death and her son's minority left her in charge. Having got rid of her Xianbi chief minister in 466 and replaced him in high office with Han Chinese, she began churning out decrees designed to erase all traces of tribal tradition: barring shamans and wizards from Confucian temples, banning mediums, soothsayers and blood feuds, encouraging agriculture and replacing barbarian sacrifices to heaven with sacrifices to ancient Chinese emperors. Peasants who fell under Northern Wei rule were organized in a thoroughly Chinese, Legalist-Confucian way, divided into groups of households under headmen responsible for delivering tax quotas. Any spare time in the winter months, Feng dictated, was to be filled by attending training courses in Confucian morality.

The dynasty's preoccupation with being and looking Chinese was driven by anxiety about the cultural and political legitimacy of their once barbarian regime in north China, and sharpened by uneasy glances at the Chinese state south of the Yangtze. Before the collapse of the Han, the undisputed heart of Chinese cultural orthodoxy had lain in the north, particularly around the ancient capitals of Chang'an and Luoyang. But after the overrunning of these two cities in 311 and 316 by Xiongnu armies, many members of China's northern aristocracy had fled from the traditional heartlands of Chinese civilization – Hebei, Henan, Shanxi and Shaanxi, around the capitals of Chang'an and Luoyang – to the south, traditionally viewed by northerners as a humid, sickness-ridden jungle wasteland. To begin with, the émigrés were horribly homesick. Everything looked different: the lush greens of forests and rice fields contrasted dramatically with the dusty yellow loess plains on which millet, wheat and beans were grown in the north. Beyond Chinese settlements lay non-Chinese, the southern *man* 'barbarians'; even today, the Chinese sometimes use the once-derogatory *man,* which literally means 'savages', as a general term for southerners.

In the early years of their exile, the émigrés stubbornly held to northern ways as culturally 'pure': they refused to appreciate the rice-based southern diet, bemoaning the lack of their favourite wheat dumplings and pancakes. At their new capital at Jiankang (present-day Nanjing), they kept up the old northern court rituals and the dialect of Luoyang, even while the flood waters of the Yangtze lapped at the hems of their gowns. But by the fifth century, the northern families had acclimatized and were eating rice, speaking the local dialect and dispatching work parties to clear uncultivated land. Soon the south boomed, thanks to its naturally fertile wetlands and the waterways that facilitated communication and commerce. And with success came a new Chinese cultural confidence that defined itself through disdain for northerners: for the way they barbarously braided their hair, for their rustic casualness. Northern literature, sniffed southern readers, was 'like the braying of donkeys and the barking of dogs'.[18] To southern sensibilities, northern women were left on a scandalously loose rein: observers commented with amazement on how women north of the Yangtze handled public family business and legal disputes. They even had the bravura to demand monogamy of their husbands, in contrast to the south, where men acquired concubines far more energetically.[19]

The ruling elite of north China – most of whom, after Chinese aristocratic migration southwards, were of Xianbi or mixed barbarian/Chinese origin – responded to southern slights with a scornful stridency that betrayed an unmistakable chippiness concerning their own claims to be the guardians of the true Chinese civilization. As they gulped their dairy products, northerners ridiculed the southerners' preference for tea: 'Tea,' one Wei official proclaimed, 'is the very slave of yoghurt!'[20] Dinner parties at which both northern and southern aristocrats were present turned with little prompting into drunken slanging matches over which side was the most civilized. At one particularly unruly occasion, a southerner's brief reference to the Wei dynasty as 'barbarian' unleashed an indecorous stream of northern vitriol. 'You have a nerve, you fishes and turtles ... Your land is wet; it is cursed with malaria and crawling with insects. Frogs and toads share the same lairs, men and birds cohabit.' Southerners, the furious northerner continued, are 'puny and tattooed', their rulers 'harsh and violent', prone to murder and incest, 'no better than birds or beasts ... You wear your hats too small and your clothes too short ... you gobble frog soup and oyster stew as great delicacies ... Clear off as fast as you can!' Although the (northern) chronicler of the conversation records that this 'elegant and cultured speech' so stunned the southerner that he fell ill with heart pains, the length and violence of the northerner's rant suggests perhaps that the semi-barbarian did protest too much.[21]

Soon enough, the Northern Wei's sense of cultural insecurity began spreading damagingly to frontier policy. In 484, Gao Lü, one of the Chinese who had been promoted to high rank immediately following Feng's execution of the Xianbi chief minister, made a policy speech that urged the court and its armies to turn their back utterly on the steppe style of fighting that had won them north China and embrace an approach to defence that was nothing if not Chinese. 'The northern barbarians,' he began,

are fierce and stupid, like wild birds or beasts. Their strength is fighting in the open fields; their weakness is in attacking walls. If we take advantage of the weakness of the northern barbarians, and thereby overcome their strength, then even if they are very numerous, they will not bring disaster to our door, and even if they approach, they will not be able to penetrate our territory ... I calculate there are five advantages to building long walls: it will end the problem of mobile defence; the nomads can graze the north, eliminating their need to raid; we can look for the enemy on top of a wall, and no longer have to wait for an attack; it removes anxiety about border defence and the need to mount defence when it is not necessary; it permits the easy transport of supplies and therefore prevents insufficiency.

Walls, Gao pointed out, playing up to his empress, had an excellent Chinese pedigree: 'In former times, the Zhou ordered Nan Zhong to build a wall in the northern region; Zhao Ling and the First Emperor of Qin built long walls, while Emperor Wu of the Han followed these precedents.' Gao then delved even deeper into the Chinese past, noting how the canonical ninth-century-BC Zhou divination manual *The Classic of Changes* referred to 'the ruler holding strong points to defend his kingdom ... Could this mean building long walls?'

At this present moment, our best plan would be to follow the ancients in building a long wall north of the [frontier] garrisons, to protect us against the northern barbarians. Although this will mean a temporary expenditure of labour, it will bring permanent advantages. Once built, the wall will benefit one hundred generations ... When the barbarians come, there will be fortifications to defend and the soldiers posted there will be able to defend them. As they can't attack fortifications, they will get nothing from their raid. Once they have used up their pasture they will leave, and the problem will be solved.

There were two stages to Gao Lü's plan: first, 'In the seventh month, dispatch sixty thousand men in six divisions … to the northern garrisons.'

In the eighth month … display our might north of the desert. If the barbarians descend, we should engage them in a decisive battle, if they don't, then the army should be dispersed over the area to build long walls. I calculate that the stretch covered by the six garrisons is no more than 1,000 *li*, and if one soldier can build three paces of wall in one month, then 300 men can build three *li*, 300,000 men can build thirty *li*, and 30,000 men can build 300 *li*, so that 1,000 *li* would take 100,000 men one month to complete. Supplying grain for one month will not be too crippling.

'And because,' he added hopefully, 'the men would understand the long-term advantages of a wall, they would work without complaining.'[22]

It is not clear from the sources that Gao Lü's plan was ever acted upon. One possibility is that his suggestions involved simply repairing or reinforcing the line that was already built in the 420s. Another is that an additional stretch of wall was built to the east of the earlier one, arcing from the mountainously rumpled terrain around Chicheng in northern Hebei, the eastern terminus of the first wall, briefly into Inner Mongolia, before ending in the rocky, forested hills of Liaoning province, joining up with the Liao River then either following or using that waterway as a natural frontier all the way down to the Liaodong coastline. The best evidence for this is a sixth-century treatise on the rivers of China which describes the situation of a frontier wall in the north-east in relation to local waterways. Archaeologists in the 1960s and 1970s found ruined stretches of wall – either stone-fronted and filled with gravel or grit, or made of earth, or incorporating natural obstacles (mountains and rivers) – perhaps datable to the period.[23] What Gao's opinions do make strikingly plain, however, is the radical transformation of the Tuoba worldview, from expansionist nomadism to insular Chinese superiority complex. In both form and content, every aspect of his speech is thoroughly Chinese, from his obsession with building excluding barriers between the Northern Wei and the barbarians at their frontiers to his dehumanization of the nomads as 'wild birds or beasts' and desire to look down upon them from the height of walls. That Gao, as a Chinese, should take this view is less than astounding; that he should present this advice to rulers of non-Chinese, nomad origin, presumably confident that it would be well received, is rather more noteworthy. Twenty years later, the military spirit among the Northern Wei had declined to the point that even veteran generals were peddling the same line to their eagerly receptive rulers:

'[Walled] defences are the best way of separating those who eat grain, live in towns and houses, wear silk and walk like scholars, from those of wild appearance, who wear wool and drink blood, who live with the birds and beasts ... We should join the old forts up between east and west, building walls and defences, stationing soldiers against trouble ... Thus, our authority will grow and the army will flourish ... bands of raiders will not dare attack walls or forts, neither will they dare penetrate south of the wall, and thus the north will be untroubled.' The emperor followed [his general's] advice.[24]

~

Whatever the reality of Northern Wei walls, soon after Gao Lü's recommendations the frontier was abandoned altogether by rulers in ever more desperate search of Chinese credibility. In 493, the emperor Xiaowen left Pingcheng with a million-strong army on a campaign against south China. Xiaowen encountered appalling weather: rain that fell so determinedly for two months the emperor's senior officials prostrated themselves in front of his horse and begged him to let them all go home. The emperor, who complained angrily that his advisers wanted to prevent him from unifying China, offered them a choice: either he could continue with the campaign or they could allow him to build his own little corner of China – a proper Chinese capital where they were presently stationed, at Luoyang, the still-ruined capital of the Later Han, which had been destroyed in 311 by the Xiongnu. Content to agree to anything that would permit them to dry off, his advisers accepted the emperor's bargain.

A true step-grandson of the Empress Feng, Xiaowen had never been happy in Pingcheng. 'This,' he had confided in a royal prince earlier that year, revealing his intention to move capitals, 'is a place from which to wage war, not one from which civilised rule can come.' The obsequious prince applauded the decision, responding that the move would doubt-less be popular among the masses as 'the central region ... is the support of the world and just the place from which to rule the Chinese and pacify the empire'. The emperor was realistic and saw trouble ahead – 'The northerners are fond of their roots, and when they hear the unexpected news of a move they are bound to be alarmed and upset' – but was not to be deflected from his plan.[25] To Xiaowen, Luoyang possessed exactly the kind of Chinese pedigree that he wanted for his regime: the site around which the oldest archaeological remains of recognizably Chinese cultures have been found, it was located in what had been from the earli-est times the very cradle of Chinese civilization, along the valley of the Yellow River. Ever since the mythical Xia dynasty had first made it their seat of power in, legendarily, the third millennium BC, Luoyang had been capital to successive imperial houses.

Luoyang also carried a range of rather less auspicious connotations, having been both raised from and razed to the ground several times thanks to the depredations of warlords and barbarians. The former cap-ital that Xiaowen first saw still lay in ruins after its sacking by the Xiongnu in 311, covered in 'weeds and thorns growing thickly as if in a forest', as one mournful witness wrote not long after the city's fall, its principal landmarks crumbling shrines and the rubble of the old imperial college.[26] Unperturbed, however, by historical precedent, Xiaowen set his archi-tects and builders to reconstructing Luoyang and embracing the Chinese way of life as never before: banning Xianbi clothes and language, and dropping the barbarian Tuoba for the more refined Chinese surname Yuan. In 494, sprawling crocodiles of humanity undertook the long, dif-ficult journey south from Pingcheng, presumably forced to wait in makeshift shelters amid the waters of Luoyang's rivers for a capital to grow up around them. For nine years, forced labour daily shifted tens of thousands of logs until the dynasty's palatial needs were more or less met;

the vermilion gates and yellow pavilions of countless luxurious residences for aristocrats, eunuchs and merchants followed over the next two decades.

The Northern Wei court at Luoyang glittered for some twenty years, made rich by grain extracted from the countryside surrounding the capital. The wealth of one prince 'embraced mountains and seas'; everywhere he went, he was accompanied by a retinue of musicians playing gongs, trumpets and flutes, whom he paid to perform all day and night.[27] Another prince – with his Persian horses dressed in gold, and precious goods in silver, crystal, agate and jade from the far west – aspired to rival the extravagance of a southern Chinese notable who dressed in clothes made from 'the fur of foxes' armpits'.[28] Yet another strolled around the palace 'with a gold cicada gleaming on his head, jade tinkling at his waist', composing spur-of-the-moment poems over breakfast and dinner.[29] Both money and time were rushed into religious endowments: the city's highest pagoda, one account claims, measured 296 metres (only four metres shy of the Eiffel Tower). Monasteries and temples lay amid orchards of juicy, out-sized pomegranates and grapes, next to limpid pools brimming with water chestnuts and lotuses, serenaded by rare birds and cicadas. In the first twenty years of the sixth century, 802,366 days of corvée labour were used up in the carving of monumental cave-temples – their interiors populated by golden-faced, ruby-lipped sculpted Buddhas, with pastel reliefs of angels, musicians and dancers – gouged into sandstone cliffs to the glory of the imperial family.[30]

~

While Luoyang revelled in its luxurious, ceremonious Chinese aspirations, events on the walled northern frontier were conspiring to destroy the dynasty and its southern capital. Ever since moving to Luoyang, Wei rulers had surrounded themselves with courtiers antipathetic to northern interests: back in 494, Xiaowen had sacked any official who opposed the move south. In 519, the court at Luoyang had even tried to ban soldiers from top government posts, at which the imperial guard – one of the last bastions of tribal military power – immediately rebelled. Not surprisingly, the old Xianbi warrior class – on whom, in the event of frontier trouble, the court depended – felt increasingly slighted. The frontier ceased to be a homeland where prestige and glory were to be won in military adventures and became instead the dynasty's dumping ground for undesirables – convicts and corrupt officials. Vigorous campaigns on the steppe had ceased after the death of the emperor Xiaowen in 499, to be replaced by walls and bribery of Rouran 'tribute' embassies to Luoyang. But static defences were both expensive to man and maintain, particularly at great distance from the political centre in Luoyang, and ultimately could only delay rather than repel or annihilate determined invaders if garrisons were not prepared themselves to launch attacks into the steppe.

By 523, those same border garrisons were unwilling to lift a finger on behalf of the pampered Northern Wei court, much less to hurl themselves into the wastes of the Gobi desert. That year, Wei walls and gifts notwithstanding, a Rouran invading force had struck across the defence lines, taking 2,000 captives and hundreds of thousands of animals, before disappearing back, almost unscathed, into the desert belt. Ill-treated and starving – their corrupt superiors had long been skimming or even totally suppressing army rations – the garrisons mutinied. Opportunistic rebellions quickly spread to the west and south of the Wei empire. A nomad leader of the forces of discontent soon emerged in the person of Erzhu Rong, chieftain of the Erzhu tribe of central and southern Shanxi, and a former horse-breeder and general animal husbander for the Northern Wei.

Erzhu Rong had remained loyal to his imperial masters through the early border rebellions, helping to suppress mutinous insurrections, if only to give his horsemen some battle practice. In 528, however, when the teenage emperor suddenly died, leaving an infant on the throne and a power-hungry empress dowager in real command, Erzhu Rong seized upon the pretext of investigating the suspicious circumstances of his sovereign's death to lead his horsemen on the capital. As his force of

5,000 cavalry – banners raised, dressed all in white, the traditional Chinese colour of mourning – approached Luoyang's city walls, the imperial court's response dripped with delusional Confucian Chinese hauteur. 'Erzhu Rong,' pronounced one of the empress's advisers, 'is a petty barbarian … a man of mediocre talents who has turned his arms against the palace without measuring his virtue and weighing up his strength. He is like a mantis trying to stop a cart-wheel at the end of its track.'[31] Shortly afterwards, this petty barbarian crossed the Yellow River, settled on a hillside outside Luoyang and invited the capital's aristocracy for a meeting at his campsite. From there, after gracelessly massacring every single member – perhaps as many as 3,000 – of this state welcoming party, and drowning the dowager empress and her child-emperor in the Yellow River, he rode into Luoyang and set about enjoying court life, until he was himself stabbed to death in 530 by the new puppet emperor he had installed. Following a plucky but doomed attempt to defend the city, the emperor was himself garrotted by the murdered leader's successors, shortly after praying to the Buddha not to let him be reborn as a king.

In 538, only fifteen war-filled years after the failure of frontier walls, Northern Wei Luoyang was pulled down on the orders of a northern warlord, its population of two million forced to flee the city and the dynasty brought to a close.[32] The desolate end of the Northern Wei – menaced by nomadic warriors from without and mutinous garrisons from within – formed a tragic monument to barbarian conceit, a lesson in the follies of capitals and walls which, in less than fifty years, had only to be learned all over again by their successors.

CHAPTER FIVE

China Reunited

In China, writing history has always been a political business. For much of the Chinese past, historians have been civil servants, appointed and watched over by the government: ever since scribes were first hired by the state in 753 BC 'to record events', the task of writing history has been wedded to the political centre, devoted to narrating and justifying the acts of rulers. History from below existed, of course, but always in a subordinate position to court records. Dynastic history was known as *zhengshi*, 'correct, standard history'; any sidelong glance away from the centre could be disdainfully classified as *yeshi*, 'wild history', a label that blurred easily into the even more disreputable category of fiction. For ordinary Chinese, the only path of entry into the dynastic annals and historical notoriety lay in disturbing the political order through, for example, launching a peasant rebellion, and thereby provoking government intervention.

By the fall of the Han dynasty in AD 220, Chinese thinkers had elaborated another important theoretical tool to help them guide history towards ever more political purposes: the idea that human (i.e. political) history was regulated by ever-repeating cycles, that what went around came around – good and bad emperors, order and chaos, unity and disunity: 'the world must unite when it has long been divided and it must be divided when it has long been united.'[1] The movement of these cycles was determined by a cosmic force called the 'Mandate of Heaven': emperors ruled only through convincing Heaven of their virtue. If a dynasty's moral character went into steep decline, Heaven would withdraw the Mandate – publicizing its decision through national cataclysms such as rebellions, civil wars and comets – and pass it to someone else. Following this logic, imperial houses were always destroyed by self-indulgent, thoroughly unworthy emperors, a fact that each new dynasty hastened to point out by compiling the 'correct history' of its predecessor within a few years of mounting the throne. By the end of the Han, historians had a bulging storecupboard of stereotypical characteristics possessed by bad, Heaven-offending emperors – extravagance, lust, unfiliality, to name but three among many – which usually materialized at the end of the Correct Histories to signpost and justify the approach of dynastic collapse, two classic cases being the emperors of the hated and short-lived Qin, the tyrannical First Emperor and his psychopathic wastrel son Huhai.

The attractions of this macro-theory to those who lived with and processed Chinese history are obvious. To overworked historians, millennia of recorded history could be organized into just so many tidy sequences of rise and fall. To rulers and their officials, meanwhile, history – if correctly manipulated – offered a bountiful cache of self-justification. If history consisted of endlessly repetitive cycles of rise and fall, kept spinning by the personal failings of previous emperors, regime change could always be validated by demonizing a dynastic predecessor. Thus when the Sui dynasty, which reunited China in 581, lasted only for two emperors and thirty-seven years, it offered up a public relations gift to its successor, the Tang. In its unification of the country after centuries of fractiousness, in its authoritarian first emperor and lecherous, spendthrift second, in its brief duration, in its huge public building projects and imperialist expansion, in its destruction by popular rebellion and, most of all, in its love of frontier wall-building, the Sui looked like nothing more than a recapitulation of the reviled Qin. The civil chaos that followed the dynasty's demise succeeded only in affirming, in the minds of the Chinese people, the association between long walls and tyranny, oppression and empire-wide disaster.

~

No single supreme steppe tribe emerged immediately out of the dereliction of the Northern Wei. The Rouran – the north-eastern underdogs during the heyday of the Tuoba Wei – took advantage of the chaos generated by the rebellion of the Wei garrisons to expand into Manchuria and Mongolia. But their authority over the steppe was never entirely convincing: too divided to create a single, unified command comparable to that of the Xiongnu under Maodun, the Rouran were forced in 546 to enlist the help of another tribe, the Tujue, in crushing the Gaoche (literally, the 'tall chariots'), a people based in western Mongolia.

After he had gone to the trouble of capturing 50,000 enemy tents on behalf of the Rouran, the Tujue leader (or khaghan), Tumen, requested a little quid pro quo: the hand in marriage of a Rouran princess. Feeling no such burden of reciprocity, the Rouran replied, by messengers, that the Tujue were impudent slaves. Tumen in turn responded by killing the envoys, striking a marriage alliance with the dynasty currently ruling north-west China and leading a rebellion against their former masters. By 552, he had defeated the Rouran, driven their leader to suicide and established his own tribe as the new pre-eminent power on the steppe.[2]

Some historians claim that the name 'Tujue' – the Chinese transliteration of a Turkic word – derives from *Türküt,* the plural of *Türk,* literally meaning 'strong'. If true, the Tujue lived up to their name: although Tumen died in 552, his sons between them destroyed the rest of the Rouran leadership, conquered other neighbouring tribes and built an empire that stretched from Manchuria to the Caspian Sea.[3] In English, the Tujue are also known as the Turks, the tribe who would come to dominate Central Asia and parts of Europe for the next millennium, and whose name lives on in their distant descendants who currently inhabit the modern nation of Turkey.

Once their military supremacy had been established over the steppe, the Turks set their sights southwards, intent on turning their empire into a vehicle for exploiting the two non-Chinese dynasties that had carved up the old northern empire of the Wei: Zhou in the west, Qi in the east. The Turks held them both in terrified thrall, as was tellingly illustrated by the web of awe-inspiring legends that the official chroniclers of the Northern Zhou spun around the tribe's early history. 'The Turks were a breed of Xiongnu,' noted the dynasty's record, 'who became a distinct horde and were afterwards crushed by neighbouring States, which utterly annihilated the clan.'

There was a lad just upon ten years of age whom the soldiers, observing his small-ness, had not the heart to kill, so they cut off his feet and pitched him into the jungly morass, where a she-wolf fed him with flesh: and when he grew up he had connec-tion with the wolf, who in consequence became pregnant. The king of those parts, hearing this lad was still in existence, repeatedly sent to kill him. The messenger, see-ing the wolf at his side, was about to kill the wolf too, on which the wolf fled to the northern mountains ... The wolf hid away ... and then gave birth to ten sons ... Their descendants increased in numbers until they gradually reached some hundred households.

Another slightly less epic version had it that the Turks were descended from one Nishitu, also born of a wolf, who married two wives, one the daughter of the Spirit of Summer, the other of the Spirit of Winter. While one turned into a white swan, the other, more conventional con-sort became pregnant and gave birth to four sons, one of whom founded the tribe of the Turks. Although, the Chinese chronicle soberly assesses, 'the above accounts differ' on incidental details concerning the Turks' origins, 'they agree so far as wolf's progeny goes'.[4]

Thus intimidated, and each extremely nervous of an alliance between the Turks and a rival court, the Qi and the Zhou both struggled to find solutions to the northern threat. Wall-building was one. Between 552 and 564, the Qi built in separate stretches a total of around 3,300 kilometres of wall in Shanxi, Hebei and Henan, reaching as far west as the Yellow River, and as far east as Bohai on the coast. In a single year, 555, the Qi emperor dispatched an astonishing 1.8 million men to build over 450 kilometres of wall from the Juyong pass between the mountains north of Beijing, past the relative flats of Datong and up to the eastern bank of the Yellow River. These walls were clearly quickly built, in a single working season: either mounded up out of local earth and stones, cut out of mountains or formed by a non-walled line of defence made up of garrison posts, watchtowers and natural barriers. Of the Qi wall, two earth-and-stone stretches survive in contemporary Shanxi, 3.3 metres wide at their base and an average of 3.5 metres high.[5] A traditional name for one of the Zhou ramparts in contemporary Hebei was the 'Red Wall', due to the reddish colour of the local soil of which it was presumably made.[6]

But no wall seemed to work as well as bribery. Both the Qi and the Zhou made the Turkish khaghan so fabulously wealthy through menace payments – between 553 and 572, one of Tumen's successors annually received 100,000 rolls of silk from the Zhou alone – that he could afford to pretend disdain for Chinese largesse: 'My children … are filial and obedient,' he sighed complacently, 'so why should I fear poverty?'[7] Even subsidies, however, were of limited success, as large-scale raiding continued. In 563, for example, the Turks plundered deep into Hebei, more than 350 kilometres south of Beijing, 'leaving not a single human or animal behind'.[8]

~

This partially successful appeasement policy began to change when north China was reunited under a single dynasty: first, briefly, by the Northern Zhou in 578, then in 581 by the Sui. Not long after destroying Qi in 577 – in the process, presumably fighting his way through a Qi wall built specially in 564 for the very purpose of fending off the Zhou – the Zhou emperor unexpectedly died at the age of thirty-six. He was succeeded by an unhinged autocrat intent on murdering his wife and replacing her with the widow of a prince whom the emperor had already driven to death.

Perhaps the new emperor would have had his way, if his wife had not happened to be the daughter of Yang Jian, a high-ranking Zhou noble with a considerable capacity for ruthless violence. After impassioned pleadings, Yang's daughter was saved, the emperor sickened and died, and Yang decided to seize power himself, assuming the regency over the six-year-old new emperor, forcing the women of the imperial family to become Buddhist nuns and executing more than sixty Zhou princes. In 581, within the space of some two months Yang Jian proclaimed himself first Prince, then Emperor Wen of the Sui dynasty. Eight years later, when Wen destroyed the remnants of the southern Chen dynasty, based in present-day Nanjing, near the south-east coast, China was reunited for the first time in almost four centuries.

Wen's resemblance to his Qin predecessor, the First Emperor, is, in places, marked. Like the first Qin emperor, Wen had made himself master of China while remaining, in personality and politics, a man of the north – a product of the semi-barbarian north-western aristocracy (some members of which spoke Turkish as well as Chinese). His family – based midway between the ancient Chinese capitals of Chang'an and Luoyang – had served and married into the non-Chinese ruling families of the north. Wen had been thoroughly trained in horsemanship and war, and married the daughter of a powerful Xiongnu clan who, in characteristically assertive, northern style, at the age of thirteen made her husband swear an oath of monogamy. Unlike retiring southern Chinese aristocratic women, Wen's wife took an active role in imperial politics. It was she who urged him to proclaim himself emperor after assuming the regency, quoting the old proverb, 'Once you're riding the tiger, it's hard to get off' (in other words, he had gone too far to turn back). After he became emperor, they would travel together to the imperial audience hall, and she would sit behind a screen to monitor proceedings, sending her eunuchs into the audiences to chide the emperor when he made a wrong decision.

Yet again, not unlike his Qin predecessor, Wen remained a harsh ruler:

subject to violent rages (he once beat a man to death with a horse whip) and deeply controlling – he even rationed cosmetics for palace women – he was also superstitiously religious and distinctly Legalist in his insistence on rigid imposition of both the law and severe punishments. Nor could he rid himself of an inherent suspicion of Confucian scholars. When one learned Confucian courtier had had the temerity to interfere in an act of political violence, urging his emperor not to execute the Zhou princes, Wen told him, 'Mind your own business, bookworm!'[9] At Wen's court, Confucian proprieties were maintained only when his advisers offered nervous admonishments. Once, in the process of beating someone in his throne hall, he accepted the remonstrance that this was 'inappropriate' behaviour for a Son of Heaven and permitted his bastinado to be confiscated. Shortly afterwards, his natural instincts prevailed once more, when he actually killed a man in the audience hall. When a military official remonstrated with him, the volatile Wen killed him also, before being stricken with remorse, sending condolences to the official's family and scolding his advisers for not stopping him.[10]

In 581, the same year that Wen made himself emperor and eight years before the entire country was reunited, he adopted a distinctly Qin frontier policy to keep the northern barbarians under control: wall-building. First of all, he put a stop to the subsidies that had made the Turks so rich. The Turks, inevitably, viewed this change with some displeasure. Like most steppe tribal leaders, the Turkish chieftain – the khaghan – relied on the rewards of diplomatic blackmail or plunder to secure supporters in a highly unstable system of rule. Theoretically, the Turkish hierarchy was organized as that of the Xiongnu had been, along three levels, each supposedly controlled by the khaghan at the centre. In reality, however, lesser khaghans appointed by the centre often carved autonomous pockets of rule out of the Turkish dominions. After Tumen died in 552, the whole succession question was further complicated by his decision to abandon primogeniture in favour of splitting his empire between his sons (who ruled the east) and his brother, Istämi (who ruled the west). When

123

Tumen's sons were outlived by their uncle and the eastern Turkish empire collapsed into civil war, Istämi seized the opportunity to become largely autonomous. Although, by 581, Shetu, a grandson of Tumen, had emerged victorious in the east, he needed all the material incentives he could muster to keep his shakily reunited followers together; the Sui decision to block payments thus came at the worst possible moment.

'Emperor Wen,' Shetu felt, had 'behaved very shabbily towards him'.[11] Anticipating trouble, the emperor turned his attention to the northern frontier, where he directed local 'barbarians' to build walls for twenty days in north-west Shanxi. At the end of the same year, Shetu broke through the frontier to take the town of Linyu, in coastal Hebei, at the eastern end of the frontier. 'Troubled by this,' one chronicle relates, 'the Sui leader repaired defences, raised long walls on the frontier ... and stationed several tens of thousands of soldiers there.'[12]

All this effort achieved, however, was to highlight the inherent limitations of walls: fortify strong points and the enemy will seek out weak ones. With the central and eastern parts of the frontier – Shanxi and Hebei – defended by recently repaired walls, the Turks pragmatically shifted their attention further westward. Goaded both by material need and by his wife, a Zhou princess who had vowed revenge on the Sui for deposing and murdering many of her relatives, in 582 Shetu led 400,000 archers on a huge raid on north-western China – Gansu and Shaanxi – following which 'not a domestic animal was left'.[13] The emperor reacted to the news with markedly Chinese fury:

In days gone by the Wei's course declined, and disasters came thick and fast. The Zhou and Qi contended, and divided the land of China. The Turk barbarians trafficked equally with the two states. The Zhou looked anxiously eastward, fearing that the Qi would get on better terms with the Turks, while the Qi looked anxiously westward, fearing the Zhou would get on more intimate terms with them. In other words: China's peace or war depended on the whim of barbarians.[14]

The emperor went on to condemn the Zhou and Qi practice of

subsidizing the Turks, 'pouring out the wealth of their treasuries and casting it out upon the desert, to the distress of China'. The Sui, by contrast,

having received the clear commands of Heaven to cherish paternally all regions, in compassion for the burden borne by our subjects, abolished the abuses of the past: we recalled the objects which used to go to the enemy as extra rewards for our officers and men. We give repose to the people on the roads, who can now devote themselves to agriculture and weaving.

But the emperor's plan to defy the nomads by cutting off subsidies and building walls had failed to pacify the north and, by provoking raids, had increased national misery. 'The ferocious monsters in their stupid ignorance,' the emperor fulminated, 'did not understand the profound bearing of Our Will ... they carry on the insolence of ancient days. Quite recently they have emerged in a body from their lair to make an attack upon our northern frontiers.' Frustrated by his lack of success, the desperate emperor placed his hopes in the supernatural. In the land of the Turks, Wen muttered hopefully, 'there are ominous signs of evil to come. During the past year beasts have been heard to speak, and men to utter supernatural things, to the effect that [their] state must perish.' Although the emperor had to admit to himself that 'so far nothing has come' of these portents, he remained confident that 'now is the time for the light and the darkness to declare itself'.[15]

In a sense, the emperor's new, passive faith in forces beyond his control paid off. While strenuous wall-building was only counterproductive, sitting and waiting for the Turks to tear themselves apart was far more successful. Within two or three years of Shetu's massive raid, the Turks were severely weakened by internal strife: Shetu attacked his cousin; the cousin fled west to the khaghan of the western Turks, who saw his opportunity to declare independence from Shetu's authority in the east. Soon, pressured by hordes of rebellious kinsmen, Shetu had no choice but to turn to the Chinese for support. The previously vengeful Zhou princess wrote to Emperor Wen, begging him to adopt her husband as a son – which, taking the request to imply vassalage, the emperor graciously agreed to do, permitting Shetu to settle with his people south of the desert, near the Chinese frontier. The emperor's second-born son, Prince Guang, the future Emperor Yang, brought the khaghan troops, clothes, food, carts and – of less obvious military use – musical instruments, all of which, the sources record, enabled him to defeat his cousin in the west. Chinese sources described Shetu's attitude towards the Chinese emperor as sycophantically grovelling, as an appropriate effusion of barbarian humility before Chinese brilliance: 'Just now the weather is fine and the elements are propitious, probably because in China a great sage has arisen ... We have now felt the effects of your purifying influence ... Morning and evening I respectfully hold my services ready.' Shetu's true motives for the rapprochement with China were far more opportunistic, his behaviour far more surly and evasive. When the emperor demanded an overt demonstration of the khaghan's vassalage, dispatching an officer to whom the khaghan was ordered to kowtow, Shetu tried to wriggle out of his obligations by pretending to be too ill to meet the envoy.[16]

The true measure of Wen's sense of Shetu's trustworthiness lies, perhaps, in the emperor's continuing passion for wall-building: three times he sent his officers and labourers back to the Ordos region – to contemporary Ningxia, Shaanxi and Inner Mongolia. In 585, some 30,000 men were sent to the area to build over 700 *li* of wall 'to prevent barbarian incursions', between Lingwu, on the western side of the Yellow River loop, and Suide, near the eastern side – not far from the line snaked by the later Ming wall across the gritty, scrubby, ochre surface of the Ordos. The following year, 150,000 were dispatched to construct a broken line of a few dozen garrison posts in the grassy, pebbly desert of Inner Mongolia, just over the border of contemporary Shaanxi. In 587, more than 100,000 men were sent on 'wall repair work' at an unspecified location – presumably working on the sections already started – for twenty days.[17]

~

In the 590s, shadows began to fall over the Sui court, distracting the emperor from his beloved frontier. To begin with, there was murderous jealousy. When, in 593, her husband strayed from his vow of monogamy, the empress took immediate and direct action, killing the unfortunate woman while her husband was holding an audience. Next came conflict – perhaps filicidal – between the imperial couple and their children. The empress's censoriousness, in combination with the emperor's paranoid insecurity – like steppe tribesmen, Wen tended to view his sons not as allies but as potential rivals – conspired to eliminate or banish from court four out of their five sons before Wen's death. The first to go was his third son, Jun: stripped of his position in 597 on the grounds of extravagance, he was mysteriously poisoned a week after the emperor's sixtieth birthday in 600. The second target of imperial condemnation was the crown prince, Yong, who first slipped out of favour in 591, when his mother began to suspect him of poisoning his wife in order to install a favourite concubine. Soon, the empress – who herself never wore elaborately dyed or embroidered fabric, on the practical grounds that it was hard to wash – began criticizing the crown prince's love of splendid clothing and ornaments. 'Since ancient times,' she warned, 'kings and emperors who love luxury have never lived long.'[10]

One individual benefited from all this imperial suspicion: the emperor's second-born, Guang, who set about portraying himself to his parents as a paragon of frugality. When his parents visited him, he made sure his servants were old and ugly, his screens and drapes simple, his instruments filled with dust, their strings snapped, convincing the emperor that he had no love of luxury.[19] By the end of 600, taken in by this display of miserliness, the emperor had demoted his first-born and elevated his second as heir apparent. Blocked by Guang from protesting his dismissal in a petition to the emperor, Yong climbed a tree in the palace garden and shouted out complaints, hoping the emperor in a nearby palace compound would hear him. This, however, only played into the hands of Guang, who convinced the emperor that his older brother was mentally unbalanced. The emperor never saw Yong again. In 602, Guang completed the job of discrediting his brothers by persuading his father that his fourth son, Xiu, was involved in a black magic conspiracy against another brother, Liang. And as Liang was powerful enough to merit such a conspiracy, the logic went, he must constitute a threat. Both were removed from their public positions.

From this point on, the Chinese chronicles – compiled by the Sui's successors, the Tang – are ever more unkind to Guang, accusing him of every possible sort of unfilial hypocrisy and infamy. In 604, as the emperor lay on his deathbed – weakened, one source claims, by sexual over-indulgence with concubines following the death of his wife and the end of his enforced monogamy in 602 – Prince Guang is said to have propositioned his father's favourite concubine, Xuanhua, who promptly denounced Guang to his ailing father. When Wen sent out for his first-born, planning to reinstate him as heir, the message was intercepted by Guang and his henchmen, one of whom went into Wen's room and told everyone else to leave. Shortly afterwards, it was announced that the emperor had died, concerning which coincidence, the official history of the Sui laconically states, 'various opinions were held'.[20] That night, with the corpse of the old emperor still warm, prurient accounts maintain, his son and heir – the new Emperor Yang – found incestuous happiness with his stepmother, Xuanhua.

After this Oedipal performance, the new emperor set about proving himself anything but the puritan his father had hoped him to be. Unmindful of its unfortunate associations with the Northern Wei's cataclysmic end, Yang diverted hordes of corvée labour into the speedy construction of a new capital at Luoyang; Yang's impatience for his new city drove the pace of construction so fast that as many as half of the estimated 2 million workers are said to have died. He ordered the digging of the Grand Canal, the man-made water system that linked northern China, from Luoyang, with Yang's southern capital, on the south-east coast, at contemporary Yangzhen. Built on the official pretext that it would facilitate the transport of food from one half of the country to the other, the canal seems to have carried Yang's lavish flotillas as often as it did barges of cheap southern rice: 'dragon boats, phoenix vessels, red battle cruisers, multi-decked transports' all pulled southward 'by ropes of green silk'.[21]

Like his father's, though, Yang's thoughts quickly turned to the frontier. The Turks had remained split by civil war throughout the transference of power from Wen to his son. As before, the weaker faction – led by a great-grandson of Tumen, Ran'gan – sought Chinese help and protection against tribal rivals. In the fifth month of 607, Ran'gan sent relatives to the emperor – who was camped between his two capital cities, Chang'an and Luoyang – to request permission to enter the frontier and visit the court. The emperor refused, but the following month, a hunting trip happened to take Yang through the north of Shaanxi and into Inner Mongolia, to the north-eastern corner of the Yellow River loop, from where he left the Chinese frontier for the dominion of the Turks.

Yang took no chances with the changeable barbarians, advancing northwards with his officials within a defensive square formation of troops. Judging from the khaghan's grovelling address to the emperor when he arrived, however, such precautions were unnecessary. Likening himself to a mere 'grain of seed', the khaghan offered thanks for the Sui's generosity in supporting his rule politically and economically, against the onslaught of tribal rivals: 'The late Emperor ... deeply pitied your servant's absolute helplessness, kept him alive even ... and sent your servant to sit as Great Khaghan.'[22] Sensing, from the elaborate precautions taken, the emperor's obvious unease, the khaghan hastened to reassure him: 'Your humble servant is no longer the frontier khaghan of former days, your humble servant is the vassal of your Great Worship.' The khaghan even begged to be enabled to abandon Turkish customs for Chinese: 'When your Great Worship takes pity on your servant, I beg that it is according to the clothes, ornaments, laws and usages of the superior

country, that all is as in China.' Whether motivated by a progressive tolerance of indigenous custom or by more hard-nosed economic considerations (the cost of fitting out the khaghan's horde with Chinese robes and
ornaments would not have been negligible), the emperor declined the
request and asked merely for allegiance: 'With the region north of the
desert not yet pacified and wars still necessary, all [the khaghan] has to do
is remain loyal and dutiful – what need is there to change your clothes?'[23]
The khaghan was, however, treated to chariots, horses, drums, banners
and a banquet for 3,500 of his men. A few months later, the emperor
unprecedentedly paid a visit to the khaghan's steppe residence, at
Yunzhong – 'amidst the clouds' – in the Mongolian grasslands a little due
east of the northernmost edge of the Yellow River loop, travelling in a
huge palace-on-wheels (protected by mobile walls), which, according to
Chinese chroniclers, had precisely the desired effect of overawing the
locals: 'The barbarians thought a spirit had come: anyone who saw the
imperial camp, from ten *li* around, fell to their knees and kowtowed.'
After the khaghan himself had kneeled and proposed a toast, the
emperor, a keen poetaster, was so delighted by his reception that he wrote
a rhapsodic ode to the exotic north:

> In a felt tent, I watch the wind arise,
> The Qionglu mountains open up towards the sun…
> Men with braids raise up to me their savoury mutton,
> Hands clad in leather falconers' gloves, they offer me the wine cup,
> Say, what do you think of the Chinese Son of Heaven
> Coming unprotected to the Shanyu's steppe?[24]

But Yang's expressions of triumphal insouciance are contradicted by
the fact that both these expeditions were accompanied by wall-building.
In 607, 'over one million men were sent to build long walls, from Yulin
in the west to Purple River in the east'. A year later, in 608, another
200,000 men were sent to build walls in the same region.[25] Roughly paral-
leling the contemporary border between Shanxi and Inner Mongolia, this

stretch was built to protect the land north of the new capital at Luoyang, which lay due south. To the east and south of the wall's eastern terminus lay a natural, mountainous barrier, but west and north the land was fairly flat. The location picked by Emperor Yang was the natural northern frontier of the yellow plain, the springboard for northern nomads to strike south into Shanxi; theoretically, the wall closed this route off. Part of a Sui wall survives in contemporary Inner Mongolia, a massy stretch of earthen rampart, perhaps 2.5 metres tall, running between solid towers looming twice as high out of archetypal Gobi vistas: 'not a desert in the Sahara sense, of mere shifting sand, but of hard sand and gravel mixed with clay, always covered at least with the thinnest of grass, and often with tufts of a grass-bushy sort,' as an American motoring through in 1923 described it.[26] One and a half millennia have left their mark on the structure, eroding great bites out of the mounded earth. Now, rising up amid the sparse, wiry scrub on the fringes of the Ordos, it looks more like a termite-infested bank than a man-made defence. Its lumpy, hole-ridden surface certainly bears no resemblance to the smooth stone slabs of later Ming walls near Beijing, although it shares a family likeness with the traditional pounded frontier walls that had been strewn across the north-west by states and dynasties since the first millennia BC.

Emperor Yang enthusiastically commemorated his wall in verse:

> The desolate autumn wind gusts up,
> We travel far, ten thousand *li*.
> Travelling so far, where are we headed?
> To cross the river and build the Long Wall.
> Does the great emperor rely on his own wisdom to build?
> No: he follows the precedent of his sacred ancestors.
> Building the wall is a stratagem that will benefit a myriad generations,
> Bringing peace to a hundred million people.
> Who would dare be troubled by anxious thoughts?
> We will be able to rest easily in the capital.

We deploy our regiments by the Yellow River,
For a thousand *li* the barbarian banner is furled.
Mountains and rivers appear and disappear off into the horizon,
Plains roll endlessly away into the distance.
Our regiments halt when the gongs sound,
Our soldiers start once more when the drums thunder.
Tens of thousands of cavalry set out,
Watering their horses below the Long Wall.
At dusk in autumn, clouds gather beyond the wall,
Mist and darkness enclose the mountain moon.
We proceed along the crags on horseback,
The beacons are lit in plenty of time.
We ask the officer of the Long Wall
Whether the Shanyu has come for an audience with the court.
The cloudy air falls still over the heavenly mountains,
Dawn light floods the northern pass.

...

When we return we will drink to our hearts' content,
And report our triumphs at the temple of our ancestors.[27]

Yang's joyful paean subverts every traditionally mournful sentiment about wall-building. Although the road is long, he preaches, the undertaking is blessed by Heaven and will safeguard livelihoods for tens of thousands of years to come. Here, beacon towers – usually an emblem of imminent attack, panic and fear – seem merely to announce that the barbarian leader has come on a social visit. The frontier is usually associated with chaotic movement – with the whirlwinds of battle, with charging horses and the frantic cut-and-thrust of fighting; Yang's wall, by contrast, is so blissfully peaceful that the air is still and its victorious soldiers can plan celebratory libations at the ancestral temple. In his anxiety to glorify walls, Yang even offers a controversial tribute to 'our sacred ancestor' – the hated first Qin emperor. The use by the Sui sources of the old

Qin term 'Long Wall' certainly invites comparisons with this inauspicious predecessor.

Given that the dynastic history of the Sui estimates that half a million of Yang's wall workforce died on the frontier, the emperor's effusion of self-congratulation rings rather hollow.[28] Other, less politically weighted poems of the dynasty suggest that popular hatred of the wall was not so easily forgotten: soldiers on duty beyond the wall are described as 'floating souls', exiled from home and civilization, enjoying no rest through sleet in winter and frost in autumn; freezing border temperatures cut even 'the frontier geese to the quick' and 'hurt the horses' bones'; border beacons 'cause a chaos of fear'; the water is so cold it 'cracks your guts'.[29]

~

Even amid the completion of Yang's imperial triumphs – his Long Walls, his Grand Canal, the submission of the northern tribes – there were signs of the frontier trouble that, walls or no, would destroy the Sui. In 607, at more or less the same time that Emperor Yang graciously received the allegiance of the Turkish khaghan, the Turkish leader was slightly embarrassed by the arrival of another visitor: a clandestine emissary from the state of Koguryo, which extended east of the Liao River, in Manchuria, into the north of contemporary Korea. Although the eastern khaghan tried to make light of this encounter by openly introducing the Korean envoy during an imperial audience, evidence of this secret contact between the eastern Turks and the Koreans was deeply discomforting to all concerned: the Chinese feared a hostile alliance across the north-east, while the eastern Turks were nervous of alienating their Chinese sponsors. The Chinese attempted to handle the situation with a show of intimidating hauteur, informing the Korean envoy that his king 'should promptly come and do homage' at the Chinese court.[30] If he failed to do so, the Chinese would lead an army on his country. The Korean ruler ignored the summons, and Emperor Yang decided to invade. The decision was fateful, as the Korean war – in addition to Emperor Yang's lavish programme of public building works – placed strains on the Sui that were to destroy an outwardly robust regime. Preparations began inauspiciously, with a Yellow River flood causing conscripts to desert. When the emperor finally set out in 612, he anticipated rapid progress on to the Koguryo capital; instead, walled cities along the Liao River withstood Chinese attack until summer rains forced Yang to return to Luoyang. The next year, the emperor went back across the Liao River but was distracted by internal revolts, many concentrated around areas recently flooded by the Yellow River. Ignoring the threat of civil turmoil, Yang puzzlingly decided to return to Korea in 614, after which expedition the Korean king still refused to pay homage at the imperial court and China duly collapsed into a mass of rebellions.

Far from cowed by the emperor's new walls, tribes on the northern frontier seized the opportunity for renewed insubordination. The effusively pro-Chinese eastern khaghan Ran'gan had died in 609, succeeded by a son, Duoji, who was far less eager to do homage to the Middle Kingdom. After Duoji suspended his visits to the Chinese court, Yang suggested another northern imperial progress to restore friendship face to face; Duoji responded to the idea by launching a raid on northern China, in which the Sui commander sent to fight the Turks was killed. In 615, as Emperor Yang holidayed at the Fenyang palace in north Shanxi, he was almost captured by a force of 10,000 sent by the new khaghan, and was forced to take refuge in the garrison town of Yanmen, about 150 kilometres south of the wall that edged along the northern border of Shanxi, and one of only two garrisons still held by the Chinese in the surrounding prefecture. The court panicked: the terrified emperor 'clutched hold of his son, his eyes bulging with fear', while his officials set loose a torrent of escape plans, the most ill-judged of which involved the emperor himself breaking the Turkish barricade with a few thousand elite cavalry. After a thirty-six-day siege – of a garrison town with only twenty days' food stores for its soldiers, not counting its unexpected imperial guests – the khaghan's men finally withdrew, lured away by a report of trouble on another frontier.[31]

Permanently shaken by his experience at Yanmen, the emperor grew increasingly depressed and distanced from reality: while famine-stricken peasants were driven to eat tree bark and leaves, soil and, finally, each other, he concentrated his attention on private entertainments, such as the catching of sufficient glow-worms to illuminate nocturnal pleasure trips. Convinced that, in Luoyang, he was too close to the geographical focus of rebellions, Yang made one last bad decision: to flee from the northern frontier to his southern capital. The entire imperial flotilla had been burned during the civil war that had interrupted the second Korean campaign, but despite the parlous national situation, a new fleet of dragon boats and floating palaces was hammered together. In the seventh month of 616, Yang set off for the south, executing any officials who dared to oppose his flight. Two years later, Yang was himself murdered in his bathhouse by Yuwen Huaji, the son of one of his most trusted generals and one of the rebel leaders, but not before he had first been forced to witness the murder of his beloved son Wang Zhaogao.[32]

~

Within two decades of Yang's murder, China's new ruling house, the Tang, in their (Correct) *History of the Sui,* were gleefully making unflattering historical comparisons that neatly slotted their predecessor into a moralistic Chinese cycle of dynastic rise and fall:

The Sui dynasty's achievements and shortcomings, preservation and destruction are analogous to those of the Qin. The First Emperor unified the country; so did Emperor Wen. The second Qin emperor was tyrannical and used force and harsh punishments. Emperor Yang, too, was malevolently cruel. In both cases their ruin began with the uprisings of rebels, and they lost their lives at the hands of commoners. From beginning to end, they are as alike as the two halves of a tally.[33]

In their anxiety to justify their usurpation of the throne, the Tang sponsored a blackening of Emperor Yang's character that turned him into one of Chinese history's legendarily evil emperors, every bit as bad as Huhai of the Qin. Page after scurrilous page catalogued his wickedness: his patricide and fratricide; the human cost of his building projects, including 50,000 buried alive in the shallows of his Grand Canal; his sexual excesses – his delight in deflowering virgins and forcing beautiful women to pull his barges up and down the canal; his extravagance (having the awnings for the imperial flotilla woven from the eyelashes of rare animals).[34] While the Tang – like almost every dynasty that preceded and succeeded them – stretched historical fact to suit their own political purposes, on one monumental issue the analogy was legitimate. For the Sui, as for the Qin, their walls proved no guarantee of permanence.

CHAPTER SIX

Without Walls: The Chinese Frontiers Expand

Like his predecessor the First Emperor of Qin, Emperor Yang of the Sui listened earnestly to the voice of portent. After the First Emperor was warned that 'Hu' would bring down the house of Qin, he immediately sent his best general, Meng Tian, on campaign against the Hu, the northern barbarians, with 300,000 troops and orders to build a Long Wall to protect his empire. Similarly, when a soothsayer prophesied in 615 that a man surnamed Li would replace the Sui dynasty, Yang diligently set about executing people surnamed Li (the Chinese equivalent of Smith or Jones), including one of his senior generals and thirty-two members of his family.

The First Emperor's pre-emptive strike had, of course, been entirely misdirected, as the dangerous Hu was much closer to home, in the form of Qin Shihuang's unbalanced son, Huhai. Yang's efforts were also doomed: although lacking only in their degree of thoroughness, they nonetheless failed to eliminate Li Yuan – the duke of Tang and first emperor, Gaozu, of the Tang dynasty – before Li Yuan eliminated the Sui. After deposing the last Sui child-emperor – no more than a puppet ruler – in 618, Li founded the dynasty that, at its peak, would extend Chinese authority from the valley of the Oxus on the edges of Persia in the north-west to the frosted borders of modern Korea in the north-east. No other ethnically Chinese dynasty stretched China as far as the Tang;

the only regime to surpass its frontiers was the Manchu Qing dynasty, which had itself begun life as a steppe power and was therefore given a territorial head-start by being able to graft its old northern homelands on to China proper. The empire of the Li clan provided a valuable lesson in frontier management that future dynasties, while revering the Tang as a political and cultural golden age, repeatedly overlooked: the conquests, wealth and vibrancy of Tang China were all achieved without long walls.

~

Although modern Chinese retain a fierce national pride in the glories of Tang China, most of these successes were, ironically, indebted to the dynasty's exposure to foreign, steppe culture. After the Tang dynasty was founded, genealogists in royal pay constructed an impeccably pure, Chinese lineage for the Tang, tracing a line of descent from Li Guang, one of Han Emperor Wu's most audacious generals against the Xiongnu. The reality of their family background, however, was cosmopolitan bordering on the barbarian. Like many of China's hardiest political survivors, the Tang were originally of mixed Chinese and northern aristocratic stock: Li Yuan's father had married into the same Xiongnu family as had the first Sui emperor. At the end of the Sui dynasty, the clan's power base centred on Wuchuan, a garrison post just inside the frontier wall near Datong, in north Shanxi.

As a high-ranking Sui official and outstanding general – a great favourite of Emperor Wen and his wife – Li Yuan remained loyal to the Sui in the opening stages of the rebellions that erupted during Emperor Yang's expeditions to Korea, defending the capital and the frontier from bandit and Turkish attack. But when Sui fortunes went into terminal decline, Li Yuan seized his moment, bolstered by hearing a popular ballad version of the pro-Li prophecy. 'I should rise up and march a thousand *li* to fulfil it!' Li Yuan is reported to have said in 617, before gathering 10,000 troops around his stronghold in Shanxi.[1]

Eight years into Li Yuan's reign as Emperor Gaozu, the Tang's tribal heritage resurfaced when, in 626, wrangles over the succession turned murderous. For a few years, Gaozu's sons had been treating each other with growing suspicion: the second son, Li Shimin, had established himself as a general far more talented than the heir apparent, winning key victories against rival warlords in the years after 618. Scenting a definite threat, the crown prince – together with his ally, his youngest brother – responded by trying to turn court opinion against Shimin. Finally stirred by a rumour that his brother was planning to murder him, Shimin accused his two brothers of having affairs with their father's concubines.

Moved to defend themselves directly to the emperor, both rode out to the entrance of the palace, where Shimin and twelve of his followers ambushed them. Shimin killed his older brother; one of his officers saw to the younger. Shimin then sent one of his generals in to the palace to inform the emperor that the question of deciding the succession had been somewhat simplified. Two months later, Gaozu was 'persuaded' to retire in favour of his one surviving son, who proclaimed himself Emperor Taizong.

Taizong's bloody management of the succession made very plain the non-Chinese influences on him and his clan. His readiness to regard his family members as rivals and mortal enemies reflected a characteristically tribal anxiety, while his murder of his brothers and demotion of his father absolutely contravened the most fundamental principle of the Chinese moral order: the Confucian commandment of filial piety.

~

A master of the steppe's fluid, unceremoniously violent style of politics, Taizong naturally had only contempt for border walls, transforming through bold military action the frontier situation that he inherited from his father. Since 618, while China righted itself after years of civil war, the Turks had been raiding or blackmailing the new dynasty, as the fancy took them, one year receiving 30,000 'pieces of stuff' as gifts from the Tang, the next removing almost all the attractive women from frontier settlements. In 625, following extended raids in the vicinity of Chang'an – involving up to 100,000 cavalrymen led by the khaghan,

Xieli, himself – the quavering Chinese court even considered moving from vulnerable Chang'an to take refuge in a more mountainous part of Shaanxi.[2]

In 627, while they mounted another raid directed at the capital, the Turks sent a spy to the court at Chang'an, who quickly demonstrated his incompetence undercover by boasting that his khaghan's army was a million strong and fast approaching. Taizong responded decisively, imprisoning the envoy and placing him under sentence of death, then riding out of the palace gates at the head of his army to meet Xieli, who had been fondly imagining that the Chinese army had been destroyed by internal strife. Taizong's measured show of force – not a single sword was drawn – had precisely the desired effect and won him a crucial psychological advantage. 'The Turks,' he reasoned, 'think that because we have recently had internal troubles we cannot muster an army. If I were to close the city, they would thoroughly loot our territory. Hence I go out alone to show that I have nothing to fear, and I make a show of force to make them know I mean to fight.' The Turks withdrew, made peace proposals and received copious gifts from the Chinese, by which Taizong planned to render them careless and decadent, before destroying them in battle at a time of his choosing. 'All this,' gasped one of Taizong's top ministers, suitably awe-struck by his sovereign's grasp of steppe diplomatic strategy, 'is quite beyond my stupidity.'[3]

The following year, Taizong's moment came, when vassal tribes rebelled against Xieli and the steppe suffered an abnormally cold winter, during which 'many sheep and horses died of starvation, and the people felt a scarcity'.[4] A year later, the Turks' troubles worsened when a rift opened between Xieli and his immediate subordinate, Tuli. One of Taizong's advisers, noticing that Xieli had moved troops to the frontier – presumably with a view to launching raids to ease the hardships of his people – suggested rebuilding and manning long walls. The emperor was not in favour:

One of the romanticized views of the Ming border wall produced by
Lieutenant Henry William Parish during the Macartney embassy of 1793.

The wall built by the state of Zhao in Inner Mongolia, *c.*300 BC.

An early twentieth-century view of a herder and his flock on the Mongolian grasslands.

A Ming Chinese sketch of
two Xiongnu barbarians.

Qin Shihuang, the First Emperor and builder of the first Long Wall (*Changcheng*) across north China.

A sketch of the tamping technique in Chinese wall building.

Aurel Stein's labourers pause to be photographed around the Han wall they have just dug out of the desert. Note the wall's stratified appearance, made up out of layered twigs and reeds.

The now barely discernible Jin wall in Mongolia, underscored by snow drifted up against one side.

A Persian depiction of Mongol soldiers in training.

The ornately decorated Cloud Terrace, the arch that the Mongols built into a pass north of Beijing.

The Turks have had hoar-frost in the height of summer; five suns have appeared at once; for three months it has been consecutively fine, and a lurid glare has covered their steppes ... They move about in an indefinite way, most of their flocks and herds have perished, which means that they are not making use of the land ... Xieli is not on friendly terms with Tuli, and they two are engaged in internecine strife ... they are bound to perish, and I will make their capture for you, gentlemen. It is not, I believe, a matter of building up defences.[5]

Exactly as Taizong predicted, by 629 the Turkish military machine had been destroyed by internal disputes. That year, Taizong sent out six generals, with a total of 100,000 troops, who took tens of thousands of prisoners and cattle, and to whom virtually all the Turkish leadership surrendered, barring Xieli, who briefly escaped on a fast horse before being captured and brought back to Chang'an by a Chinese officer. When the emperor received Xieli in the capital, he roundly and publicly chastised him for his crimes, but ultimately desisted from executing him, choosing instead to 'lodge' (diplomatic parlance for 'imprison') him in the capital. Xieli spent his remaining years in depressed denial, mooching around Chang'an, spurning the house provided for him in favour of a tent pitched in his courtyard. 'For a long time he was apathetic and listless,' records the *History of the Tang,* 'singing melancholy songs with the people of his household and weeping in company with them.' When the emperor tried to cheer him by giving him an estate with hunting land, Xieli churlishly declined. After his death in 634, he was given the posthumous nickname of 'ungovernable'.[6]

The same year of Xieli's capitulation, 630, the remaining defeated Turkish leaders travelled to the Chinese court and requested that the emperor assume the title of 'Heavenly Khaghan'. This was unprecedented: China and the steppe had been engaged in almost constant hostilities for over a millennium, and although northern tribes had managed to take substantial slices of China, the Chinese before Taizong had never managed to abandon their hobbling sense of cultural superiority, and the love of walls that came with it, for long enough to understand and defeat the nomads on their own terms. Taizong was as to the manner born in his new role, holding himself up as a paragon of tolerant multiculturalism. 'Since Antiquity,' Taizong gushed, 'all have honoured the Chinese and despised the barbarian; only I have loved them both as one, with the result that the nomad tribes have all held to me as to father and mother.'[7] An eighth-century Turkish inscription tells a rather different story about the Turks' relationship with their Chinese 'father and mother': 'The sons of the Turkish nobles became slaves to the Chinese people, and their innocent daughters were reduced to serfdom.'[8]

Taizong, in any case, wasted little time squaring his rhetoric with his actions, and concentrated instead on encouraging murderous infighting among the western Turks. Until 630, the khaghan of the western Turks commanded an empire that stretched from the Jade Gate extremity of western China to Sassanid Persia, around the Caspian Sea, and boasted of alliances as far west as Byzantium. One or two years before this empire began to fall apart, a Chinese Buddhist monk called Xuanzang happened to pass through the khaghan's dominions while on a pilgrimage to India and left a detailed account of the splendid court encamped at the town of Ak-beshim, now a sun-baked ruin in western Kyrgystan but in the seventh century a bustling link in the Silk Road, 3.5 kilometres in circumference, teeming with bazaars and passing caravans. He described a ruler dressed in green satin, his hair bound with yards of silk, surrounded by hundreds of brocade-dressed officers and a multitude of mounted troops so great

that the eye could discern no limit to it ... The khaghan dwelt in a large tent ornamented with golden flowers that dazzled the eyes ... Although this was a barbarian ruler sheltered by a felt tent, one could not behold him without esteem ... Meanwhile, the music of eastern and western barbarians sounded its noisy chords. Half-savage though these airs were, they charmed the ear and rejoiced the heart. Shortly afterward, fresh dishes were brought in, quarters of boiled mutton and veal, which were piled in abundance before the revellers.[9]

Fortunately for the Tang emperor, this flourishing regime was to collapse in one of the sudden turnabouts typical of steppe politics. After the
khaghan was assassinated in 630 by a rival tribe, Taizong sowed constant
discord by supporting first one, then another leadership faction,
promptly causing the spurned faction to murder the favoured. After ten
years of what was in effect civil war, one of the pretenders for the western Turk khaganate – still failing to grasp the undermining influence of
Chinese interference – requested a marriage alliance with a Tang princess.
Taizong deftly requested, as a modest betrothal gift, five oases in the
Tarim basin, south of the Tianshan mountains. Combined with Taizong's
policy of military intervention – in 638, an oasis king is said to have died
of fright at the news that a Chinese army was nearing his kingdom – his
diplomacy enabled him to establish Chinese suzerainty over the oasis
kingdoms of Central Asia, through which the Silk Road ran to Persia and
the Eastern Roman empire. Between 640 and 648, Taizong extended control over most of the Tarim basin, establishing in 649 a protectorate-
general as far west as Kucha, in the middle of the Taklamakan desert,
which he confidently named Anxi (literally, Pacifying the West).
Garrisons were stationed in these far outposts of the Chinese empire, but
Taizong continued to scorn walls, jubilantly proclaiming to one of his
generals that 'instead of appointing men to protect the frontier, Emperor
Yang exhausted the country in building long walls to defend against
attack. Now I use you to protect the north and the Turks dare not come
south – you are much better than a long wall!'[10]

~

By the first half of the eighth century, Tang China was reaping the material benefits of its foreign policies. Under the reign of Emperor
Xuanzong (712–56), exotic luxuries flowed into China from all directions;
Iranian, Indian and Turkish decorations appeared on every kind of
household object. The northern Chinese became so accustomed to the
transportation of outlandish animals from the south that when the supply northwards dried up after a eunuch insurrection in Canton in 763, the

poet Du Fu plaintively remarked that 'recently the provision of a live rhino, or even of kingfisher feathers, has been rare'.[11] Major cities hosted substantial foreign populations: Arabians, Ceylonese and, above all, merchants from Sogdiana (contemporary Uzbekistan), their presence brightly noted in a distinctly Tang sculptural vogue for big-nosed, dark-skinned, slightly caricatured figurines. The capital, Chang'an, contained an estimated 25,000 foreigners, Canton perhaps as many as 120,000, some of whom attained high office. While the aristocracy grew addicted to polo and the emperor took a dancing girl from Tashkent as his concubine, green-eyed, golden-haired Western dancers offered wine in amber cups to Chang'an *flâneurs* with disposable income:

> The barbarian houri with a flower-like face
> Stands at the wine-kettle, and laughs with the breath of spring
> Laughs with the breath of spring, dancing in a dress of gauze.[12]

Men wore leopard-skin hats; women exposed their faces under Turkish caps and went about in public dressed in men's riding clothes. (Women probably enjoyed more freedom during the Tang than during almost any other ethnically Chinese dynasty; the crippling practice of foot-binding did not begin until the Song dynasty, two centuries later.)

Few individuals were fonder of foreign and specifically Turkish ways than Taizong's eldest son, Li Chengqian, who chose only Turkish or Turkish-speaking retainers, dressed like a khaghan and erected a yurt in his palace courtyard complete with wolf's-head banners, where he sat, slicing hunks of mutton with his sword. The towns and cities of China's western outstretch were, inevitably, the most cosmopolitan of all, hosting an array of Iranian fire-worshippers, merchants, musicians, acrobats, conjurors, contortionists and twirling Sogdian dancers – these a particular favourite of Emperor Xuanzong – who tripped and span over the tops of balls rolling about a stage.[13]

For its first 150 years, the Tang empire often resembled nothing less than an antipodean fantasy world, in which all the conventions and values

of imperial China could be turned upside down, to spectacularly successful effect. Walls, with their ability to lay down in earth and stone the
sharply exclusive distinctions that the Chinese cultural superiority complex found so appealing, were spurned in favour of tactics – military
campaigns and fickle diplomatic sleight-of-hand – which came straight
from the steppe. While not quite eradicated, the Middle Kingdom worldview – the belief that China occupied the centre of the civilized world –
was certainly challenged by worship of foreign exotica, and the Tang
even opened the door, if temporarily, to a sexual revolution in politics. It
was during the early Tang that China was ruled by its first and last
empress, Wu Zetian, who, taking power after her husband's death in 690,
inverted every convention of the Confucian patriarchy for her own,
proto-feminist purposes: eliminating most of the male Tang line to
found her own matrilineal dynasty; taking male concubines; spending
state funds on aphrodisiacs so potent that she reportedly sprouted new
teeth and eyebrows at the age of seventy, with a view to deriving maximum enjoyment from a new pair of lovers she had taken. Perhaps most
enraging of all to her male aristocratic contemporaries was her decision
to dispatch her great-nephew as a hostage bridegroom to the daughter of
the eastern Turkish khaghan, rather than the usual princess that had been
the standard offering since the Han. In Wu's beleaguered male courtiers
– until then terrorized into submission by her secret police – something
seemed to snap at this latest and most outrageous reversal in traditional
sexual politics. 'Never since ancient times has there been a case of an
imperial prince being married to a barbarian woman!' protested the most
frank, and courageous of them, who was himself promptly relegated to
serve on the frontier.[14]

~

Yet despite the successes and abundances of the high Tang, the wheels of
Chinese frontier history – powered by long-standing prejudice against
the practices of the barbarian north – would soon turn again. During the
eighth century, the political focus of Tang power moved steadily to the

south, away from both the northern homeland and the ways of life that had helped the dynasty to dominate the steppe tribes. As mass migration into central and southern China took place, the standing of the southern aristocracy was strengthened at the expense of the old, semi-Turkish northern warrior elite, resulting in a neglect of the northern frontier in favour of the gentler climate and pursuits of the south.

At the start of the dynasty, frontier defence was handled by teams of militia still attached to the land, who performed revolving shifts at the capital and at the frontier, respectively for a month and three years at a time. In the early Tang, moreover, militia service was an honour rather than an imposition, largely restricted to members of the upper classes. The net result was that military power became centralized around the capital, ensuring that alternative power bases were not formed in distant provinces, and that a career in the military remained a prestigious choice in the eyes of the ruling classes. As the aristocracy shifted southwards, however, responsibility for manning frontier posts was passed increasingly to elite, professional forces, many of whom were made up of and led by hardy Central Asians with fraying loyalties to the Chinese regime.

The most historically significant of these was the Sogdian general An Lushan. Born around 703, after an early career as a sheep-stealer, he climbed through the ranks of the Chinese army until, as the personal favourite of the dictatorial chief minister Li Linfu, he was given command of a massive force at the border post of Yingzhou on the northeastern extreme of the frontier – the southern reaches of Manchuria – a strategically crucial region with a long history as the launching pad for successful takeovers of north China. While Emperor Xuanzong lost himself in an ever deepening infatuation with his favourite concubine, the renowned beauty Yang Guifei, An Lushan rose up the military and political hierarchies, viewed by the court as too much of a fat, illiterate buffoon to pose any kind of political threat. (As a sign of her affectionately mocking regard for the commander, Yang Guifei publicly dressed the enormous An entirely in baby clothes on his birthday in 751, at a ceremony in which she jokingly adopted him as her son.)

An, however, was ambitious for more than imperial layettes. Realizing the weakness of the emperor's army relative to his own frontier command, in 755 he led a force of 200,000 men and 300,000 horses on the Chinese capitals, Chang'an and Luoyang. Both fell without any struggle. The emperor fled west, before being forced, heartbroken, by his mutinying troops to execute Yang Guifei, whom they blamed for distracting Xuanzong from his political duties. Although the rebellion was finally put down in 763, with the help of Uighur mercenaries, Tang China was never the same powerful state again, collapsing increasingly into provincial military protectorships. The empire's frontier defence disintegrated: the Uighurs took over Gansu, the Tibetans made their way into the Central Asian oases and in 763 advanced into China as far as Chang'an. From 790 onwards, all territories west of the Jade Gate were lost to China. At the same time, the dynasty was beginning to eschew the cosmopolitanism that had accounted for much of its early vigour, instead turning inwards and towards an increasingly xenophobic vision which held that a pure, simple Chinese culture had been corrupted and enfeebled by Buddhism. In 836, Chinese were forbidden to have dealings with 'people of colour' – Sogdians, Iranians, Arabs, Indians.[15] Nine years later, an empire-wide proscription of Buddhism began, secularizing 260,000 monks and nuns, seizing their property, reinventing monasteries as public buildings, melting down bells and statues into coins that the faithful populace, terrified of sacrilege, refused to use. But these efforts to shore up Chinese backbone by rounding on the foreign did not stop the rot setting in across the empire. By the ninth and tenth centuries, the emperors of the once great Tang family were at the mercy of warlords, Turkish and Mongol invaders, bands of robbers and hordes of feuding eunuchs, until, in 907, the dynasty petered to a close.[16]

~

Curiously, although the Tang built no walls, the idea of a Long Wall was not forgotten during the dynasty. Quite the opposite: the frontier and its walls loomed in popular consciousness as never before, thanks indirectly to a seventh-century bureaucratic reform – the reinstatement of the civil service examination.

Because of an age-old high cultural bias against business and commerce, for most of imperial Chinese history, government service remained probably the most socially attractive career option for educated Chinese men. The sanctity of emperorship – ordained, as it was, by the Mandate of Heaven – ensured that working for the imperial state would invariably be viewed as honourable and righteous in all but the most exceptional circumstances (for example, when Heaven was in the process of handing its mandate from an unworthy to a worthy recipient). And in addition to a fixed salary, an official post offered the creatively corrupt bureaucrat abundant opportunities for self-enrichment.

Chinese emperors had been using exams in a fairly unsystematic way to select their officials since the second century BC, testing candidates' detailed knowledge of the canonical works that were central to mainstream political culture: the Zhou dynasty texts venerated by Confucius, together with collections of his and his most famous disciples' sayings. After they were reintroduced by the Sui and Tang dynasties, following centuries of post-Han disunity, the civil service examinations slowly became the dominant path of recruitment to coveted jobs in the imperial bureaucracy. By the late imperial period, the examination system had evolved into a sophisticated and thoroughgoing system of educational torture and Confucian thought control, in which examiners delighted in pushing the limits of candidates' Confucian erudition to pointlessly obscure extremes, asking their victims, for example, to identify where in his *Analects* Confucius had used a particular word. During the Ming and Qing dynasties (1368–1911), the civil service examinations became an intellectual tyranny that absorbed the mental energies of an enormous empire's educated adult males from conception to old age. Prenatal manuals lectured pregnant women on maintaining the posture that would best aid the development of an embryonic graduand, while at the opposite end of the human life span, despite an official cut-off age of fifty, men of seventy or more persistently tried their luck at taking the exams, attempting to disguise themselves as younger men, sometimes so effectively that even their wives didn't recognize them.[17] By the nineteenth century, the minuscule ratio of passes to fails, combined with the lack of alternative prestigious career options for over-educated men, had created a pressure-cooker society, primed to explode with male status frustration. The most destructive popular rebellion of the nineteenth century, the Taiping, was led by a provincial school teacher who, delusional with despair after failing the civil service examinations for a second time, suffered a nervous breakdown in which he hallucinated that God told him he was the younger brother of Jesus Christ. When his breakaway Heavenly Kingdom was finally annihilated after fourteen years by the Chinese government in 1864, it had left millions dead and almost brought the ruling dynasty to its knees. (Although the examination system was finally abolished in China in 1905, controversially replaced by tests of knowledge in more modern arts such as science and technology, it lives on in spirit in Britain's own civil service exams, which are based on the Chinese imperial model.)

Then at a less mature stage of its development, however, the civil service examination was a more relaxed institution in the seventh century. The most important change introduced by the Tang in 681 was to reorganize the curriculum so that success depended less on detailed exegesis of the classics and more on literary and, in particular, poetic composition. Associated with state ritual since at least the Zhou period, when odes were sung to accompany court ceremonies, poetry now explicitly became the ladder to orthodox political power. In 722, Emperor Xuanzong forbade imperial princes from keeping large entourages of poets, viewing such groupings as a direct threat to his own political prestige. Poetry remained enmeshed in Chinese politics for the next 1,500 years: although, like Plato, keen to throw other poets out of his Republic, Mao Zedong was himself an enthusiastic amateur versifier.

Thanks to the universal popularity of the imperial bureaucracy as a career choice, and because handling verse was a prerequisite to professional advancement, poetry-writing boomed during the Tang: most poets, including the great ones – who became the celebrities of Tang China – were either serving or aspiring civil servants, often famed more for their ability to handle couplets than administrative departments. Even the wildest poets aspired to be state-sponsored eccentrics rather than free-wheeling bohemians. Li Bo – perhaps the most famous of the Tang poets: a drunken, duelling, romantic wanderer who is said to have drowned after leaping, drunk, into a river to embrace the reflection of the moon – took care to pursue official advancement while he constructed his own cult of exotic genius, by marrying a relative of a high-ranking local minister and winning a government post as poet in the Imperial Academy.[18]

Unfortunately for the masses of aspiring poet-bureaucrats, the supply of plum jobs in attractive, central locations fell far short of demand. As a consequence, in a culture where being sent just a few hundred kilometres from the capital was seen as exile, many officials were forced to take up undesirable posts on China's remote northern frontier, in the hope of eventually being promoted to less arduous positions nearer to the Tang capital of Chang'an. And so the frontiers were populated by wistful, homesick poets stuck in an alien and highly dramatic landscape – a sure recipe for a massive outflow of lyrical sentiment. China's most renowned poets of wilderness expressed mainly horror and loneliness at the sight of the northern deserts and mountains – raging like discontented tourists against the unreasonable coldness of the frontier's winters, the offensive heat of its summers, the violence of border warfare and the pointlessness of long walls – and freely admitted they would far rather be enjoying the comforts of home in the Chinese hinterland. Poetry about the empire's northern borders and walls had existed since the Zhou, but it was the Tang's institutionalized poetry boom that turned it into an independent literary genre: *sai shi* (frontier verse).

Cen Shen (715–70), who spent nine years serving as a minor official on the frontiers in the mid-eighth century, was typical of his class of frustrated literati officials. At the age of twenty-nine, desperate for a promotion after ten years of largely fruitless struggles to advance through the official hierarchy, he took the dramatic career gamble of a move to Anxi, in Chinese Turkestan, where he served on the staff of two frontier generals for eight and three years respectively. A mildly tragic figure, he never attained the senior bureaucratic position for which he was hoping. He was still marooned in his desert oasis in 756, when his career prospects were mangled by An Lushan's rebellion and its chaotic aftermath. With the court in disarray, after 757 he was given a series of insignificant posts near and around the capital, before being sent out to govern the anarchic province of Sichuan, in central and western China. When he was finally recalled to Chang'an in 768, his return was prevented by a bandit insurrection. He died two years later, still in Sichuan.[19] Languishing, in the 740s and 750s, in a sandy outpost north-west of Dunhuang, Cen expressed the plaintive and representative sentiment:

> Over the desert I watched the sun rise
> Over the desert I watched the sun set.
> How I regret journeying here – across ten thousand *li*!
> Fame, success – what are these things that drive us on?[20]

His frontier verse is a poetry steeped in mournful regret, haunted by the mournful melodies of the barbarian flute:

> Have you not heard that the sound of the barbarian pipe is the saddest
> > of all,
> Played by the purple-whiskered, green-eyed barbarians?
> Their unending song
> Kills with its sadness our lads on campaign in the northwest.
> During the freezing autumn, in the eighth month on the way out west,
> The North wind blows and snaps the grasses of the Tianshan mountains.
> In the Himalayas, the moon is poised to slant downwards,

As the barbarians lift their pipes up to it.

...

In the frontier towns you will have sad dreams every night,
Who wants to hear the barbarian pipe played to the moon?[21]

Cen, as he repeatedly made clear, wanted only to be back with congenial friends in the centre of civilization, the Tang capital at Chang'an. His short poem 'Meeting an envoy on his journey back to the capital' spills over with lachrymose homesickness:

I gaze eastward toward my homeland, along the endlessly stretching road,
My two sleeves drenched with never-drying tears.
Encountering you here on horseback I have no paper or brush;
I trust you to take back word, that all is well.[22]

So overwhelming was the longing of frontier poets for their Chinese homeland that their literary powers of vision were often blindfolded by nostalgic denial. Despite the obvious physical differences between the respective geography of China proper and its frontiers, many of the stock images of frontier verse – its plants, animals and weather – are drawn from the standard symbolic repertoire of Chinese landscape poetry: heavenbound geese to denote loneliness, rolling tumbleweed to symbolize the poet set far adrift from his native roots. Even if a poet forced himself to confront the alien reality of the frontier in his poetry, he underlined the strength of his homesickness by mapping his surroundings in terms only of their *lack* of the conventional features associated with poetic descriptions of the Chinese landscape. 'The mountains are not green, the waters are not clear,' one writer notes wistfully, 'The breath of spring does not pass through the Jade Gate.' 'There are no flowers – only the cold,' another sighs, 'No sight of the hues of spring.'[23]

More than most frontier poets, however, Cen Shen struggled to describe the frontier and its wars on their own terms, finding the repertoire of comparatively temperate images inspired by the landscapes of

China proper little use when faced with the climatic extremes of the Gobi and the Taklamakan deserts:

> …
>
> The level sands are wide and bleak, their yellowness reaching to the skies,
> In the ninth month, the wind howls at night
>
> …
>
> The Xiongnu's grass is yellow, their horses fat.
> West of the mountains, the smoke and dust of flight rise up.
> The Great General of China leads his troops westward,
> Even at night, he wears his golden armour
> And his troops advance, their spears clattering.
> The wind cuts our faces like a knife.
> The horses wear snow, their breath and sweat steam,
> Their coats are spun into ice.
> In the tent, a summons to war is drafted, but the water on the inkstone is
>   frozen solid.
> Hearing this, the barbarians respond with fear, not bravery.
> Their short weapons, I predict, will not dare to engage you in close
>   combat.
> Let us await reports of victory.[24]

When Cen's thoughts turned from the cold – the snowy autumns, the 90-metre stretches of ice criss-crossing the Gobi, the biting winds and blizzards that made fox-fur robes feel thin and insubstantial, that so froze bows and armour they became unusable – they lurched immoderately towards its climatic antithesis, the searing heat of modern Xinjiang and the Central Asian republics:

> I have heard the barbarians at Yin Mountain gossip
> That on the western shore of the Hot Lake,* the water seems to boil.

* Lake Issyk-kul in contemporary north-west Kyrgystan, but within the Tang Anxi Protectorate.

Flocks of birds dare not fly over,

Beneath its surface, the carp grow long and fat.

By the bank, the green grass never withers,

In the sky, white clouds spin off into oblivion.

The steaming sands and molten rocks ignite the barbarian clouds,

Boiling waves, flaming breakers sizzle the Chinese moon.

Hidden fires heat the stoves of Heaven and Earth,

Why must they incinerate this corner of the west?

. . .[25]

Sometimes, of course, frontier poets – who were, after all, representatives of the state, however junior – had to set aside their sense of melancholy and alienation for a gung-ho enthusiasm that glorified Chinese military imperialism and praised the courage of generals and soldiers. Wang Changling's 'Army Song' puts a very public face on frontier affairs:

The great general goes out with his army on campaign,

Daylight darkens over Elm Pass.

Golden armour glints in all directions,

The Shanyu retreats, his courage broken.[26]

In 'Under the Wall', however, the poet reveals his private feelings:

The cicadas chirrup in the empty mulberry wood,

In the eighth month, the pass is desolate.

Passing in and out of the frontier,

There are yellowed rushes everywhere

. . .

My horse crosses the river in autumn,

The cold wind off the water cuts like a knife.

Across the desert flats, the day is not yet finished,

I can dimly make out Lintao.

In olden days, battles along the Long Wall

> Were described with praise and awe.
>
> But today, the past is no more than yellow dust
>
> White bones jostled amongst the grass.[27]

In Tang frontier poems, the wall was reinvented as a stereotypical allusion designed to evoke the absolute loneliness of its setting, the inhumanity that enshrouded its construction, the futility of the expansion that it supported.

> To the west of the Chinese beacons, where the surrendered Turks camp,
>
> The Long Wall is propped up on yellow sands and whitened bones.
>
> We have inscribed our achievements on the mountains of Mongolia,
>
> But the land lies deserted, the moon shines for no-one.[28]

In the sure hands of the best Tang poets, however, dusty stereotype could be powerfully transformed into pacifist polemic, as expressed by Li Bo's pair of songs, 'War South of the Wall':

> Last year we fought at the source of the Sanggan River
>
> This year we fight on the roads by the river Cong.
>
> We've rinsed our weapons in the seas of the far west
>
> We've pastured our horses in the frosted grasses of the Heavenly
>> Mountain.
>
> Wars of ten-thousand-mile marches,
>
> The Three Armies are old, exhausted.
>
> The Xiongnu live not by ploughing, but by killing,
>
> And so it has been since antiquity, only fields of bleached bones
>> and yellow sand.
>
> The Qin emperor built the wall to keep the barbarians out,
>
> The Han kept the beacon fires burning.
>
> And still they burn, untiringly,
>
> Unceasing wars and marches.
>
> On the battlefield the fighting's hand to hand, to the death,

Injured horses whinny their sorrow to heaven,

Hawks and crows peck guts out of bodies,

Then fly off to drape them over withered trees.

Soldiers are smeared over the wild grasses,

But the generals persist in futility.

Truly the tools of war bring nothing but brutality,

The sages only used them as a last resort.[29]

The battlefield is dark with confusion,

The soldiers swarming like ants.

The sun is a red wheel suspended in turbid air,

The brambly weeds dyed blood-purple.

Beaks full of human flesh, crows

Uselessly flap their wings, too full to take flight.

The men on the wall yesterday

Have become the ghosts at its feet today.

Flags glimmer like scattered stars,

The drums keep rattling, the slaughter is unending.

Our men – husband, sons,

They're all there, amidst the rattle of the drums.[30]

~

In 880, a bandit-turned-rebel leader by the name of Huang Chao trundled into the Tang capital, Chang'an, in a golden carriage, followed by a brocaded retinue several hundred thousand strong, rich from the profits of a furious sacking of Canton and Luoyang. After slipping away, shortly before, from his doomed capital by night, the pen-penultimate Tang emperor was by this point scuttling over the wild peaks and gorges of the Jinling mountains to take refuge in Sichuan, where he was to become a virtual prisoner of his powerful chief eunuch. Despite their ceremonious entrance, the rebel forces soon began to treat Chang'an as they had China's other two great metropolises: looting, killing, punishing the city for its luxury and privilege.

Two years later, in the spring of 882, a poem appeared on the gate of the Department of State Affairs in Chang'an. More satirical than lyrical, it poked fun at the city's new rulers, in whose anarchic regime the capital's literati bureaucrats had been forced to serve. The rebels responded swiftly, killing every official in the offending department, pulling out their eyes and stringing up their corpses. They then proceeded to execute everyone in the capital – for centuries, the centre to which the elite of China's poet civil servants had been drawn – who could write poetry.

The year 907 is the traditional date for the close of the Tang – when a regional warlord murdered the last Tang child-emperor – but it was, perhaps, the events of spring 882 that drew a decisive and horrific line under the dynasty and the gilded age of Chinese poetry it had ushered in. After the emperor had abandoned his capital to bandits and government commanders reinvented themselves as independent warlords, foreigners along China's northern borders began to seep southwards, founding their own states in Manchuria, Shanxi and Hebei.

It was thanks to the most successful of these peoples, the Khitan Liao and the Jurchen Jin, that, despite the Tang's best efforts to tear down frontier barriers physically and figuratively, walls would start to spring up once more, only to fail China at a critical moment: the Mongol invasion led by Genghis Khan.

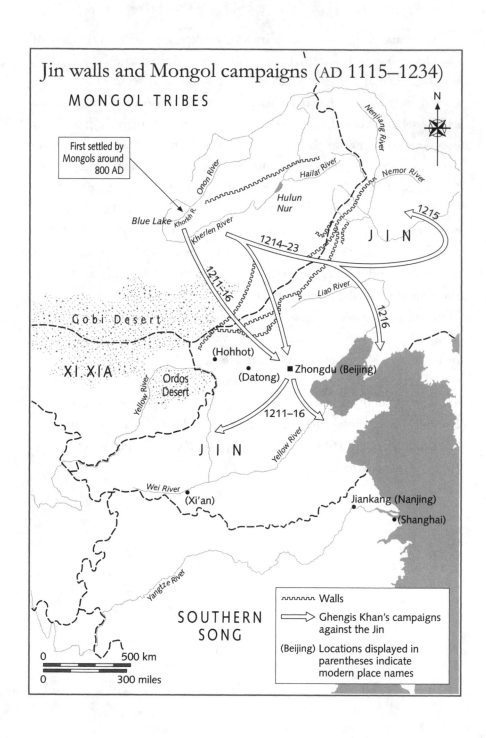

Jin walls and Mongol campaigns (AD 1115–1234)

MONGOL TRIBES

First settled by
Mongols around
800 AD

N

Onon River

Nenjiang River

Hailar River

Nemor River

Blue Lake *Khorkh R.*

Hulun
Nur

1215

Kherlen River

1214–23

J I N

1211–16

Liao River

1216

Gobi Desert

XI XIA

● (Hohhot)

Ordos
Desert

(Datong) ■ Zhongdu (Beijing)

Yellow River

1211–16

J I N

Yellow River

Wei River

● (Xi'an)

Jiankang (Nanjing)
● (Shanghai)

Yangtze River

SOUTHERN
SONG

0 ————— 500 km

0 ————— 300 miles

〰〰〰	Walls
⟹	Ghengis Khan's campaigns against the Jin
(Beijing)	Locations displayed in parentheses indicate modern place names

CHAPTER SEVEN

The Return of the Barbarians

For eight years, between 1194 and 1202, the state of Jin, which then controlled most of northern China, deliberated over which one of the five cosmic elements – earth, wood, metal, fire or water – should represent the dynasty. Courtiers, officials and learned scholars divided into factions, marshalled arguments and – that age-old bureaucratic resort – drew up illustrative charts. Since Jin meant 'gold' in Chinese, some reasoned, the dynasty should choose metal. But, others countered with scissors-paper-stone logic, as the Song dynasty, the Jin's rival that ruled over south China, was already represented by fire, and fire overcame metal, this would be an inauspicious choice; water – the natural vanquisher of fire – would be far preferable. And so it went. In the end, the earth faction triumphed, arguing that, according to millennia-old patterns of cosmic sequencing, earth inevitably succeeded fire, as the Jin would inevitably succeed the Song. Well into the thirteenth century, the question still refused to go away, with debate reopening in 1214. This time, the metal faction went on the offensive, arguing that the dying fires of the militarily weak Song could not destroy strong, tempered metal, while one rogue element argued for fire on the less circuitous grounds that the Jin in its early years had used red as a flag colour. And so it went.[1]

In normal Chinese circumstances, there would have been nothing particularly eccentric or pettifogging about such a debate. The Five Elements theory of dynastic succession was simply the Middle Kingdom's answer to the problem of legitimizing rulership in a pre-democratic age, the Chinese equivalent of European divine right. Since the first millennium BC – the formative centuries of the Chinese state – the achievement of political legitimacy had been rationalized into a set of quasi-religious principles that harmonized political change with the workings of the natural universe. A few hundred years after the Zhou dynasty established that emperors ruled by winning the mystical Mandate of Heaven, Zou Yan, a thinker of the third century BC, theorized the passing of the mandate into cycles of the five basic elements: the power of these waxed and waned in sequence – as revealed by cosmological phenomena and heavenly portents – with each holding sway over the world throughout fixed periods of time. As each dynasty attached itself to a particular element, so its power would rise and fall with the natural processes of the cosmos.

Zou Yan's idea soon gained momentum, and from the Qin emperor onwards, rulers of China agonized long and hard over which element to attach their reign to; anyone staking a claim to China – conquerors, usurpers, rebels – had to become fluent at reading heaven's cosmic intentions. Thus, when China disintegrated into civil war – for example, during the fall of the Han – rebel groups fought each other as vigorously with cosmological propaganda as with weapons, each commandeering a particular element and bombarding rivals with heavenly manifestations and prophecies to prove the ascendance of their own cosmic force.

But for the Jin court, these were neither normal nor Chinese circumstances. For one thing, the Jin were not a Chinese dynasty, but a Manchurian tribe – the Jurchen – that less than a century ago had swept down from the conifer-forested mountains of the chilly north-east to conquer swathes of north China. In theory, they were perfectly free to ignore the convoluted cosmological dilemmas of Chinese political tradition. Secondly, and more significantly, a threat was looming over the Jin far more disquieting than that of elemental discontinuity. Ten years earlier, in around 1190, a once marginal and poverty-stricken tribesman of the northern steppe had persuaded his people to elect him leader. At the time of the Jin's scholarly debates, this tribesman was on the point of overcoming his remaining nomadic rivals and drawing them into a united Mongolian nation. Not long afterwards, in 1206, his people proclaimed him Genghis Khan, supreme leader of the Mongols and the architect of an empire that at its height in 1290 would stretch across Asia from Russia's eastern coast to the shores of the Black Sea; throughout the intervening decades, the Mongols would plunder land and devastate populations with a mindless thoroughness that provoked one observer of China after Genghis to comment, 'If for a thousand years to come no evil befalls the country, yet it will not be possible to repair the damage, and bring the land back to the state it was formerly.'[2] In 1214, in fact, as metal and fire factions continued to argue the toss at the Jin court, Genghis Khan was at the very walls of Beijing, having captured most of Jin China north of the capital, sweeping past thousands of kilometres of border walls in the process. What led the Manchurian Jin to waste its time on Chinese philosophical abstractions when the Golden Horde of Genghis Khan's Mongols was snapping at its heels?

The Jin, the latest in a succession of barbarian steppe clans to rule north China after the collapse of Chinese imperial authority (in this case, following the fall of the Tang in 907), found themselves torn between the two archetypal dilemmas of foreign, northern conquerors of China: how to adapt their traditions of steppe pastoralism to govern Chinese farmers, and how, in the process, to avoid swapping the nomadic military discipline that underpinned their success over the Chinese for a more settled way of life that would in due course expose them to attack by tougher, genuinely nomadic tribesmen. Again, like the Northern Wei before them, the Jin tried to meet these challenges by maintaining a two-tier system of government – one for the farmers that came under their sway, one for the nomads – and by maintaining an intimidating military presence on the steppe. Yet finally, showing a staunch disregard for the lessons of history, the Jin trod precisely the same path that had destroyed the Wei: first, undertaking energetic sinicization (to the point of nominating themselves the cosmological heir to the Chinese Song dynasty); secondly, adopting a very Chinese solution to frontier policy – wall-building; and thirdly, suffering annihilation by steppe forces, in this case by the Mongols under Genghis Khan.

~

The Jin's own progress to power had been achieved in 1124 by beating back to the steppe another sinicized barbarian dynasty, the Liao. In 907, the year that its founder, Abaoji, took power, the Liao had enjoyed as impeccable a steppe lineage as the Jin, having begun life as the Khitan nomads from Manchuria, in the north-east. The Khitan had been bothering the Chinese empire since the Sui dynasty, but only managed to expand southwards in the early tenth century under the direction of Abaoji, who dragged his fractious followers and their north-eastern Chinese conquests together into a state through a creative combination of tribal and Chinese approaches: having first exterminated all his rivals and opponents, he then hired a band of Chinese advisers who helped him to exploit agrarian land, choose a Chinese reign title, introduce a linear succession and publicly endorse Confucian philosophy. In 913, his uncle sarcastically expressed the Khitans' sense of culture shock: 'At first I did not realise how exalted a Son of Heaven is. Then Your Majesty ascended the throne. With your guards and attendants you were extremely dignified and in a different class from the common run of people.'[3]

Pausing only briefly to execute his rashly critical relative, the first Liao emperor built walled cities, introduced a script based on Chinese characters and divided his kingdom into northern and southern halves, the former governed in the nomadic fashion, the latter in the Chinese. His dynasty even took on the Chinese examination system to recruit officials, although knowledge of the steppe rather than of Confucius seemed to be key to success. In one examination paper, candidates had to compose an essay on 'Killing Thirty-six Bears in One Day', while an official's ability to dispatch three hares with three successive arrows was prized just as much as his ability to write poetry.[4] His approach seemed to work: by 937, Liao had acquired parts of northern Hebei and the key passes into northern China, including Datong in Shanxi.

Within a few decades, the Liao set its sights on territories further south. The areas of China beyond Liao control had known a brief period of reunification during the 960s and 970s, when a successful general established his own dynasty, the Song. In its three centuries of existence, the Song would harness the fertile wealth of the southern ricelands to fuel a bustling urban economy, a flourishing luxury commodity trade and a renaissance in Chinese art, poetry, science, mathematics and philosophy, assisted by the development of wood block printing. But it would never manage to reunite the Chinese empire. In 979, riding high after a campaign that had destroyed a last pocket of resistance by independent warlords in Shanxi province, the Song emperor dragged his exhausted army on to northern Hebei, intending to take back territories won by the Liao in 937. The expedition turned into a fiasco: the Song forces were routed south-west of Beijing, with the emperor wounded by an arrow and forced to escape back south in a donkey-cart. The Song never managed to regain military dominance over the Liao, who in 1004 invaded north China and annexed areas of the Yellow River region. At its peak, the Liao empire extended southwards down to the pale brown, farmed flats of present-day Tianjin, and further east into Hebei; to the west, it intersected the eastern side of the Yellow River loop almost in the middle, and stretched north to include Manchuria and the north of Korea, as far as the banks of the Sungari River. Centuries after the dynasty's collapse, Liao domination over north China was still commemorated in Europe, where China was commonly identified as

Cathay, a name derived from that of the Liao's original tribe, the Khitan.

In keeping with their ambitions to become both China and Chinese, the Liao built walls in the north-east, as early as 908, to protect themselves from hardier steppe peoples further north, in Manchuria. But maintaining the frontier – with walls and garrisons manned by 22,000 regular troops – proved a crushing burden. The defence bill was generously footed in part by the Song dynasty, who, made rich by the introduction of double rice-cropping, a boom in handicrafts and the markets flourishing along their southern waterways, were blackmailed in 1005 into paying the Liao menace-money to the tune of 200,000 bolts of silk and 100,000 ounces of silver. But Liao fortifications also relied on a punishing and highly unpopular system of military conscription. Any family left without able-bodied males was economically ruined by the need to hire substitutes, which often had to be financed by the selling of children and land. Made rich by generous subsidies from the Song, the once aggressive Liao dynasty grew defensive in its dotage – and while this conservative policy suited the court well, it generated discontent among frontier garrisons, as there was reduced opportunity for the nomadic army to acquire plunder and profit.

The true weakness of Liao walls became fully apparent when the empire was conquered by one of its tribal vassals, the Jurchen – another Manchurian people, from the northern borders of the Liao empire. Resentful at seeing his people cheated and beaten by frontier officials, at a feast held to enable vassal tribes to pay homage to the Liao in 1112, a Jurchen leader called Aguda flatly turned down the Liao emperor's drunken request to dance. The refusal was not as pettily churlish as it sounds: in north-eastern tribal etiquette, dancing was traditionally symbolic of submission. Enraged, the Liao emperor wanted to execute his defiant vassal, but was finally dissuaded by his more temperate but, as it transpired, ill-advised chancellor.

Skilled warriors on horseback, toughened by their lives of hunting and trapping among the forests and mountains of northern Manchuria, the Jurchen had destroyed a Liao army of 700,000 men, conquered most of Manchuria and founded their own dynasty, the Jin, all within three years of Aguda's challenge to the emperor. By 1126, the Jin and the Liao had effectively traded geographical and political places: the Jurchen had taken over the Liao state and the Liao had fled north to the Jurchen's old homeland. Misguidedly thinking to exploit the Jurchen to weaken the Liao, the Song assisted in the Jurchen attack. But with the Liao dislodged, Aguda promptly demanded from the Song almost twice the annual subsidy that had been paid to the Liao: 200,000 ounces of silver and 300,000 bolts of silk. Not content with this level of extortion, in 1125 the Jin drove the Song dynasty south from its capital, Kaifeng, in present-day Henan, taking prisoner an abdicated Song emperor and his son, whom they delighted in renaming the 'Marquis of Muddled Virtue' and 'Double Muddled' respectively. Pushed down to a new, southern capital at Hangzhou, near the eastern coast, the Song were largely saved from total extermination by the swampiness of south China's rice fields, through which the Jin's fearsome cavalry could only squelch ineffectively.

But once in power, the hard-riding Jin also began to reinvent themselves as Chinese, maintaining a curious mix of nomadic and Chinese habits (the Jurchen were, after all, outnumbered ten to one by Chinese in their newly expanded empire). The fourth Jin emperor, for example, retained an attachment to nomad-style blood feuds: his decision to execute all surviving male relatives of the Liao and Song families left in Jin territory, together with his habit of transferring the wives and concubines of murdered rivals into his own harem, gained him an enduring place in Chinese pornographic history as a bloodthirsty lecher. At the same time, however, he was a great admirer of Chinese culture, an avid reader of the Chinese classics whose enthusiasm for chess and tea won him the Jurchen nickname of *Boliehan* – Aping the Chinese.

The Jin soon began to build their own walls in the north of their kingdom, far beyond the line of the Great Wall later set down in stone by the Ming dynasty: in Manchuria and in Mongolia in the years 1166, 1181, 1188, 1193, 1196 and 1201, mobilizing as many as 750,000 men at one time.[5] Jin walls were a technical improvement on past constructions, including, at their most complex, an outer moat, outer wall, inner moat and main wall; the inner moat could range from ten to sixty metres in width. Jin walls also made use of beacon towers that raised the alarm with fire at night and smoke during the day, of semicircular platforms on the outside of the wall from which attacks could be launched on marauders, and of battlements and parapets on the wall itself that protected defenders. Rather than build just a single line of wall – which, if it failed, could endanger an entire empire – the Jin erected a comprehensive network of defences. The outer wall stretched some 700 kilometres from Heilongjiang, in northern Manchuria, westwards into Mongolia. The inner network of walls expanded around 1,000 kilometres north and north-east of Beijing, sketching out a broadly elliptical web of fortifications roughly 1,400 kilometres along its longest diagonal and 440 kilometres along its shortest.[6]

The bleak remoteness of some of the defences from China proper, far north of the line currently marked by the Great Wall, a couple of hours' drive from Beijing, is conveyed in the travelogue of a Daoist sage's disciple, who left north China in 1222 with his teacher to meet Genghis Khan in Afghanistan. Seven days after setting off northwards from Dexing, a town some 160 kilometres north-west of Beijing, their party reached 'Gailibo, where the ground consists entirely of small salt-tumuli'.

Here we encountered the first signs of human habitation, a group of about twenty houses standing to the north of a salt-lake which winds about for a considerable distance towards the north-east. After this point there are no rivers, but frequent wells dug in the sand, from which sufficient water is procured. One may also travel due north for several thousand *li* without coming to a single high hill. After five days on horseback we crossed the line fortified by the Jin ... After six or seven days we suddenly came to the great sand-desert.[7]

Around 1,800 metres above sea level, this is one of the emptiest, least welcoming of north China's historical frontiers. Now, almost the only man-made shelters to be seen are Mongolian yurts or the earthen roofs of herdsmen's cellars, partially submerged pillboxes crouched down into the desert amid the winter snows, their entrances marked by single, padlocked wooden gates set in their low front walls, rising up out of the ground like square, thickly hooded eyes. While in some places the wall remains substantial – around two metres high and wide at the top – in others it has practically disappeared, swelling out like a prominent vein underneath the carpet of scree, forcing the stony desert to mound gently over it.[8] The flattened rampart becomes significantly easier to spot in winter, when windblown snows drift up against one shallow side, underscoring the wall's slight elevation. In both name and reality, the Jin defences bear little resemblance to what we now call *Changcheng* or Great Wall: indeed, contemporary sources studiously avoid that Qin term, favouring instead 'border fortress', 'barrier', 'rampart' or plain 'wall'.[9]

The whole question of wall-building provoked controversy: great numbers of officials were drawn into the consultation process, some of whom displayed an open scorn for walls. When natural and economic circumstances – the consequences of a serious drought – brought a halt to wall-building, a defence official argued that this pause should become permanent: 'What has been begun is already being flattened by sand storms, and bullying the people into defence works will simply exhaust them.' Yet the economic calculations of the then prime minister won the day: 'Although the initial outlay for the walls will be one million strings of cash, when the work is done the frontier will be secure with only half the present number of soldiers needed to defend it, which means that every year you will save three million strings of cash ... The benefits will be everlasting.' The emperor quickly approved, perhaps already redistributing in his head the saved three million into alternative projects.[10]

~

While thousands of kilometres of wall were built during several decades over sand-blasted mountains and plains in the north, it evidently never crossed the minds of the Jin emperor and his officials to go to the trouble of building any defences to the south, against the Song. On the contrary, to the Jin the south was a punchbag, to be insulted, invaded and pillaged as the need arose. A new treaty of 1141–2 had negotiated an even bigger indemnity for the Jin, which henceforth addressed the Song as a vassal state. This rhetorical shift was practically unprecedented in Chinese dynastic history: although the tributary system had often worked at a loss for the Chinese, they at least felt they were holding to the moral high ground. After all, the primary significance of tribute relations was that barbarians acknowledged inferiority by kowtowing to the Chinese; it was only of secondary importance that the northern barbarians were invariably presented with money and gifts far more valuable than the tribute goods they themselves offered China. In the agreement of 1141–2, the Chinese were robbed even of this source of 'face': the traditional roles of the tribute system were reversed, with the Song termed the 'insignificant state' existing on Jin sufferance, the Jin the 'superior state', and the annual indemnity paid by Song named as 'tribute'. Not surprisingly, Song sources tried to excise this humiliating episode from history by managing to mislay their copy of the decree; happily for posterity, Jin officials were not so careless, setting it into their dynastic records. As late as 1206, even with Jin strength severely reduced by natural disasters – in 1194, the Yellow River had catastrophically changed course, resulting in serious flooding in central and eastern China, while areas of Shandong had been blighted by drought and locusts – a Song offensive was easily neutralized into a peace treaty.

The situation looked very different on the Jin's northern borders, as the ruling dynasty glanced uneasily back towards its own origins, towards the precarious, nomadic existence of tribes that had little to lose and much to gain from continuous warfare. Fortunately for the Jin, however, for most of the twelfth century the landmass now known as Mongolia remained a mess of tribal rivalries which the Jin managed to control with moderate ease through a combination of campaigns, fortifications and diplomacy. Until the thirteenth century, the Mongols, a people who had settled around the River Onon in north-east Mongolia around AD 800, were one nomadic group among many – the Naiman, the Kerayit, the Tatars – on the northern steppe, herding or hunting, and living in tents of felt on the plains, or of birch in the forests. If the area around the Onon looked in 800 much as it does now, the Mongols would have found it a relatively hospitable environment: a well-watered, tree-dotted savannah of lush grasses, with good deer-hunting in the steep valleys further north.

The Jin first set about securing their northern borders with the steppe tribes around 1140, when the Mongol khaghan, Kabul, great-grandfather of Genghis, was invited to the Jin capital, Zhongdu (now Beijing), and lavishly banqueted, with a view to forging some kind of alliance. Relaxed by the important diplomatic lubricant of fermented mare's milk, at an advanced point in proceedings Kabul leaned over to the Jin emperor and tweaked his beard. Whatever Kabul's intentions, they were interpreted negatively by the emperor's incensed officials, who were in the process of reinventing themselves as etiquette-conscious Confucian Chinese and consequently refused to strike any kind of agreement with the presumptuous khaghan. They let him leave peacefully enough, but soon dispatched a force to ambush him. Although Kabul escaped back to his steppe stronghold, relations between the two powers deteriorated from this point on. Shortly after, the Jin directed their desire for revenge at Kabul's nephew and successor, Ambakai, who, on being captured by the Tatars, a buffer tribe situated between Jin and Mongols, was handed over to the Jin and subsequently executed in a particularly brutal way: crucified on a contraption known as a 'wooden donkey'.[11]

The Jin pursued a successful policy of divide and rule for the next sixty years, ensuring that no single tribe remained powerful for long enough to pose too great a threat. After the betrayal of their leader, the Mongols fell upon the Tatars. When the Tatars beat off the Mongols to become the dominant steppe power, the Jin reallied with the Mongols to destroy the Tatars. It was in connection with this campaign against the Tatars that the Jin first approached Genghis Khan, then one of several men competing for the Mongol leadership, and asked him to join them. Born in 1162 to a clan head called Yesugei, the young Genghis had strong personal reasons for hating the Tatars. It was after eating food offered by a Tatar that Yesugei fell ill and died, leaving behind a wife with six children. Deeming Yesugei's sons too young to inherit their father's position, the clan abandoned the entire family to survive by foraging fruit, roots and fish along the banks of the Onon. Worse was to come when the thirteen-year-old Genghis, after settling a childish quarrel with one of his brothers over a bird and fish by shooting him dead, was captured and enslaved by rival clansmen. Escaping from a wooden pillory and a gang of pursuers, he returned to his family and spent subsequent years gathering allies and sworn brothers about him. Unsurprisingly, Genghis leapt at the invitation to attack his old enemies, the Tatars, and personally captured the Tatar khan in 1196. The Jin rewarded their new vassal Genghis by giving him the title 'Keeper of the Frontier', an act that, within twenty years, had begun to look like a highly injudicious historical decision.

In 1206, after eliminating his rivals to the leadership of the Mongols, Genghis called a *kuriltai,* a national assembly, at Blue Lake in central Mongolia, a natural conglomeration of limpid blue sky and waters, and luxuriant green grasses that offered all the twelfth-century conveniences a tribesman could hope for: protection by surrounding foothills, water, good pasture and a 100-metre peak from which a commander could survey his forces. There, he lavishly rewarded loyal followers with titles and honours, and proclaimed himself 'unifier of the people of the felt-walled tents'.[12]

Genghis's steppe regime boded ill for the Jin dynasty on two counts. First, he created a new model of Mongol society, in which power was no longer inherited – leading inevitably to destructive rivalries among and between families – but guaranteed by loyalty to one broadly acclaimed leader (himself). Instead of directing their considerable military energies towards liquidating each other, the now united steppe tribes were ready to hurl themselves, in an alarmingly cohesive formation, at states beyond the steppe. The Jin would henceforth have to take on, as one force, the tribes whom, until very recently, they had been dividing and ruling. Second, the new Mongol alliance made its component peoples more outwardly aggressive. Genghis recognized that the fractious tribes of the steppe had lost, in each other, a significant source of plunder, and that they would only stay under a single Mongol command if he could ensure they were well rewarded with booty. He would have to find new raiding targets further afield.

Such is the historical fascination generated by Genghis Khan's empire of atrocities that the rationale behind his devastating path to conquest is sometimes obscured by simple enumeration of where he went, and whom, what and how he annihilated: the millions of Muslims killed in Central Asia, the defeated Russian commanders slowly suffocated to death under the banqueting table of victorious Mongol generals, the Chinese cities entirely massacred except for a handful of craftsmen and actors (even barbarians, it seems, sometimes needed distracting). The geographical variety of his targets – China, Central Asia, Persia, Russia – makes it hard to elucidate a single cause of his aggression such as a particular racial hatred. His desire to conquer is probably best explained as the pastoral nomad leader's impulse to loot carried to extremes: the loyalty of his men depended on generous rewards more luxurious than those afforded by the grassy steppe plains. Genghis's brutality towards the populations encountered in his campaigns – more than 1.3 million in the Central Asian oasis city of Merv were said to have been killed in a few days, each Mongol soldier dispatching 400 people – points to an obsession with the instant gratification of plunder, and a fundamental lack of interest in territorial acquisition for its own sake; any conqueror who wants to make long-term profits out of an empire takes care to ensure there are producers left to work it. The Mongol conquest thus happened almost by accident. The Mongols under Genghis Khan started off as no more than a phenomenally successful version of the steppe plunderers who had been harassing China and other sedentary societies since the first millennium BC. The difference was that the Mongols took the business of raiding rather more seriously than their predecessors, laying utter waste to any area towards which they directed their horses. After stripping an area bare, they had no choice but to move on to another – hence the piecemeal acquisition of China between 1213 and 1279.

~

It did not take Genghis long to set his sights on the opportunities for plunder offered by the Jin, who had in turn been profitably plundering Song China for years. Surprisingly anxious to find a moral pretext for invasion, he began by searching for Jin transgressions of his military code of honour (throughout his fighting career, he persistently maintained that he attacked only in response to perceived affronts or betrayals of loyalty). While his desire for war could historically be traced back to the Jin's crucifixion of his great-uncle, Ambakai, more immediately, Genghis decided that remaining a vassal of the Jin had become an insult to his dignity. When an ambassador from a new Jin emperor, who had come to the throne in 1208, arrived at Genghis's steppe stronghold demanding a tribute offering to confirm Genghis's continuing vassal status, Genghis retorted that the new emperor was an imbecile: 'Why should I kowtow to him?'[13] After spitting in the direction of the south – where the Jin capital lay – he then galloped off. Genghis spent the next three years preparing for invasion, and in spring 1211 led 100,000 men and 300,000 horses south-east from the Gobi towards the Jin capital of Zhongdu.

The Jin failed to respond in any positive way, hamstrung as much by psychological as by military weakness. Already by 1210, Jin fear of the Mongols had gained the upper hand over reason: terrorized by stories of Mongol strength, the Jin court 'forbade the common people from spreading rumours about border affairs'.[14] Whether sensible counter-measure against public hysteria or ostrich-like act of denial, this did little to hold up the advance of the invaders. Crossing over the threshold between China and the steppe north-west of Beijing, the Mongols dodged round the end of the Jin walls and heavily defeated a much bigger Jin army, leaving the bodies of the Jurchen forces 'piled like rotten logs' over fifty kilometres of the valleyed frontier.[15] Ten years later, the Daoist pilgrims passing through the old borderland on their way to Genghis's court noted the corpses that were still scattered over the landscape. 'Northwards lay nothing but wintry sands and withered grass. Here China – its customs and climate – suddenly comes to an end. . . [The disciples] pointed to the skeletons lying on the battlefield and said: "Let us, if we come home safely, say Masses for their souls...".'[16]

As the Mongols closed in on the capital, leaving the Jin's first, outer line of defence days of riding behind – it took the Daoist party, who were doubtless rather slower on horseback than a Mongol horde, ten days to reach the wall from the frontier battlefield – the Jin attempted to reinforce their forts and to sue for peace. But the Mongol generals moved too fast for the auxiliaries to be effective, and took insufficiently manned garrisons and walled cities to the north of Beijing with little difficulty; meanwhile, terrified peace envoys promptly defected and revealed the Jin's battle plans.

It is sometimes supposed that the Jin fell because the long frontier walls were crumbling after centuries of neglect, that they were by then a millennium-old institution in need of dedicated renovation. Before the Tang, however, practically every dynasty with authority over north China had built and manned their own walls, and far more recently the Liao and the Jin had done the same. There was little wrong with the Jin walls and forts beyond the two fundamental military limitations of static defences. First, the defensive efficacy of walls, as Genghis Khan was allegedly fond of pronouncing, depended on the courage of those defending them. Many of the Jin frontier garrisons were made up of unreliable Khitan (formerly Liao) rather than Jurchen troops, whose loyalty to the Jin soon wavered before the Mongol onslaught. A fortress north-east of Beijing, at Gubeikou, fell after no kind of fight at all, thanks to the treachery of a Khitan commander.[17] Secondly, walls and forts create illusory boundaries: they themselves might be impregnable, but the defensive voids existing beyond their limits are not. All too often, the strength of their fortifications gave the Jin a false sense of security, as they sheltered behind their walls while the Mongols tirelessly plundered the surrounding, undefended countryside. Only one fortified pass was stormed on Genghis's advance towards Beijing – the substantial Juyong fortress, blocking a pass between two mountains north of the city. Finding himself briefly held up, Genghis's most senior general, Jebe, employed one of his favourite tactics: staging a mock retreat that drew the Jin garrison out of the pass in pursuit, he then ambushed the garrison and charged through the open gates of the fort. The Mongols also had at their disposal a formidable repertoire of siege-breaking techniques. One was to demand as a ransom all the animals of the city or town. After a relieved population had duly handed them over, the Mongol leaders would attach firebrands to each animal and set them loose. The terrified creatures would flee back to their homes, spreading fire and panic throughout the settlement and distracting any resistance to the Mongol attack. Another, even more devastating tactic was to turn Chinese prisoners into a human shield which was then driven towards a town, thoroughly weakening the resolve of the walls' defenders.

In 1214, finding Beijing and its forty-three kilometres of city walls too well defended to fall after anything less than a lengthy siege, Genghis agreed to withdraw his forces after extracting from the Jin a vast indemnity of silk, gold, horses, boys and girls, and one of the emperor's daughters. But soon another pretext arose to resume the invasion: the flight of the Jin court and government further south to Kaifeng, the former northern capital of the Song. Genghis responded in outraged tones: 'The Jin Emperor made a peace agreement with me, but now he has moved his capital to the south; evidently he mistrusts my word and has used the peace to deceive me!'[18] In 1215, the Mongols returned to besiege, then sack Beijing – some parts of which burned for a month – massacring its starving and traumatized inhabitants. The fate of the Jin capital became a sickening warning to later rulers contemplating resistance to Genghis's horde. When, one year later, an ambassador from one of Genghis's future targets in Central Asia came to investigate the truth of Beijing's total devastation, he relayed back to his sovereign that human bones were mounded throughout the city, that the earth was smeared with human grease, that typhus spread by rotting corpses was epidemic.

By 1217, after swift, final blows against Manchuria, the former Jurchen homeland, Genghis Khan, the Jin's former 'Keeper of the Frontier', was keeper of all China north of the Yellow River. The Jin would not be fully dislodged from Kaifeng until 1234 – for the Mongols, the intervening twenty-odd years were filled with distractions such as conquering the sprawl of territory that lay between China and the eastern shores of the Black Sea – but their final collapse was only a matter of time. A song from the time of the Mongol invasions sums up the sense of the Jin Wall's futility: 'The Wall was built, with cries of pain and sadness; the moon and the Milky Way seem low in comparison with it. But if all the white bones of the dead had been left piled up there, they would reach the same height as the Wall.'[19]

~

Once the Mongols held north China, the fall of the south was inevitable. The Mongols were unbeatable in cavalry engagements, particularly now that they controlled the northern trade in horses on which the Song depended, thus ensuring that the Song were sold only sick, stunted mounts, sometimes no bigger than large dogs. Where cavalry was useless – in the wet paddy fields of the south – the Mongols adapted to the new watery terrain by creating a navy, beating the Song ever further back to the very edges of south China, until the last child-emperor was killed in a sea battle at Canton in 1279.

~

So resistant were the early Mongol rulers of China, the sons and grandsons of Genghis Khan, to the idea of any accommodation with the Chinese way of life and its softening influences – the downfall of so many previous non-Chinese dynasties – that one nomad extremist even suggested depopulating (massacring) north China and turning it over to pasture. Fortunately, a Khitan adviser persuaded the khan that more money, and therefore power, could be generated by letting the inhabitants live, as people tended to pay more taxes than horses. Although no wholesale liquidation of the Chinese took place, the new regime tried to ensure that the natives were kept out of the business of government by devising a system of ethnic ranks – Mongols, western and Central Asians, northern Chinese and southern Chinese – which decided the allotment of official posts. The first two categories – about 2.5 per cent of the entire population of China – held the majority of the most powerful positions.

Although Khubilai Khan, the grandson of Genghis and first Mongol emperor of all China, succumbed to moderate sinicization, maintaining – controversially, in the view of the old tribal elite – that more than Mongolian battle skills would be needed to rule China, he did manage to avoid building border walls. Marco Polo, who allegedly spent years at the court of Khubilai, gasping at the size and magnificence of everything from palaces to pears, conspicuously fails to mention any kind of a frontier wall in his *Travels*. Polo's doubters have used this omission to argue that he never got anywhere near China but instead embroidered sketchy tales related to him by Persian or Arab merchants. Yet while there is plenty to suspect in Polo's account – his claims, for example, that he was present at a siege that ended two years before he supposedly reached China, that he was made governor of the southern metropolis Yangzhou, an appointment puzzlingly omitted by exhaustive Chinese bureaucratic records – there are nonetheless enough corroborated factual observations, such as those concerning foot-binding and burial practices, to make it at least partially convincing.

When it came to building his capital, Dadu, on the site of contemporary Beijing, Khubilai proved more susceptible to Chinese influence, setting his own palace, according to Polo, within four walls: the 9.5 kilometre-square city wall, an outer palace wall (both whitewashed and battlemented), an inner wall and, finally, a marble wall providing a kind of terrace around the palace itself. Inside, Khubilai nodded briefly to his tribal heritage – draping his interiors with curtains of ermine – but otherwise eschewed the traditional Mongol simplicity dictated by his ancestors' nomadism. The walls of the halls and chambers, Polo recounted, were 'all covered with gold and silver and decorated with pictures of dragons and birds and horsemen and various breeds of beasts and scenes of battle.'

The ceiling is similarly adorned, so that there is nothing to be seen anywhere but gold and pictures. The hall is so vast and so wide that a meal might well be served there for more than 6,000 men. The number of chambers is quite bewildering ... The roof is all ablaze with scarlet and green and blue and yellow and all the colours that are, so brilliantly varnished that it glitters like crystal and the sparkle of it can be seen from far away.[20]

Outside the palace, the city itself was no conglomeration of makeshift yurts, but 'full of fine mansions, inns, and dwelling-houses ... the whole interior of the city is laid out in squares like a chess-board with such masterly precision that no description can do justice to it'.[21]

Curiously, the Mongols – renowned more as burners and pillagers than as aesthetes – contributed one of the most exquisite constructions that now forms part of the walled fortifications near Beijing: the Cloud Terrace (Yuntai), a white stone arch, 7.3 metres high, built at the Juyong pass north of the capital. Covered in Buddhist inscriptions in six different languages, in carvings of precious jewels, animals and dragons, the arch is a monument to the cosmopolitan Pax Mongolica that rose up from the dust and carnage of Mongol empire-building, an open gateway mocking with its elaborately, uselessly ceremonial decoration the functional failure of the supposedly fast defences against which it was set. Rather than obstructive walls, the Mongols favoured free-flowing trade and communication routes throughout their enormous empire: at the end of Khubilai's reign, Mongol China had 1,400 postal stations, kept functioning by the 50,000 horses at their disposal. The Cloud Terrace was the portal through which emperors and commoners travelled from Beijing to the steppe and back, toing and froing within the pan-Eurasian empire of the Mongols.

But the very lack of walls may yet have contributed to the collapse of Mongol rule in 1368. From 1300 onwards, widespread poverty in south China triggered rebellions of increasing frequency and intensity against the government. Medical historians have theorized that Chinese impoverishment was due in part to depopulation caused, or at least aggravated, by the shifting of trade routes from the deserts of the Silk Road to the grassy steppes, bringing the plague down through China in the flea-ridden saddlebags of Mongol tribesmen. Just as, during the Western age of exploration, indigenous peoples of the New World were devastated by the arrival of European diseases such as smallpox and measles, in some parts of China as many as two-thirds of local populations were wiped out by pestilence spread during the Mongol conquest.[22] By this reasoning, it was the absence of walls in Mongol China that, for once in Chinese history, brought disaster on a dynasty. For it was through one of these insurrections – the revolt of the Red Turbans – that Zhu Yuanzhang rose up to found the Ming dynasty, the greatest wall-builders in Chinese history and the architects of the Great Wall as it is now visited.

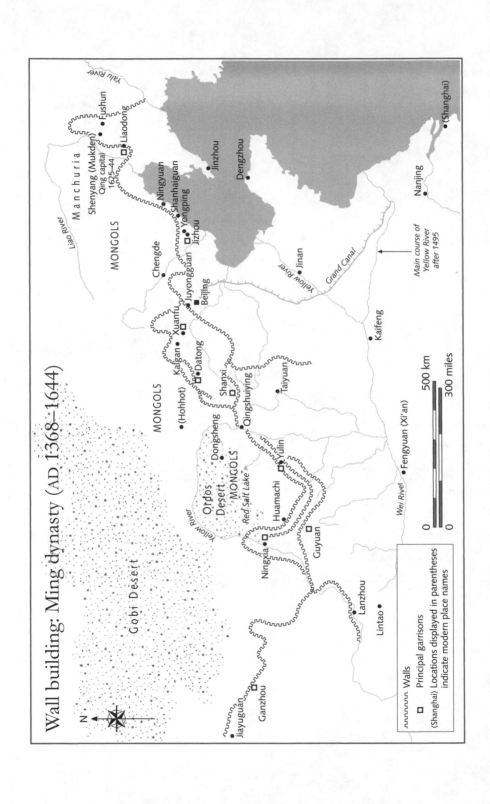

Wall building: Ming dynasty (AD 1368–1644)

Yalu River

Fushun
Liaodong

Manchuria

Shenyang (Mukden)
Qing capital
1625–44

MONGOLS

Liao River

Ningyuan
Shanhaiguan
Yongping
Jizhou

Chengde

Juyongguan
Beijing

Xuanfu
Kalgan (Hohhot)
Datong
Shanxi
Qingshuiying
Taiyuan

MONGOLS

Dongsheng
Ordos
Desert
MONGOLS
Red Salt Lake
Yulin
Huamachi

Yellow River

Ningxia
Guyuan

Lanzhou
Lintao

Ganzhou
Jiayuguan

Gobi Desert

N

Jinzhou

Dengzhou

Jinan

Grand Canal

Yellow River

Kaifeng

Wei River
Fengyuan (Xi'an)

Nanjing

(Shanghai)

Main course of
Yellow River
after 1495

0 ____ 500 km
0 ____ 300 miles

∿∿∿ Walls
□ Principal garrisons
(Shanghai) Locations displayed in parentheses
indicate modern place names

CHAPTER EIGHT

A Case of Open and Shut: The Early Ming Frontier

On New Year's Day, 2 February 1421, after sixteen years of dedicated construction by more than 200,000 labourers, the Ming emperor Yongle inaugurated his new capital, Beijing, on the site of the former Mongol city of Dadu. Almost the first brickwork to go up had been the city wall, a ten-metre high, twenty-three-kilometre perimeter, within which were built in due course the iconic structures that still define the city today: the vermilion Forbidden City; the massive red, walled portal that divides the palace from the expanses of Tiananmen Square; the city gates, enormous wooden doors set into stone arches that tower over choked roads.

Rejecting the moderation of thirteenth-century Chinese architectural fashions, Ming buildings instead veered towards an overwhelming monumentality. While the calling cards of earlier Chinese architecture were still very much present in the high Ming style – the curved roof, the overhanging eaves – Ming architecture became a distorting mirror of the past, replacing Chinese builders' earlier concern for harmony of proportion with a worship of overblown scale: sacrificing the height of walls to length and exaggeratedly deepening roofs. In the Forbidden City, the results were overbearing: huge, heavy, tiled roofs slipped, like oversized hats, over foreshortened walls, all seemingly groaning under the weight of their own self-importance. The gaudy imperial colour scheme – its huge expanses of white marble, golden-yellow roof tiles, deep red walls, blue, green and gold mosaic – adds an extra over-emphasis to the outlines of the entire ensemble. There is nothing subtle about the appeal of the Forbidden City: it impresses through the size of the imperial conceit, through its succession of enormous, white-stone courtyards, its string of raised audience halls, its marble bridges and stairs, all set with rigid symmetry within a rectangle 1.1 kilometres on its longer edge. Its proportions dwarf visitors, compelling a slow progression through the complex, forcing them to submit to an oppressive imperial vision of time and space. Never intrinsically beautiful, the Forbidden City impresses mainly with its authoritarian pomposity, with its aesthetic of thuggish grandiloquence.

Yongle's architectural schemes rivalled and perhaps outdid those of his predecessor, the First Emperor of Qin, in their desire to imbue the institution of absolute imperial rule with an exclusive grandeur and sanctity expressly designed to intimidate both Chinese and foreigners alike. The huge public spaces, ceremonial halls and mazes of living quarters and administrative departments that filled the Forbidden City nestled within three concentric sets of walls: its own, that of the larger imperial city (which included imperial ministries, granaries, factories) and that of the main city. South of the city lay the Temples of Heaven and Earth, a complex of state-constructed temples and altars set amid parklands almost as expansive as the area reserved for the Forbidden City. Every aspect of the new capital's architecture was thus laden with heavy-handed, autocratic symbolism. The situating of the Forbidden City at the centre of a triple set of square excluding walls, orientated to the points of the compass, bludgeoned visitors towards only one inexorable conclusion: that the Chinese emperor, the Son of Heaven, enthroned, enclosed, imprisoned at the centre of his capital – the universe in harmonious microcosm – both physically and spiritually represented the cosmic centre of the world.[1]

The choice of Beijing, which was much closer to Mongolia than the old, southern capital in Nanjing, as imperial headquarters projected a definite message about the new Ming empire. After more than 450 years of foreign occupation of China before 1368, the founding year of the Ming dynasty, Yongle's decision to move the capital to Beijing, so near to the steppe, emanated a new and total confidence regarding the dynasty's ability to keep its empire safe and the frontier in peaceful thrall.

Yongle wanted as many witnesses to his New Year's Day ceremonies as could be mustered. Assembled in Beijing in 1421 were thousands of ambassadors from Asia and the coasts of the Indian Ocean, all required to kowtow before the Chinese Son of Heaven. The veneration offered by these dignitaries was the fruit of two decades of the emperor's concertedly outward-looking foreign policy. By 1421, he had led two out of a total of five campaigns against the Mongols and wooed into diplomatic neutrality the tribes of the far west. Since 1405, exploiting a maritime technology far in advance of anything achieved by the West at that time, Yongle had dispatched six separate fleets of huge junks – each one over sixty metres long, several times bigger than Columbus's *Santa Maria* – from China's east coast on missions of exploration and diplomacy to Java, Ceylon, even as far as eastern Africa, bringing back exotic goods, animals and hordes of diplomatic representatives from distant kingdoms anxious to establish tributary, and therefore trading, relations with Ming China. The Chinese vessels were called 'treasure ships', laden on departure with the emblematic treasures of Chinese civilization – porcelain, silk and jade – designed to dazzle the rulers and peoples of the dozens of countries that the fleet's admiral, the eunuch Zheng He, claimed to have visited. Almost a century before Columbus set off for the Americas, China had invented its own brand of borderless maritime imperialism, its expansionist approach the polar opposite of the insular wall-building favoured by so many of Yongle's predecessors.

~

Some 200 years later, Ming China looked very different. Yongle's hands-on policy of open expansionism had been abandoned by stay-at-home emperors prone to frequent-to-constant bouts of acute political isolationism. The Forbidden City was no longer a cosmopolitan magnet for foreign exotica but a vermilion prison for its imperial residents, Beijing a city as often besieged by acquisitive Mongolian raiders as by admiring bringers of tribute. By the seventeenth century, the Ming dynasty had turned in on itself, attempting to set a lock around China's borders: around its exposed coastlines, with a prohibition on foreign trade; on its northern frontier, with the most substantial, expensive and elaborate system of walled border fortifications that any Chinese dynasty had constructed, some in the lavishly towered and crenellated, bricks-and-mortar form by which the Great Wall is now known to its millions of visitors. But even as parts of this wall were still being built and repaired in 1644, foreign invaders from the north-east were surging through it to conquer the empire it was meant to protect.

For those willing to see them, the seeds of Ming China's destruction were already sown in Yongle's grand designs. In his triple-walled Forbidden City, Yongle had constructed an emblem of the rigidly enclosed ceremonial of Ming rule, the coffin in which his dynasty would later suffocate. And for all their apparent cosmopolitanism, Yongle's maritime enterprises were as much an exercise in imperial Chinese self-love as a pragmatic, entrepreneurial colonial initiative. A primary aim of the expeditions seems to have been an elaborate, international hunt for kowtows: to persuade as many foreigners as possible to acknowledge China's cultural supremacy, to confirm and celebrate China's position at the centre of the world, surrounded by tributary vassals. When money for these expeditions ran out, China's emperors simply became ever more entrenched in their own Sino-centric worldview, ever more walled in – figuratively and physically – by their own visions of supremacy.

~

In the early years of the Ming, nonetheless, little of this was apparent. The border wall, for one thing, did not exist; not even an idea of it. On 7 September 1368, the year that Ming rule was founded, the current representatives of the Mongol Yuan dynasty scuttled out of Dadu and through the white stone arch of the Cloud Terrace, heading for the 'stately pleasure dome' of their summer capital at Shangdu (or Xanadu, in Coleridge's transliteration), on the southern steppes of contemporary Inner Mongolia. The Mongol emperors annually progressed between their capitals, making the twenty-three-day trek in late spring to escape the stifling heat of a Beijing summer for the cooler, mountainous and forested surroundings of Shangdu, with its marble palace, vast hunting ground and pastures filled with specially bred white mares and cows that produced milk only for the khans and their family.

This time, however, their departure needed to be unceremoniously quick, as the Mongol royal family were fleeing more than a hot, dry Beijing summer, which would in any case have been well past its worst by early September. On the day that they left, Xu Da, a general of the first Ming emperor, defeated the capital's army to the east of Dadu; a week later, Ming forces scaled the city's walls and took the city. In a final, emphatic gesture of victory, the Ming changed the city's name from the Mongol choice of Dadu (literally, 'Great Capital') to Beiping ('The North is Pacified'), shifting their own capital south to Nanjing ('Southern Capital').

Zhu Yuanzhang, who proclaimed himself first Ming emperor, Hongwu (literally 'Overwhelming Military Force'), in 1368, was a man elevated by desperation. Born in 1328 to a destitute peasant family, he slowly hauled himself from the very bottom rung of Chinese society to the top, somehow surviving the pestilence, hunger, bandits, pirates and civil war that had dispatched millions of his compatriots over the past century and a half. When Zhu was sixteen, most of his family died within some three weeks of each other from a combination of famine and disease. After the destitute, orphaned Zhu's last refuge – a Buddhist temple at which he had become a mendicant monk – was destroyed by Mongol soldiers, he turned to a rebellious rural Chinese sect called the Red Turbans, a millenarian cult that rallied suffering peasants to rise up against the Mongol authorities in preparation for the allegedly imminent arrival on earth of Maitreya, the Buddha of wealth and king of radiance. The cult spread over much of central and southern China, acquiring regional power bases and leaders, among whom Zhu Yuanzhang emerged supreme after a series of spectacular victories over his rivals, including a naval triumph of 1363 in which his guerrilla battalions dynamited an enemy force of perhaps 300,000 men in south-east China.

In 1368, ignoring his – and his generals' – fatigue, Hongwu almost immediately sent Xu Da north of Beijing, to fortify frontier passes, close on the heels of the departing Yuan. His primary target was the first pass north of the city, Juyongguan – the one pass that had seriously held up the Mongols on their rampage towards the capital 150 years previously, the pass that the Mongol dynasty had robbed of its defensive properties by installing within it the open, decorative Cloud Terrace. Ever since the Warring States period, the Juyong pass had been classified as one of the key 'fortresses under Heaven', a fifteen-kilometre-long valley a mere sixty kilometres north of the capital, nestling among green mountains, the largest and nearest of which was Badaling, rising up to close off the eastern side of the valley. According to one source, Xu Da's fort 'straddled two mountains, spread over an area of thirteen *li,* and rose up forty-two feet high'.[2] Elsewhere, Xu Da is described as 'piling up stones into a fort, which within three years hosted a thousand-strong defence garrison'.[3] The Chinese, Hongwu's message ran clearly, were back in charge, firmly bolting the steppe wolf out.

Ming emperors never forgot the humiliation of Mongol occupation. Memory of the Mongol conquest haunted them, turning security against the north into an obsession that would, ultimately, paralyse and bankrupt the dynasty. The Ming hostility to foreigners was universal in scope, but not in degree. The Japanese, Koreans and Annamese, sneered Hongwu, were 'no more than mosquitoes and scorpions', but the northern barbarians were a continuous and vital 'danger to our heart and stomach'.

Ever since ancient times, rulers have governed the empire. It has always been a case of China occupying the interior and managing the barbarians, and the barbarians being outside and submitting to China. There was no such thing as the barbarians occupying China and governing the empire. From the time the Song fortunes declined, the Yuan was created by northern barbarians entering and residing in China. As for our Chinese people, it must be that Heaven's will is that we Chinese should pacify them. How could the barbarians rule the Chinese? I fear that the heartland has long been stained with the stink of mutton and the people are troubled. Therefore I have led forth armies to make a clean sweep. My aim is to chase out the Mongol slaves, to do away with anarchy and assure the people of their safety, to cleanse China of shame.[4]

Yet despite Ming China's hatred of the 'northern barbarians' and its powerful sense of shame at having succumbed to foreign domination, Mongol bloodthirstiness changed Chinese political culture for ever, stripping the soft ceremonial flesh of Chinese absolutism away to reveal its cruel, despotic bones. The Mongol conquest injected a new acceptance of extreme violence into Chinese society, inuring its inhabitants to unprecedented levels of brutality. Pathologically suspicious of conspiracies around him, from 1380 until the end of his reign Hongwu launched a series of purges that began with his chancellor Hu Weiyong, who was suspected of plotting with the Mongols, and ended with the execution or forced suicide of many of his best generals. By the close of the purges – in which even his son-in-law was forced to kill himself after being accused of selling tea illegally – some 40,000 people, and many of his most able officials, had lost their lives. Not long into his reign, educated men began to dread an imperial summons to serve in government; those unfortunates already corralled into service took the precaution of bidding their final farewells to their families if called to an imperial audience, and of swapping congratulations with their colleagues if their heads remained in contact with their bodies by nightfall.

Again, like the Mongols, the early Ming rulers had minimal interest in extensive border fortifications, and little intensive wall-building was done before the late fifteenth century. Although concern about the Mongols uniformly preoccupied the dynasty, early emperors chose not to hide behind walls, but to imitate the tactics of the enemy, attacking deep into the steppe. The main reason that the early Ming rulers neglected to build walls is that they simply did not need them. With a well-organized, battle-hardened army, Hongwu and his son Yongle could launch campaigns into the steppe to keep the Mongols in line. Instead of walls, the early Ming emperors relied on the less tangible but rather more effective quality of military 'awesomeness' *(wei)* to cow the northern steppe peoples.

Hongwu's main contribution to frontier defences was the fortification of two lines of strong points – one inner, one outer – scattered across Mongolia and north China, designed to function not as a fixed frontier but as bases from which to launch further campaigns and influence steppe affairs. Zhu's most trusted subordinates were sent to border areas to build linchpin forts between the two linear extremes of Jiayuguan in the west (literally, the Pass of the Pleasant Valley) and Shanhaiguan (the Pass between Mountain and Sea) in the east. Both locations have obvious strategic advantages, the former a sandy oasis settlement sandwiched towards the end of the Gansu corridor between two mountain ranges, the latter blocking free passage along the coast between China, and Manchuria and Korea. Yet this was no Long Wall: eventually, Ming emperors would link individual strategic strong points and passes along the inner line of northern fortresses with winding stretches – in some places doubled or even tripled – of wall; but not yet. In the meantime, the outer line of forts – which spanned from the eastern edge of Liaodong to the top of the Yellow River loop, bulging out at its northernmost point about 250 kilometres north of Beijing – represented the main focus of Ming policy towards the steppe. A long way – at its remotest point, nearly 200 kilometres – clear of the line that would later become the Ming frontier wall, it was much too far from China proper to have any purely defensive significance; instead, these forts formed the backbone of early Ming expansionism, itself a Mongol-style policy of governing both steppe and China.

Commanders sent by Hongwu to the frontier to supervise the building of forts became neurotically obsessed with fulfilling their missions without reproach from their exacting ruler. Legends tell of the anxiety suffered by the general sent to build a wall six metres high and some 700 metres long around Jiayuguan, as he struggled to keep to the schedule of time and costs he had originally submitted to the emperor, and thereby to avoid terrible punishment. His triumph when he did so is attested by a legendary single brick – the one brick that was left over from the building materials he applied for in advance – placed on one of the fort's eaves.

Hongwu's confident military start to the dynasty was continued in spirit by his son Yongle, who personally led campaigns deep into Mongol territory. But Yongle crucially undermined Ming defences by withdrawing garrisons from seven of the eight forts established in the steppe by his father, leaving only the Kaiping garrison due north of his new capital, Beijing. This garrison was itself withdrawn six years after his death. Establishing a magnificent capital so close to the steppe, then abandoning the military structures necessary to maintaining a secure, dynamic presence on the steppe turned Beijing into an obvious target for Mongol raiders, and forced later Ming emperors to fall back, as a last resort, on an impoverishing policy of static defence – wall-building.[5]

~

Although by moving his capital within striking distance of Mongol riders Yongle created the geopolitical foundations on which thousands of kilometres of Ming frontier walls would later come to be built, it was the actions of three others that ensured the wall as it is now known went up: a foolish young man who became Chinese emperor in 1436, a grasping eunuch and an ambitious, charismatic Mongolian. None of these three ever so much as picked up a shovel or heaved a brick, but their collision in 1449 destroyed the possibility of any useful diplomatic dialogue between the two sides, driving the Chinese towards stubborn isolationism and the Mongols towards further aggression.

In 1448, a party of 2,000 Mongols reached Beijing. The purpose of their mission was ostensibly peaceable: they had come to participate in what passed, in Ming China, for diplomacy – the great, elaborately choreographed charade of the Ming tribute system. Mongol hopes for profit were high. Ever since the tribute system – in which foreigners ostensibly subordinated themselves to the Chinese emperor by presenting gifts and performing prescribed rituals of vassalage – had been systematized during the Han dynasty, it had operated at an economic loss for China. The Chinese maintained 'face' and had their Sino-centric view of the world confirmed; the non-Chinese effectively were given money, and both essential and luxury Chinese goods at knock-down prices, in return for a number of kowtows and a few of their own commodities.

By 1448, the Ming tribute system was less amply funded than it had once been, but stories of the riches offered to those willing to touch their foreheads to the ground in front of the Chinese Son of Heaven in previous decades would have persisted. The travelogue of a Persian embassy fortunate enough to be present in Beijing in 1421, at the time of the capital's inauguration, is stuffed with tales of fabulous banquets – an apparently inexhaustible supply of 'geese, fowls, roasted meat, fresh and dry fruits', of 'filberts, jujubes, walnuts, peeled chestnuts, lemons, garlics and onions pickled in vinegar', washed down with 'various kinds of intoxicants consisting of wines and liquors' – the most magnificent of which was a thousand-dish feast in which the emperor's food was prepared behind a wall of yellow satin, and brought in to the accompaniment of an orchestra, the twirling of ceremonial umbrellas and spectacular displays of acrobatics. After sufficient (eight) prostrations had been completed, presents were distributed to the embassy: to one sultan alone, eight bags of silver, three suits of royal robes with lining, twenty-four undergarments, ninety-one hawks, two horses, 100 arrows, five spears and 5,000 currency notes. After every banquet, the travellers retired to digest in lavish accommodation, on brocade pillows, coverlets and cushions, waited on by 'servants endowed with great beauty'. The Mongol embassy must have been salivating at the very prospect.[6]

Yet behind the decorous satin wall of tribute relations – the training courses in Chinese rites compulsory for 'barbarian' embassies, the imperial processions, the kowtows, orchestras, acrobats, banquets and exchange of gifts – tension between Mongols and Chinese had been developing over several years. Neither side felt that the tributary system was delivering what it wanted. To the Mongols, the profits of tributary embassies were beginning to appear threadbare. Their expectations no doubt inflated by memories of the extravagant gifts distributed in Yongle's time, by 1439 the Mongols were grumbling that tributary gifts were much smaller than they used to be. To the Chinese, these complaints looked simply greedy and undignified – inappropriate for a vassal who should be abjectly grateful for any celestial crumbs scattered from the Son of Heaven's table. Mongol politics, however, checked any impulse to compromise over the size of handouts. In the 1430s, the tribes of Mongolia were reunited, for the first time since the collapse of Mongol power in China, under one leader, Esen. Within ten years, Esen was in control of the enormous swathe of territories that stretch between contemporary Xinjiang and Korea. Unity put tremendous economic demands on the Mongol overlord. In order to keep this vast spread of tribal peoples content and united under his leadership, Esen needed to supply material incentives; given fifteenth-century Mongolia's relative scarcity of natural resources, the need for abundant procurement of Chinese goods, most straightforwardly and peacefully through the tribute system, became paramount.

Soon enough, Esen began sending annual 'tribute' missions to China, ostensibly to bow down before Chinese suzerainty, but in reality to receive Chinese goods – including basics such as clothes and grain – in exchange for a degree of subordination on his part, and for steppe products such as horses and furs. (Esen's 1446 tribute mission to China brought, among other items, 130,000 squirrel pelts.) Very quickly, the Chinese began to feel that Esen was taking advantage of the tribute cha- rade. First, he was bringing extravagant quantities of steppe commodities into China, thereby putting pressure on the Chinese to offer ever more extravagant gifts in return; by 1446, the Chinese government was refusing thousands of animal skins. Second, one of the great subsidiary expenses of the tributary system for the Chinese was the entertainment – ban- quets, daily rations, accommodation – of the embassies. The bigger the embassy and the longer it stayed in China, the larger the entertainment allowance had to be. By the 1430s, the Chinese strongly suspected that the Mongols were taking advantage of their hospitality: the tributary sys- tem, in short, had become a barbarian confidence trick at Chinese expense. As early as 1424, a dynastic record complains that '[s]ince Barbarians are so eager for profit no month goes by without some com- ing or going to present tribute, and soldiers and common people … have to escort them and wait on them'.[7] In 1437, one particularly blatant mis- sion from the north-east dispatched between thirty and forty men as escorts for no more than five tribute horses. Before the 1440s, Mongol missions had numbered no more than a few hundred; between 1442 and 1448, however, Esen dispatched an average of 1,000 men per year, all of whom needed feeding and rewarding, and many of whom – in the opin- ion of Chinese officials – were disgracefully behaved and brought tribute of poor quality.

Mutual suspicion dramatically intensified in 1448, when a 2,000-strong embassy declared a non-existent extra 1,000 men, in order to wrest more gifts from the unwilling Chinese. The discovery of the fraud gave the Ming court the perfect excuse to reduce their quota of presents by 80 per cent. Further enraged after a misunderstanding by which he had been led to believe his son would be allowed to marry into the Chinese imperial family, Esen mobilized forces against the north-west and north-east of Beijing.

The Chinese responded ineptly, lurching from unconcern to outraged militancy. They began either by ignoring reports that Esen was gathering his forces for an attack or, little better, merely dispatching mild-mannered envoys to enquire of him whether the reports were true. The Tianshun emperor, an immature twenty-one-year-old, then suddenly announced plans for a retaliatory expedition against Esen in the north-west. His officials carefully dressed their opposition in humble Confucian platitudes, but their horror at the idea was patent: 'The Son of Heaven, although the most exalted of men, should not get personally into these dangers. We officials, although the most stupid of men, insist that this must not occur.'[8] Unfortunately, the emperor was encouraged in his delusions of generalship by his former tutor Wang Zhen, one of the first catastrophically overweening eunuchs of the Ming dynasty.

Although employed by every Chinese dynasty since the Shang – primarily as trustworthy males to guard the palace harem, later as personal factotums, functionaries and even de facto prime ministers of the emperor – eunuchs have received a universally bad press throughout Chinese history, their reputation for perpetrating political infamy matched only by that of women. A poem from the *Classic of Poetry* (*Shijing*), one of the canonical Zhou texts of the early first millennium BC, expresses the orthodox historical view:

> Chaos is born not of heaven
> But of women.
> Nothing good, no education, no instruction
> Ever comes from wives and eunuchs.[9]

This age-old imputation of villainy is partly a problem of sources. For the majority of the Chinese past, those who have wielded pens, or brush and ink, have been male, Confucian scholar-officials – natural arch-rivals in power-holding to eunuchs and women. Yet although the written histories are undeniably biased against eunuchs, there is an excellent case to be made for the corrupting effect that some of them had on political practice.

The fact of this influence became a particularly intractable problem during the Ming dynasty, when numbers of eunuchs were to rise dramatically, partly because of social deprivation (voluntary castrations became commonplace, as families saw an emasculated career in the imperial palace as more secure than a chancy existence in the poverty-stricken countryside), partly because of fashions in imperial gift culture (eunuch servants became a prized and frequent item of exchange between the emperor and his extended family) and partly through the actions of certain emperors. When Yongle usurped the throne in 1403, he had to rely heavily on an army of eunuchs – a band of men personally bound to him – rather than civil servants and advisers, to fight, administer and spy for him, to root out opponents among the traditional ranks of imperial officials to his murderous coup against the designated heir. His pattern of dependence was followed by most of his successors: soon enough, the imperial city, indeed the empire, was swarming with eunuchs and eunuch-run bureaus. The imperial city alone was a mass of departments, treasuries, warehouses and factories managed by eunuchs, producing both everyday and luxury goods. Across the empire, there was no area of government devoid of eunuchs competing with and spying on their civil servant counterparts.

In theory, there was nothing wrong with a duplicated class of functionaries: the more servants of the state, the more that could be achieved. In practice, however, although there were hard-working, talented eunuchs, the rise of eunuch power led to inefficiency and division. The principal problem with eunuchs, as with palace women, was that they were not taken on to the imperial staff through a regularized system of recruitment – unlike Confucian bureaucrats, who toiled to pass the civil service examinations – but on imperial whim. This meant that they had no stable, secure career ladder to clamber up, and that their personal prospects depended on the emperor's favour and whatever they could squeeze out of the court. Their appeal to emperors lay precisely in this dependent, personal relationship: emperors made use of them as an inner circle of personal loyalists to be played off against civil servants. The eunuchs became a tool of absolutism, the ugliest manifestation of which was the eunuch secret police, an organization reaching out far and wide across the empire, torturing with grim assiduity anyone suspected of anti-imperial insurrection.

One of the most damaging long-term effects of this dispersal of ad hoc agents of despotism throughout Chinese society and government was to destabilize politics. Any decision or policy came down to the whim of the emperor, or of his personally appointed agents, making it formidably difficult to establish any rational system of policy evaluation. Winning a policy argument depended on identifying and currying favour with the emperor or his favourites of the moment; as these latter individuals could change more than once in the space of any protracted discussion of policy, careful, long-term planning became a near impossibility. The Ming culture of violence, meanwhile, meant that the penalties for failing or displeasing the emperor were terrifying: between 1641 and 1644 alone, three high-ranking ministers were driven to suicide by imperial will. Serving in Ming government was murderously stressful.

In frontier matters above all, the two prerequisites of eunuch career success – greedy self-interest and the need to pander to imperial whim – combined to particularly deleterious effect. Although the dangers of campaigning – the expense, the military superiority of the enemy, the impossibility of chasing the Mongols to a final, decisive victory in the vast steppelands – were obvious to many, the idea of a big, showy, risky expedition to the steppe was peculiarly attractive to a palace eunuch such as Wang Zhen. First of all, a major frontier campaign offered an ambitious and avaricious eunuch a clear opportunity to assemble plunder and glory, thereby assuring his pre-eminence as court favourite. Secondly, a eunuch's own career depended on pandering to his emperor, and more often than not during the Ming dynasty this meant eunuchs encouraging their militarily incompetent imperial patrons in their bellicose delusions of grandeur towards Mongolia, and reassuring them that they were fully qualified to teach the treacherous Mongols a lesson in battle.

Yet the military pretensions of an emperor and his eunuch did not by themselves automatically spell disaster. In combination with dramatic military decline, however, they were able to bring the dynasty to its knees and forced a radical rethink of frontier defence. By 1449, the once impressive Ming military machine was in no condition to challenge united Mongol forces. Back in the late fourteenth century, Hongwu's scheme for guaranteeing military security had consisted of creating a hereditary class of soldiers, with their own dedicated farming land. As long as officers and rank-and-file kept procreating, Hongwu theorized, a constant supply of soldiers would be guaranteed, and one that would feed and clothe itself.

Fifty years into the Ming dynasty, this grand plan was encountering serious problems. Hongwu's policy of military inbreeding did not suc-ceed in isolating a gene for military talent: he and most of his founding generals failed to pass on their battlefield valour to their descendants. Both Ming emperors and officers grew increasingly less vigorous as the dynasty went on, with the army being increasingly administered by civil-ian officials, and often adversely influenced by political rather than strate-gic interests, by imperial whim rather than by rational planning. Furthermore, there was always a way out of hereditary army obligations for those with money: rich families paid the poor to substitute for them. Corrupt commanders transformed the Ming military into a racket, turn-ing military land into their own private estates, demoting the rank-and-file into serfs to work their land and build their palaces, embezzling wages, rations and uniforms out of state allowances. Although, as the hereditary military families procreated so the army ranks theoretically swelled, in reality a majority of those on the military rolls had gone AWOL. By the middle of the fifteenth century, the quality of the Ming army – corrupt, under-disciplined, under-trained and under-supplied – was already noticeably deteriorating.

The 1449 expedition to chastise Esen in the north-west, over-enthusi-astically supported by the profit- and glory-hungry eunuch Wang Zhen, was a disaster from start to finish, mired in heavy rain, incompetence and melodrama.[10] On 4 August, as the emperor set out from Beijing for the frontier zone of Datong at the head of an army half a million strong and assembled in a frenzied two days, a high-ranking civil servant threw him-self in front of his ruler's palanquin, begging him to think of the coun-try, not just himself. The emperor remained silent, letting Wang Zhen shout abuse at this bringer of unwanted advice, before proceeding on towards the border.[11]

By the time the army crossed the Juyong pass, pounded by unseason-ably torrential rain storms, the sixty-five-year-old minister of war – a civil servant with no military experience – had already seriously injured him-self by falling off his horse several times.[12] When the Chinese finally completed the 340-kilometre, thirteen-day trudge west to Datong, pur-sued ominously all the way by glowering black clouds, they came upon a battlefield strewn with Chinese corpses: the casualties of a resounding defeat already inflicted on the Datong garrison by Esen. 'The chill of ter-ror,' the chronicle of the expedition reports, 'gripped all hearts.'[13] Finally, implored by one of his eunuch lieutenants to give the expedition up, Wang Zhen ruled to declare it a triumphant success and that the army should return to Beijing. The Chinese army might perhaps have beaten a safe retreat, if Wang Zhen had permitted the army to travel along a southern route, passing by his home county. Afraid that the soldiers might damage his enormous personal estates, however, Wang insisted on a more exposed, north-eastern passage.

Having so far remained eerily concealed from the increasingly unnerved Chinese, on 30 August Esen's men struck the army's rearguard. Valiant Chinese officers fought to their last arrow, even struggling on, using their empty bows as clubs, before being torn to pieces by the Mongols. Two days' march ahead, the emperor's entourage might have managed to slip safely through the Juyong pass and back to the capital if

Wang Zhen – concerned that his personal baggage train of a thousand wagons had been delayed – had not called a halt at the ill-defended post station of Tumu to check on the whereabouts of his valuables. When the long-suffering minister of war protested that a quick escape was vital, Wang Zhen shouted, 'You idiotic bookworm! What do you know about military matters? One more word out of you and I'll have your head.'[14] The minister spent the night of 31 August weeping in his tent with his colleagues, while Esen and his cavalry swiftly surrounded the camp.

Despite the earlier heavy rain, the Chinese found Tumu bereft of supplies of water, the one nearby river blocked off by Esen's men. Parched, hungry and terrified, they were destroyed by a full-scale Mongol attack on 1 September 1449.

The Chinese army broke, chaotically gave ground and became a mob. 'Throw down your arms and armour and be spared,' shouted the Mongols. Ignoring their officers, the Chinese soldiers went wild, stripped off their garments, and ran toward the Mongol cavalry, only to be cut to pieces. The air rained arrows, as the Mongols closed in. The emperor's personal cavalry guards surrounded him and tried to break through but made no headway. Dismounting, the emperor sat on the ground amidst a hail of arrows that killed most of his attendants.[15]

Calm and miraculously unharmed, this was the state in which the Mongols found and captured him.

~

All was not lost for the pragmatic Chinese, who recovered remarkably well from the shock of losing their Son of Heaven. Quick-thinking officials in Beijing dubbed the captive Tianshun 'Grand Senior Emperor' – in other words, kicked him upstairs – and elevated his younger brother to the position of junior, or real, emperor. The one courtier unwise enough to protest was summarily executed. The new regime then set about preparing for the defence of Beijing against a Mongol onslaught. When Esen arrived at the gates of the city, planning to restore the old emperor as a puppet ruler married to his daughter – in return, naturally, for a staggering ransom – he was politely but firmly informed: 'It is the altars of the Earth and of Grain that are of great importance, while the ruler is unimportant.'[16] Put another way, interests of state outweighed those of an individual leader, and one substitute emperor was very much like another. Esen vented his frustration on the surrounding countryside but failed to break into either Beijing or any other walled cities before retreating north again. Once the Chinese had, with little more than restrained regret, let Tianshun go, his value as a hostage plummeted and in 1450 Esen handed him back in exchange only for resumption of tribute relations and some insultingly paltry gifts. The former emperor was immediately bundled off into a corner of the Forbidden City on the orders of his younger brother, who was less than overjoyed to see him back. After failing to reap the rich rewards he had hoped to gain by ransoming the emperor, Esen seriously lost face among his subordinate tribes and was assassinated in 1455 by one of his own people.

Esen's original antagonists, the eunuchs, also suffered in the aftermath of Tumu. After Wang's death in battle, officials took a terrible revenge on Ma Shun, one of Wang's surviving eunuch lieutenants at court. In an extraordinary scene, unprecedented and unrepeated in Chinese political history, a bloody fistfight broke out at an imperial audience when, unable to restrain his hatred of his eunuch rivals any longer, a censor rushed at Ma, wrestled him to the ground and bit him. Other officials immediately abandoned all sense of decorum and leapt into the scrum. Lacking in conventional arms, the struggle was brutishly drawn out with improvised bludgeons: officials eventually blinded and battered the eunuch to death with his own boots. The nervous new emperor tried to escape the bloody fray by tiptoeing out of the audience chamber, until the new minister of war grabbed him back by his robe, forcing him to condone this spontaneous execution scene.[17]

In spite of the government's regrouping and the death of Esen, the disaster at Tumu set Ming frontier policy on a self-destructive course. Never again would the Mongols be overawed by the prospect of Ming military action. With a few notable exceptions, the process of military decline well under way by 1449 continued apace in the following decades. By the late fifteenth century, Ming emperors were even more manifestly incapable than Tianshun of leading campaigns into the steppe. When the earnest but weakling Hongzhi emperor (r. 1488–1501), perhaps the most unlikely field commander of the entire dynasty, ventured, 'Our dynasty's emperor Taizong [Yongle] often led campaigns beyond the Great Wall; is there any reason why We cannot do the same?', his stunned secretary of war had just enough presence of mind to suggest diplomatically, 'Your Majesty's godlike military qualities certainly are in no way inferior to those of emperor Taizong, but now our generals and their foot and mounted forces are far inferior.'[18] Tumu annihilated the Ming's military reputation in the north and gave the Mongols the courage to redraw the frontier. Both Hongwu and Yongle had laboured to create a buffer zone around their borders, making treaties with friendly tribes, and posting garrisons and watchtowers hundreds of kilometres out into the steppe, but after 1449 Mongol tribes seeped down into the Ordos region, settling around the Yellow River loop, drawing ever closer to China proper.

Secondly, although Tumu illuminated a serious conflict in foreign relations – Mongol desire for and Chinese aversion to trade relations – that the Chinese were now too weak to resolve by force, neither would the Ming court accept a diplomatic solution. While raids and trade, both undertaken by individual tribes, straggled on through the rest of the century, the Chinese emperor and his officials fretted and fulminated increasingly about the growing Mongol presence in the Ordos area. Tumu further entrenched and institutionalized Ming Chinese feeling against the Mongols. After 1450, rhetorical and physical attacks on Mongols – especially those living in China – grew in both frequency and virulence. Until 1450, despite the traumatic historical memory of Mongol occupation, Ming China was content to accept the services of Mongolian soldiers in its armies, and allowed loyal Mongols to settle on the northern border areas and even in the capital: fifteenth-century Beijing hosted a population of perhaps 10,000 Mongols. In the aftermath of Tumu, attitudes hardened, to the point where it was reported that problematic Mongols should be executed as a public example. 'If they are not of our racial kind,' a top civil servant pronounced grimly, 'their hearts must be different.'[19] A new political orthodoxy was being established, according to which any compromise with the Mongols was treason, while offensive or defensive defiance – however many lives on the frontier and ounces of silver it cost – represented the apogee of virtuous patriotism.

Most significantly, perhaps, the Ming court proved incapable of learning anything from the political debacle of Tumu, of drawing any lesson from the destructive influence of violent factionalism on government, or of fostering a spirit of greater conciliation and cooperation in the political sphere. The bloody revenge exacted by civil officials on their eunuch rivals only heightened the sense of mutual acrimony between the two power groups; another bloodbath followed the palace coup of 1457 that restored the formerly captive emperor, in which those who had stepped up to save the Ming state in 1449 were strangled, beheaded or exiled. Court intrigues intensified, leading to a near-total paralysis of policy. Frontier policy became a political football passed between court factions, each mouthing angry patriotic platitudes, each vying to win favour with unpredictable emperors who sat, cloistered in the Forbidden City, angrily nurturing a futile sense of superiority over the foreigners snapping at the frontier.

Against this backdrop of racist arrogance, military incompetence and murderous factionalism, only one course of action was beginning to look both defensively viable and psychologically satisfying: wall-building.

~

While courtiers battered each other to death with their boots, frontier officials on the ground suffered the consequences of political paralysis at the centre. Although, after Tumu, orders were sent out to strengthen border defences, a despairingly frank report of 1464 bemoaned the state of the frontier:

The Mongols are notorious for their propensity to raid, but our border commanders follow their routine and grow completely lazy. The cities and fortifications have
not been repaired, ammunition and arms are in a pitiful state. Crying abuses are
being practised: the rich soldiers bribe their superiors every month, thus avoiding
their services. But the poor ones must either endure cold and hunger, or desert. This
is why the guarding of the frontier is in such a deplorable state.[20]

Among these long-suffering local governors was Yu Zijun, a hard-
working official devoted to improving conditions in the north-western
region under his supervision. And for inhabitants of the provinces spanning the base of the Yellow River loop, life was generally miserable. Parts
of these provinces – eastern Gansu, Ningxia, Shaanxi – have always
counted among the poorest regions of China: mountainous, often
parched, blighted by unreliable rainfall and scoured periodically by sand
carried southwards by Inner Mongolian gales. Farming was possible, but
dedicated irrigation constantly necessary. In the war-stricken China of
the 1930s, Mao Zedong was to choose this very region as a relatively safe
headquarters for his beleaguered Communist guerrilla forces, as an area
whose poverty and isolation gave pause to both the right-wing
Nationalist government forces, which had been determinedly trying to
annihilate the Communists since 1927, and Japanese invaders from the
north-east, notorious for the consistent, thorough brutality with which
they approached their attempted conquest of China in the years preceding and during the Second World War. In the Ming period, economic
conditions here were even worse, and foreign raiders from the Ordos
region to the north far less nervous about striking across the dry loess
hills of the region, relieving the settlements of anything useful (cloth,
grain, metal, animals, women, children) and destroying what they could
not use or easily enslave – houses and the male population. The populace
that Yu Zijun encountered was impoverished, harried and badly in need
of security. Several years of good works in this poor and isolated region
– founding a school, encouraging students, teaching the locals to farm,

promoting self-defence by manufacturing metal weapons, pacifying the Mongols with trade – focused the governor's mind on the need to resolve decisively the problems caused by the region's dangerous proximity to the Ordos, which had been overrun by Mongols. In 1471, he submitted a memorial to the emperor, recommending the construction of a wall, about nine metres high, between Chinese settlements and the Ordos, to protect the local people.[21]

Back in Beijing, the minister of war was unenthusiastic, but lacking any better ideas. Arguments about the frontier had by then been rumbling on indecisively for well over a decade. Still smarting at the loss of the Ordos, the court refused to view Mongol occupation of the area as anything more than a temporary setback and produced a stream of unrealistic military schemes – such as sending a vast force out along the Shaanxi border, or dispatching a crack detachment of 3,000 men to hunt down and massacre the Mongol leaders – most of which found favour with the emperor but were never implemented. Walls, however, were still not an attractive option, tarred as they were by association with their unfashionable and short-lived aficionados, the Sui and Qin dynasties, by their expense and by their tendency to collapse. (In the first reference to Long Walls – the Qin term – in the dynastic record of 1429, one of relatively few such mentions, they are inauspiciously described as having fallen down after heavy rain.[22]) Their heads firmly in the clouds, the planners in Beijing nonetheless thought it would be cheaper, better and – still more far-fetched – easier to solve the problem by pushing the nomads out of the Ordos by force. In May and June 1472, as the sandstorms of the cursory Beijing spring died down into the still, sweltering humidity of the summer, ministers found themselves stuck in yet another meeting about the frontier problem.

Into the meeting, and the entire impasse, rushed Wang Yue, a talented forty-six-year-old soldier-official who had some twenty years of experience in public office, but was still anxiously searching for the dramatic military victory that would make his reputation as a general, assuring him

fame, fortune and, or so he hoped, a safe hereditary title for his descendants. Although he had begun his career climbing up the civil appointments ladder, graduating from the examination system at the relatively
young age of twenty-five, Wang was, by temperament, an unceremoniously brisk and practical military man. Even when summoned to an
audience with the emperor, he maintained his custom of wearing the
characteristically long sleeves of his mandarin's gown short, refusing to
sacrifice his habitual freedom of movement to imperial etiquette.
Perhaps scenting in Wang a hunger for glory, or perhaps simply because
there was no one else desperate enough to accept the post, the court
appointed him as second-in-command on a campaign to clear the
nomads out of the Yellow River loop. Wang Yue was made chief of staff,
and his immediate superior optimistically acclaimed the 'General Who
Pacifies the Barbarians'.[23]

Wang Yue was ambitious, but not insane. The bureaucrats in Beijing,
despite instructing him to thrash once and for all the northern barbarians
out of the Ordos – a region of some 80,000 square kilometres – had provided him with only 40,000 troops for the purpose. The outlook for supply was also poor: the northern provinces, Shaanxi and Shanxi, were both
yellow with drought, and moving fast through autumn towards their bitter winters. Potential conscripts, not surprisingly, were fleeing before the
unappealing prospect of either starving or freezing to death even before
they reached the icily desolate Ordos. But when Wang, stationed on the
chilly, friable, open 800 kilometres of the north-western frontier, prevar-
icated and asked for more men, he was accused of cowardice by politicians sitting behind two, if not three protective walls in Beijing. Bai Gui,
the minister of war, scoffed from inside the imperial city that a single
nomad could scare off thousands of Ming troops.

The result was stalemate, with Wang refusing to budge without more
troops and the government refusing to provide them. It was at this
moment that Yu Zijun chose to remind the government of the benefits
of building a wall across the region: that it would require only 50,000 local

people, compared with the 150,000 soldiers and 110,000 porters required for a campaign (all of whom would have to eat, somehow, off the poor land of the north-west); that it could be cut out of local materials; that the work could be completed in about two months. Finally, perhaps as a sop to the warmongers in Beijing, Yu added that it would give the region a chance to recover before any new, large-scale offensive was launched on the north. In January 1473, Yu, Wang and his senior, the General Who Pacifies the Barbarians, forged a compromise alliance between war and wall factions, planning a small-scale punitive raid to intimidate, temporarily, the Mongols out of the area, followed by a season of wall-building.

The new strategy made more troops unnecessary, since Wang Yue decided to fight not in the Chinese fashion, relying on immense armies trailing huge, unwieldy and vulnerable baggage trains, which trumpeted their intentions weeks or even months before they came within sight of any enemy, but with nomadic chutzpah. In other words, he fought dirty. On 20 October 1473, he led 4,600 hand-picked swift horsemen on a two-day and two-night gallop into the desert, to Red Salt Lake, on the liminal zone along which the Ordos became desert. There, as he expected, Wang found not a force of nomadic warriors oiling their bows for battle, but rather a scene of Mongol domesticity, a settlement of felt tents in and among which the Mongol women went about their daily business: fetching water, washing, cooking, minding the animals, processing them into the comestibles and objects on which they subsisted (cloth, hides, meat, milk). Practically every Mongol man able to fight had galloped off south-west to raid a Chinese garrison. Apart from a small force of guards, the only males left were those incapable of offering resistance: the very young or the very old. None of the camp – guards, women, children, the elderly – stood a chance against Wang Yue's horsemen. Their tents were ranged against a lake, thereby blocking any escape route. Hundreds were killed, the tents looted and then burned, the animals – 133 camels, 1,300 horses, 5,000 cattle, 10,000 sheep – captured as booty. The outlook for the survivors – robbed of shelter and livelihood, in an area where winter came early, where even in October temperatures could approach freezing – was bleak. When word reached the Mongol raiding party further south, they rushed back to their womenfolk and promptly fell into a Ming ambush. Intimidated, for the first and last time in a long while, by the Chinese military, the Mongol survivors limped back up north, temporarily chased out of the Ordos.

With the coast briefly, exceptionally clear, Yu Zijun stepped in to build the longest continuous wall so far seen in the Ming dynasty. 'With the troubles of the inner territories thus eased,' recalls the *History of the Ming,* 'Zijun was given command of a corvée force.'

He dug banks, built walls and sank moats in a continuous line over more than 1,770 *li,* from Qingshuiying in the east, to Huamachi in the west. Every two or three *li* he built towers and ridges to accommodate a warning system, and shorter walls against empty ridges, forming basket-shaped enclosures to shelter lookouts from arrow-fire. Spanning eleven forts, fifteen border towers, seventy-eight small towers and 719 cliff-top stockades, the work employed 40,000 corvée labourers for less than three months. The land within the wall was turned over to farming, yielding sixty thousand *tan** of grain at each harvest.[24]

Yu's wall snaked some 910 kilometres from east to west, punctuated by more than 800 strong points, sentry posts and beacon towers, over the natural frontier zone enclosed by the Yellow River through which China began to turn into Mongolia. This, however, was still not the permanent construction of bricks and mortar that is enshrined in the popular imagination as the Great Wall of China: a later chronicle refers to doubters of Yu's wall, who feared that 'the walls made of sandy earth would easily collapse and could not be relied upon when the raiders came'.[25] Yu himself, in one of his memorials on wall-building submitted to the throne, emphasized that his proposed wall was to be made not of brick or stone, but by hacking away the loess soil of the north-west into a barrier.

* One *tan* = 3,990 tons

'Today,' he wrote in the early 1470s, 'of the old frontier, only stones are left, but tall mountains and steep cliffs remain. We should construct a border wall that follows the shapes of these mountains and the contours of the ground, sometimes shovelling and gouging, sometimes building ramparts, sometimes sinking trenches, joining everything up into one, continuous line.'[26] Note Yu's careful use of the term 'border wall' *(bian qiang)* and his cautious avoidance of the term *changcheng,* Long Wall, implicated still in the dynastic cataclysm of the Qin.

If the wall was truly built to the nine-metre height originally recommended by Yu Zijun, relatively little of it survives today in the form in which it was initially constructed. As with the Han wall in the far west, gale-blown sands have long since eroded or buried much of this wall, itself built on and out of loess only a little less friable than the particles which were to cover it. (Seventy-five per cent of the land on which sits Yulin, one of the crucial garrison cities along the drag of Yu's wall, is sandy.) The process of dilapidation began early: by the seventeenth century, a French Jesuit tourist remarked that the wall around Yulin was so thoroughly and densely concealed by sand that one could gallop over it on horseback.[27] What do remain are lengths of yellow-brown, tamped-earth embankment which close off the edge of the loess highlands from the Mongolian desert plateau they become further north. Almost any walls once made or clad in stone have long since been exfoliated by peasants, seeking building materials for their own private use, leaving only tamped-earth cores behind. Here, the ruins of walls seem to form an organic part of the landscape itself, sandcastle-like ramparts mounded out of the soil and steadily returning to their source, like scar tissue healing over and disappearing. None of the largest, most impressive surviving forts of the area seems to have formed part of Yu's original magnum opus: the Tower for Suppressing the North – a vast, four-tiered, thirty-metre-high wedding cake of a fort, about seventy-eight metres long by sixty-four metres wide – was built in brick only in 1608.

Yet despite its impermanence, Yu's wall provided a physical template for the wall-building boom of the sixteenth century, as well as prefiguring in every way the circumstances in which the bricked frontier wall would go up during the following 150 years: general military decline, diplomatic intransigence, court intrigue and paralysing political delusions. But the negative factors that permitted the north-western wall to be built were quickly forgotten. By 1482, Yu's wall seemed already to have proved its worth when a gang of Mongol raiders was trapped within the walls and trenches. 'Confused and unable to find a way out, they were driven out with bloodied noses, after which the border people admired Zijun's achievements all the more.'[28] Frontier walls, for the time being, had shaken off their bad historical reputation and started to find favour with the Ming.

~

Given the choice, Yu Zijun would not have ended his wall in the north-west, just shy of the eastern side of the Yellow River loop. Following continued Ming military decline in the late fifteenth century, the capital at Beijing, once a symbol of Ming confidence towards the steppe, had turned into a defensive liability, a favourite raiding destination for nomads further north, protected only by two garrisons, Xuanfu to the west and Datong to the north. Conditions in Xuanfu and Datong were fairly comparable to those in the Yellow River loop before Yu had brought his benign influence to bear: peasants and soldiers were desperately impoverished and fortifications – both natural and man-made – poor (the land between Datong and the steppe to the north is largely flat, offering no natural, protective barriers). In 1484, Yu was put in charge of the military garrisons of Xuanfu and Datong, and, predictably, advocated more earthen wall-building.

But by 1484, moderation was on the wane. Even in the 1470s, Yu's conciliatory combination of tamped walls and trade narrowly escaped the policy-makers' veto, as warmongering ministers tucked up safely in Beijing argued themselves to a standstill not over whether to throw troops against the Mongols, but over how many they should send. A decade later, Yu Zijun's new wall-building plans fell foul of court intrigue and Wang Zhi, the all-powerful head of the eunuch secret police who, like Wang Zhen before him, was anxious to enhance his standing further with the emperor by winning military glory on a border campaign and threw his support behind the war party at court. Yu's former ally Wang Yue happily lent his energies to another campaign, while Yu protested about the actions of border military commanders who provoked the frontier peoples with acts of violence. This time, the balance of power at court was against him. Believing that eunuchs were 'defective human beings' who deluded 'witless and young rulers', he unwisely said as much in a memorial to the emperor, urging that eunuchs be demoted back to duties of minding household affairs of the palace.[29] Shortly afterwards, work on Yu's new wall was halted after eunuchs seized on an inspection report which claimed that the construction was too expensive and was causing popular discontent, and which accused Yu of corruption and nepotism. Yu was to die in 1489, spending the last eight years of his life moving in and out of office, between active service and retirement, attempting to avoid a slew of slander and disgrace. Yu had offered the Ming court one of its last chances to escape from a downward spiral of expensive confrontation with the north, through a moderate, cost-effective combination of defence and diplomacy. But once Yu's way of compromise had been rejected, Ming emperors of the sixteenth and seventeenth centuries were to exhaust first of all their armies, then their treasuries and labour forces with unending wars and walls.

CHAPTER NINE

The Wall Goes Up

Two boys were born in 1507: one in Hubei, the central, rice-basket province of Mainland China; one in Mongolia. The first, Zhu Houcong, became emperor of China; the second, Altan Khan, the great sixteenth-century unifier of the Mongol tribes. Although they never met – the former would not countenance such a slight to his imperial majesty – their clash of worldviews generated the diplomatic stalemate which in turn created the Great Wall of brick and stone that so enraptured Lord Macartney at the end of the eighteenth century.

His ministers probably never hoped or expected that Zhu Houcong would express anything as assertive as a worldview. He was chosen as emperor precisely for his apparent lack of personality. When Zhu Houcong came to the throne in 1522 as the Jiajing emperor, the government was still recovering from the idiosyncrasies of his predecessor, Zhengde, a fecklessly eccentric philanderer much given to excessive drinking, war-gaming with tigers and kidnapping women for his harem, but allergic to the everyday routine that kept government and country ticking over: audiences with officials, meetings with envoys, elaborately symbolic ceremonials. When Zhengde suddenly died, aged thirty-one, after a boating accident, leaving no heir or named successor, his nephew Zhu Houcong was the solution improvised by an energetic grand secretary, in the hope, no doubt, that he would prove more blandly malleable than his unruly predecessor. Zhu Houcong's family had no great palace presence, no influence in the court intrigues that usually determined the outcome of imperial power struggles: at the time of his accession, his blind, elderly grandmother had been exiled to the imperial laundry, while his mother, the daughter of a palace guard, was a provincial dowager, living on the family estate in Hubei.

But it was Jiajing's very obscurity that made him a rigidly intolerant and uncompromising ruler: towards his officials, wives and, most of all, towards the Mongol 'barbarians', whose very existence he regarded as an outrageous personal affront. Jiajing suffered from the pettifogging obsession with etiquette and public appearance that plagues only the truly socially insecure. At the root of his anxieties lay the irregularity of his route to the succession. Lacking either an overwhelming blood claim to the throne or the natural, outgoing charisma of leadership (as a boy, Zhu Houcong had been quiet and book-loving), the new emperor sought to root his legitimacy in a relentless pedantry over questions of ritual and ceremony, tweaking or hijacking precedent to bolster his own position, ruthlessly eliminating opposition to his status-seeking alterations. Two years into his reign, seventeen officials were beaten to death and another 163 banished for disputing the emperor's wish to promote his once obscure natural mother to empress dowager. Although this approach strengthened his authority as emperor, permitting him to enjoy, at forty-four years, the second-longest reign of the Ming period, it also made him inward-looking, grudge-bearing and pompously over-conscious of his own dignity.

The implications for frontier relations were serious. The emperor's preoccupation with personal prestige critically exacerbated in him the traditional Chinese cultural superiority complex towards, and contempt for, the north. As he aged, his sense of animosity only intensified, reaching ever greater heights of small-mindedness: in his later years, he began to demand that whenever mentioned in edicts or memorials, the characters for 'northern Mongols' should be written as small as possible. If the

Mongols' mere existence enraged him, the idea of trading or treating with them was violently out of the question. And it was trade, above all, that the Mongols now needed and wanted, but which had been cut off in any regular form in 1500. A vicious diplomatic circle resulted: the more offensive the emperor found the Mongols, the less he permitted trade; the more they raided, the more he hated them; and so it went on.

By the 1530s, Altan Khan, the baby boy born the same year as Zhu Houcong, had grown up to become the Chinese emperor's Mongolian *bête noire*. After inheriting command over the tribes north of Shanxi, Altan transformed his subjects from a piecemeal raiding rabble into a unified force of invaders. He created a new centre of operations on the steppe at Hohhot, the present capital of the Inner Mongolian Autonomous Region, only 200, 300 and 400 kilometres north-west of Datong, Xuanfu (the two key defensive garrisons in the north) and Beijing respectively. Far more than a glorified steppe campsite, Altan's Hohhot was an impressive agglomeration of Chinese-style buildings – erected with the help of Chinese who had fled into Mongolia – the most magnificent of which was a walled imperial palace based on the Ming architectural style. An inscription hanging above a palace gate, 'overawe Chinese and barbarians', hinted at the scale of Altan's ambitions, and his new city left him and his cavalry poised to swoop on the power centres of China in a way that the old Mongolian capital of Karakorum never had.[1]

But Altan was in fact no Genghis Khan: his raids were conducted in search of Chinese silk, clothes and food rather than land, and a conciliatory Chinese policy of allowing trade and tribute would have dramatically lowered tensions across the border. Not for Altan was the overwhelming sense of Mongol racial superiority and mission that drove Genghis south of the steppe, that led the Yuan dynasty to try to legislate out of government any native Chinese, that propelled the first generation of Mongol rulers of China to advocate massacring the population and turning the country over to pasture. Altan never showed any interest in acquiring territory in China proper beyond the liminal pastoral-agrarian zone of the

Ordos, and even demonstrated an admiring appreciation of the fundamentals of Chinese political culture. If Jiajing had ever been minded to
stroll around Hohhot, on the main gate of the palace he would have
approvingly read an inscription bearing the unmistakably sinophile sentiment 'Civilizing and Developing Government'.

The middle decades of the sixteenth century were lean times on the
steppe – only rarely did Altan's tribes shake free of the menace of famine
– making the question of tribute and trade (horses and furs for grain and
beans) truly a matter of life and death. 'In spring,' a Ming official
observed of Altan's tribesmen, 'they often beg our patrols to buy their
cattle: one ox for a *picul* or so or rice or beans … Those who are worse off
would take off their fur coats or bring hides or horse hair hoping to stave
off starvation for one more day.'[2] Yan Song, a grand secretary of the
1550s, probably had it about right when he described Altan and his horde
as 'merely a group of food-looting bandits – nothing to worry about'.[3]
But when the emperor refused to countenance the trade that, to the
Mongols, made the difference between survival and starvation, they
vented their frustration and satisfied their hunger in raids across north
China.

In 1541, not for the first time, Altan submitted a petition, via envoy, to
present tribute. Jiajing ordered that it be rejected, reinforced the garrisons
at Xuanfu and Datong, and put a price on Altan's head. The following
year, Altan sent another envoy to Datong, to repeat the request.
Accurately gauging the political winds blowing from Beijing, the governor arrested the envoy and dragged him to the city's bazaar, where he was
chopped into pieces. Delighted by this diplomatic treachery, the emperor
made his pleasure and approval apparent by promoting and rewarding all
those involved.

Altan Khan was outraged by this breach of faith and China's northern
provinces – particularly Shanxi – suffered the terrible consequences of
the Chinese emperor's intransigence in the eight particularly black years
that followed the butchery of Altan's envoy in 1542. 'The bandits were

indignant,' the *History of the Ming* reports somewhat anaemically, 'and carried out a great invasion, massacring villages and fortresses.'[4] This was nomadic raiding in its most punitive form, visiting a storm of destruction on its settled targets, scouring villages for any item of use: 'every time they invade China they take every inch of iron and every foot of cotton cloth,' sighed one official.[5] Soon, a devastated Shanxi – barely subsisting at the best of times – was starving. As the 1540s progressed, the Mongols pushed deeper and deeper into China, burning, killing, above all taking whatever they felt they should have been able to obtain through trade but had been denied them by Ming obduracy: grain, and goods both everyday (metal and pottery) and luxurious (although, no doubt, disappointingly little luxury was to be found in China's parched border provinces). In 1545, the cycle of starvation, petition, violence and retribution began yet again: famine and disease in the north pushed Altan to sue for trade; hoping for rewards similar to those doled out in 1542, the servant of a Chinese officer murdered the Mongolian envoys. The emperor neglected to punish him in any meaningful way. In 1547, yet more heads of Mongol envoys were sent to the Ming court. Two years later, retreating after a raid on Xuanfu, west of Beijing, Mongol forces issued a dire threat, through a message attached to an arrow shot into a Chinese camp: if trade was not reopened, the Mongols would attack the capital that autumn.

This degree of stalemate between the Chinese empire and the steppe was practically unprecedented. No other dynasty had so consistently refused contact with the north – compare, for instance, the frequent tribute missions entertained by the Han court, its dispatching of princesses, the Sui emperor's processional tours. And it was not long before diplomatic stonewalling took on a more physical form. With the Mongol headquarters at Hohhot glowering over the plains leading down to Datong, Ming commanders of the 1540s began building up walls to the northwest of the capital, on the barren plains north of Datong and Xuanfu, a double border forming a defensive ellipse, starting on the eastern side of the Yellow River loop, bulging north of Datong, then arcing south, before meeting the northern side not far from the Juyong pass. The idea was to protect the regions of Shanxi that had been so ravaged in raids of the 1530s and 1540s, and to safeguard doubly or even triply the passage to Beijing from Hohhot and the Ordos, filling the gap in defences left by Yu Zijun's north-west barricade (which, by the 1520s and 1530s, was in any case crumbling). Although the terrain supporting the outer, north-ernmost wall was high – at an average altitude of 1,000 metres – and con-sequently cold, dry and inhospitable, it was periodically flat and lacking in natural obstacles. Further south, the inner line ran over, and made strate-gic use of, more dramatically mountainous terrain; the pass at Yanmen, due south of Datong, lies among a line of peaks between 1,500 and 3,000 metres high. Some of these are China's holy mountains: Mount Wutai, Mount Heng – pilgrim destinations on which eaved Buddhist temples now sit, one, the Temple in Mid-Air, lounging nonchalantly across beams bored into a cliffside.

By 1547, the commander in charge of building commented, a few more months' work would complete a 500-kilometre-long barrier sep-arating 'the Chinese and the barbarians'.[6] In combination with building work carried out by other commanders in the area, the lozenge of defences drawn up north and west of Beijing would steadily grow, throughout the remaining decades of the Ming, to around 850 kilometres of wall, sometimes in doubled, tripled or quadrupled stretches, the line broken every few hundred metres by towers and signal beacons. Of the original 1540s work, relatively little remains prominently visible today: none of the earth forts around Datong were bricked, in the style of the tourist Great Wall, until the 1570s. Today, in among the deep, desiccated fissures sunken into the raw brown landscape around Datong, run ruined, predominantly earth walls, continuous, at most, for a few dozen kilometres, and battered by wind, rain and sand, and once again by both the depredations of local peasants – who have recycled earth and stone into their own houses, or sunk graves into the original walls – and the Japanese invasions of the 1930s. But where they survive, original, eight-metre-wide foundations, exaggeratedly wide to support ruins now only three or four metres high, suggest the physical statement that the walls must have originally made, as they rose up out of the bleak flatlands in north Shanxi. Names of surviving forts assert the trademark bombast of Ming China's defensive imperialism: 'Overawing the Goat-like Barbarians', 'Winning Victory'.[7]

For the rest of 1549, the court sat tight in Beijing, trusting in the righteousness of its obstinacy and in the fastness of its new border walls. Up to a point, the ramparts built during the 1540s worked: Altan Khan's nomads were unable to smash their way through the several hundred kilometres of wall covering the north-west approaches to Beijing. But after this point – the point at which the nomads galloped as far as the eastern- or westernmost extent of the walls – they failed. Until the Chinese were prepared to create a continuous perimeter fence around the full extent of their territories – a plan adopted, at least in theory, later in the century – and mobilize almost every man in the empire to guard it (this the Ming never accomplished), the nomads were going to find a way round at either or both ends, flowing, like water, along the path of least resistance.

By 1550 Altan Khan and his Mongols had realized that all they needed to do to circumvent the wall was ride far enough towards the defensive blank north-east of Beijing. To the west, Datong and Xuanfu held, partly because the Datong commander bribed the nomads – starving after five months of drought – not to attack. But by late September – peak raiding season, with the fields of north China full of crops and harvesters, exposed and vulnerable beyond their city and town walls – the Mongols had galloped to the north of the capital and camped little more than thirty kilometres east of Beijing, in Tongzhou, the last city at which the Ming armies had paused for breath before sweeping on to expel the Mongols from Beijing in 1368. They then looted and burned the capital's suburbs for three days. True, the suburbs were not the city itself, the centre of government with its nexus of imperial buildings. But they were strategically and symbolically vital to the city. The immediate north of Beijing was a favoured destination of Ming tourists – a green, pleasant and gently undulating spread of pavilions, villas, streams, temples and lotus-filled lakes that existed alongside clustered settlements where daily life and production went on for a few dozen kilometres, after which this sedate landscape became the wild, scrubbily forested mountains over which the Great Wall of the popular imagination winds. As his final insult, on 30 September Altan personally led 700 men up to the northern face of the city walls, to bang on Anding Gate – literally, the Gate of Safety and Security, originally designed as the triumphal entry point for emperors returning from victorious northern campaigns.

Panic and recrimination spread through the capital. As city-dwellers watched impotently from the towers over the city gates while the suburbs burned, the wealthier among them – thinking of their estates to the north of the city – complained that officials were holding back the army and allowing the Mongols to pillage at will. They were right: the grand secretary, Yan Song, had advised the minister of war not to dispatch the capital's army, pointing out that while military disasters near or in the steppe, hundreds of kilometres from Chinese civilian witnesses, could be reinvented at court as great victories, a defeat just below the city walls would be impossible to conceal from the crowds watching from the parapets. While calculatedly face-saving, Yan's advocacy was also based on practical considerations. Although, according to official registers, the capital garrisons were 140,000 strong, far less than half of these were signed up to military duties, the rest being diverted into construction work (not necessarily for the state: soldiers were often high-handedly requisitioned by senior nobles or eunuchs for their own private purposes).[8] Those gathered together to fight in 1550 were a sorry bunch: the *History of the Ming* reports that the army of 50–60,000 men led out to face the enemy 'began weeping and snivelling at the first sight of the Mongols, and refused to fight. The officers turned ashen, and could do nothing but gape in terror at each other.'[9] Although reinforcements arrived, the city had no provisions for them, and the starving auxiliaries simply joined in with the looting hordes, raiding whatever they could find.

Jiajing was unforgiving in his distribution of blame. On 2 October, he broadcast, via proxies, from the south gate of the Forbidden City – the front that now overlooks the expanses of Tiananmen Square – that all his officials were irresponsible and derelict. On 6 October, the battle-shy minister of war was executed and replaced with the pragmatic governor of Datong who had bribed the Mongols to bypass the fortress under his command. Perhaps only a stroke of personal misfortune saved the head of Weng Wanda – the official overseer of the new walls around Datong – from rolling in the immediate recriminations conducted by the emperor: following the death of his father, he had abandoned the court and his official position in 1549 and returned to his home province of Guangdong in the south to mourn.

Altan dispatched a Chinese prisoner to deliver another message to the emperor, asking, yet again, for permission to present tribute (in effect, to trade). Unwilling, as ever, to countenance intercourse with barbarians, the court stalled Altan with a remarkable diplomatic sleight of hand. They first evaded the direct request in the letter by doubting its authenticity, on the grounds that it was not written in Mongol. They then instructed Altan to return to Mongolia and submit a request for trade through the correct bureaucratic channels – the governor of the border town of Xuanfu.

Despite having brought north China to its knees, Altan Khan astonishingly agreed to this demand and docilely left the perimeters of the capital. Predictably enough, the emperor never delivered the desired trading agreement. Succumbing to a brief attack of diplomatic realism after the Khan's raid on Beijing, Jiajing allowed trading markets to open in 1551 and 1552.[10] But by 1552, nauseated anew by the humiliation of treating with barbarians, he had already thought better of the new policy, executed the official responsible for opening markets and forbidden anyone henceforth even to mention the possibility of trade with the Mongolian hordes, ruling that any official who permitted markets would be punished by death.[11] Raiding continued apace, while realistic border officials who had to deal with the consequences of imperial obduracy and who argued against this policy of non-compromise lived in fear of their lives. Yang Shouqian, a military official in the north-west, remembered how 'the governor of Datong was severely punished for allowing communication with foreign barbarians ... those in responsible positions are afraid.'[12] Even relatively moderate, pro-trade officials deeply imbibed the contemporary culture of racist scorn, referring to the Mongols as greedy 'dogs and sheep', harbouring 'animal-like desires, deep as gorges'.[13]

The upshot of this policy, apart from bloodshed – in 1567 alone, tens of thousands of Chinese were killed in Mongol raids on Shanxi, Hebei and the Beijing area – was the completion of China's walled border, across the exposed defensive blank to the east of the capital penetrated by the Mongols in 1550, a previously open frontier of approximately 1,200 kilometres.[14] And while this gap was being filled, with stone ramparts and 1,200 towers, existing forts in the west were being reinforced in materials as hard as the government's political line: the Great Wall in the brick and stone, as opposed to tamped-earth, form as it is now recognized, finally sprang up during the mid- to late sixteenth century.[15] Even so, its builders were clearly less impressed by their work than later tourists: like Yu Zijun before them, contemporaries identified the mature Ming wall not as 'Great' or even 'Long', but simply as the 'Border Wall', or the 'Nine Border Garrisons', visualized as nine strongholds stretching between Liaodong and Hebei in the east, and Gansu in the west, strung together by walls.

The last, north-eastern additions to the wall remain among the showpieces of the 6,000-odd kilometres of the entire structure, providing the world-famous landscapes of stone and brick snaking over the spines of scrubby mountains. At the same time, expensive and lengthy repairs were ordered for walls further west: three years at a cost of some 470 ounces of silver per kilometre in Xuanfu, five years at a total of 487,500 ounces of silver around Datong.[16] By 1576, renovation of the wall in the north-east was deemed necessary. From this point on, until the fall of the Ming dynasty in 1644, some of the largest, most impressive surviving show-pieces of the wall were built in brick: in 1608, the thirty-metre-high Tower for Suppressing the North near Yulin in the north-west; in 1574, 'the great northern gate to the capital', the twelve-metre-high brick arch-way over Zhangjiakou – halfway between Hohhot and Beijing, strung out between China and Mongolia – in the outer line of wall; that same year, the southern gate of the Fort for Obtaining Victory near Datong, again rising twelve metres from the ground, with the stalwart characters for 'Guarantee' carved on its outer wall, and those for 'Obtaining Victory' confidently chiselled inside.

~

From its westernmost extreme, among the desert oases of Jiayuguan, to its eastern endpoint, where it tumbles into the coastline at Shanhaiguan, every rampart, fort, crenellation and plaque in the Ming wall seems calcu-lated to make physical statements about the country over which it stands guard and the Ming government that masterminded its construction: to define, enclose and exclude.

These two endpoint fortresses were originally announced by near-identical plaques, reflecting an unmistakable cultural self-confidence across the thousands of kilometres of frontier that separated them. In the far west, on the gate of Jiayuguan, a plaque (destroyed in the twenti-eth century) once proclaimed to all-comers 'The First Fortified Pass Under Heaven'; at Shanhaiguan in the east, facing out over the sea, a sur-viving inscription still announces to the waves and rocks that this is 'The First Pass Under Heaven'. The wall's architects designed their work to project a clear message: to set the limits of the (civilized, Chinese) world. With their curved roofs and tidy, even walls, both Jiayuguan and Shanhaiguan ensure that the wall draws to an official close with a very Chinese fanfare; even though fortifications do, in fact, extend beyond these two passes, fading out into the western desert and winding towards

Manchuria in the north-east, the two passes are the dramatic limits that stay in the memory. Both are elaborate fort complexes, the western occupying 2.5 square kilometres, the eastern almost 1.5 kilometres, a cluster of gates, towers, government offices and even – in the case of Shanhaiguan – temples. Jiayuguan – the carved eaves of its triple towers set within a perfectly regular, crenellated square of walls – rises incongruously up out of the western desert like a prize-winning Chinese sandcastle, transplanted far from the cramped agricultural patchwork of China proper. In the east, the grey-brown bricks – the characteristic colour produced by the Chinese brick-firing process – of the main fortress of Shanhaiguan keep guard over the coast and mountains to the north, its rather grim, windowless, penitentiary-like walls topped, again slightly incongruously, with the jaunty carved eaves characteristic of Chinese architecture. At Jiayuguan, a gate facing east carries the inscription 'The Gate to Glorious Civilization'; another inscription over a gate facing west intones, with paternalistic imperialism, 'Treat distant lands with kindness.'[17] In its 6,000-kilometre extent, in its architecture, in its attached forts, the completed Ming frontier wall is a monument to the self-perception of the country that erected it: to the unified cultural psychology that, at least in theory, held together a land of dramatic natural contrasts, of desert oases to the west and forested mountains to the east.

But it should not be imagined that the wall, now overgrown or frequently in ruins – these days, the severe, windowless tiers of the vast Tower for Suppressing the North rakishly sport crops of grass, even the odd, hardy tree – ever snaked uniformly or even completely over this terrain. The term 'Great Wall', rarely if ever used by its Ming builders, evokes one monolithically crenellated barrier stretching from west to east, in the style of the best-known, north-eastern sections. But as one of the contemporary names for the Ming wall, the Nine Border Garrisons, indicates, defences along the general route taken by the walls were organized around regional key points, in places in the form of a single, double or even triple wall, sometimes meandering off into puzzling diversions, with gaps and weaknesses plugged by towers, forts and strongholds, some of which lie north or south of the general line.

Moving east from the sands of Jiayuguan, the wall guards thousands of kilometres of border, the zone of interface between Chinese and non-Chinese. Across Shaanxi and Shanxi, the provinces that bore the brunt of nomad trading and raiding, towers rise up around the wall, sentry posts from which traffic with northern barbarians – only tolerated on grudging official sufferance, at best – was policed. A fitting monument to official suspicion of such trade are the oppressively high, bleakly unembellished walls of the Tower for Suppressing the North, built to superintend trans-actions between Mongols and Chinese at horse fairs. This western-central stretch of the wall often feels like classically wild frontier territory: the land bare, flat, given to depressing into sudden, dramatic crevasses, marked with the unmanned vestiges of a wall long since abandoned, the ruins of a derelict system of foreign relations.

If, in its westward manifestations, the wall sometimes appears a slightly earthbound construction, ambling along the flatlands and plateaux out of which it was made, north and east of Beijing it succumbs to ostentatious exhibitionism, as if unable to resist showing off the ingenuity of Chinese architects and engineers. Here, crenellated brick- and stone-walled corri-dors, sometimes up to fourteen metres high and almost six metres wide at the top, punctured with squinting arrow slits and spy holes, and punc-tuated by forts and towers, rise and dip, clinging somehow on to the crests of the mountains that dimple the landscape, winding their way eastward to the sea, hanging all the while on to the peaked high ground, sometimes diverting away from the main thrust towards the coast in meandering fronds of auxiliary ramparts that bolster the principal line. These are the admired, guidebook vistas of the Great Wall, as exempli-fied by the airbrushed sections most visited by tourists, the Badaling or Mutianyu stretches a few dozen kilometres north of Beijing.

A detour to nearby, more crumbling sections – at Jinshanling or Simatai, for example – gives a better, rawer sense of the wall-builders' virtuosity. Here, where the wall-walker's path has not been calibrated into tidy steps by labourers conscripted by state tourism bureaux, where the crenellations are not inevitably splotched with fresh Communist cement, where the trees and bushes native to the mountain terrain have edged their way back from exile over and through the stonework, where the corridor on which you walk is not always reassuringly walled on both sides but sometimes crumbling down the sheer slopes, you get a clearer vision of the obstacles posed by the terrain, of the tenaciousness of the bristly greenery pushing through the stones, of the narrow, precipitous spines of the mountains over which the wall winds. Here, where there are no cable cars, you are forced to ascend as did the original builders – soldiers and peasants fulfilling their corvée obligations, or convicts. To re-create a very muted version of their fatigue, pick up a twenty-kilogram stone slab and the experience becomes more authentic still. When you pause for breath in one of the towers that bulge up every sixty to 200 metres, and look through the jaggedly ruined arched windows, it is easier to get a sense of the isolation of the construction work, of the solitude of guarding the wall, of the quiet that might have preceded carnage, as you imagine would-be raiders lurking in the dense vegetation lower down the slopes.

How did they do it?

Wall-building had always created logistical problems for Chinese governments, notably how to find and provision the necessary manpower. The mature Ming wall, however, presented an entirely new scale of difficulty. In the past, even as late as Yu Zijun's wall of the fifteenth century, Chinese walls had made use of materials available on site: tamped earth or reeds fronted with local wood or stones. But late-sixteenth century Ming walls were an altogether more substantial affair, made of bricks and stone slabs, studded with additional towers between 250 and 500 metres apart, signal-beacon platforms and larger bricked forts, all of which required greater and more skilled manpower and resources – stone masons, an extensive network of brick kilns, quarries and transport routes and, inevitably, upwardly spiralling quantities of government silver.

Ever since walls have been built across the north of the Chinese empire, their process of construction has become overlaid with a thick crust of supernatural legend – recall earlier stories of the First Emperor's magic horse and whip, or his creation of nine suns to drive his workers to constant toil, or the formation of the Great Wall out of an exhausted dragon collapsing to the ground – as if a feat of construction as monumental as long border walls defies the possibilities of mortal engineering. No dynasty's wall has become more heavily enshrouded in myth than that of the Ming, and in particular the brick-clad version of the sixteenth century.

The fairy-tale explanations for the Ming wall's most dazzling feats of engineering cited by folk chroniclers tend to be a variation on the following formula. A despairing overseer, unable to eat or sleep for worry about the terrible punishment that awaits him for failing to complete his section of the wall on time, restlessly wanders at night the hills and rivers around his building site until he meets a mysterious old man who, asking him the cause of his obvious distress, offers to build the wall for him. The precise nature of the old man's solution varies from story to story. In one account of the building of Zijing (literally, Purple Bramble) pass, about 110 kilometres west of Beijing, the old man knits the pass out of brambles which, after a few days, miraculously turn into stone. In another story, an elderly Daoist enlists an army of spirit soldiers to help a government official pining away with anxiety as he attempts to build a sluice gate across a particularly treacherous mountain pass.

Sometimes, fantastical animals come to the rescue. One story resolves the mystery of how building supplies were transported to the Huairou stretch of wall across the hills and mountains north of Beijing. Here, the mountainous terrain made it unfeasible to carry up enormous, heavy stone slabs, but neither were there any flat expanses of soil nearby from which earthen bricks could be fired. The overseer is stymied until a local man, Li Gang, informs him of a suitable field ten kilometres away and is dispatched to make the bricks. So far so plausible, until Li Gang is confronted with the problem of how to transport the bricks up to the builders on the mountaintops. Luckily, he takes a nap, during which he dreams that the Lotus Fairy hands him an ox whip and tells him to go and fetch a magic ox from behind Lotus Mountain that will help him move the bricks. Off Li Gang goes and, as promised, the sturdy ox soon shifts tens of thousands of bricks. After congratulating the ox on this feat, Li Gang wakes up, sees that the bricks have all gone and, hurrying to the building site, discovers that the workers are already using them. Another legend relates that a divinity cracks his whip at some enormous stone slabs, which then transform into mountain goats and skip up the hillside of their own accord. When they reach the top, the spirit cracks his whip at them again and they morph back into stones, docilely awaiting their transformation into walls and towers.[18]

Extrapolating from the nature of the terrain and the materials used in the wall's construction, it is possible to describe the circumstances of building in more matter-of-fact terms. Whenever they were available, materials were procured from nearby and used in as raw a form as possible: earth, stones, wood and reeds were all employed to fill or finish walls. The basic building technique remained an old and familiar one: tamping down these rough-and-ready materials between fronts made out of wood, stone or bricks, ideally fired from local earth. Several types of mortar were used to sandwich bricks into facings, but one recipe favoured by Chinese wall-builders made prominent use of sticky glutinous rice. In some places, particularly across the cold, open spaces of the Yellow River basin, the earthen core is all that remains; the outer, protective shell has either been eroded or stolen by locals for their own uses, or never existed, the wall originally being little more than a tightly compressed mud embankment. Further east, however, and further into the Ming period, these mounded walls started to acquire bricked fronts. In the area around Datong, for example, first heavily fortified in the sixteenth century, only fifteen out of the seventy-two large forts built in the region were built by 1425; fifty-two were constructed mainly between 1540 and 1570, and only three of these were bricked before 1571; for the rest, the hard facing came in the final seventy years of the dynasty.[19] In open, flatter areas, local soil could be dug up and fired into bricks in a process that took between eight and fifteen hours in small, domed-roof furnaces set up near the building sites. If no suitable open ground was found nearby, the bricks had to be transported from further away – a brick at the western end of the wall system, stamped with its date and place of firing, was manufactured eighty kilometres away. Over relatively straightforward terrain, bricks – the largest of which were around 60 × 24 × 18 centimetres – could be carried by both humans and animals: on backs, in carts, in barrows or, where there were rivers conveniently close, by boat. When human backs were involved, the carrying pole was favoured: two baskets balanced on ropes or chains on either side of a rod slung over the shoulders. Where the terrain was precipitous to the point of making progress with heavy burdens inefficiently dangerous for individuals, human chains would be set in place which passed materials up mountainsides from hand to hand.[20] Where the terrain made brick construction almost impossible, builders would actually chisel the wall out of the mountaintop.

The height of walls was determined by the nature of the terrain: walls rose up higher (seven or eight metres) on relatively open ground than on mountains, where the ridges on which foundations were lodged provided walls with a natural defensive advantage, requiring the walls themselves to be no more than a few feet in height. In all cases, however, the ground from which the wall would rise had first to be evened out by preliminary layers of stone and brick. The floor along the tops of walls would, where possible, be paved to permit horses to gallop along their length – at their widest, on the stone walls north of Beijing, perhaps five abreast. Where bricks were used, crenellated battlements topped the entire structure, providing a shield from behind which patrols and guards could peer out.

Punctuating the wall were raised platforms, towers and forts – north, south and integrated into the wall – serving a variety of functions but forming part of a complex tactical defence network, used for observation, communication, fighting and shelter. The frequency of these posts depended on the security risks associated with the surrounding terrain: in militarily beleaguered spots, towers might be only thirty or fifty paces apart, although the norm was probably somewhere between 500 metres and four kilometres. Beacon stations, naturally, had to be within sight and earshot of each other; alarms could be given with smoke (by day), fire (by night) or cannon.[21] If these signals functioned adequately, the border walls became a communications system that, theoretically, linked China's western extreme with its eastern counterpart: already in the Tang, signals could travel some 1,000 kilometres in one day and night. Although relatively little is known about how the beacons worked – Ming sources in fact say little concrete about the nature of the signals, either to keep them secret or because the codes were already well known to their operators – a Tang manual gives a flavour of the system, describing three fire 'cages' set on the top of towers, transmitting morning and night messages of calm (one fire), intimations of danger (two fires) or actual sightings of battle (three fires). A Ming military manual explains how alarms were transmitted from the frontier to political centres:

On every observation tower, whether during the day or at night, three men will have three torches, one cup-size gun and two hand guns. If outside the borders or on the sea shore, patrols meet with an enemy landing party, in daytime they will wave flags and fire cannons as the signal; during the night they will light torches and fire cannons as the signal. Those on the towers will easily receive the signal, and in the daytime they will reel out twelve large white flags, and neighbouring towers will hoist the great flag. These signals in one direction are to go straight to the seat of the prefecture, and in another direction as far as the town where the military commandery is located. If it happens that during the daytime the sky is overcast or there is a fog, and no flags can be seen, then they must light a shelf of reeds prepared in advance. They will light them in sequence: if one is lit and the neighbouring tower lights its fire in response, they may stop; but should the neighbouring tower not light its fire in response, then they must light another shelf of reeds. If there is an alert during the night, patrols on observation towers near the sea shoot fire-arrows, make noise, and set fire to one shelf of grass only, because in the night it should shine brightly, and there is no need for a second shelf. The neighbouring towers, too, immediately all together light a shelf of grass. The tower near the exact spot where the enemy arrived dispatches a man to proceed by shortcuts to the commandery seat and other official places to announce the number of the enemy and time and circumstances of the landing.[22]

Signal towers also had codes for communicating the numbers in an enemy approach: one fire and one cannon salvo for up to 100 raiders; two of each for 500 to 1,000; three for 1,000 and more; five for 10,000.[23]

Towers varied in size: some were ordered to be built twice the height of the wall, others nine metres high, others again half that size. Two main categories existed: the solid (which were little more than platforms for watching and fighting) and the hollow (which could serve as storehouses, beacon towers and accommodation). Although harder to construct, the hollow towers possessed a greater variety of functions than the solid, and they lacked the serious security drawback of solid towers – if a patrol had to make a dash back to the wall to escape raiders, a solid tower offered no shelter inside; guards could reach safety only by heaving themselves up the side of the wall on ropes. In 1553, after a skirmish with some Mongols near Datong, one Chinese soldier barely escaped alive, by being hauled up the outside of a tower on a rope by the crew on the top. The hollow towers, designed to accommodate guardsmen for months of service at a time, contained stores – a bed, cups, saucers, water, grain, salted vegetables, fuel (mainly oxen or wolf dung). Hollow towers also offered a windowed bunker from which to take potshots – with arrows or firearms – at approaching raiders. Beacon towers might house between five and ten operators, while towers for watching or fighting functioned like miniature garrisons, sheltering fifty men or more; among the biggest was the 'Tower for Receiving Distant Nations', at Xifengkou along the eastern stretch of the wall, a vast structure able to accommodate 10,000 men.[24]

Such was the theory, if not necessarily the reality, of a grand imperial scheme. Take, for example, the Tower for Receiving Distant Nations, which dilapidated during the last century or so of the Ming, until it seemed, to the Mongols passing by, no more than a symbol of Chinese decadence.[25] Throughout the intensive era of Ming wall-building, the calls for repair came so frequently that the wall could never have functioned effectively as a single unit along its entire length.

The costs were inevitably huge: the stretch of wall built in the east in the 1560s and 1570s began with a projected budget of 65,000 ounces of silver. Finance for repairing walls both to the east and west was also constantly required: in 1574, almost 21,000 ounces of silver were allocated to the strengthening of the eastern stretch. Further fortifications in 1576 were projected to cost over 3.3 million ounces of silver – well over three-quarters of central government's annual revenue by the late sixteenth century. The Ming government consistently underfunded these projects – in 1576, the ministry advanced a paltry 54,600 ounces of silver – suggesting that the results could not possibly be as impregnable as their builders would have liked.[26]

This parsimony perhaps explains the ease with which the Manchus broke through from the north-east to conquer China between the 1620s and 1644; the reality of the Ming wall no doubt constantly fell far short of the ideal. But this line of reasoning maintains too much faith in the basic strategic soundness of wall-building. Ming weakness rested more crucially with the men who directed frontier policy and with the soldiers who manned the frontier. By the late sixteenth century, the Ming military was in a state of abeyance – underfinanced, poorly organized and lacking in discipline – and no match for crack Manchurian troops. The proliferation of Ming walls tied the Chinese to a policy of static defence that was fundamentally ill-suited to cope with their supremely mobile adversaries, who, as Altan Khan demonstrated in 1550, inevitably ignored solidly fortified routes in favour of those that were not.

~

The political and social consequences of a walled stand-off between Chinese and Mongols were obvious to anyone who spent any time near the frontier. 'Corpses of soldiers were exposed in the fields,' recalled a border official in the 1570s, 'people wandered homelessly, cities and towns were ruined, food supplies were exhausted, border officials were unable to protect even themselves and the court was so occupied that there was no time to eat.'[27]

In 1571, however, a remarkable diplomatic opportunity presented itself to the Chinese and was seized by two politicians intelligent, pragmatic and brave enough to argue that simply hiding behind walls would never create peace; that only diplomacy and trade could bring the north to heel. Furious that a bride promised to him had been married off to another nomadic king, Altan Khan's beloved grandson fled inside China and surrendered. The Ming grand secretary, Zhang Juzheng, together with a governor of the north-west called Wang Chonggu, persuaded the court to use the grandson as leverage over Altan, compelling him to swear allegiance to the Ming as a tributary and bribing him to good faith by opening border markets. Altan leapt at the offer, even agreeing to change the name of his capital at Hohhot – the perch from which he had swooped down on China for decades – to the condescending Chinese choice of Guihuacheng: 'City Returning to Civilization'. On 13 June 1571, on the Terrace for Airing Horses just outside Datong, the garrison he had terrorized for the past forty years, Altan was enfeoffed as the *Shunyi wang* – the Obedient and Righteous Prince. 'Listen, the 800,000 mounted troops of China and the 400,000 mounted troops of the northern barbarians,' proclaimed Altan to anyone who might listen. 'Never again will we violate China's borders.'[28] Tribute and gifts were exchanged and merchants summoned from south China to trade at the northern borders, while Zhang Juzheng hoped to make use of the respite to rationalize and improve border defences. 'From then on,' the *History of the Ming* recounts, 'the frontier areas were released from their sufferings. From east to west, all soldiers and civilians of the seven garrison districts along the several thousand *li* of the border enjoyed happy times. No weapons were used, and military expenditures were reduced by 70 per cent.'[29]

In 1582, however, both Zhang Juzheng and Altan Khan were dead, and with them the desire for compromise. As confrontation escalated once more, so did wars and costs, leaving a terminally declining Ming army defenceless against a new great power rising up in the north-east, where, around the rivers, fields, forests and steppes of Manchuria, a tribal small-fry called Nurhaci was starting to build himself an empire. Sixty years later, Beijing would be added to his dynasty's conquests, but not without the assistance of a crucial gap in the border wall, created by one Wu Sangui, the Chinese guardian of the gateway pass between China and Manchuria, who in 1644 abandoned the moribund, many-walled Ming and invited the Manchu invaders into the Middle Kingdom.

CHAPTER TEN

The Great Fall of China

Anyone choosing to stroll about Shanhaiguan, the pass in the frontier wall that controlled access from the fields, forests, steppes and
rivers of semi-barbarian Manchuria to the agrarian plains of north-east
China, around Chinese New Year in 1644 might have sensed nothing
particularly untoward occurring around its web of greenish-brown-grey
walls. Life for those working on the walled fort was probably continuing
largely as it had done, on and off, since about 1381, the year in which the
Ming dynasty began building the fort on the east coast: tamping earth,
firing and heaving bricks, building and reinforcing walls. Even today, in
only partially preserved condition, the walls around the town are 4.3
kilometres long, fourteen metres high and seven metres thick, converging on the centrepiece, two-storey fortress that proclaims itself 'The
First Pass on Earth', its blank, solid fourteen-metre-high ramparts
crowned with heavy curved eaves. In 1644, they would have been more
redoubtable still. The previous century, security-minded planners had
strengthened the western rear of the fort with the *Gongzhen men* – the
Gate at Which the Border Tribes Come to Pay Homage. Beginning in
1643 and continuing throughout 1644, builders worked on reinforcing
the new gate of imperial hospitality with yet another outer wall to the
west. (Both constructions have since crumbled away.)[1] Presumably, if
circumstances and time had allowed, layer upon layer of outer wall

would have been added, to appease the Ming planners' frontier anxieties.

History has not recorded what was in the minds of those corralled into work on this latest reinforcement of the wall in the sub-zero temperatures of north-east China in January: whether, in addition to the usual sources of wall-builders' discontent (fatigue, backache, insufficient clothing and food, maltreatment by overseers), they felt a certain sense of *fin-de*-dynasty futility about the whole enterprise; whether they realized they were building endless, useless walls around an irredeemably decayed political centre. But it is possible, even likely, that rumours had begun to filter out east about catastrophic events shaking the centre of the world, Beijing: that revolts beginning in Shaanxi fifteen years ago had swallowed up north and central China, that rebels were about to overrun the capital, that the Ming dynasty, bankrupt and abandoned by its civil servants, was on its last legs, that a former shepherd had as good as proclaimed himself Son of Heaven. It was even more likely that the workers of Shanhaiguan would have known theirs was practically the last Ming outpost in northeast China: that the Manchu barbarians had been steadily acquiring Chinese strongholds in the north-east for the past twenty or thirty years and were now hovering over Shanhaiguan, waiting their moment to surge through this final fortress and pick over the carcass of the Ming. And still they kept building.

~

That same New Year's day, 1,100 kilometres west of Shanhaiguan, in the ancient capital of Chang'an, a new dynasty, the Shun, was being inaugurated. After more than eight years of dedicated plundering through north China, Li Zicheng, a shepherd turned postman turned rebel leader from Shaanxi – the northern stronghold of so many of China's most successful conquerors, usurpers and revolutionaries – resolved to grasp the Mandate of Heaven, set loose by the decadent Ming, for himself. Li, who liked to call himself 'The Dashing Prince' *(chuang wang)* had virtually no sense of how a country might be governed but a cause that brought to his side practically every fighting male his forces encountered: justice for ordinary people, against the extortions of the Ming government. Between him and Beijing lay 800 kilometres of countryside and towns whose inhabitants were already humming hopeful hymns of praise to the Dashing Prince, in anticipation of their liberation from crushing burdens of taxation and corvée.[2]

Some 375 kilometres north-east of Shanhaiguan, in the city of Mukden, Manchuria, another family of aspiring emperors was poised to make its own strike on the Ming capital. Like Li Zicheng's, the origins of the Manchu Jin dynasty were humble: only a few generations before, they had been semi-nomadic ginseng traders descended from decadent barbarians expelled from China by the Mongols in the 1230s. Ambition, audacity and rigorous military discipline, however, had within three decades transformed their leader Nurhaci from a small-timer with only thirteen suits of armour to protect his followers into the founder and ruler of a Manchurian state fully independent from Ming China. Soon enough, Nurhaci – like many Manchurian candidates before him – began laying acquisitive eyes upon China itself. In 1629, the Manchus had advanced as far as the outskirts of the capital, falling back for lack of manpower and cannons, but gathering up, as they retreated north-east, Chinese artillery experts whose knowledge would offer them the key to overcoming the Ming fortifications that had so far held them off. During available moments in the next decade – years mainly taken up with battering and slowly breaking down the forts and walls that made up the Ming line of defence in the north-east beyond Shanhaiguan – the Manchus would concentrate on making themselves appear qualified to rule China: encouraging the Chinese under their jurisdiction to work the fields rather than hunt and trap; setting up a government that mirrored that of the Ming; organizing examinations to recruit their bureaucracy; choosing a new dynastic name, Qing, that sounded reassuringly like Ming. They even built their own, smaller-scale replica of the Forbidden City in their capital, Mukden. Although the twelve-acre palace complex here was less than a tenth the size of the Beijing original, its low red walls and weightily eaved, yellow-tiled roofs groan with the same self-importance of its older, bigger Chinese predecessor. All the Manchus needed to do now was stand ready to swoop while China tore itself apart. They were not kept waiting long.[3]

~

About 300 kilometres west of Shanhaiguan, in Beijing, the situation was every bit as cataclysmic as the enemies of the Ming dynasty to the east and west hoped. As Li Zicheng prepared, with his million-strong army, for his final advance across north China, an apocalyptic pall seemed to descend over the capital. Their maudlin tendencies heightened by the vicissitudes of a Beijing winter – temperatures plummeting as low as minus 20° centigrade, accompanied by scouring, sand-laden winds – pedestrians passing by the gates of the Forbidden City claimed they could hear spectral noises of battle and cries of woe. For officials massed outside the main gate of the palace at dawn on New Year's Day, there was a more mundane explanation for any audible wails: a weeping emperor, huddled up inside the Forbidden City, too depressed at the disaster enfolding him to receive the New Year's wishes of his dutiful officials. Making their way back to their residences as dawn broke, the officials and anyone else out on the streets would have kept their heads firmly down, trying to shelter from the dust storm that was lacerating the early morning and from the pestilence – probably smallpox – then raging through north China and the capital.

The emperor was right to be depressed: his government lay in tatters around him, his officials paralysed by financial and strategic bankruptcy, his army practically unpaid and barely functioning. In mid-April 1644, the minister of finance estimated that '[i]t takes 520,000 ounces of silver a month to meet the cost of military provisions for defending the frontiers. In the first month, we still had [taxation] receipts coming in ... In the second month, the receipts stopped entirely.'[4] An official audit of the Ministry of Finance that year revealed the imperial treasuries contained only 4,200 ounces of silver; by early 1644, the government owed several million ounces of silver in army salaries alone. As Li Zicheng's forces closed in on Beijing, the capital garrisons had been neither paid nor fed properly for months. When the emperor demanded to inspect in person the contents of his personal treasury chamber in the Forbidden City, the doorman tried to stall him by pretending that he could not find the keys. When the emperor finally barged his way past, he found nothing but a red box containing a handful of receipts.[5]

The main reason for the bankruptcy of the Ming military was that historically there was no provision within the state budget for paying an army. The original plan of the Ming founder, Hongwu, had been that the military should be self-sustaining: as part of his project to repopulate and revitalize rural China, Hongwu gave over large slices of temporarily devastated but nonetheless prime agricultural land to the army. He then granted each of his hereditary military families up to fifty *mu* (some 7 acres) of arable land, from which to provision themselves. During the fifteenth century, however, as Ming emperors led by example in becoming increasingly palace-loving and unwarlike, the social prestige of army service bled away and the hereditary military effectively became a malfunctioning racket. The most powerful army families turned ordinary soldiers into personal servants, while entrepreneurial officers made a tidy profit out of 'selling leisure' to their men: charging a monthly fee that bought exemption from military duties. Those who could not afford 'leisure' simply deserted, leaving behind only those too weak or incapable to run away. Although, by the late sixteenth century, the military rolls officially contained about 1.2 million soldiers, many garrisons were operating at 20 per cent of their official strength. Nowhere was Ming military decline more obvious than in the state of the capital garrison in 1644. As Li Zicheng marched on the capital, only between 10 and 20 per cent of the 700,000 soldiers on the official roster could be found. Most of these were elderly, weak and starving.[6]

The only way of persuading men to fight was to pay and provision them adequately. But what little money was officially made available

A Ming sketch of a kiln and carrying pole, both important tools in the building of the Ming border wall.

A recent view, through the window of a ruined watch-tower, of the partially restored stone Ming wall cresting the hills at Jinshanling, near Beijing.

A Ming map of the Nine Border Garrisons around which the border wall was organised.

The Ming wall in the Ordos country in northwest China. Note the contrast between this mud embankment and the solid brick-and-stone wall north and northeast of Beijing.

An early twentieth-century photograph of the Ming wall built across a village in northeast China.

An early twentieth-century view of the First Pass Under Heaven at Shanhaiguan, the north-eastern gateway through which the Qing and the Japanese armies advanced from Manchuria to attempt their conquests of China.

Aurel Stein's photograph of Jiayuguan, the westernmost pass in the Ming border wall, rising up out of the sands of northwest China.

Li Yongfang surrenders to the Manchus, the first Chinese general on the northeast frontier to do so on the Qing progress towards conquering China.

melted away on its journey towards the soldiers who most needed it: when the emperor tracked the progress of 52,000 ounces of silver earmarked for garrisons on the north-east border, he discovered that every single piece became unaccountably lost on its journey to the frontier. Little wonder that the Ming rank and file lacked the physical strength and determination to take on the dynasty's enemies. 'When you whip one soldier,' a Ming general sighed, 'he stands up, but another one lies down.'[7] The semi-mercenary, semi-conscript army that resulted caught the worst of both military worlds: an expensive rabble of, for the most part, uncommitted incompetents. 'All those under arms,' wrote Matteo Ricci, the Jesuit priest who settled in China between 1583 and 1610, 'lead a despicable life, for they have not embraced this profession out of love of their country or devotion to their king or love of honour and glory, but as men in the service of a provider of employment.'[8]

The Ming coffers were empty for two very straightforward reasons: there was too much money going out and not enough coming in. Ever since the fifteenth century, but especially in the sixteenth, Ming emperors had been throwing money at projects both personal and political – 10.4 million ounces of silver spent on the Wanli emperor's tomb, 33.8 million on war in Korea at the end of the sixteenth century, each within the space of a few years; the exorbitant costs of intensive wall-building have already been noted. Ming emperors almost never separated public and private when allocating the imperial budget: in the sixteenth century, imperial palaces were rebuilt at least four times after destruction caused by carelessly started fires; the last reconstruction alone cost more than 730,000 ounces of silver. And the emperors led by example: if they were not going to stint themselves, neither were their relatives. At the start of the dynasty, the imperial family had been given enormous estates and generous stipends at safe distances from the capital, in order to neutralize them as political threats to the emperor. As the dynasty wore on and the clan inevitably multiplied, the civil list swelled until, by the close of the seventeenth century, allowances for the imperial family were gobbling up half the tax revenue from two major provinces, Shanxi and Henan. The government even took the desperate measure of suspending marriage permits to princes, presumably to put a brake on their alarming rate of reproduction.

But Ming China was a large country, and a very rich one in places, and should have been able to provide the government with the taxation revenue needed to fund its projects. By the late Ming, China was probably the leading supplier in a global luxury goods trade – particularly in ceramics and textiles, porcelain and silk – sucking great quantities of New World and European silver into the country via the Portuguese, Spanish and Dutch traders docked around its peripheries. Although the benefits of this trade did percolate through all layers of Chinese society – the arrival of hardy New World crops, especially the sweet potato, often made a vital difference to those living off China's poorest, driest land – it was the minority of Chinese city-dwellers who profited the most. As silver increasingly became the dominant means of payment, making resources and workers far more mobile, the agrarian economy – which traded in kind – declined relative to the urban and mercantile. Towns and cities boomed, as the well-off funnelled their capital away from agriculture and into industrial production: handicrafts and the processing of cash crops such as sugarcane, cotton and tobacco. But this frenetic and highly profitable urban economic activity had a seriously impoverishing and destabilizing effect on China's rural majority. Those who could abandon the countryside did so: landlords became increasingly absentee, moving to the towns; skilled workers commanded decent wages in urban workshops; the unskilled waited to be engaged for miserable industrial labour. The bottom fell out of Chinese rural communities unable to leave for the cities: with the focus of their capital shifted to the towns, the landlord elite no longer provided investment in community projects such as irrigation works, which were crucial to rice cultivation. To this elite, their rural estates became more a cash cow – their tenant farmers financing life and business projects in the towns, the silver they generated keeping financial agents such as merchants and pawnbrokers in profitable employment – than a living, functioning community which supported individual livelihoods. Rural incomes plummeted: as the urban economy boomed and prices rose, the value of agricultural land fell; as population increased – a growth fuelled by New World crops – rural wages also declined.

Although distressing on a human level, the decline of rural communities need not have spelt penury for the imperial coffers. After all, there was just as much (if not more) money in circulation as there had always been; it was simply that the focus of wealth had shifted from the countryside to the cities. The government, however, failed to adjust sufficiently to this new reality. The Ming founder had known from bitter personal experience the horrors of rural poverty, having lost his entire family to famine and disease. After he had expelled the Mongols, rebuilding the rural economy took up the greater part of his energies: irrigating, reforesting, repopulating land, pampering peasant farmers with grants and tax exemptions. (Between 1371 and 1379, the land in use almost tripled.) But China's farmers ultimately paid a heavy price for this early, sympathetic treatment: Hongwu's focus on the rural economy meant that his successors inevitably came to regard farmers as the principal source of state income. As a result, Ming taxation never adjusted to the massive diversion of wealth into the cities and continued to attempt to squeeze more and more out of the countryside: grain taxes and corvée for public projects, or cash for avoiding corvée. Those most able to pay had either migrated away or were excused; the government handed out great sheaves of corvée exemptions to the local scholar-gentry – successful candidates in the state bureaucratic examination – and their retinues. As the task of extracting resources from the countryside became more difficult, because both money and humans were in flight from it, the government concentrated ever more of its own energies on obtaining its tax quotas, diverting attention away from some of its other important, community-maintaining tasks, such as public works and institutions.

The fragile Chinese economy was further hard-hit by the global depressions of the 1620s and 1640s. A Dutch blockade, a Spanish clampdown on exports of Acapulcan silver and political turmoil in the South Sea islands (the Philippines, Sumatra, Indonesia) drastically reduced the flow of silver into China. As the surge of bullion into the country had been the only factor enabling certain sectors of the Chinese population to keep silver-fuelled inflation at bay, when that surge suddenly dried up, even the richest areas fell headlong into depression.

So in 1644, as the last Ming emperor wallowed in self-pity over the state of the economy and government, a secretary in the Ministry of War was no doubt correct when he explained the problem to the emperor thus:

The gentry and the wealthy presently clothe themselves with rent and feed themselves with taxes, sitting at their leisure while they suck the bone marrow of the population. In peaceful times they manipulate trade so as to subordinate the people and monopolise vast profits. When there is trouble, ought we expect the people to share the vicissitudes of the gentry and the wealthy, putting forth efforts on their behalf? When the rich grow richer, fleecing the people, and the poor grow poorer, until they are unable to survive at all?[9]

The fundamental problem for Ming China was that it had ceased to function as a single imperial unit. Holding together the massive political conceit of the Chinese empire depended on its administrators maintaining a sense that government was for the benefit of a unified community. As China's imperial institutions – taxation, army, government at both the highest and the lowest levels – foundered in profiteering, self-interest and inefficiency, the sense of loyalty to Ming authority frayed, destroying the sense of psychological unity that was vital to China's political cohesion in the centuries before the efficiencies of modern technology began helping a totalitarian system to control sprawling populations. The servants and people of Ming China were at best listlessly patching the threadbare garment of the empire, waiting for a better alternative to present itself; at worst, like Li Zicheng, they were actively working for its destruction.

One last chance, however, remained for Beijing. Although the quality of the imperial armies had been concertedly declining for about two centuries, although allegiance to the Ming was disintegrating everywhere, one final fighting force, miraculously, held firm in quality and loyalty: the surviving garrisons on the north-east frontier wall around Shanhaiguan. The Ming wall and its men were about to undergo their greatest test.

~

At the start of 1644, as China disintegrated into chaos, disloyalty and incompetence, as Li Zicheng and his army marched east towards the capital, as the straggling, depleted garrisons of Beijing spread themselves across the city walls, only one man to guard every nine metres, the defence of the north-east at the crucial junction of Shanhaiguan depended on the last great Ming general, Wu Sangui. Only thirty-two in 1644, Wu – a native of Liaodong, the north-eastern province bordering between China and Manchuria – had clambered up the military hierarchy in his home province with unusual speed. Ever since the Manchu declaration of war on the Ming, the north-east had become the most pressurized stretch of frontier in the empire, more threatened than the border with the Mongols. Wu began serving in the north-east at the age of twenty-two; five years later, he was commanding 1,600 soldiers; three years after that, in 1642, he was appointed brigade-general of the province, an extraordinary commanding post created in times of war.

Wu's rapid promotion came about partly through his own military talents and partly through the abrupt departure from the Ming army in Liaodong of some of its most senior commanders. When the Manchus began intensively campaigning against the Ming in 1618, Ming defences in the north-east had stretched out in a great garrisoned and walled loop over the north of Shenyang, the old Manchu capital Mukden, before dropping south to meet the Yalu River on the Sino-Korean border. From 1618 onwards, the Manchus picked these remote border garrisons off one by one, beginning with Fushun, ten kilometres east of Mukden, in

1618. Rather than throw his troops – who lacked artillery at this point – at an assault on the walled garrison, the Manchu leader, Nurhaci, laid out an alternative to Li Yongfang, the Chinese general in charge of Fushun, in a calmly worded letter. 'If there is a battle then the arrows shot by our soldiers will strike all in sight. If you are hit, you will surely die ... The old and young inside the city will surely be in jeopardy, your official salaries will be taken away and your ranks will soon be reduced.' If, by contrast, 'you come out and surrender ... I will let you live just as you did before ... I will give you a higher position than you have and treat you like one of my officials of the first degree.'[10] In short, Nurhaci was offering Li – marooned in a freezing, cash-starved, barbarian-harassed outpost of the malfunctioning Ming empire – a peaceful entrée to collaboration. The general accepted Nurhaci's terms after just one Manchu attack.

The surrender of Fushun – the first of many such Chinese defections in the north-east – came as an extraordinary blow, both strategic and psychological, to the Chinese court. On a military level, China's only advantage over the Manchus lay in holding out behind walls. Once a walled fort was surrendered, it would never be recovered by the Chinese in open battle, in which the Manchus were manifestly superior. On a psychological level, by agreeing so easily to collaborate, Fushun's commander made a mockery of the chauvinistic imperialism that coloured every aspect of Chinese policy towards the north, that drove the construction of the wall and filled it with structures and posts such as the 'Tower for Suppressing the North', the 'Gate at Which the Border Tribes Come to Pay Homage' and the 'Official Who Pacifies the Barbarians'. There was, Li Yongfang's eager defection plainly announced, nothing special about (Ming) Chinese culture in comparison with the 'barbarian' regime of the north-east, and certainly nothing that was worth dying for.

Loyalty to the government was not something that guarding the Ming wall tended to encourage, at either the highest or the lowest levels of the army. For all concerned, frontier service was at the best of times a cold, lonely and thankless task, and for none more so than the common soldiers. The frontline of wall service was performed by crews of the thousands of towers dotted over its 6,000-odd kilometres. Of these towers, the most comfortable – although, for wall service, this adjective can be understood only in a relative sense – were the hollow ones, which offered shelter from Mongolian and Manchurian winds and snow, and provided for the storage of basic supplies. For those not fortunate enough to be stationed in these rudimentary shelters, spells of guard duty were spent on the exposed tops of 'solid-core' towers built of solid earth. 'In every border district,' a Ming military manual glibly explained, 'most towers are built of solid earth; on one side hangs a rope ladder which makes it very easy for the tower crew to climb up or down. But it happens regularly,' the manual proceeded contradictorily to caution, 'that when the Barbarians come close, our soldiers cannot get up or down in time with the result that they have failed to give the signals.'[11] Whether inside or outside the towers, crews were always vulnerable. In 1573, a group of twenty Mongols began climbing up a tower while its guards slept; the Chinese soldiers were only alerted to the danger when they were woken by the snorts of the Mongolian horses below.[12] Alternatively, crews remaining inside the towers could be smoked out or suffocated when Mongols made a hole in the brickwork and lit fires that fanned in smoke. More often than not, wall guards felt too isolated and outnumbered to put up effective resistance: as one sympathetic inspector phrased it, 'How could they have handled dragons and snakes with their bare hands?'[13]

The cause of the soldiers' suffering came as often from within as without the wall: as the Ming army, from the fifteenth century onwards, steadily transformed itself into an enormous racket, border guards were at the mercy of their officers, who regularly diverted rank-and-file salaries into their own pockets, or turned soldiers into personal serfs. Officers, however, were themselves always open to offers and a cessation of suffering could generally be bought – for a while, at least. One Ming military manual sternly but tellingly commanded that tower crews must not bribe officers.[14] With temperatures plummeting tens of degrees below zero in winter, frostbite was probably a greater danger than raiders, and government directives publicly made a great fanfare about issuing crews with fur coats, padded coats, trousers and boots. Critical inspection reports indicated otherwise: that clothing issues were inadequate, that mouldy and ill-fitting clothes and shoes were issued perhaps once every three years. The remoter the area, of course, the less reliable the supply lines. Regardless of whether supply lines were interrupted by greed and corruption or by incompetence and inefficiency, poor provisioning had a devastating effect on border troops. In 1542, one frontier report, lamenting the particular sufferings of southerners – unacclimatized, unprepared for the bitterness of a northern winter – sent to guard the border, claimed that 80 or 90 per cent of tower crews died during their watches. Food – at best only just adequate – was a similarly serious problem: inspection reports suggest that malnutrition and slow starvation were the norm. In any case, particularly when hostilities between those on either side of the wall were intense, Chinese soldiers often used up their salary allocations in bribing Mongols not to attack.[15]

But life as a regular guardsman was a junket compared to the hardships experienced by the most put-upon members of the wall establishment, the *yebushou* (literally, 'not recalled at night') or spies. Theoretically, spies had a crucial role to play in bolstering the defensive work of the wall, making night-time sorties into enemy territory disguised as Mongols, detecting and sabotaging planned raids and insurrections – sometimes carrying out assassinations – long before Mongol horses could actually be heard snorting at the foot of the wall. In practice, however, appalling working conditions undermined the quality of their performance. Although the nature of the job – nocturnal operations on China's inhospitable northern frontiers – demanded great sacrifices of the spies, the Ming military establishment did not seem to think to reward them especially, or to try to attract skilled, committed scouts with bonuses, or even adequate salaries. 'They may be away for months or years without returning to base camp, and their wives and children, lacking clothes and food, are in desperate conditions,' observed one report. 'True, they receive a monthly salary, but very often they have to spend it on weapons or horses, and they suffer indescribably from hunger and cold.'[16] As a result, officials complained almost constantly that spies were lazy, lax, negligent, 'loafers and slippery types who use substitutes'.[17]

As the final insult, there appears to have been no rigid timetable for border service, no official, set time limit on which guardsmen could set their sights: different sources speak of a month of service, four months, three months, ten days, nineteen months and so on. In short, neither the Ming command nor the hapless frontier soldiers probably had any idea when leave might be granted. Service on the wall was a particularly elastic form of torture.

The hardships of frontier life were compounded if the wall was in poor repair and offered little shelter against weather and attackers. Constant and urgent requests from the borders to the government to mend towers indicate the rate at which they disintegrated, battered by wind, rain, assaults and depredations. At the end of the sixteenth century, a Liaodong official reported that local walls had shrunk to shoulder height. 'For years now, the Manchus and the Chinese frontier people have been systematically breaking them down', stripping bricks and wood for use in private building projects.[18] Near Datong and Xuanfu, it was reported in 1552 that passing Mongols had torn down 'five to six tenths of the wall'.[19] In 1609, a commander-in-chief described the state of defences in Liaodong, ten years before the Manchus began their onslaught:

Moats are filled with sand until they are flush with the ground, and are no longer dug back out. Walled fortresses are in an even worse state of ruin. Many lack gates, and one can no longer move around on the walls. Anyone who tries to walk on them has to hang on to the battlements, his legs often left hanging into a void.[20]

As the towers dilapidated, so the frontier guards abandoned them. Often, crews dared not raise the alarm – by smoke signals or cannonfire – as the

enemy army approached, presumably because the towers were so vulnerable that the enemy would soon be upon them and tacit cooperation
looked a more appealing prospect than hopeless resistance.

The combination of lassitude and disaffection induced by such
extreme physical danger and discomfort meant that soldiers guarding the
Ming wall adopted, at best, a live-and-let-live attitude towards the potential aggressors beyond the walls and towers of the frontier; at worst, they
actively collaborated, as allies, spies and welcoming gatekeepers.
Although the wall, with its towers and guards, was designed to obstruct
and police Mongol entry into China, permitting access only at set times
in set places, as often as not the Mongols were reported as breaching or
scaling the wall wherever they pleased. Traffic going the other way
slipped through with equal ease: prisoners returning to Mongolia 'gave
the towers a wide berth'; despite the impression given of a continuously
defended line of wall, there were clearly gaps.[21] When Esen led his
Mongols through north-west China to Beijing in 1449, frontier guards
simply abandoned their towers in advance. A hundred years later,
observers were noting that tower crews fled in terror when the Mongols
crossed the wall. If guards did stand their ground as Mongols
approached, they looked the other way and pretended not to have seen
them, raising the alarm only after the danger was well past. Often, however, the contacts were more friendly and partisan: as the towers were
located on the very cusp of Chinese and Mongolian or Manchu territory,
frequent contact between the two sides was inevitable. In 1570, the gov-
ernor-general of the north-east referred to the dozen-strong tower crews
along the border simply as the 'twelve traitors'.[22] In 1533, an official
claimed that the Chinese *yebushou* spies were in fact serving as guides for
gangs of raiding Mongols. The cause of this insubordination was plain to
those with any experience of frontier conditions, such as this inspector of
1553: 'We must treat the crews better, and then from being the enemy's
eyes and ears, they will again be our eyes and ears.'[23]

While officers did not have to endure the acute, day-to-day physical suffering of the rank and file, they faced another, higher-level kind of nightmare: the public disgrace, and often execution, that followed failure and defeat. The Ming founder and his son, Yongle, had set the despotic tone for the dynasty by scouring the ranks of their officials for imagined traitors and critics, creating a terrorizing culture of responsibility and recrimination. As military disasters multiplied in later centuries, their successors held fast to this precedent, dealing ruthlessly with scapegoats wherever they were to be found. Between 1619 and 1625, three commanders in the north-east were executed on charges of treason after retreating to the south-west from positions made hopelessly isolated by the defections of other Ming officers. The head of the last of these victims was paraded along the frontier as a warning to others of the punishment for 'treachery'. In 1630, the minister of war in office when the Manchus had surged past the wall east of Beijing and approached the capital the previous year was dismembered in the marketplace, and his entire family executed, enslaved or exiled. Another two commanders were executed in 1643, a third mercifully permitted by the emperor to take his own life, thereby avoiding execution by slow strangulation. In 1621, two failed generals, recognizing the fate that was inevitably theirs, committed suicide in Liaoyang. With this level of penalty for failure in a war that was becoming increasingly hopeless and destructive for a rapidly declining Ming army – 45,000 Ming troops were massacred in one campaign of 1619 alone – it is little wonder that following Fushun's docile example, frontier commanders, together with their ill-provisioned men, seized the opportunity to survive under the Manchus.[24]

For those facing death in the line of active duty, the nature of the war in the north-east suggested that the end would rarely be quick or painless. As the Chinese strength lay in fortifications, the only way to resist the Manchus was to take refuge within walled garrison towns and to try to outlast any siege. One of the most brutally drawn out of these took place in 1631 at Dalinghe, a garrison fortress about 150 kilometres north-east of Shanhaiguan. After an encirclement lasting eighty-two days, only

11,682 out of an original 30,000 survived; nearly 20,000 were dead of
starvation and its inevitable consequence, cannibalism. As the days
advanced, those most dispensable to the war effort were systematically
butchered for food: first the workmen, followed by merchants, followed
finally by the weakest of the soldiers. Eventually, the officers sustained
themselves by killing and consuming their rank and file. After the
Chinese general finally decided to surrender to the Manchus, only one
officer refused to switch allegiance from the Ming. The Manchus granted
him a dignified execution, but when his body was taken back inside the
gates of the fortress, the starving masses fought among themselves to rip
the flesh from his body for food.[25]

By 1642, all the major forts and strongholds north of Shanhaiguan but
one had surrendered. Under the command of Wu Sangui, only
Ningyuan, about 75 kilometres north-east, halted the Manchu advance,
standing guard over Shanhaiguan, the critical, thickly walled bottleneck
leading on to the plains of China. When advisers urged him to rush on to
the Chinese capital, the Manchu leader refused. 'Shanhaiguan,' he said,
shaking his head, 'cannot be taken.'[26] The youngest of a dynasty of successful Liaodong career soldiers, Wu was almost the last general in his
north-east clan – indeed in the entire north-east – still loyal to the Ming.
(One of his uncles was the commander who had surrendered Dalinghe;
in the thirteen years since that harrowing siege, his remaining uncles and
cousins followed, relinquishing the north-east to the Manchus as far as
Wu's own stronghold at Ningyuan.) Wu Sangui, in whose hands the fate
of the empire rested, now faced a choice: to fight for the flailing cause of
the Ming Son of Heaven, as his professional responsibilities bound him
to do, or to sacrifice the emperor to family loyalty and self-preservation,
adding his men to the surging ranks of the ascendant, barbarian
Manchus.

~

In Beijing, as the capital began to feel a little spring warmth in April 1644
and Li Zicheng's army prepared to breach the double line of walls in

Shanxi, to the west of the capital, the emperor considered his options. First, he tried appointing a new military commander to resist the advance from the north-west. The commander chosen responded to the honour by bursting into tears. 'Even if I go,' he protested, 'it will be useless.'[27] On 7 April, the wall garrison of Datong fell to Li Zicheng; within ten days, Xuanfu had also surrendered. In both cases, firm resistance was scarce; the Ming military had long since lost confidence in itself. Only the Juyong pass now protected the capital.

On 10 April, another crushing blow was dealt. The Department of Astronomy soberly reported that the Pole Star – traditionally symbolic of the emperor – had slipped down in the heavens. Perhaps in reaction to this news, the emperor took the step that he had hesitated over for months: summoning his last loyal general, Wu Sangui, from the north-east to defend Beijing. Twelve days later, as the emperor conducted his regular morning audience in the Forbidden City, an out-of-breath courier dashed into the audience hall with an urgent, highly confidential note for the emperor. 'As he read it, his expression changed. He arose and went into the inner palace. After a long time, he dispatched an order for the officials to retire. This was the first they were to know of the fall of Changping.'[28] South of the final Ming-held stretch of wall around the Juyong pass, Changping was a mere 65 kilometres north of the Forbidden City. Two weeks earlier, its unpaid garrison had mutinied.[29] Changping's collapse meant that the Juyong pass too had fallen to the rebels; the Ming commanders sent to hold the pass had simply let them through. The Ming wall, festooned decoratively over the rippling mountains, had watched impotently as its gates were held open to the dynasty's enemies.

A day later, the emperor held his final audience, at which he announced his plan of last resort to the gathered ministers: 'The civil officials can each commit suicide.'[30] On the following day, he conducted his final negotiation as emperor, receiving his former favourite, the eunuch Du Xun, who two days before had relinquished the Juyong pass to the rebels under Li Zicheng. In exchange for 1 million ounces of silver and a private kingdom in north-west China, Li offered to defeat other rebel groups and the Manchus. Reluctant to go down in history as an appeaser of rebels, the emperor refused. After Du Xun departed, the emperor violently knocked over his own throne.[31]

Not long after midnight on 25 April, the last emperor of the Ming appeared, drunk, disorientated and possibly blood-spattered, for his predawn audience. The evening of the previous day he had spent soaking himself in alcohol and dispatching his consorts: although one empress had saved him the trouble by committing suicide, others clung stubbornly to life, forcing him to kill one and sever the right arm of another. Fortunately for the dignity of the imperial person, none of the emperor's officials arrived for the audience to see him in this state. Blaming everything on 'the mistakes of treacherous ministers', the emperor then staggered past the imperial pleasure garden of twisted trees and rocks of the Forbidden City, out of the palace's back gate and up a man-made mound called Coal Hill a short distance further north.[32] On Coal Hill – still a popular viewing point over Beijing today – he may have paused for a moment to contemplate his predominantly low-rise capital: its palaces and temples, its maze of grey-bricked alleyways sprawling busily between the two great symbolic coordinates of the city – the vast courtyards and pavilions of the Forbidden City and the blue-tiled roof of the Hall of Prayer for Good Harvests, the circular centrepiece of the Temple of Heaven complex south of the city walls, that rises, like a space rocket, out of the surrounding parkland. He may also have heard a buzz of civilian panic and the tramp of an exuberant peasant army as Li Zicheng and his followers entered the city. Shortly before one a.m., he made his way inside the red pavilion on the hill that housed the Imperial Hat and Girdle Department and hanged himself with his sash. Three days later, his body, dressed in a blue silk robe and red trousers, was found, identifiable by a note bearing two explanatory characters written in his own hand: *Tian zi* – the Son of Heaven.[33]

Like many things occurring that year in China, it remains unclear precisely when Wu Sangui decided to join his uncles and cousins in abandoning the Ming dynasty to its own fate. While he did not publicly contemplate disloyalty until after the dramatic events of 24 April, neither did he exactly hurry to the emperor's aid in the middle weeks of the month. Puzzlingly, after receiving his 10 April summons, it took him until 26 April to cover, with his 40,000-odd frontier troops, the less than one hundred kilometres from Ningyuan to Shanhaiguan, after which he had travelled halfway across the monotonous yellow-brown flats of Hebei to Beijing, some further 140 kilometres, when reports reached him, a few days after the fact, of Beijing's fall. Other sources, however, claim that the emperor may have delayed sending for Wu Sangui until 22 April, in which case Wu's failure even to near the capital in time for Li Zicheng's assault can be more innocently explained.[34]

Even after the emperor had committed suicide and the capital had fallen, all was not yet lost for the Ming. Although the capital was in enemy hands, there were probably enough Ming loyalists in the south to mount a counter-offensive against the northern rebels. Aware of this, but personally isolated, Wu Sangui returned to Shanhaiguan to ponder his next move.

Recognizing the importance of Wu Sangui as the commander of the last significant Ming army in the north, Li Zicheng immediately tried to win him over by means of two letters. The first, from a surrendered Ming general, praised Li Zicheng's moral character. The second, probably dictated by one of Li's henchmen, was supposedly from Wu's father, Wu Xiang, a former Ming general and now hostage of Li Zicheng in Beijing. His father's letter – a very thinly disguised ransom note – turned on a nice point of Confucian morality. In ordinary, harmonious times, Confucius deemed the demands of filial piety entirely compatible with the loyalty owed to the emperor: 'Let the ruler be a ruler, the father a father, the son a son.' Indeed, the correct performance of every social role was necessary to spread peace and prosperity throughout the empire. But these were not harmonious times and the usual rules of loyalty to the emperor no longer applied: returning the emperor's favour, the letter argued, was no longer Wu's primary obligation. If he surrendered to save his father's life, he would earn eternal fame for his filial devotion. The letter, further-more, offered Wu Sangui both title and rank in Li Zicheng's new Shun regime; the military envoy who brought the letter enlarged the overture by delivering with it 10,000 ounces of silver and 1,000 ounces of gold.[35]

The next part of the story is, again, confused. One version has it that Wu Sangui wrote back a priggish letter to his father, chastising him for his submission to Li Zicheng and paraphrasing Confucius back at him, to counter Wu Xiang's arguments about filial piety and justify his refusal to submit and consequent sacrifice of his father: 'If my father cannot be a loyal minister, then how can I be a filial son?'[36]

By another, more romantic and popular version of events, Wu Sangui is less a sanctimonious son, more a bewitched lover. As he contemplated his next move, rumours supposedly reached Wu Sangui that his beloved and legendarily beautiful concubine, Chen Yuan (worshipped by one of her many besotted admirers as 'a lone phoenix fluttering behind a screen of mist'), had been stolen by Li Zicheng. Mad with jealousy, Wu allegedly forgot his father's predicament and began dreaming up desperate schemes to take revenge on Li.[37] This story of war-estranged lovers entranced generations of Chinese, turning Chen Yuan into another Yang Guifei, 'a woman lovely enough to cause the fall of a city or kingdom', and Wu Sangui into a rather more dynamic version of the Tang emperor Xuanzong.[38]

Such a scenario was, however, probably dreamt up by later authors of historical romances, keen to discredit Wu Sangui as an unreliable loose cannon, driven by passions and unable to subordinate his physical desires to the general political good. It is rather more credible that, as another account has it, after receiving the letter and gifts from Li Zicheng, he deliberated for several days before deciding to transfer his allegiance to the new master of Beijing. Shortly after setting out for the capital, however, he had a disturbing encounter that changed everything. At Yongping, little more than fifty kilometres south-west of Shanhaiguan, he was surprised to meet one of his father's concubines. She provided a horrifying account of recent events in Beijing: that Li Zicheng, reading Wu Sangui's silence as defiance, had butchered almost the entire Wu household – thirty-eight people in total – and hung Wu Xiang's bloody head from the city wall. Wu was only the latest victim of the rebel leader's reign of terror against surviving Ming officials, whom Li Zicheng despised as turncoats for not having taken their own lives as Beijing fell to his rebels. A week after he had entered Beijing, financial pressures intensified Li's hard line towards scholar-officials. Eagerly expecting to find bulging imperial treasuries with which to pay his armies, Li had been shocked to find almost nothing at all. On 1 May, he began trying to extort tens of thousands of ounces of silver from former Ming officials; those who failed to pay up were assiduously tortured by Li's sadistic senior general. Some thousand died within vices specially constructed to crush human bone; a grand secretary died after five days of torture, his cheekbones split from repeated beatings. The rebel troops, who had remained moderately orderly on first entering Beijing, soon followed the brutal example of their leaders, forcing open 'doors, seizing gold and silver, violating wives and daughters. The people began to suffer. Every nightfall was the same.'[39]

Wu immediately repealed his decision, halted his progress to Beijing, turned back to Shanhaiguan, where he had left the majority of his 40,000 troops, and prepared for battle with Li Zicheng. It came in less than three weeks. On 18 May, with a characteristic fanfare – beheading sixteen Ming officials at the eastern gate of the Forbidden City – Li Zicheng led 60,000 troops out of the capital and on to Shanhaiguan. This time, outnumbered by 50 per cent, Wu Sangui had to think fast. With both his father and the emperor now dead, the only loyalty that remained for Wu was to his uncle and cousins who had sided with the Manchus. On 20 May, Wu dispatched a letter north-east to the Manchus in Mukden: 'I have long deeply admired Your Highness's majestic authority, but according to the obligations of the Spring and Autumn Annals, borders are not to be crossed, and I have therefore not communicated directly with you before now.' Wu quickly went on to explain the critical nature of the situation, that 'roving bandits ... a mob of petty thieves' had overthrown the emperor. While Wu was sure they could be defeated by 'righteous armies', his own forces were not large enough to guarantee success, and he had 'wept tears of blood in search of help'. If the Manchus would step in now to help, they would not only 'rescue the people from fire and water' but also share in the 'gold and silks, the boys and girls' amassed by the bandits. 'Once the righteous troops arrive, that will be theirs.'[40]

Wu Sangui's letter reached the Manchu Forbidden City in Mukden at a momentous time: on the day that the Manchus had at last learned of the Ming emperor's suicide, almost a month earlier. With the Mandate of Heaven floating free, with an entry to Shanhaiguan being offered, the Manchus were now ready to intervene, but on their and not Wu Sangui's terms. 'If,' the Manchu regent Dorgon – the real power behind the youthful emperor – wrote back to Wu, 'you were to lead your army and surrender to us, we would assuredly enfeoff you with your former territory and bestow a princedom upon you.' Without waiting for Wu's answer, Manchu troops somewhere between 45,000 and 100,000 in number moved towards Shanhaiguan at roughly the same speed as the letter itself, stationing themselves at Wu's old stronghold of Ningyuan. On 25 May, with most of Li Zicheng's army now at the edge of Shanhaiguan and the nerves of his local gentry allies jangling in the face of Li's show of strength, Wu Sangui accepted the Manchus' terms.[41]

At sunrise on 27 May, after a night spent eight kilometres from Shanhaiguan, sleeping in their armour, their weapons by their side, the Manchu soldiers arrived at the gates of the fortress town. Following a quick formal, and secret, surrender – now, with the cannons of Shanhaiguan rumbling in the early skirmishes of battle, was not the time for elaborate ceremonial – Wu ordered his men to attach pieces of white cloth to the back of their armour, so that the Manchus could easily distinguish them in battle from the other Han troops of Li Zicheng.[42] He then placed his soldiers in the frontline of the Manchu army and led the first charges against Li Zicheng's army, which was arrayed in a broad sweep to the west of Shanhaiguan. The rebel army fought Wu's troops practically to their knees, driving them up against the western wall of the fort, while the Manchu troops deliberately held back, letting both sides exhaust themselves, thus ensuring that Wu would be all the more dependent on reinforcements. When Li was on the point of proclaiming victory, however, the weather dramatically intervened, in the form of a blinding sandstorm. As Li's troops peered through the gritty fog, they suddenly perceived on their left flank the gleam of hairless scalps: the clean-shaven foreheads of Manchu warriors. To cries of 'The Tartar troops have come', Li Zicheng's exhausted army began to break, then retreat, then collapse into a rout, scattering and straggling back to Beijing, with Li Zicheng among them.[43]

Beijing was to know another week of terrible, bloody uncertainty, as Li's army, drunken and defeated, sacked and burned large parts of the city with the uncaring, mindless destructiveness of those who instinctively felt they would soon be gone. With the Manchus temporarily too exhausted to pursue him immediately, Li had just enough time in Beijing to hold an accelerated coronation ceremony – previously, he had always called himself prince rather than emperor – before, on 4 June 1644, he set fire to the Forbidden City and rode west out of the city walls, 'smoke and flames filling the sky'.[44]

The residents of the capital took a rapid revenge on any rebel soldiers too drunk or disorientated to follow their masters out of the city, hurling them into blazing buildings or cutting their heads off in the streets. Soon, however, a new cloud of dread settled over the city, as citizens began nervously debating the identity of their next imperial masters, spreading anxious rumours about a 'grand army' sighted from the east, about a proclamation announcing a 'Great Country of Qing'.[45] Through unthinking force of habit, even though the city lay burning and smouldering around them, the upper classes spent the night of 4 June dredging the wreckage of their property for suitable ceremonial outfits in which to receive the vanquishers of Li Zicheng, whom most automatically assumed to be the still-loyal Wu Sangui and the Ming crown prince.

Early the next day, the surviving ministers arrayed themselves along the approach to Beijing, up to ten kilometres outside the city, to greet their new ruler. When the grand army drew near, however, the harassed officials were presented not with a restoration of the old dynasty but with tens of thousands of shaven foreheads and glossy black pigtails belonging to barbarian – Manchu – warriors. No doubt after a certain amount of uneasy jostling, a member of the welcoming party was propelled out of the crowd and nervously volunteered to escort the strangers into the city. Proceeding through streets lined with citizens proffering flowers and burning incense in welcome, the troops wound up to the eastern gate of the Forbidden City, where an official 'had prepared the imperial regalia'. 'One of the barbarians dismounted and climbed upon the imperial chariot. He spoke to the people: "I am the Prince-Regent. The Ming heir apparent will reach all of you in due course. He has assented to my being your ruler." Astounded, everyone in the crowd gaped uncomprehendingly.'[46] Although Dorgon continued to speak, his words were lost amid the growing buzz from the crowd as it absorbed this latest shock and sought to explain the identity of this stranger; one of the more creative rumours instantly circulated was that their new ruler was descended from the Ming emperor taken by the Mongols in 1449, the result of a Ming–Mongol steppe liaison. In the meantime, escorted by the imperial silk brocade guard, Dorgon 'proceeded to enter the Forbidden City', or at least the one palace left standing after Li Zicheng's torching of the complex.[47] And so, in such confused circumstances, after decades of disaffection, disloyalty, dereliction and incompetence, and despite the unending efforts expended on the Ming wall, the barbarian Manchus slipped through to take their place in the vermilion inner sanctum of the Chinese empire.

~

Slowly, to general astonishment, a shaken normality returned to the capital, even though the streets and markets were once again filled, as they had been 300 years before, with northern barbarians. The new Qing dynasty offered conciliation and appointments to traumatized former officials of the Ming, burying the dead emperor and dispatching generals – Wu Sangui included – over the country to root out the forces of Li Zicheng. 'It's just like old times,' remarked one scholar with satisfaction, as officials went back to gathering and gossiping in the Chang'an market.[48]

Remnants of the Ming dynasty straggled on in the south; eighteen years later, Wu Sangui captured and delivered up to his Manchu overlords the last member of the Zhu clan to call himself a Ming emperor, a cousin of the emperor who had killed himself rather than see rebels take Beijing. A few months later, the last of the Ming was quietly executed. Perhaps reflecting on this, and events of twenty years earlier, the Qing emperor later addressed this poem about the border wall to the Ming dynasty:

> You built it for 10,000 *li,* stretching down to the sea,
> But all your expenditures were in vain.
> You exhausted the strength of your people,
> But when did the empire ever belong to you?[49]

~

True enough, to any Chinese with a sense of history, this looked like the familiar old cycle of vigorous barbarian conquerors falling in with Chinese ways. And like so many non-Chinese before them, within 250 years the once vigorous Manchus would be so bound and constricted by the ritualized Chinese superiority complex they had inherited that they were unable to contemplate useful dialogue with the next wave of barbarians – the West – to launch themselves on the Middle Kingdom.

But for the wall and what it specifically represented – centuries of tragic conflict between those living either side of it – things would never be quite the same again. Rather as the Mongols had done before them, the Qing dynasty blurred many of China's northern frontiers with a Pax Manchurica over China's former frontiers, obliterating the old military *raison d'être* of the Long Wall. After some hundred years of concerted bloodshed, China, Inner and Outer Mongolia, Tibet, Central Asia as far as Lake Balkash, Taiwan and, of course, Manchuria were all in Qing hands, forming an empire that makes the contemporary People's Republic look shrunken by comparison. Once the Qing dynasty had united the territories north and south of the wall, the old frontier lost its strategic role as a defence against invaders. When the Western barbarians approached China, in any case, they did so not over the landlocked north, but over the seas, rendering the wall a physical irrelevance.

The wall also lost its old significance as a dividing line between civilization, to the south, and barbarism, to the north. Like the Mongol Yuan dynasty, however, the Manchus were anxious to emphasize certain racial distinctions – between those north and south of the former barrier – as a way of imposing their authority, as foreign conquerors, over the vanquished Chinese. This was done in two ways. First, by coercion: the Qianlong emperor, in the late eighteenth century, systematically censored and destroyed all writings, both ancient and modern, in which 'barbarians' were criticized, while all Chinese after 1645 were compelled, on pain of death, to adopt the Manchu hairstyle of shaved forehead and long pigtail. And second, by segregation: in an effort to preserve the Manchu rulers' tough nomadic-military mystique, Manchuria – geographically, historically and racially, a thoroughly mixed, steppe-agrarian environment – was reinvented as an ethnic homeland of mythical, nomadic purity from which the Chinese, with their polluting, decadent habits, had to be banned. Now that the barbarians could travel wherever they liked in the empire, they turned the tables on the Chinese: after 1668 the Qing barred Chinese from moving north of the Great Wall. Lord Macartney, on his way to the Qing emperor's summer refuge in 1794, noted the defiance of a Manchurian towards the Chinese after passing through the wall, sensing that another authority, beyond the grasp of the ethnic Chinese, ruled in the north-east.

A Tartar servant of the lowest class attending at the Palace had, it seems, stolen some of the utensils furnished for our accommodation, and when taxed with the theft by [our Chinese guides], answered with so much impertinence that they ordered him to be smartly bambooed on the spot. The moment he was released he broke out into the most insolent expressions, and insisted that a Chinese Mandarin had no right to bamboo a Tartar without side of the Great Wall.[50]

To this end, the Qing attached some importance to maintaining defences in the north-east. Stories abound concerning the Kangxi emperor's (r. 1661–1722) eccentric habit of testing the fastness of this artificial ethnic frontier by travelling to Shanhaiguan in mufti, to ascertain whether he, disguised as a commoner, could easily pass through. The stories always confirm the tightness of Qing security. In one version, Kangxi tries to saunter through the pass on horseback. The suspicious guards, unconvinced by his claim that he is a Beijing hat merchant, cuff him and send him back on his way. (The story ends tragically for the assiduous guards. Later, when Kangxi sends for them to reward their diligence, they hang themselves, appalled to learn they have struck the Son of Heaven and certain that a terrible punishment for such lese-majesty awaits them.)

But otherwise the wall – parts of which were still being built and repaired even as the Ming collapsed – became after 1644 a Chinese Maginot Line, particularly in the eyes of China's scholar-official class, which had presided over and felt deeply responsible for the failures of the late Ming: a symbol of Ming Chinese military weakness, collapse and conquest by, yet again, foreign 'barbarians'. Wan Sitong, a late-seventeenth-century historian and poet only six years old at the time of the fall of the Ming, was in a better position than most to pronounce on questions of the recent past, as one of the authors hired by the Qing government to compile the standard *History of the Ming* in the early decades of the new dynasty. He spoke for everyone – and particularly for anyone who had given up part or all of their lives building frontier walls – in expressing the sense of absurdity and futility that clothed the raising of walls by all dynasties since the Qin, but especially the Ming:

> The men of Qin built the Long Wall as a defence against the barbarians.
> Up went the Long Wall and down came the empire.
> People are still laughing about it today.
> Who would have imagined, then, that the Ming, to protect themselves
>> from northern enemies
> Would also decide building walls was the answer to all their problems.
> They called theirs the border wall, instead of the Long Wall.
> Endlessly they built walls, without ever pausing for breath.
> As soon as it was announced the walls were built in the east
> It would be reported that hordes of barbarians had raided in the west.
> They rampaged through collapsed walls, as if over flat ground,
> Plundering whatever and wherever they liked.
> When the barbarians retreated, up went the walls again.
> The builders worked from dawn till dusk, and what was the use?
> The gentry and ministers all squandered government funds
> Wasting money needed for farming.
> …
> Why did we build walls for 10,000 *li*?
> Dynasty after dynasty has done the same thing.
> So why do we only laugh at the First Emperor of Qin?[51]

Now that the wall had officially ceased to perform, amid such disgrace and humiliation, its intended practical function, the stage was set for it to become a decorative tourist attraction, a vainglorious historical fudge; in short, for the wall by all the names it had been known over its 2,000-year history – the Long Wall, the Frontier, the Border Wall, the Nine Border

Garrisons – to become wrenched from its ignominious history and rechristened Great, by impressionable visitors unfamiliar with the true extent and complexity of its failures, and determined only to worship it unconditionally.

CHAPTER ELEVEN

How Barbarians Made
the Great Wall

In 1659, the thirty-six-year-old son of a Belgian tax collector sailed into Macao, the island off the south coast of China claimed by Portuguese traders and missionaries a century earlier. It soon became apparent to the new arrival, an astronomer and missionary called Ferdinand Verbiest, that he had reached the Middle Kingdom at a deeply inauspicious moment in Sino–Western relations. A year or so later, Verbiest made his way to Beijing, where he embarked upon the defence of Adam Schall, a German astronomer accused by xenophobic Confucian ministers of plotting insurrection against the emperor. The imperial verdict does not, perhaps, testify to Verbiest's skills in advocacy: Schall was condemned to death by strangulation, while Verbiest himself was imprisoned. Fortunately for the two northern Europeans, an earthquake in 1665 shook the emperor's confidence in his own judgements and an amnesty secured their release. Schall, broken by his captivity, died within a year. Verbiest, a better astronomer than advocate, however, stayed on in Beijing until 1669, when an incompetent Confucian official gave him an opportunity to win the favour of the new, teenage emperor, Kangxi. On Christmas Day 1668, the president of the Bureau of Astronomy – Schall's former accuser – published a calendar for 1669; Verbiest challenged it and volunteered to prove his superior expertise in a competitive experiment. Two weeks and a correct prediction of the height and angle of the sun later, Verbiest became the new director of the Bureau of Astronomy; his opponent was dismissed and arrested.

By his death in 1688 — at which point he was fluent in six languages, including Chinese and Manchu — Verbiest had laboured for almost two decades on behalf of the imperial court. He had drawn up calendars, built huge and elaborate astronomical instruments, as well as an observatory in which to use them, and overseen the forging of 132 large cannons (on which he eccentrically inscribed the names of male and female Christian saints), subsequently used to arm China's city walls. When not engaged in state projects, he was occupied in devising more frivolous knick-knacks for the emperor's pleasure: sundials, water clocks and pumps for water features in palace gardens. Perhaps his most innovative moment was an early attempt at an automobile, in which he strapped a boiler on to an oven, attached a paddle wheel, gears and wheels, and steam-motored around the corridors of the Forbidden City for an hour or so. In the process, he struck up a close and affectionate working relationship with Kangxi, whose civil servant he effectively became.

By most reckonings, Verbiest was a remarkable man: to travel to the Far East and become the favourite astronomer-inventor of the Chinese emperor was, by seventeenth-century Belgian standards, unusual. Among his immediate peers, however, his career and travels were not entirely exceptional. Verbiest, like Schall, was one of several hundred Jesuits dispatched to China from the sixteenth century onwards, part of the proselytizing Catholic diaspora to the new, extra-European world in the wake of Columbus's voyages of discovery, and one of a handful of these priests who won access to the heartland of imperial power.

As a firm imperial favourite, in the early 1680s Verbiest accompanied his Qing patron twice — on one trip alone with 60,000 men, 100,000 horses, a 'massive equipage of drums and musical instruments' and the emperor's grandmother — on safari in Manchuria as measurer-in-chief. 'I was to be always at the Emperor's side,' Verbiest recorded, 'so that I might make in his presence the necessary observations for determining the state of the heavens, the elevation of the Pole, the grade of the terrain, and to calculate with my mathematical instruments the height and distance of the mountains. He could also conveniently ask me to tell him about meteorites, and any other problems of physics or mathematics.'[1]

Far more than imperial pleasure trips, Kangxi's northern expeditions fulfilled a crucial symbolic and practical function in early Manchu rule over China. They gave the emperor an opportunity to demonstrate the continued vitality of his nomadic heritage, proving to his 60,000-strong retinue that his competence in the arts of riding, archery and hunting in the terrain of his homeland matched the robust example of his conqueror ancestors. In Kangxi's case, his passion for safaris was no cosmetic exhibition: on hunts, he displayed a boyishly ingenuous enthusiasm, making painstaking inventories of his kills. Furthermore, outings beyond the old border wall line provided the Manchu troops with vital field training: shooting, making camp, formation riding.[2] At the same time as flaunting their steppe traditions, however, the Manchu emperors also adapted significantly to the country they had conquered, making great show of educating themselves in the civilizing ways of the Chinese. After an initial period of brutal conquest, the Qing wooed the native literati into enormous, state-funded classical Chinese publishing ventures. Qianlong, Kangxi's grandson, claimed to be the author of 42,000 poems, energetically collected Chinese calligraphy, paintings, porcelain and bronzes, and even kowtowed before Confucius's tablet in the sage's native province of Shandong. Kangxi, Yongzheng and Qianlong, the three rulers who, between them, steered Qing China into and through its eighteenth-century 'Prosperous Age' (Qianlong's own phrase), attempted to tread a workable middle way between these two political traditions, more or less successfully presenting themselves as dynamically in touch with their muscular Manchu roots, and at the same time upholding bookbound Confucian orthodoxy. (By the close of Qianlong's reign – the last decade of the eighteenth century – cracks in the Manchu imperium were beginning to show. With the population more than doubling to 313 million in the second half of the eighteenth century, with resources and opportunities severely strained, authoritarian emperors at the political centre and an overstretched, underpaid regional bureaucracy had become incapable of meeting local needs; late-eighteenth-century China was an endemically corrupt society on the cusp of tumbling into a century of rebellions and insurrections of increasingly cataclysmic magnitude.)

While, back in the more vigorous 1680s, the Kangxi emperor enjoyed himself dispatching bears, wild boar and tigers, his excursions north-east may have given Verbiest the opportunity to research another of his declared interests: a possible new route for missionaries to pass between Western Europe and Beijing, via Moscow, less fraught than the pirate-infested voyage from Europe to Macao.

Establishing a precursor of the Trans-Siberian Railway lay beyond the abilities of even this exceptionally inventive priest and Verbiest seems to have made little headway with his scheme. However, it was perhaps the fruitless reconnaissance trips for this route that turned Father Verbiest into a passionate admirer of the structure originally designed to prevent precisely the free passage between China and foreign lands further north that he hoped for: the old Ming border wall.

Verbiest was, quite understandably, impressed by what he saw. The wall he visited would have been the bricked line of defences snaking vertiginously over the peaks north-east of Beijing, from Gubeikou to Shanhaiguan, the undulating vista celebrated in a thousand awe-struck tourist brochures. What he probably would not have seen was the mud embankment that the wall became further west, or the holes ripped in remoter parts of the defence line by Mongols and by Manchus earlier in the century. 'That prodigious wall of China,' Verbiest exclaimed. 'The seven wonders of the world put together are not comparable to this work; and all that Fame hath published concerning it among the *Europeans,* comes far short of what I myself have seen.'[3]

On his original passage to China, Verbiest had been accompanied by another Jesuit, a skilled cartographer and middle-aged China hand called Martino Martini, who was making a return to China after a ten-year absence. Although Martini died shortly afterwards, in 1661, the crowning achievement of his life's research had been published eight years earlier: his *Atlas Sinensis,* a province-by-province collection of the most complete and authoritative maps of China to date, accompanied by short descriptions of the country, that won him acclaim among European cartographers as the father of Chinese geography. Martini's map gave a physical form to Verbiest's hyperbole, drawing a thick, continuous, crenellated line across the north of China, interrupted only by a group of mountains and the occasional river. 'This celebrated wall,' enthused Martini, 'is very famous ... longer than the entire length of Asia.'

[I]t circles the entire empire ... I find that it exceeds three hundred German leagues in length ... It is nowhere interrupted except in the northern parts, at the city of Xiuen in the province of Pequing, where a small part is composed of horrible and inaccessible mountains which join onto the sturdy wall ... The rest is uniform ... The height of the wall is thirty Chinese cubits, and the width is twelve, and often fifteen.[4]

After making such wild generalizations about the state of the entire wall based, presumably, only on observations of its condition near Beijing, Martini proceeded to set in place another cornerstone of the modern myth of the Great Wall: its extreme antiquity.

The person who began this work was the emperor Xius ... He built this wall starting in the twenty-second year of his reign, which was 215 years before Christ ... In the space of five years, which is incredibly short, it was built so strongly that if anyone was able to slip a nail between the cut stones, the builder of that part would be put to death ... The work is magnificent, huge, and admirable, and has lasted right up to the present time without any injury or destruction.[5]

The Jesuits were not the first Westerners to report on the wall. Since the days of the Roman empire, when Ammianus Marcellinus had described the land of the Seres (silk – the commodity synonymous with China in the minds of Roman consumers) as surrounded by the 'summits of lofty walls', Europe had possessed a vague, mythical awareness of a Chinese wall.[6] During the first millennium AD in the Middle East, legends sprang up around the idea of an iron wall built in Central Asia by Alexander the Great between two mountains known as the 'Breasts of the North', designed to imprison the fiendish northern hordes of Gog and Magog, who, the Old Testament prophesied, 'shall wait until the appointed time and then descend upon the land like a storm bringing death and devastation in the last days of the earth'.[7] As over the centuries the steppe generated wave upon wave of belligerent horsemen – Scythians, Turks, Mongols – it began to resemble more and more plausibly the spawning ground of Armageddon, and Alexander's mythical wall blurred into reports of Chinese walls that began to seep into the West after Europeans and their religious ambassadors started taking to the seas. Catholic missionaries, merchants and historians of China in the decades predating the Jesuit invasion – none of them eyewitnesses – had reckoned the wall to be between 320 and 2,400 kilometres long, an exercise in gap-filling between natural, mountainous defences.[8]

While not exactly precise in their descriptions of the wall, these accounts at least avoided outlandish exaggeration. But it was the installation of the Jesuits in the seventeenth century that inflated earlier, more restrained Western reports of Chinese walls into one, overwhelmingly Great Wall. In its Jesuit version, moreover, the wall was not permitted to exist in isolation, as a monument to be admired simply because of its prodigious size; the idea of, and reverence for, the Great Wall were an integral part of Jesuit adulation of China itself. In the most glowing Jesuit accounts, authors begin to wax analytical and philosophical, as well as descriptive, about the virtues of the wall and the people who built it: '[W]e cannot but admire the Care and Efforts of the Chinese, who seem to have made use of all the Means, which human forecast could suggest, for the Defence of their Kingdom, and for preserving the public

Tranquility.'⁹ The most famous and successful Jesuit travellers to China had to love China and its achievements – including the Great Wall – because they had invested so heavily in integrating themselves into the country (in the interests of winning the population over to Catholicism), to the point of compromising elements of the Christian mission that had drawn them there in the first place. This construction of the Great Wall in Western imaginations overlaid a significant shift in early modern European attitudes to China: the realization that, while clear superiority in weaponry was still lacking, extracting anything out of China – whether trading profits or converts – would require Western envoys to massage the Chinese worldview; to embrace Chinese mores and thereby prop up the empire's age-old cultural superiority complex.

That the Jesuit missionaries should have fallen so deeply in love with China in general, and with its wall in particular, is one of the historical ironies of the seventeenth century. The Jesuit presence in China, a branch of Catholic expansionism, sprang directly out of a new, imperialist and profit-hungry European impulse to trade and conquer. As fifteenth-century Europe recuperated from the devastating wars and plagues of the previous hundred years, it started to nose its way outward along unexplored trade routes. In 1428, attempting to recoup losses incurred in assaults by the Mongols and Turks, the sultan of Egypt squeezed his European customers by raising the price of pepper by more than 60 per cent. The need to repair their ruined profit margins impelled European merchants to search for an alternative sea route to the spices of the East, one that bypassed Alexandria and its exorbitant demands. Under the helmsmanship of their monarch, Prince Henry the Navigator, Portuguese sailors crept down the African coast, capturing Ceuta in the north, rounding the Cape of Good Hope and mooring at Calcutta, confronting Europe with a mass of alien lands, peoples and opportunity. To monarchs and merchants, these discoveries offered power and profit. To the Catholic Church of southern Europe – spurred by a newly aggressive self-confidence following the recent expulsion of the Moors from

Spain – they promised a potentially huge harvest of pagan souls.

The expansion of Europe was powered by an intolerant alliance between state and Church, for both of whom the earlier Crusades had legitimized the use of force to spread the Christian faith. Scenting massive opportunities for conversion, fifteenth-century Popes sanctified imperialist conquest by successively granting the Portuguese political power over lands conquered from heathens. After Columbus accidentally discovered the Americas, thinking they were the Indies by another route, South America took the full weight of this belligerent, nationalistic Catholicism, its people soon too weakened by exposure to new European contagions to resist. Paganism provided the rationale behind the conquest and exploitation of the New World: because the inhabitants of America were pagans, went Catholic writ, they deserved to have their wealth taken away from them, to undergo any oppression necessary to convert them into God-fearing Christians.

The Portuguese – the first Europeans to reach East Asia in significant numbers in the era of maritime exploration – would have used precisely the same forceful approach to bring China to heel, if they had not encountered substantial opposition from a regime well able to stand up for itself in battle. When, early in the sixteenth century, the Portuguese tried to barge their way undiplomatically on to the mainland at Canton – building a fort, buying Chinese children, trading at will – the Ming government dispatched a war fleet, sank a number of Portuguese junks and executed all the prisoners they took. (In the process, the Ming did not neglect to make careful note of the design of Portuguese cannons, replicas of which were subsequently installed on the forts of their Border Wall.) It was later thanks only to internal Chinese turmoil rather than Portuguese negotiating skill that, around 1557, the Europeans were able, finally, to inveigle their way on to Macao, where they built themselves houses and churches, and from which island the missionary effort was launched.

At the outset, European missionaries – many of them Dominicans and Franciscans, the orders that had fallen upon the opportunities offered for conversion by South America – made exactly the same errors as their merchant counterparts. Arrogantly Euro-centric, the first missionaries landed in China without authorization or knowledge of the language and still expected converts to come flocking. They were quickly sent back to Europe by brisk officials, where they dropped heavy hints to figures in authority that there 'is no hope of converting [the Chinese], unless one has recourse to force and unless they give way before the soldiers'.[10] A commando-style landing by four Franciscan priests in 1579 resulted in their capture and the death of one in a Chinese prison. 'No monastery of nuns,' sighed a wistful Spanish court historian contemplating the Chinese empire, 'better observes the rule of cloister.'[11]

Instead, it took a radical accommodation with Chinese custom and language for the missionary effort even to be permitted to exist on the mainland, an accommodation that was accomplished by the Jesuit order, whose missionary activities were predicated on the principle of cultural adaptation. First of all, St Ignatius of Loyola, the founder of the order, decreed that his followers should study the language of whichever country they operated in, and stipulated no distinctive habit, thus enabling, at least in theory, members of the order to integrate themselves into their local environment. Secondly, the Jesuit order concentrated on instructing its members in the most advanced aspects of Western culture and learning, in order to be able to sell European religion as part of a complete and practical package of civilization and knowledge to potential believers. Recognizing China as the sophisticated, highly literate society that it was, the Jesuits were well equipped to tackle two tasks there: to please the Chinese by demonstrating that they were both sufficiently morally and intellectually elevated to study Chinese culture, and to achieve sufficient fluency in the Chinese language to convey to potential converts the merits of their own Christian culture and learning. In 1577, the senior Jesuit in charge of the East Asian operation ordered priests to start learning

Chinese. Five years later, after the Jesuits had started to learn how to observe Chinese etiquette – above all, how to kowtow – they were granted a small patch of land on the southern Chinese mainland where they would build a house and church. The diligent application of Matteo Ricci – the most famous Jesuit, and the first to reach the Chinese capital – to the scholarship of both Europe (science, mathematics, geography, theology) and China (its language, its Confucian literature and philosophy) during the twenty-three years he spent in China won him an invitation to Beijing, where he lived for the last nine years of his life, thereby establishing at the very centre of the Chinese world a Catholic presence that was inherited by his successors, including the unfortunate Adam Schall.

Thanks to Ricci's linguistic brilliance and hard work, Catholic priests were no longer facing inevitable imprisonment, torture and expulsion (dead or alive) from China (though the Jesuit position was always vulnerable to the jealousy of court astronomers eager to discredit their rivals as foreign traitors, as Schall painfully discovered). But an objective assessment of the career of Ricci, and of later Jesuits whose position in Beijing was made possible by his diligence, suggests that on both material and psychological levels China emerged the victor of this East–West encounter. The Chinese were able to enjoy the most advanced fruits of Western learning, as expounded by the learned Jesuits: Qianlong's disdain for Lord Macartney's technological offerings of 1793 could in part be explained by the fact that the Jesuits resident at his court had long since furnished him with equally, if not more, sophisticated gadgets. And seeing some of Europe's most gifted, erudite men voluntarily immerse themselves in Confucian philosophy could only have confirmed confidence in the superiority of the Chinese worldview: that the externals of Western civilization (maps, astronomical instruments, cannon) could be safely and even usefully absorbed into the fundamentals of Chinese culture, without in any way threatening the pre-eminence of the latter; that China was the magnetic centre to which tribute offerings were inevitably brought by admirers, but to which serious, radical cultural alternatives could never be envisaged.

A few years into his stay in China, beyond his facial features and abundant beard, Ricci looked and behaved overwhelmingly like a Chinese: wearing the hat and the long purple silk robe of the Chinese scholar-official, debating the Confucian classics, bowing and kneeling exactly when required. If practical Western learning and technology were originally meant to be the spoonful of sugar disguising the bitter medicine of Christianity, Ricci's patients proved adept at guzzling the former and spitting out the latter. A few of his many visitors, admittedly, converted to Christianity; most, however, simply wanted to see his clocks and globes, his map of the world, to wonder at this barbarian's ability to master Chinese. In a similar way, the demands of Verbiest's court position – as astronomer and adviser to the emperor – forced him not only to reduce his efforts to make converts; he even had to abridge his own devotions. And Ricci's struggle to translate Christianity into Chinese resulted in his Confucianizing Christianity rather than Christianizing Confucians. To avoid alienating potential converts, Ricci bent over backwards to accommodate traditional Chinese beliefs into Catholicism. Ancestor worship, for example, the ritual cornerstone of Confucian morality, Ricci deemed entirely compatible with Christian belief, deciding it was merely an act of respect, devoid of religious implications.

Most usefully of all, the Chinese – without making any conscious attempt to do so – gained in the Jesuits a largely creditable, influential group of enthusiastic Western propagandists. Having invested so much effort in ingratiating themselves with the Chinese, Jesuits such as Ricci and Verbiest were committed to justifying their life's work by proselytizing the virtues of China in the letters, diaries and book-length accounts they sent to Europe. When, back in the European heartland, the seventeenth-century Catholic establishment began excoriating the Jesuit accommodation of Chinese rituals as unacceptably heterodox, the Jesuits felt obliged to compose ever more extravagant paeans to the glories of China, to create in their writings the image of a glittering civilization whose fundamental virtues would justify their own compromises with a pagan society.

To Ricci, China presented a salutary example of order, unity and moral orthodoxy to a Europe being torn apart by post-Reformation religious conflict. Its crops and fruits were appetizing and abundant, its flora rich and varied, and the government of 'this wonderful empire' dominated by regard for dignity, honour, merit, learning, impartiality and moderation.[12] 'The ancient kingdom of China derived its name from the universal practice of urbanity and politeness,' he exulted, 'and this is one of the five cardinal virtues esteemed by them above all others'.[13] Even Chinese wine, Ricci observed, seemed thoughtfully brewed to avoid giving the drinker a hangover.[14]

The Jesuit cult of the Great Wall was merely one of the most obvious ironies of their decision to serve as propagandists for China in the West, and illustrates better than anything else the degree to which their critical faculties were blunted by the need to defend their investment in China: they were, in effect, worshipping at the shrine of a structure expressly designed to keep people such as themselves out of the country. During the sixteenth and seventeenth centuries, under the Jesuit gaze, China's border defences metamorphosed from the plain 'wall' of earlier travellers' accounts, to 'a tremendous wall' (1616), 'this famous wall' (1681) 'that prodigious wall' (1683), 'this great Wall' (1693) and, finally, 'the GREAT WALL' (1738).[15] By the late seventeenth century, the celebrated, painstaking erudition of the order had, in the case of the wall, been waived in the interests of propaganda: ignoring the bad geographical fit between the description of the sketchily constructed Qin 'long wall' in Sima Qian's *Historical Records* and the brick-and-stone reality of the Ming wall near Beijing, Jesuit observers combined the two and proclaimed their amalgamated Great Wall 'almost all built with brick ... above 1,800 Years' old, and miraculously 'scarce the worse' for its age.[16]

Although a handful of well-travelled priests tried to tone down the cult by pointing out the wall's less substantial appearance beyond the main passes, the tone of most reports remained rapturously overawed. After 1735, when another Jesuit, Jean Baptiste Du Halde, published *A Description of the Empire of China* – a compendium of the accounts of other Jesuits, including Verbiest, that found its way on to the bookshelves of many of the eighteenth century's most interested Western observers of China – the Jesuits had sealed the West's view of the wall: 'terrassed, and cased with Brick ... wide enough for five or six Horsemen to march abreast with ease'.[17] Gone, for the time being, was any sense of the wall's historical failings, of its gaps and ruins, of the relative youth of the Ming wall in the north-east. Even the wall's ignominious role in permitting the Manchu conquest of 1644 provoked only a phlegmatic sigh of 'Such is the vicissitude of human Affairs.'[18]

~

In 1703, a nine-year-old French boy called François Arouet began his studies at the College of Saint Louis-le-Grand, behind the Sorbonne in Paris. At the time the most prestigious and fashionable school in France, the Jesuit-run college would nurture some of eighteenth-century France's most notorious intellects – including Robespierre and the Marquis de Sade. Arouet would himself become one of its best-known and, for the most part, celebrated alumni under the pen-name that he adopted in 1718, after a year spent imprisoned in the Bastille for spiking his verse with social criticism: Voltaire.

Despite the famed excellence of his Jesuit teachers, Voltaire was generally unaffectionate in later reminiscences about his educational experiences at Louis-le-Grand. In his *Philosophical Dictionary,* he recalled that as a child he 'learnt Latin and nonsense'.[19] While dining at the house of Mr and Mrs Alexander Pope in London, he cheerfully unearthed a barely repressed memory of unhappy times at school. Asked why his constitution was so poor by his early thirties, he informed his nonplussed hostess that 'those damned Jesuits, when I was a boy, bugger'd me to such a degree that I shall never get over it as long as I live.'[20]

In his lifetime, Voltaire was not the Jesuits' only critic. As the Rites Controversy – which turned on the allegation that, in their desire to make converts beyond Europe, the Jesuits were unacceptably distorting the faith to acclimatize it to local conditions – gathered pace throughout the eighteenth century, opposition to the Jesuits within the Catholic Church intensified. To their clerical detractors, Jesuit activities in China – where the most prominent Jesuits dressed as Chinese scholar-officials and became part of the state's Confucian machine – were a perfect example of the order's opportunistic capitulation to pagans.

Beyond the rigid doctrinal confines of the Catholic establishment, however, Jesuit reporting about worlds beyond Europe was being embraced by some of the most original and enquiring minds of the era. By the late seventeenth century, Europe was starting to break out of an intellectual universe circumscribed by classical orthodoxy and the Old Testament, to comprehend that world history went beyond Christian Europe's boundaries of understanding. The elastication of Europe's temporal and geographical frontiers had begun: with the first glimmerings of geological enlightenment that, within a hundred years, would stretch the history of the earth from 6,000 years into millions, making a mockery of the Bible's Creationist timeline; and with the awareness of new societies around whose edges Europeans had so far only skirted. The erosion of old, Euro-centric certainties encouraged thinkers to prize individual reason over inherited theological orthodoxy, to search for relativistic, tolerant intellectual frameworks that could absorb the sense of shock generated by dramatically expanding horizons.

Probably no single non-European country posed as much of a challenge to Christian Euro-centrism as China. As the first Europeans – most of them Jesuit priests – took up residence in China and began to send back detailed reports of the Middle Kingdom, Europe became aware of a state that existed far beyond the pale of Christian civilization and that, in the eyes of many *philosophes,* compared more than favourably with its European counterparts: more rational, more orderly, more tolerant, more scholarly. In Jesuit histories of China, scholars of the eighteenth century identified a continuous history that existed without reference to Christian chronologies, that stretched back almost 5,000 years, to 2952 BC, 600 years before the supposed date of the Flood. Intellectual admiration was reinforced by an appreciation of China's material artefacts. As the Portuguese, Spanish and Dutch levered open the doors to trade, more and more Far Eastern objects found their way into European homes: soft silks, delicate porcelains and carved cabinets that for decades would prove beyond the technical skills of European imitators. By the late eighteenth century, the love of Chinese goods had percolated into the consciousness of European designers and architects, into the lacquer craze of Madame de Pompadour and Marie Antoinette, into the extravagant copper dragons of the Prince Regent's Pavilion at Brighton.

For Voltaire, an incorrigible, polemical critic of dogma, a true man of the Enlightenment, China represented a particularly choice counter-example to the France of his day. As Louis XIV's reign drew to a close amid a welter of insolvency, military defeats and religious intolerance, French despotism in its present manifestation seemed to have little to recommend itself to Voltaire, who spent substantial portions of his adult life imprisoned in or exiled from his native France, fleeing censorship and persecution for his feuds with nobility and Church. In China and its national philosophy, Confucianism, Voltaire identified a highly literary civilization distinguished by its antiquity, its abundance of population, its elevation of literati to positions of national leadership, its tolerance of faiths, its lack of an oppressive church bureaucracy, its enlightened rulers. (Voltaire was helped towards his laudatory conclusions about the Chinese empire through being roughly contemporary with Qianlong, the last of the three great Qing emperors, who between them had overseen an unprecedented expansion in China's frontiers and population, while being themselves energetic sponsors and practitioners of the literary arts.) In short, Voltaire summarized in his *Philosophical Dictionary,* the constitution of [the Chinese] empire is in fact the best in the world, the only one founded entirely on paternal power ... the only one in which the governor of a province is punished when he fails to win the acclamation of the people upon leaving office; the only one that has instituted prizes for virtue, while everywhere else the laws are restricted to punishing crime; the only one that has made its conquerors adopt its laws ... four thousand years ago, when we couldn't even read, the Chinese knew all the absolutely useful things we boast about today.[21]

Although Voltaire was often at loggerheads with the Jesuits as representatives of the Catholic bureaucracy, he swallowed their version of China whole, filling his bookshelves with Jesuit pro-China propaganda, including Du Halde's 1735 *Description*. And like the sinophile texts that he devoured, Voltaire loved the Great Wall – most of the time. 'The great wall,' Voltaire expounded in 1756, '[which] was built one hundred and thirty-seven years before our aera, subsists to this day; it is five hundred leagues in circumference, rising on the tops of mountains, and descending down precipices, being almost everywhere twenty feet broad and above thirty feet high: a monument superior to the pyramids of Egypt, both by its utility and dimensions.'[22] Eight years later, in his *Philosophical Dictionary*, his wall-worship was undiminished: 'It isn't worth my while here to set the Great Wall of China up against the monuments of other nations; the Wall simply leaves them all behind in the dust. Neither is it worth reiterating that the pyramids of Egypt are merely childish and useless heaps in comparison with this great work[.]'[23]

Voltaire's love of China sometimes got the better of him, leading him into situations perilous to his artistic integrity and personal dignity. In 1755, he completed *The Orphan of China*, a roughly historical play set in the time of Genghis Khan that he turned into a fairly blunt instrument for hammering home his own view of the superiority of Chinese civilization, as 'a great example of the natural superiority which reason and genius provide over blind force and barbarousness', and to glorify the importance of the arts to contemporary France.[24] In the play, Genghis

Khan and his Mongol hordes conquer China by force, only to be conquered in turn themselves by the sciences and arts of the vanquished
nation. Years later, the septuagenarian Voltaire was still sufficiently in
love with his depiction of Genghis to cast himself in the role in a domestic production of the play, performed for the benefit of an unlucky
Edward Gibbon, who afterwards declared himself 'much struck with the
ridiculous figure of Voltaire at seventy acting a Tartar conqueror with a
hollow broken voice, and making love to a very ugly niece of about
fifty'.[25]

Perhaps the greatest damage that China did to Voltaire was to his intellectual consistency. Voltaire studied Chinese history and society not for
the advancement of scholarly accuracy – he never made any effort actually to see China for himself – but for the sake of whichever polemic he
happened to be concentrating on at any one moment: against the clerisy,
in favour of the arts, against the political institutions of contemporary
France. Like the Jesuits before him, Voltaire had distinctly ulterior
motives for lauding China. As a result, his sinophilia wavered according
to the case he was wanting to make at the time. By 1766, perhaps
responding to the seeds of absolute scepticism planted by Hume in his
1757 *Natural History of Religion,* Voltaire was starting to judge China and
its achievements no longer as a single, unified counter-example to everything he disliked about contemporary Europe, but on more selectively
utilitarian grounds. While still able to praise China's laws, and Confucius's
maxims, Voltaire began to find his earlier vision of China 'over exalted'.[26]
Why was their knowledge of science currently as advanced as that of
'Europe in the tenth, eleventh and twelfth centuries'? 'Their great
progress in antiquity contrasts puzzlingly with their present ignorance. I
have always thought that their respect for their ancestors – a form of religion for them – was a paralysis that prevented them from progressing scientifically.'[27] He now refused to speak further of 'this five-hundred-league
wall, built 220 years before our era; it is a work as futile as it is vast, and
moreover unfortunate in having seemed at first useful, since it was not

able to defend the Empire'.[28] When Voltaire took the side of the Moderns against the Ancients in their famous Quarrel – which resurfaced in the eighteenth century, focused on contemporary discussions of ancient republicanism – he forcefully declared China's wall 'useless'.

The Chinese, more than two hundred years before our vulgar era, built this great wall which could not protect them from the invasions of the Tartars ... The great wall of China is a monument to fear ... testifying to the patience of the Chinese, but to no superior genius. Neither the Chinese nor the Egyptians were able to make a single statue that bears comparison to the work of our sculptors today.[29]

As Voltaire dithered over China and its wall, as both lost the wholehearted support of one of Europe's most agile minds, the eighteenth-century pendulum of opinion on China began to swing decisively. No longer lauded as a repository of political virtue and reason, China in European eyes started to become an empire paralysed by worship of the past, exhausted by emblematically vast, pointless projects that had failed to prove themselves by modern, utilitarian standards. The Great Wall had completed its journey from fact, to myth, to defining symbol of the country it wound across.

~

England was China's great rival for Voltaire's affections. In 1725, he fled over the Channel, escaping a feud with a brutish French aristocrat and expecting to find a sanctuary of liberty and reason, peopled with readers of Locke and Newton. He was inevitably disappointed by reality, but not sufficiently to tarnish his praise for the nation's free-thinking virtues in an intellectualized travel book, *Letters Concerning the English Nation*.[30] Between Voltaire's two foreign passions themselves, however, there was little love lost.

Ever since the Portuguese first reached the south China coast at the start of the sixteenth century, eventually winning for themselves Macao, several of Europe's imperial naval powers, including England, had struggled for a similar trading foothold at the edge of the Middle Kingdom.

Many learned from Portugal's early mistakes, especially the Dutch, who, from their first trade mission of 1655 onwards, bent over backwards – or rather, in practice, forwards – to please the Chinese by complying with every element of Chinese tributary etiquette, and particularly the kow-tow. England's representatives, however, were not prepared to take such a straightforwardly pragmatic approach. England's earliest major trade expeditions to China coincided with an intensification of national self-importance and of the aggressive, self-confident impatience that would drive the acquisition of the British Empire, with advances in technology and weaponry, and with the willingness to use them in the furthering of colonial expansion. Unlike the Enlightenment *philosophes,* British military men and merchants wasted little time theorizing about the virtues of the Chinese system of governance; they wanted the treatment and conces-sions owed to them as upstanding members of a global system of diplo-macy and trade they were building for their own benefit. When the English were stonewalled by China's own older and even more entrenched view of international diplomacy, relations soured.

The tone of the British Empire's belligerent stance towards China was set by a 1748 travelogue of an abortive stay in China written by Commodore George Anson, who in July 1743 sailed his battered warship into Canton, demanding help with repairs and supplies. Instead, he spent a frustrating and sultry two months being ignored by the Chinese viceroy, who, Anson was informed by proxies, was too busy and too hot to hold an audience. In his resulting account of China, Anson replaced the sedate, idealizing intellectual tourism of the French Enlightenment with the contemptuous impatience of British jingo imperialism. Anson was frankly disgusted by China – its 'rude and inartificial' written language, its 'second rate' technical skills, its 'poverty of genius'. Remarking on the weakness of its defences, he remarked hopefully that the 'cowardice of the inhabitants, and the want of proper military regulations' doomed China 'not only to the attempts of any potent State but to the ravages of every petty Invader'.[31]

Anson may well have taken lessons in style from that barometer of eighteenth-century British opinion on China, Daniel Defoe. After bankrupting himself by the age of thirty, in middle age Defoe came to depend precariously on his success in wooing middle-class readers through his polemical articles, pamphlets and fiction. In *The Farther Adventures of Robinson Crusoe,* opportunistically flung out on to the printing presses in 1719 only four months after the phenomenally successful *Robinson Crusoe,* Defoe painted a raw picture of ebullient, gunpowder-fuelled English imperialism. After Crusoe sets out on a second bout of travels, he is forced into an accidental landing on the south coast of China. From the coast he makes a long journey inland, up to Nanjing and then Beijing, his account of which is geared so as to pour the maximum amount of scorn on his host country, and reflect the maximum amount of glory on to Europe, and England in particular.[32] Eventually, Crusoe makes his way to 'the great *China* wall' north of Beijing, where he 'stood still an hour to look at it on every side, near, and far off'. He finds very little about it to his liking, beginning with a distinctly backhanded compliment to its builders and engineers: 'a very great work it is, going over hills and mountains in a needless track, where the rocks are impassable, and the precipices such as no enemy could possibly enter'. Asked his opinion by an irksome guide, 'who had been extolling it for the wonder of the world', Crusoe snidely replies that 'it was a most excellent thing to keep off the *Tartars*', a joke which his dense Chinese interlocutor naturally fails to understand. After this restrained opening skirmish, Crusoe can control himself no longer:

Well, says I, seignior, do you think it would stand out an army of our country people, with a good train of artillery; or our engineers, with tow companies of miners; would not they batter it down in ten days, that an army might enter in battalia, or blow it up in the air, foundation and all, that there should be no sign of it left?

Crusoe ensures we know that he has had the last word to his Chinese guide about 'this mighty *nothing* call'd a wall': 'when he knew what I had said, he was dumb all the rest of the way, and we heard no more of his fine story of the Chinese power and greatness'.[33]

Defoe's armchair fulminations against China and its wall – his crude, chauvinistic confidence and pride in European technology, his contempt for China and its pretensions to greatness – could have come out of the mouth of any of nineteenth-century Britain's gunboat diplomats. At the time of their writing, admittedly, Crusoe's threats were more imperialist bluster than political reality. Far from overawing future colonial peoples, throughout the eighteenth century over-adventurous Britons were often humiliatingly bested and held captive in the diverse parts of the world in which they were aspiring to build their empire: by Barbary corsairs, Algerian slave-owners and Mughal emperors.[34] But as the eighteenth century became the nineteenth, as the industrial revolution and international competition for wealth, territory and power gathered steam, and put muscle on the bones of wishful imperialist rhetoric, the favoured topics of the Enlightenment – science, universalism, progress for the betterment of mankind – survived, barely recognizably, in more intolerant, actively belligerent guises. Stoked with self-confidence by technological great leaps forward, propelled onwards to new forceful acquisitions by rivalries with neighbouring states, the imperialist European nations became convinced that they, and they alone, had invented the way of modernity and progress for the contemporary world. Far from searching for inspiration from non-Western models, they now embraced a mission to disseminate (by force if necessary) their vision of Progress – the inalienable right to free trade, the sovereignty of the nation-state, both buttressed by the triumph of Western science – to those unfortunate parts of the world as yet unenlightened. To brashly self-assured British visitors to China of the nineteenth century and beyond – Robinson Crusoe's intellectual descendants – the Great Wall became a double-edged symbol: an unarguably impressive fixture on the anthropological museum tour that was leisured travel around the imperial world, but also the emblematic folly of a crumbling, atavistic power and a needling reminder of the inevitable decline that beset all empires.

~

In July 1861, as summer burned so intensely in Tianjin, the port city south of Beijing, that thirsty soldiers preferred to take their port ration frozen, George Fleming, army doctor and intrepid Victorian traveller, applied for and obtained from the local British consulate a passport to travel over the Great Wall and into Manchuria. Three years previously, such a permit would have been unthinkable, but fortunately for Fleming's plans, twenty-six British and French gunboats, 18,000 troops and an Opium War had since intervened. In 1856, after British dignity had been purportedly outraged by Chinese disrespect to the national flag, Anglo-French forces had surrounded and captured Canton. In April 1858, the allied forces had moored gunboats at the coast near Tianjin, stormed Chinese defences and demanded negotiations. On 26 June, the Qing government had signed the Treaty of Tianjin, granting to the British the right to install ambassadors, consuls, missionaries and jurisdiction over their own subjects in China, to travel, trade, work and hire wherever and howsoever they wanted; in short, to do whatever they liked in the previously locked and bolted realm of Qing China. Loudly and clearly, the treaty demanded 4 million silver *taels'* compensation from the Chinese for British trouble and expense incurred; quietly and more murkily, it legalized the opium trade.

The following year, the Qing court – still suffering from intense waves of the Middle Kingdom superiority complex that it had inherited from the empire it had occupied in 1644, still unable to accept the fact of its military inferiority and political weakness – had thought better of the treaty and taken revenge by sinking four European gunboats on the coast south-east of Beijing. In 1860, 18,000 British and French soldiers had returned to the site of the previous year's debacle and battered the coastal forts for two and a half hours, until white flags were raised. Incensed, the Chinese had responded by kidnapping the thirty-eight members of an

Anglo-French negotiating party, of whom twenty-six died in captivity. But allied forces – led by Lord Elgin – had finally silenced Chinese resistance by looting and burning the Chinese emperor's pleasure sanctuary, the Summer Palace north-west of Beijing, a 60,000 acre complex that included a palace built in the European Baroque style by eighteenth-century Jesuits: 'A memorable day in the history of plunder and destruction,' as one of the British captains present described it.[35] By November 1860, the 1858 treaty had been confirmed, the indemnities quadrupled, and the stage set for a British merchant and missionary invasion to succeed the military. The era of imperialist tourism in China had been born, and George Fleming was to become one of the first to take advantage of it.

By the middle years of the nineteenth century – the decade of the first Opium War – the Qing empire's attempt to combine the martial vigour of the old, steppe-based Manchurian way of life with a Chinese-style administration managed by scholar-officials selected through a Confucian examination system was falling apart. Perhaps the most significant cause of social and political instability was the rampant population upsurge that started in the eighteenth century. For a time, this increase – nourished by New World crops hardy enough to flourish on previously unworkable, peripheral land; fuelling a booming domestic market for regional goods – succeeded in plumping out a surface impression of Chinese prosperity. But as the eighteenth century drew to a close, the strains brought by dramatic population growth were outweighing its benefits, causing acute land shortage, rural destitution and rising food prices. A series of devastating domestic rebellions ensued, often launched by groups driven out by overcrowding or desperation into marginal regions where, remote from local government control, other, heterodox allegiances (to religious fraternities and secret societies) more easily took hold. And at the same time that the land problem began to tear Qing China apart, government armies no longer seemed able to pull off the decisive victories over forces of discontent that had kept the empire more or less pacified since the late seventeenth century. Overstretched by campaigns on its far-flung frontiers, the Qing state was forced to rely increasingly on militias conscripted by local elites to suppress local insurrections, a dependence which steadily leached power and initiative from the political centre.

But it was the assertion of an increasingly insistent and intransigent foreign – and, in particular British – trading presence off China's south coast that triggered some of the nineteenth century's most dramatically damaging assaults on Qing authority. The clash between Britain and China escalated, in part, out of the uncompromising Qing diplomatic worldview, which had, if anything, intensified the traditional imperial Chinese superiority complex towards the outside world. Qing emperors saw themselves not only as rulers of the Chinese *tianxia,* all under heaven, but also – thanks to the massive sprawl of their territories across Mongolia, Manchuria, Xinjiang, Tibet, Taiwan, Yunnan, Burma – as the overlord of lords as far as the diplomatic eye stretched, as heirs to Genghis Khan's vast imperium, as the 'Khan of Khans'. The Qing state, in other words, inherited the long-standing universalistic pretensions of Chinese emperorship and gave them real, political form by expanding its dominions to subsume many of the Chinese empire's traditional challengers. Small wonder then, perhaps, that when the bewigged and frock-coated representatives (Macartney and company) of a small, distant island nation in 1793 petitioned for Qing China to lift trading restrictions against its domestic manufactures and allow it to establish a permanent embassy on Chinese soil – rather than meekly consenting to be expelled, like all other normal tributary barbarians, after a stay within the Celestial Empire legislated to the last nod by Qing guest ritual – the imperious Qianlong gave them short shrift.

Less than fifty years later, in the 1830s, the British were justifiably certain that the Qing empire lacked the ability to resist a reiteration of these demands, provided they were backed by military reinforcements from India. In the intervening decades, the British discovery of opium as the wonder product for which the Chinese could supply an apparently insatiable demand to counterbalance the British lust for tea had critically checked the eighteenth-century rush of foreign silver into China. And yet the British, they constantly reminded the Chinese, still wanted more: they wanted Chinese markets to be opened to Britain's factories and mills. Just as constantly, the Qing government refused, clinging to hubristic ideas of China's military superiority, of its ability to bring foreign barbarians to heel by its civilizing influence, and of its possession of uniquely alluring goods capable of subduing all – even the most unruly – foreigners into tributaries.[36] As he counselled continued resistance to British demands on the eve of the first Opium War, Lin Zexu – the emperor's man in Canton in 1839 – informed his ruler that British gunboats were too big to sail into Chinese rivers, that English soldiers did not know how to use their 'fists or swords. Moreover, their legs are firmly bound with cloth, and consequently it is extremely inconvenient for them to stretch … what is called their power can be controlled without difficulty.'[37] This, as the British, equipped with the very latest weaponry, sailed upriver into the mainland and routed outmoded Chinese fleets and undermanned, disorganized garrisons. The bemused Chinese government responded, insufficiently, by gathering bandits and smugglers into unruly emergency defence militias and by hiring martial arts masters – boasting of their ability to lie underwater for ten hours without needing oxygen – to conceal themselves on river beds and drill holes in barbarian hulls, until official hostilities were stilled by the 1842 Treaty of Nanjing, which forced the Qing to unlock five ports to the principles of British Free Trade; the events of 1858–60 confirmed and continued a process already begun, wrenching China's gates wider apart.

The arrival of European gunboat diplomacy turned the customs and values of Qing China upside down. With the most sanctified spaces of the empire violated, pillaged and destroyed by barbarians, what had been enclosed was now forced open. Between 1840 and 1860, China became the latest and probably the most reluctant corner of the globe to be violently converted to the nineteenth-century orthodoxy of borderless free trade: 'Vast hordes of populations,' exulted the *Illustrated London News* at the conclusion of the first Opium War in 1842, 'breaking through the ignorance and superstition which has for ages enveloped them, will now come out into the open day, and enjoy the freedom of a more expanded civilization, and enter upon prospects immeasurably grander.'[38] The actions of the Europeans even reversed the historical function of the frontier, transforming the Middle Kingdom into the battleground of barbarians and forcing the emperor to flee north in 1860 *beyond* the wall to take refuge at Jehol.

Fleming's reaction to China, as related in his 1863 account of his journey, *Travels on Horseback in Mantchu Tartary,* was so scornfully adverse that the reader cannot help wonder why he went there in the first place, then spent so many months engaged in uncomfortable travel between Tianjin and Manchuria. Like Anson before him, Fleming found practically everything intolerable: Chinese calligraphy was 'grotesque', the language a string of 'harsh guttural aspirations' and musical instruments 'weapons of torture'.[39] Once Fleming started on Chinese standards of hygiene, he was almost unstoppable: the smells of China were at best 'villainous', at worst 'revoltingly vile', villages 'wretched', winds 'sickly and feverish'.[40] Encountering a town, he asserted that 'nothing living, I am confident, could exist near it for a few hours but Chinese and cesspool rats.'[41] Pigsties encountered were so 'degradedly filthy' that they put him off sausages (or 'fragrant intestines', as they are termed in Chinese) for the rest of his stay in China.[42] He saved his very few good words for opium – that great British import – which, he observed, was 'a very quiet and unobtrusive way of getting dead drunk'.[43] The best compliment he found to pay the Chinese is that they were the most 'improvable of all eastern nations [if] permitted ... to see the glimmer of a modern world and a new civilisation, and to hold intercourse with a new race of men some twenty centuries younger and yet more advanced in whatever pertains to human greatness'.[44] 'China,' he concluded, 'has exercised but little influence in modifying or directing the progress of either the antique or modern world.'[45]

But Fleming's tone radically changed when, within 10 kilometres of Shanhaiguan, he caught sight 'of the world-famed barrier whose wonders have been sounded for centuries in the West ... There could be no hesitation now in consoling ourselves for the suspense we had endured'.[46] After a tussle with the local authorities for a permit to climb up to the wall, the redoubtable, muscular Fleming, leaving his weakling, breathless Chinese minders far behind, hurled himself up some 'savagely perpendicular' heights towards a tower in the wall. At around midday, he 'won the coveted peak, and completed the ascension by toiling into the summit of the little ruined tower', feeling 'unmingled pleasure ... as I stood on that pinnacled mountain-top where the foot of European had never before trodden, where the most adventurous of the dwellers beneath would never dream of coming, and where, perhaps, the presence of man had been unknown for long centuries'.[47] Eager to justify his tourism with a smattering of morally virtuous scientific investigation, he hastily set out a barometer and thermometer to take a few perfunctory measurements, then abandoned himself entirely to gasping at this 'world-renowned monument ... a little more than two thousand years old', at its athletic twists, turns, dives and ascents ('I feel as if looking at some vast monster since it began its heavenward rise'), as it 'goes away bounding magnificently up hill and down dale ... like the body of a rider when his horse is clearing a succession of stiff fences'.[48] Such was Fleming's admiration for the 'petrous girdle' before him that he started to revise his general disgust for everything else to do with China and the Chinese, celebrating instead 'the Herculean efforts of a great nation in byegone ages to preserve itself from invasion and subjection'. 'Even to a Westerner, who has seen some of the triumphs of nineteenth century engineering ... it seems all but impossible that any people could set themselves down to the performance of so monstrous a difficulty.'[49]

After scratching a record of his visit on to the tower wall, Fleming began a hair-raising descent. A dedicatedly scientific Victorian, he had chosen to haul up his barometer and thermometer instead of water; as he came down, dehydrated, the sun at its peak, with one hand he clung to 'narrow crags, shelves, and hair's-breadth projections that would have bothered the sure eyesight and surer footfalls of the chamois ... the other being engaged in carrying the inconvenient barometer'.[50] Parched, sunstroked, completely lost – despite, or rather because of his compass, as the burden of his precious instruments forced him to take an unfamiliar path down – and with his ankle sprained, he passed out for an hour or so. Finally, at sunset, with 'an almost superhuman effort of strength and mind', the indomitable Fleming staggered his way up to some Chinese labourers, who, offering him food and water, struck him as the 'finest peasantry in the world'.[51] Needless to say, his scorn for the Chinese returned as soon as his hunger, thirst and fatigue retreated. The next day, his accommodation was, as usual, 'villainous and miserly', officials 'childish and supererogative', and so on and so forth, all the curmudgeonly way into Manchuria.[52]

Fleming was not the very first European tourist to take advantage of the Treaty of Tianjin to make a pilgrimage to the Great Wall. A year previously, he had been pipped to the post by Henry Russell, another energetic Victorian traveller, approaching from the opposite direction, southwards from Siberia and Mongolia. Russell, who was every bit as much the genuine imperialist article as Fleming, climbed to the top of the wall, shot a revolver to mark his triumph and gathered together stones to place in museums back in Europe, where he described the Great Wall to interested parties as 'snaking across the landscape like a tapeworm'.[53] Fleming's *Travels on Horseback* did, however, formulate the standard mid- to late-nineteenth-century European response to China and its Great Wall, subsequently becoming an inspirational guidebook for later wall-walkers.

Fleming was a typical Victorian globetrotter, a traveller created by the victories of British gunboat diplomacy and its fixation with opening musty old China to the fresh sea breezes of free trade between nations. His successful, death-defying storming of that mighty symbol of

Chinese enclosure, the Great Wall – against the wishes of local officials – was both made possible by and recapitulated, in spirit, the Anglo-French destruction of the walled compounds of the emperor's inner sanctum, the Summer Palace, replaying the brutish, scornful victory of British imperialism in China.

Fleming's pretensions to scientific exploration provided the supposedly objective, intellectual veneer to contemptuous racism characteristic of much high-imperial British travel writing. The founding of the Royal Geographical Society in 1840, with its declared devotion to 'scientific travel', entrenched a fashion for 'scientific' travelogues, which justified themselves through their claims to apply and further (geographical, horticultural, ethnographic and so on) knowledge – hence Dr Fleming's determination to take barometer and thermometer readings on the wall, and his desperate clinging on to his outsized instruments, even though they were nearly the end of him. The sense of moral and intellectual supremacy fostered by Britain's technological superiority over a scientifically petrified China both informed and fuelled Fleming's unthinking contempt for almost everything and everyone he encountered there. Like many of his Western contemporaries in China, Fleming was obsessed with Chinese hygiene, or the lack of it, coming as he did from a Britain where the new science of sanitation was becoming the marker of civilization, with dirt the emblem of social, racial and moral inferiority.

Given Fleming's revulsion for all things Chinese, we should, perhaps, therefore be surprised by his veneration of the Great Wall. Why, when confronted with this massive embodiment of Chinese isolationism, with the ancient (or so he believed) bricks-and-stone antithesis of modern free trade, was his impulse not to telegraph to his regiment back in wretched Tianjin and tell them to hurry north with their biggest guns to destroy the largest Chinese cordon of all, as Defoe had suggested a century earlier?

Victorian imperialists might have been bumptiously Christian, but they were not puritans. Quite the contrary: they adored bombast, both in spectacle (consider the Diamond Jubilee of 1897, a 50,000-strong procession of troops – including Canadians, Hong Kongese, Malays, Jamaicans and Cypriots – through London, all led by the tallest man in the British army) and in architecture (think of the Gothic cathedrals built to loom unexpectedly out of imperial landscapes in India, Australia and Canada, the vast palisade of government buildings in Bombay). The sheer immensity of the Great Wall, this potent image of imperial grandeur, spoke directly to the nineteenth-century British love of monumentality.

As a monument, moreover, universally trumpeted as being deeply ancient, unchanged over 2,000 years and uniform across thousands of kilometres, the wall offered Fleming and those who followed in his footsteps justification for locking China into a global cabinet of ancient, ethnographical curiosities, providing irrefutable proof that China was no more than a venerable fossil in comparison with the imperial masters of the modern world, the British. It was safe to admire the visible achievements of the Chinese of two millennia previously, as they set into even greater relief the degeneration of the contemporary Chinese and their inability to match, let alone improve upon, the application of their distant ancestors.

The historical function of the wall – built to protect China from the Mongols – also appealed to the utilitarian tastes of Victorian imperialists, contrasting most favourably with what Fleming described as the 'unmeaning [and therefore] unsightly' pyramids of Egypt.[54] At the same time, the Great Wall, ultimately 'impotent against such intrepid barbarians', did not shake the British superiority complex.[55] Its failure to keep out nomadic invaders – the Mongols of Genghis Khan, the Manchu Qing – and the ultimate futility of the staggering, slavish obedience of the Chinese labourers to their imperial architects exhibited the fundamental flaws of isolationist wall-building as a strategy and of the Chinese as a race, and augured the inevitable universal victory of free trade. As another visitor of the early 1860s put it, 'when the fact is realised that for thousands of miles this extraordinary product of masonic art pursued its serpentine course, all other so-called wonders of the world fade by comparison with this lasting memento of a despot's folly and the involuntary labour of a submissive people.'[56]

~

Fleming's successors echoed his sentiments about both China and its wall in ever more strident choruses. For all imperialist tourism's pretensions to scientific objectivity, almost every visitor unquestioningly swallowed, parroted and often inflated erroneous and unverified assumptions about the wall: about its length (which some made out to be 1,500 miles, others 2,000), its age (at least 2,000 years), its builder (Qin Shihuang), its speed of construction (somewhere between five and fifteen years) and its uniformity (most based their unstinting admiration for the wall on a visit to the bricked stretches north of Beijing; few troubled to investigate its very different appearance to the west). A 1923 *National Geographic* feature on the wall piled fiction upon fiction: 'The Mightiest Barrier Ever Built by Man Has Stood Guard Over the Land of Chin for Twenty Centuries ... According to astronomers, the only work of man's hands which would be visible to the human eye from the moon is the Great Wall of China ... COMPLETED IN 15 YEARS.'[57] Coexisting with this adulation, however, was a delight in dwelling on the ponderous, petrified symbolism of the Great Wall as Great Anomaly: that despite the impressively 'prodigious extent' of its wall, China's institutions were 'for much above five-and-twenty centuries ... never changing or varying ... so that [the Chinese] exhibit the only instance in the history of our species of improvement being permanently arrested in its progress'.[58]

And yet one wonders if a degree of unease does not lie behind this breathless Western obsession with the Great Wall, behind travellers' denunciations of its futility; one wonders if the Western tourist sometimes protests too much. When, in 1924 – two decades after the Indian National Congress had been radicalized by militant Hindus, a modernized Japanese navy had defeated the Russians at Tsushima and anti-imperialist, nationalist parties began springing up all over Africa and Asia

– an American visitor to north China called the Great Wall 'a tombstone to … imperial vanity', it is hard to believe that the resonances of imperial decline could have been lost on all his readers.[59]

In many of the hundreds of books published after 1860 by Western travellers in China (not to mention the countless travel articles printed in periodicals such as *Macmillan's Magazine* and *Once a Week*), tales of visits to the Great Wall, together with standard-issue sketches and photographs of ramparts and towers festooning mountains, became so commonplace that travel writers, concerned to differentiate themselves from the regular herd, began to search for ever more flamboyant rhetorical devices to embellish their descriptions, or gimmicks to differentiate their visit from the masses of I-Saw-the-Wall accounts. As global adventurism evolved into mass tourism, as intrepid globetrotters were joined by Thomas Cook's organized crocodiles of sightseers, a conventional journey on foot, by horse or cart, and cries of 'stupendous' or 'wonderful' ceased to be sufficient. One senses precisely this desperation to be different in Luigi Barzini, an Italian journalist who, accompanying the aristocratic Prince Borghese on course to win the Peking–Paris Great Automobile Race of 1907, passed the Great Wall by the (then) still novel means of the motor car. To Barzini, the Wall was 'faintly jagged, like a thing with teeth … a prodigious architectural moulding … a fantastic freak of the earth, thrown up by some great unknown natural force', its towers 'like a row of giants at their watch-posts'.[60] For the overexcitable Italian, the symbolism of poop-pooping by motor car through the wall proved just a little too much:

We experience the inebriation of conquest, the exaltation of triumph … We feel as if we were breaking the stillness of a thousand years, as if we were the first to give with one rapid flight the signal of an awakening out of some great sleep. We feel the pride of a civilisation and a race, and are conscious of representing something more than ourselves … The great longings of the Western soul, its strength, the true secret of all its progress, is resumed in the short word – Faster! Our life is pursued by this violent desire, this painful insatiability, this sublime obsession – Faster! Here in the midst of Chinese immobility we truly carry with us the essence of our feverish advance.[61]

Thirteen years later, an American visitor exclaimed that the wall 'would make a cracker-jack highway ... if Mr Ford should take a few millions and buy the old thing for the benefit of his future patrons in China'.[62]

The truly jaded simply omitted to describe a visit to the Great Wall. Already in 1880, a British army captain on his way to Tibet had tersely remarked that an 'excursion to the Great Wall ... need not be here recounted'.[63] In 1921, a traveller on his way to Mongolia noted 'that wonder of the world, the Great Wall, winding like a gray serpent over the ridge after ridge of the mountains ... I had seen all this before ... It was too near, and the railroad had made it commonplace.'[64]

The one-upmanship of travel writers had little effect on tourists panting to see the famed Great Wall for themselves. Ever since the organized-tour business reached China at the turn of the nineteenth century, the Great Wall has been essential viewing for foreign visitors, the linchpin of trips to the north. As pompous imperialist sermonizing slowly slipped out of fashion, contradicted in no small part by the rise of an assertive modern Chinese nationalism, Western visitors shed their ambivalence towards the wall as an impressive but dusty emblem of defensive failure, thereby extinguishing the only shadow of critical nuance complicating their appraisal of its history. The Great Anomaly became plain Great.

Throughout these heady years of wall-worship, very few Western visitors remarked on the genuinely Great Anomaly of the wall: that this foreign obsession was in no way mirrored by Chinese interest. Describing his difficulties in gaining a permit to visit the wall, George Fleming remarked that obstructive bureaucrats explained not only that 'the sun was very hot, there were no roads, the hills were a long way off, and covered with stones' but also that 'the Chinese never went up there'.[65] Fleming made his expedition on his own because his pragmatic Chinese minders were unwilling to risk their lives hurling themselves up walled mountaintops, unlike their crazy foreign devil master. (Fleming, of course, readily dismissed their antipathy to 'clambering up ... nearly inaccessible rocks' as another example of the Chinese lack of physical backbone, and thought no more of it.[66]) But early in the twentieth century, the Chinese, initially nonplussed by the barbarians' zeal for the wall, slowly began to reconsider their own view, to be convinced by the instigators of their international humiliation, by the appalling Fleming and others like him. When China, after decades of bruising encounters with its uninvited Western guests, began to piece back together its national self-respect, the Great Wall was the most obvious piece of imperial wreckage to hold on to.

CHAPTER TWELVE

Translating the Great Wall into Chinese

O n the warm spring afternoon of 4 May 1919, urban China caught fire. At one o'clock that day, some 3,000 student protesters gathered in front of the Forbidden City in Beijing under two large, white funeral banners. Although the banners were inscribed with the names of two intensely unpopular members of the Beijing government, the assembly was sparked by a sense of mourning for something far bigger: China itself. A few days previously, the country had received some unfortunate news. Thousands of kilometres away, at Versailles, the American president, Woodrow Wilson, the British prime minister, David Lloyd George, and his French counterpart, Georges Clemenceau, decided, in recognition of Japanese naval assistance rendered against the Germans in the world war just ended, to reward Japan by transferring to them Germany's former territorial rights in Shandong, a large slice of north-east China. The representatives of the Beijing government at the Paris peace talks – a delegation propped up by corrupt Chinese warlords and amply bribed by Japanese loans – had unsheathed their pens and prepared to sign.

From Tiananmen, the students headed east, towards the embassies, hotels, banks, shops, churches, brothels and polo field of the foreign-legation quarter of the city that the imperial powers had carved out for themselves in the early years of the century. When foreign and Chinese police barred their advance through the quarter's perimeter wall, the crowd diverted to the house of one of the government's most prominent appeasers of Japan. On discovering that its occupant had narrowly escaped them by jumping over his back wall, the protesters vented their frustration by burning his house down and by seizing and beating sense-less a fellow member of the government.

For eighty years, since China had lost the first Opium War, foreign powers had, in the phrase of anxious Chinese patriots, been 'carving China up like a melon': docking gunboats, razing palaces, extracting indemnities, asserting extraterritoriality and hacking out 'spheres of influence', great swathes of territory whose natural resources they claimed privileged rights to develop and exploit. For these same eighty years, Chinese governments had hesitated before the challenge from the West, havering between the desire to meet (and perhaps even beat) the imperialists on their own terms with modern gunboats and weapons, and the fear that such a course would subsume Chinese culture in barbarian ways.

The humiliation of the Versailles decision was the firebrand to Chinese nationalism, setting off the explosion of cultural and political protest across China's cities that is now known as the May Fourth Movement. Over several decades, Chinese reformers had, at varying speeds, been working round to the uncomfortable conclusion that the traditions of imperial government and society – the veneration of antiq-uity and of Confucius, the failure to develop Western-style science and technology – represented a historical dead-end. Both before and even more so after 1905, when the millennia-old Confucian examination sys-tem was finally abolished, young men were laying aside their classical primers and flocking to military and technical academies – many of them abroad, in France, Japan and England – to learn the wealth- and power-generating ways of the modern West, to acquire military and industrial technologies, to study medical science, and to develop the political vigour and unity that spring from a sense of nationhood. Anxieties about capit-ulating to barbarian values were theoretically quelled by the neat *ti–yong* (essence–practice) formula, a late-nineteenth-century sop to cultural conservatism which hypothesized that the Chinese 'essence' (moral and philosophical values) could be strengthened but not threatened by the selected application of Western 'practice' (science and technology).

Seized in the wake of Versailles by a newly intensified sense of national crisis and desperate for a national revival, the May Fourthers lost patience with earlier half-measures designed to counter the imperialist menace. Abandoning the quest for a harmonious reconciliation between modern Western and traditional Chinese values, May Fourth thinkers, writers and marchers decided it was time to bring about an absolute rupture with the decadent, backward past that had led China into its disastrous present: with its classical language, with its closed Confucian system of government, thought and social relations, with its superiority complex and innate distrust of anything foreign, with its veneration of the old and denigration of the young. The basic task, proclaimed Chen Duxiu, one of the intellectual leaders of the May Fourth Movement, 'is to import the foundation of Western society, that is, the new belief in equality and human rights. We must be thoroughly aware of the incompatibility between Confucianism and the new belief, the new society, and the new state.'[1] Openness was the key to survival; old-style isolationism the road to extinction. 'Be cosmopolitan, not isolationist,' lectured Chen. 'He who builds his cart behind closed gates will find it not suited to the tracks outside the gates.'[2] On street corners, in lectures, in pamphlets and journals in cities up and down China, young intellectuals cried out to replace the ancient autocracy of Confucius with modern Western science and democracy.

~

A year earlier, in 1918, a fifty-two-year-old Chinese gentleman called Sun Yat-sen had taken up residence in a villa on 26 rue Molière, one of the quieter streets set among the leafy avenues of the French Concession in Shanghai. From May to June 1919, outside his pocket of tranquil seclusion, the city sank into turmoil: perhaps a quarter of the workforce went on strike, with impromptu anti-imperialist demonstrations and plays being acted out on street corners. Like many of urban China's fifty-some-things, however, Sun seems to have taken little active part in the May Fourth Movement, dominated as it was by students. His working time was spent in scholarly pursuits, revising and editing his writings; his hours of relaxation playing croquet with his wife on the lawn of their villa or entertaining friends to dinner.

But in most other respects, Sun was anything but an average middle-aged Chinese urbanite. In 1919, he was a former revolutionary leader and president of the Republic of China; decades later, when he was safely dead, he would be embalmed in the Chinese political limelight – a world away from the sedate bookishness of his life on rue Molière – acclaimed by governments in both Taiwan and the People's Republic of China as the 'Father of the modern Chinese Nation'.

Like the May Fourth demonstrators, Sun Yat-sen was obsessed by the question of a Chinese national revival. Unlike his youthful counterparts, by 1919 he had already been worrying about it for many years. After almost three decades of international fund-raising, lecturing, meeting, greeting and manoeuvring on behalf of China's anti-dynastic forces of revolution, Sun had enjoyed a brief recompense when, following the national revolution of 1911 (prematurely sparked by a botched bomb explosion), he had been invited to become president of the new Republic of China. By 1913, after barely one year in office, Sun had resigned his job to Yuan Shikai, a former Qing general and the military power behind the revolutionary regime. Yuan had promptly begun to ignore the new con-stitution: accepting foreign loans without parliamentary approval, assas-sinating the prime minister, and finally, on 1 January 1916, inaugurating himself as emperor. At this last act, consternation quickly spread throughout the country. That same year, as, one by one, provinces declared against their tubby, moustachioed emperor and for independ-ence from Beijing, Yuan sickened – quite possibly from rage-induced stress – and died. Following the death of this military authoritarian, who had at least held together the country's armies, if not its hopes for a republic, the united façade of the new regime collapsed into feuding between regional warlords.

While the power-hungry mustered their own armies, the rest of the nation went to hell. Although the revolutionaries who had toppled the Qing in 1911 were unclear about many of their shared aims for building government, one issue above all others had unified them: the need to mount a strong nationalist challenge to the incursions of imperialist powers. No foreign power was more assiduous in asserting its interests than Japan in the north-east: after tussles with both China and Russia, Japan had by the 1910s established itself as the dominant power in Manchuria. Taking full advantage of China's post-revolutionary chaos, in 1915 the Japanese government served Yuan Shikai with the Twenty-one Demands, asserting greater Japanese economic and political sovereignty over areas of Manchuria and Mongolia; after a few months of negotiations, Yuan capitulated. Four years later, at Versailles, despite China having contributed hundreds of thousands of Chinese labourers to the Allied war effort, a decision by the Americans, British and French ensured that the cause of Chinese national sovereignty took its next dramatic turn for the worse.

It was at this critical junction for modern China that Sun Yat-sen had retired to his quiet corner of Shanghai and prepared to regroup. In 1917, after the warlord fashion of the day, he had headed south to Canton and tried, briefly, strutting about in full military fancy dress (plumed helmet, fringed epaulettes, white gloves) and calling himself Grand Marshal. Seeing little future in remaining a marshal without much of an army – Sun could muster, at the peak of his command, some twenty battalions and one gunboat – he discarded his braided uniform for the traditional Chinese scholar's robe and began work on a Plan for National Reconstruction. Replenishing his energies before his next attempt to realize his dream of a unified, republican China, the revolutionary wheeler-dealer started to transform himself into political theorist, and set about countering the radical visions of the May Fourth with his own schemas of reform.

Sun disagreed with the iconoclastic May Fourth approach, fearing that a wholesale repudiation of Chinese tradition would sever psychological links with past political culture and make it impossible to re-establish a unified state to succeed the old imperial model. Instead, he searched for ways to rehabilitate useful parts of this tradition into contemporary schemes of modernization. This has been and, to an extent, remains the central, crippling psychological dilemma of modern China: what to do with the extraordinary accumulation of experience and achievement that made China the most powerful country in the world until the eighteenth century, but left it practically helpless against the imperialist West a hundred years later. In the eyes of troubled patriots, Chinese history was responsible for China's dire predicament, but it was also precisely what made twentieth-century China – 'the Sick Man of Asia' – worth saving. Passionately wanting to be strong and modern like the West, at every turn Chinese modernizers have glanced uneasily over their shoulders back at the past to ponder whether they are still 'Chinese'.

In its main thrust, Sun's Plan for National Reconstruction laid out an improbably bold and thoroughly Westernized scheme for modernizing China: demolishing entire towns, taming the Yangtze, building a rail link between Beijing and Capetown. The modern West was everywhere as a model: Sun called for industrial development in the style of 'Europe and America', a northern port 'as important as New York' – all to be achieved under the guidance of foreign experts, with foreign capital and equipment.[3]

But even as he proposed to throw China's doors open to modern Western technology and investment, Sun did not neglect to massage the bruised Chinese sense of national worth. Sun cast about for a symbol that was solidly three-dimensional enough to boost the national ego, to show that Chinese tradition was capable of technical genius and dynamism, and one that was, at the same time, sufficiently abstract and historically vague not to bring with it any troublingly specific factual associations. Ensconced in his Shanghai retreat, he cast his eyes north.

China's most famous work of land-based engineering is its Great Wall. Qin Shihuang sent Meng Tian north to build the Great Wall, to defend China from the Xiongnu. Stretching from Liaoshen in the east to Lintao in the west, it runs for five thousand *li* over mountains and valleys. Unequalled throughout all antiquity, it is a miracle, a historical one-off. At the time of Qin, science was as yet undeveloped, and tools and instruments had not been invented. Human labour was not as plentiful as it is today, and knowledge of physics and engineering was nowhere near contemporary levels. How, then, could such a great monument be built? ... Because necessity is the mother of innovation ... Harassed beyond endurance by the Xiongnu, Qin Shihuang ruled that the best solution was to complete one mighty work to safeguard the future: to build the Great Wall as defence. Although he was not himself a perfect sage ruler, his Great Wall benefited his descendants as much as did the flood control measures completed by the Great Yu ... if we Chinese hadn't had the protection of the Great Wall, China would have been conquered by the northern barbarians during the Han, long before the Song or the Ming, and the Chinese race would not have flourished and developed as it did during the Han and Tang, and assimilated the peoples of the south. And after our country had fully developed its powers of assimilation, we were able even to assimilate our conquerors, the Mongols and the Manchus.

Although Sun used the old, ill-reputed Qin term 'Long Wall' throughout, the object of his adulation was clearly the two-millennia-old, unchanging Great Wall built and maintained by the Jesuits, Voltaire and the Victorians. For Sun, the Great Wall symbolized the triumph of the can-do spirit in Chinese antiquity and a blind, single-minded determination to hurl labour and resources at a project, regardless of technological or logistical obstacles, a spirit that, for the time being, had been well and truly lost. 'If today someone were to try to imitate Qin Shihuang in building another Great Wall, it would never come off.'[4]

While he took a disapproving stance towards the intellectual ferment of 1919, Sun in many ways shared common political cause with the May

Fourth protesters. By vocation, he was a cosmopolitan republican, not a cultural conservative. Born into a peasant family only sixty-four kilometres north of Macao, schooled in Hawai'i and Hong Kong thanks to the wealth of a brother who sailed off to make his fortune overseas, Sun was the archetypal product of China's forced opening to the West, exposed to the new hybrid of ideas and organizations that sprang up amid the trade, newspapers, schools and industries of the treaty ports. Under death sentence in China after a failed revolutionary uprising, in 1895 Sun fled to Hong Kong and Japan; subsequently, he probably spent more of his life outside than inside China. (It was only leafing through the newspapers before breakfast at the foot of the Rockies that he came across a report of the 1911 revolution.) Travelling endlessly between Japan, Europe and the USA, Sun was a truly internationalist opportunist, constantly two-timing foreign allies and sponsors in his fund-raising efforts for the Chinese republican project. In 1923, not long after he began negotiating a lucrative alliance with newly Communist Russia, Sun was taking tea in Hong Kong drawing rooms with wealthy local notables and proclaiming that 'we must take England as our model and must extend England's example of good government to the whole of China'.[5]

Even if we take into account the growing conservatism and traditionalism that may accompany the passage into late middle age, Sun's veneration of the Great Wall – this outstanding symbol of imperial Chinese dictatorship and isolationism – would seem to be incompatible with every single one of his pro-foreign, republican political convictions. But the solution to this paradox lies not in puzzling over but simply accepting the key internal inconsistency of modern Chinese nationalism and its proponents: their unstable combination of hatred and admiration for the imperialist West, and of scorn and veneration for China and its past. Towards the end of his life, Sun held imperialism to blame for all of contemporary China's problems, even as he energetically sought foreign funds for his political projects. While he appealed to his compatriots to 'recover our ancient morality', he castigated pre-modern Chinese for failing to defend their country from barbarians.[6] Even the May Fourth Movement, with its apparently straightforward message of total Westernization, was riddled with such contradictions: goaded by hatred of Western imperialism, May Fourthers cried out to import the Western spirit of science and democracy into every aspect of Chinese society, in order to save their ancient country from imminent extinction.

With this in mind, the Great Wall becomes a perfectly appropriate mascot for modern Chinese nationalists: built by the indomitable Chinese against foreigners, then worshipped by foreigners, who conveniently divorced it from its troublingly complex history and reinvented it as simply 'prodigious'. Sun's praise for the Great Wall was clearly part of his quest for a symbol or philosophy around which China (in his own words, 'a sheet of loose sand') could rally as a nation, and from which it could draw the necessary self-confidence to see off the imperialist threat. But in fixing upon the Great Wall, Sun revealed more his own cosmopolitanism than his respect for Chinese history, as his remarks on the wall – on its age, its position, its general greatness – seem to be lifted directly from one of any number of gushing, historically challenged Western travelogues. Sun, as his observations about the wall made very clear, was no classical scholar; nowhere does he give any sense of the fragmentary nature of the wall (in both chronological and geographical terms), of the relative youth of the showpiece stone-built sections, of the sense of historical debacle which followed the wall's failure to prevent the Manchu conquest of 1644 (a conquest he reinvents glibly as a victory for Chinese civilization over rough barbarians). Sun translated into Chinese the Western misreading of the wall as great, erasing, in the process, much of its inglorious history, and by doing so began modern China's love affair with the Great Wall.

In one further respect, it was no coincidence at all that Sun developed a fondness for the Great Wall. Although he began and notionally ended his political life as a democrat, he did not believe China needed democracy as it had evolved in Europe, as the fight for individual freedom.

China's problem, he considered, was not too little but too much individual liberty, preventing its people from uniting to resist the enslaving of the nation under imperialism. Instead, 'we must break down individual liberty and become pressed together into an unyielding body like the firm rock which is formed by the addition of cement to sand.'[7] Sun's emphasis on the freedom of the nation over that of the individual, and his insistence on a period of tutelage of unspecified length during which the Chinese people would be 'taught' to be democratic under a military dictatorship, gave his espousal of democracy a hollow, authoritarian ring. They certainly offered his political protégés – modern China's two most powerful parties, the Nationalists and the Communists – an easy route to dictatorship, and help to explain his attachment to the Great Wall, that millennia-old monument to the autocratic Chinese state.

Six years later, in 1925, Sun was dead, of liver cancer. He died without seeing his dream of China reunited as a republic realized. But his nationalist activism, his ability to contemplate bold schemes of national modernization, and, most importantly, his sponsorship of the Nationalists and the Communists guaranteed that when, in the years and decades to come, the two parties grew up to found their own authoritarian states, both would acclaim him as Father of the Nation and venerate as many of his pronouncements as fitted their political needs.

~

Sun may have been one of the wall's first modern Chinese admirers of any note, but it was years of war – of desperate struggle for national survival – rather than Shanghai theorizing that were firmly to install the Great Wall as a symbol of national strength and endurance in the popular imagination.

To begin with, the war was civil. In 1923, Sun Yat-sen struck a deal with Soviet Russia. The Russians would provide his Nationalist Party (the Guomindang, or GMD) with funding, arms and political and military training; Sun, in return, would allow members of the young Chinese Communist Party, founded in 1921, into the ranks of the Nationalists.

Sun would receive the financial backing he and his party desperately needed to defeat the warlords who had carved China up among themselves. The Russians would secure for themselves a regional ally against anti-Communist Japan, and further their long-term aim of world revolution by driving forward in China what they viewed as a primary political stage – national bourgeois revolution assisted by Chinese Communists – from within which Communist revolution would then naturally spring.

While Sun Yat-sen lived, and while the Nationalists still felt they stood to gain significant advantages by keeping in with the Russians, this United Front between the two Chinese parties more or less held together. In 1926, when Soviet-trained and armed troops of the Front drove up from Canton into central and eastern China, dislodging a handful of warlord regimes, the alliance substantially furthered Nationalist ambitions for reunification. But in 1927, with Sun two years dead, with his self-appointed heir, Chiang Kai-shek, on the brink of taking the great urban prizes of Shanghai and Nanjing, and with the Communists becoming, in the eyes of the right-wing Chiang, unacceptably radical in their efforts to mobilize urban and rural populaces against wealthy landowners and businessmen, the alliance fractured violently. On 12 April 1927, after months of secret negotiations with Shanghai's wealthiest financiers and their private underworld enforcers, the Green Gang, Chiang set an armed force of some 1,000 men – all Green Gang members – at the city's labour unions, the hubs of Communist activity; 100 unionists were gunned down at a single protest rally alone. Forces rallied by the Communists were similarly massacred in Changsha, Wuhan, Nanchang and, finally, Canton, where leftists were quickly identified by the dye marks round their necks from their red kerchiefs and drowned in bundles of ten or twelve in the river by the city.

While Generalissimo Chiang's political star climbed into the ascendant, as he defeated and negotiated northern warlords into nominal submission to his goal of national reunification, Chinese Communist forces spent much of the next eight years on the run, through China's most inaccessible and least desirable areas, where, or so they hoped, the sheer difficulty, poverty and isolation of the terrain would overcome even Chiang's rabid determination to hunt down his former allies. For several years, however, they chose their refuges badly. In 1929, they settled upon Jiangxi, the mountainous, infertile south-eastern province whose impoverishment seemed to make it an obviously volatile breeding ground for radical social discontent and Communist revolution. But it was also within striking distance of Chiang Kai-shek's own power centres at Shanghai and Nanjing on the east coast. Three major Nationalist campaigns hammered the Jiangxi Soviet between 1931 and 1932; a ring of newly built roads and blockhouses encircled the entire area, trapping the Communists inside.

In the autumn of 1934, after much planning undertaken in great secrecy, about 80,000 Communist troops broke out of the weakest, south-western corner of the blockade and began a year-long, 13,000 kilometre escape trek that traced a massive, reverse L-shape across some of the country's wildest, least developed terrain – hills and forests inhabited by hostile southern aborigines, the freezing peaks of Tibet, the boggy plains of the far north-west, where soldiers slept standing up because the ground was too wet for them to lie down, through rapids jostled between mountains, across hammock-like bridges suspended with iron chains over perilous rocks and whirlpools, and eventually ending in the bleak, crumbly landscapes of Shaanxi in north-west China. This manoeuvre became known, in Communist lore, as the Long March, a name that makes it sound more like an extended bout of field exercise than the running battle with Nationalist forces that it is generally thought to have been. Of the 80,000 who began the trek, only 8,000 or so are said to have completed it.

In absolute terms, the Long March – which left them driven out into China's starving north-western borderlands – was no more a victory for the Chinese Communists than Dunkirk would be for Britain five years later. In relative terms, however, the surviving Communists were bolstered both symbolically and strategically by their arrival in Shaanxi.

Admittedly, the north-west was unfamiliar, poor and liminal, a land ruled by the light, capricious yellow-brown loess soil out of which its hills were blown by Central Asian and Mongolian winds into 'an infinite variety of queer, embattled shapes', as the American journalist Edgar Snow observed during a visit to the Communist headquarters, 'hills like great castles, like rows of mammoth, nicely rounded scones, like ranges torn by some giant hand, leaving behind the imprint of angry fingers. Fantastic, incredible, and sometimes frightening shapes, a world configurated by a mad god'.[8] If thoroughly irrigated by rainfall, the light soil was fertile and easy to work. Rainfall, however, was reliably unreliable, while further north, Snow remarked, the 'crops grown are strictly limited by the steep gradients ... There are few genuine mountains, only endless broken hills, hills as interminable as a sentence by James Joyce, and even more tiresome.'[9] But the Communists had won themselves a breathing space, and – through the propagandist legends about the march fed to Snow announced to the world that, despite the human cost, they were able to fight a running guerrilla war with the Nationalists and survive.[10]

To one of them, an experienced and ruthless revolutionary called Mao Zedong, originally a native of the emerald-green rice paddies of south China, and now about to seize absolute authority over the soldiers he had led north, one feature of this ochre landscape alone stood out as an emblem of the struggle that lay behind and before him, overshadowing and judging his actions, providing an inspiring symbol of the nation for which he was fighting:

> The heavens are high, the clouds are pale,
> We watch as the wild geese disappear southwards.
> If we fail to reach the Great Wall we are not true men,
> We who have marched more than 20,000 *li*.[11]

After the Communists took power in 1949, when Mao completed his transformation from revolutionary leader to deity, when his words acquired the sanctity of gospel and the Great Wall became a tourist industry, his 1935 verse about the Great Wall enjoyed a vigorous afterlife in a rough new translation popular among visitors eager for Great Wall memorabilia. The Chinese language does not have to specify pronouns, and Mao's third line omitted them, leaving later Chinese and translators free to understand his words in a more vernacular sense: 'You're not a real man if you've never been to the Great Wall.' The quotation is now carved and printed on to rocks and signs at wall tourist sites, while T-shirts and hats emblazoned with the dictum offer solace to any visitors susceptible to crises of masculinity.

Back in 1935, however, the high regard of neither Sun Yat-sen nor Mao Zedong was as yet sufficient to guarantee the immortality of the Great Wall as a national emblem. Although Chiang's government had posthumously transformed Sun into a political icon, Sun's own legacy looked far from assured. While Sun lived, many felt that his revolutionary vision had yielded little more than violence and factionalism. After the foundation of the nominally unifying Nationalist regime in 1928 by Sun's old party, doubts persisted. On taking power, Chiang Kai-shek often looked like little more than a glorified satrap with pretensions to ruling all China, his government one that both peasants, starving in their millions in Shaanxi in the late 1920s, and intellectuals, harassed and sometimes assassinated for even whispers of left-leaning dissent, found politically bankrupt. Beyond his band of Communist revolutionaries, who were beginning to hero-worship him above any other leader, Mao in 1935 still looked, to all intents and purposes, to be a political small-timer and minor amateur poet, driven to the north-western margins of China by the Nationalist armies and doomed to remain there.

One factor intervened to rescue the wall from historical obscurity and transform it into a symbol, indeed a theatre, of the indomitable Chinese will to resist – Japanese invasion. From the 1890s onward, Japanese forces had been settling in steadily growing numbers north of the Great Wall, in Manchuria. In 1931, after decades of extending military and economic control over the region and its rich natural resources, confident

Japanese officers moved to formalize Japanese authority by provoking a full-scale confrontation with Chinese soldiers near Mukden, Nurhaci's old capital. Already overstretched by conflicts within his own government, Chiang Kai-shek ordered the morphine-addicted warlord who controlled Chinese forces in the north-east simply to withdraw south of the wall. Later that same year, the Japanese enticed the last, deposed emperor of the Qing, Puyi, back to Manchuria to head a new, independent state north of the Great Wall.

Like almost every other vigorous Manchurian power of the previous two millennia, however, the Japanese soon began to express an interest in the rest of China – not least because they were anxious to create a buffer zone to the west and south of their new possessions. As in 1644, Shanhaiguan provided the gateway to the Middle Kingdom. On New Year's Day 1933, a mysterious explosion was heard not far from the headquarters of the Japanese military police in the town. Japanese and Chinese explanations for the disturbance later diverged, the former declaring it an anti-Japanese bomb, the latter dismissing it as a few New Year firecrackers. Whatever the truth, Japanese militarists let loose their troops and aircraft on Shanhaiguan. By 3 January 1933, an estimated 2,000 Chinese soldiers and an unknown number of civilians lay dead, and the First Pass Under Heaven was in Japanese hands.[12]

Less than two months later, 20,000 Japanese troops advanced into Jehol, the north-east province visited by Macartney and his entourage in 1793 on their trade pilgrimage to the Qing emperor. Chinese resistance, offhandedly directed by avaricious warlords unwilling to sacrifice their private armies, was practically non-existent. By the first week of March, the provincial capital, site of the Qing emperor's former summer palace and hunting ground, had fallen and the entire 192,180-square-kilometre province collapsed.

A few days later, the Japanese advanced on to the Great Wall, deploying aeroplanes, artillery and tanks against Chinese forces sheltering in showpiece passes – behind walls, in towers and between crenellations –

north-east of Beijing, among the mountains that make up Great Wall country north of the capital. The Chinese, a ragbag of former warlord armies, were heavily outgunned: one frontline division of 15,000 men possessed merely ten field and mountain cannon, 100 heavy machine-guns and only two light machine-guns in each company. Some of the most vigorous fighting by the Chinese was done hand-to-hand with broadswords, and on one occasion even succeeded in beating off Japanese forces that had advanced under the cover of aerial bombard-ment. Nonetheless, by the end of May 1933, after two months of intense conflict, the Japanese had occupied all the key north-east wall passes and were in a position to swoop on Beijing.

On 31 May, Chinese and Japanese delegations signed the Tanggu Treaty, which stipulated a 250-mile-long demilitarized zone south of the Great Wall, ending just ten miles north of Beijing, thereby safeguarding Japanese control of the north-east. The Japanese army would wait another four years before provoking the skirmish that would bring about the fall of Beijing itself. In 1937, on the pretext that the Chinese had cap-tured one of their soldiers, the Japanese attacked and, three weeks later, took the Marco Polo Bridge, the junction that controlled access to north-ern China, from Shandong in the east to Shanxi in the west. By the end of July, Beijing and the surrounding region would be in Japanese hands.

As far as both China and the great majority of the Chinese were con-cerned, these defeats were tragic, leaving Japanese armies poised to initi-ate a conflict that, by 1945, would leave between 15 and 20 million Chinese dead – perhaps as many as 300,000 of them in the seven savage weeks of the Rape of Nanjing in 1937, when Japanese troops butchered the inhabitants of the Nationalist capital. But one monument, the Great Wall, and one man, Mao Zedong, were ultimately to profit from Chinese military collapse in the north.

Although Chinese resistance along the wall proved futile, although the physical wall was battered by modern warfare and by the heavy tramp of thousands of soldiers (the broader sections were used as military transport routes), the wall became a password for patriotism in a rash of popular nationalist songs. 'Go! Go! We must go together to the front to resist! To the front to resist! The blood-stained Great Wall is glorious!' ran the last verse of the song 'Defend Our Great Wall', sung by Chinese troops as they attempted vainly to defend the passes north of Beijing.[13] The Chinese broadsword divisions at the Great Wall became a byword for a new, vigorous spirit of national resistance, one capable (however briefly) of gaining the upper hand over the abundant modern weapons of the Japanese. 'Until now,' exulted a northern newspaper in March 1933,

most of our country's leadership wanted us to believe that we Chinese had no way of resisting Japan, of recovering our lost territory. The kind of heroism that we have seen at the Great Wall passes shows how wrong they are … that it's not a question of whether we can recover our territory, but whether we want to. It's not a question of weapons and technology, it's a question of courage and loyalty.[14]

The wall was again immortalized in music by a song composed for a Shanghai film entitled *Ten Thousand Li of Mountains and Passes (Guanshan wanli)*, planned after the Marco Polo Bridge incident of 1937. The film was never made but the song remains popular up to the present day, celebrating the Great Wall as a monument uniting – no longer dividing – the rightful territories of China both to north and south.

The 10,000-*li* Great Wall is 10,000-*li* long,
Beyond the Great Wall lies our homeland,
The sorghum is ripe and the soybeans are fragrant.
The whole area used to be bathed in gold, untroubled by disaster.

But since catastrophe has arisen from its plains,
Rape and pillage have afflicted the land,
In the midst of great troubles, we are exiled to other places,
Our flesh and bones are scattered, our parents mourn.

Even when our teeth have been drawn, we cannot forget our enmity and
    hatred,
Day and night we think only of returning to our homeland.
We are all working to fight our way back,
However brutally the Japanese slaves tyrannise us.

The 10,000-*li* Great Wall is 10,000 *li* long,
Beyond the Great Wall lies our homeland.
The hearts of our 400,000,000 compatriots are as one,
The new Great Wall is ten thousand *li* long.[15]

In 1936, a death sentence had been served on Mao Zedong's Communist revolution. That winter, almost four years after the Japanese had taken their first base in China proper, Chiang Kai-shek flew into Xi'an, the old north-western capital, convinced that one last encirclement campaign would destroy the Communists once and for all. Throughout the years of steady Japanese invasion before the Second World War, Chiang had focused his energies not on national resistance but on suppression of the Communists. When Shanhaiguan fell on 3 January 1933, Chiang was in Jiangxi, encircling the Soviet base area, and refused to break off to direct resistance in the north. The Japanese invasion was, he declared, merely 'external ... like a gradually festering ulcer on the skin. The [Communist] bandit disturbance is internal. It is ... a disorder of the heart. Because this internal disease has not been eliminated, the external disorder cannot be cured.'[16]

This was not how popular opinion saw matters: Chiang's rabid anti-Communism in the face of foreign invasion was rapidly building him a national public relations disaster. In 1933, as the Japanese moved further west into north China, as news of Japanese attacks there filtered down through the country, Chiang's critics multiplied, accusing him of 'sitting safely' in the south, of 'losing the nation'. Sun Yat-sen's widow accused Chiang and his government of 'betrayal, cowardice, and non-resistance'.[17]

Outrage intensified after the signing of the Tanggu Treaty: the southern press openly called Chiang a 'traitor', while a northern journalist declared that 'China does not now have a leader'.[18] In 1935, tens of thousands in cities across China marched to protest against Japanese aggression.

But as the Great Wall suffered in war, so its poet-admirer, Mao, seized his opportunity to benefit from the public feeling aroused. In 1936, thousands of kilometres from Shanghai's film studios, in a cave dwelling carved out of the loess cliffs in north China, Mao had himself versified the Great Wall as a monument to national unity.

> Here is the scene in the lands of the north:
> A thousand *li* sealed with ice,
> Ten thousand *li* of swirling snow.
> Both sides of the Great Wall
> The land rolls into one single immensity.
> From source to mouth of the great river,
> The torrential current freezes over and is lost.
> The mountains dance like silver snakes,
> The plateaus gallop away like waxen elephants,
> Striving to reach as high as the Lord of Heaven.
> On a clear day
> The white silk drapes blush with rouge
> Bewitching the beholder.[19]

While public sentiment against Chiang and his civil war seethed, Mao Zedong artfully proposed abandoning his old war against the Nationalists in favour of forming an alliance against Japan, changing his old platform of 'Resist Japan, Oppose Chiang' to 'Oppose Japan, Stop the Civil War'. He was suggesting the previously unthinkable: a second United Front, less than ten years after the first had ended in a bloodbath of betrayal. In a great public relations coup, Mao in 1936 was to win Communist China an American fellow-traveller for life by allowing Edgar Snow, a journalist from Kansas, to visit his headquarters in the north-west. Offering Snow exclusive access, Mao promoted himself to Anglophone readers not as a fanatical red revolutionary, but as a pragmatic and, above all, patriotic national freedom fighter, steadfastly opposed to appeasement of Japan: 'For a people being deprived of its national freedom, the revolutionary task is not immediate socialism, but the struggle for independence. We cannot even discuss communism if we are robbed of a country in which to practise it.'[20]

Chiang refused to countenance any suggestion of an alliance with his domestic enemies and on 4 December 1936 bustled into Xi'an, determined to finish off the Communists. At this point, however, even Chiang's closest allies refused to pursue his civil war at the cost of losing more of China to Japan. On the evening of 11 December, a warlord-turned-Nationalist commander called Zhang Xueliang ordered his personal bodyguard to arrest the Generalissimo. After a brief and futile escape into a hillside cave, Chiang – dressed only in a nightshirt and speechless after leaving his false teeth behind – was brought back to Xi'an, where Zhang offered him terms of release: end the civil war against the Communists and resist the Japanese. Although Chiang wriggled out of signing anything, his verbal agreement was given. On Boxing Day 1936, Chiang was allowed to fly back to Nanjing, with the basis, at least, for a new United Front shakily in place. The decisive Nationalist assault on Mao's base area had not only been called off; the Communists were now a legitimate political party, helping China fight for national survival.

Mao and his Communists, the Great Wall and calls for resistance against Japan thus allied to establish a powerful new platform of nationalist survival and recovery. One of the earliest set-piece United Front victories occurred among the passes around Yanmenguan, the mountainous walled pass between Hebei and Shanxi provinces, where Nationalist troops saw off a Japanese attack from the east, while Communist soldiers destroyed an enemy division from the rear. Years later, Mao remained incongruously grateful for the political boost that the Japanese invasion of north China brought him. In the early 1960s, a Japanese delegation visited Mao in Beijing and attempted to offer an apology for atrocities committed against the Chinese in the Second World War. Mao batted it away: 'Only when the Japanese Imperial Army had occupied most of China, only when the Chinese had their backs up against the wall did they awaken and take up arms ... This created the conditions for our victory in the war of liberation ... If I ought to thank anyone, it should be the Japanese militarists.'[21]

By 1945, eight years after a warlord's intervention had forced a tooth-less, shivering Generalissimo to pause before the final destruction of his internal enemies, Communist armies had grown almost tenfold, from some 85,000 troops in 1937 to more than a million, and the population under their control from 1.5 million to perhaps 90 million. After another four years of Nationalist mismanagement – spiralling inflation, persecution of intellectuals, pardoning of collaborators, incompetently fought campaigns – practically all China was in Communist hands. A blurry photograph on display in the main fortress at Shanhaiguan shows cheering locals lining the approach to the fort in 1949, as Communist troops marched through the open archway of the First Pass Under Heaven, the latest army to do so on their way to conquer China.

~

Mao Zedong did not quickly forget his old symbolic ally, the Great Wall, in his New China. A marching song written for a 1935 film, another paean to the wall as an emblem of national resistance, was adopted as the new anthem for the People's Republic:

> Arise, ye who refuse to be slaves.
> Let us build a new Great Wall out of our flesh and blood.
> The Chinese race has reached its moment of greatest danger.
> Everyone must go on to the last cry.
> Rise up! Rise up! Rise up!
> We the masses are of one heart and mind.

March on!

Into the fire of the enemy!

March on! March on! March on! On![22]

In real-life, bricks-and-mortar terms, however, the war had been disastrous for the Great Wall. Exposed to decades of warfare of varying intensity, the wall – particularly along the sections winding over the hard-fought north-east – was in a poor state of repair by the early 1950s. Badaling, the section nearest Beijing, was sadly dilapidated: its fort enclosure half destroyed, its walls, battlements and towers crumbling. Between 1953 and 1957 – perhaps in recognition of services rendered – the Communist government had a token 1,300 metres repaired, ironing out uneven floors for the benefit of the thin soles and high heels of future visitors, steadying wobbly crenellations to support the elbows of later tourist hordes. The Great Wall was entering its next phase of transformation: from idealized symbol of national resistance to manicured tourist attraction.

Some continuity with the wall's historical function in imperial China, however, remained. The original proposal for refurbishing the wall came in 1952 from Guo Moruo – a strident Romantic versifier in his youth, a high-ranking bully in the new Communist cultural bureaucracy in his middle age – who suggested that Badaling be repaired to provide a day out for diplomatic visitors to Beijing. Although embassies to China no longer approached bringing horses and pelts, the Great Wall was still the obligatory ceremonial gateway through which petitioners to the Middle Kingdom had to pass. On 19 March 1960, Badaling opened for diplomatic business, with a visit from the Nepali prime minister. In the next sixteen years – drought years for official foreign visits to the People's Republic – forty-three dignitaries followed. Hundreds have since done so.

Other parts of the wall, beyond the gaze of the few foreigners allowed past Mao's Bamboo Curtain, did far less well out of the People's

Republic. For Mao, the problem with history – both as an idea and as a material reality, in the form of artefacts left over from the past – was that he could not quite make up his mind what role it should play in his empire. In his own way, Mao – who lined his study with some of China's most ancient texts – was as conscious of history as any of his imperial predecessors: 'We should sum up our history from Confucius to Sun Yat-sen and take over this valuable legacy,' he pronounced in 1938. 'This is important for guiding the great movement of today.'[23] But while he was clear that history should serve the glorious, socialist present, any unruly aspect of the past that refused to fit his Marxist-Leninist purposes should be ignored or, ideally, erased. 'In studying history,' Mao lectured elsewhere, 'unless you take a class-struggle view as the starting-point, you will get confused.'[24] As Communist officials extended political control down to China's rural grass roots, one of the first ideological forces that they hurried to harness was that of public memory. At mass 'Speak Bitterness' meetings, the past was shut in a dark, airless box called the 'Old Society', the forerunner to Mao's dazzling New China – a simple, dishonest world in which landlords oppressed and peasants suffered.

Any other, more complex view of history, however, was for the dustbin. Obliteration was Mao's favoured solution to episodes from history that defied party control: in Communist China, anything vaguely antique has lived on borrowed time. At the same time as the People's Republic was actively turning the past into a pre-socialist nightmare to reinforce its own vision of the present, it was busy demolishing parts of the old architectural landscape of China that did not sit with its own modernizing vision and constructing its own new national set-pieces. The monumental heartland of Chinese political power, the old imperial city clustered around the Forbidden City, was radically remade in the 1950s. The walled park and Ming buildings directly south of the vermilion walls from which Mao announced the founding of the People's Republic in 1949 were bulldozed to create the vast, faceless plaza of present-day Tiananmen Square. The huge emptiness of the new square – the largest urban public space in the world – was edged with massive showpieces of socialist architecture (the Museums of Chinese History and Chinese Revolution, the Great Hall of the People) intentionally leaving the individual human visitor dwarfed by the full, overbearing ensemble. The Forbidden City itself was spared – perhaps in part because its overblown proportions shared the spatial values of socialist architecture, and its ethos of enclosure and secrecy mirrored the political values of China's new rulers. The old Beijing city wall was replaced by a ringroad, its stones finally carted away in 1969 to build shelters against Soviet bombs; only a few vast stone gates of the old wall now survive, rising up over slow-moving streams of traffic. In 1966, Mao launched his last and most ferocious attack on the past, his Cultural Revolution against the 'Four Olds' – old ideas, culture, customs, habits – in which countless irreplaceable temples, porcelain, paintings, sculptures and books perished at the hands and feet of Mao's revolutionary youth, the Red Guards.

Beyond a few tidy kilometres, the museum-piece passes near the capital on display to visitors as an airbrushed fantasy of ancient Chinese greatness, Mao had little interest in preserving the Great Wall's remaining sprawl, which was left to dilapidate further, a process accelerated by Communist utilitarianism. Acquisitive farmers peeled away outer layers of stone and rock or scooped out tamped-earth cores to use as fertilizer; along some stretches, bricks were prised off to build roads and reservoirs; elsewhere, the wall was dynamited to render its materials into saleable stone. The historical reality of the wall – its true age, function and non-uniform appearance, the errors and cataclysms associated with it – was forgotten, leaving only the occasional neat stretch to serve as an advertisement for Mao's China. In any case, by the time that Badaling had been repaired, Mao's regime had resculpted Beijing in its own modern, socialist image, and had no further need to renovate any more stop-gap monuments from a past towards which Mao felt, at best, ambivalent.

But as an idea, as the embodiment of an autocratic political philosophy, the Great Wall possessed a powerful and enduring appeal for Mao.

He passionately embraced the isolationist psychological outlook that the wall ostensibly expressed. When it suited him, Mao liked to think of himself as an internationalist, as a dynamic representative of the Communist world revolution. In practice, however, Mao's Communist belief was rooted in his suspicion of the corrupting influence of foreign ideas and thought. When he was not destroying evidence of China's past, Mao concentrated on eradicating among the Chinese masses any traces of the foreign, which, in his mind, were elided into the capitalist, the bourgeois and the dangerously anti-Communist. After Mao's Bamboo Curtain descended, leaving China became impossible for almost anyone unwilling to slip into the sea off China's south coast and risk swimming to Hong Kong. The Chinese were locked not just within their national frontiers but within cities, towns and villages. Regional markets for goods and services collapsed, after an almost inescapable Communist system of household and work-unit registration tied individuals to the job allocated to them by the state. Not content merely with preventing his subjects from leaving the country physically, Mao was determined also that their thoughts and customs should remain strictly within the bounds of an ever narrower Communist definition of Chineseness. By the start of the Cultural Revolution in 1966, the most mundane and innocuous objects – make-up, high heels, printed clothes, tight trousers, pets – had been labelled bourgeois, foreign and thus ideologically suspect; individuals daring to wear or harbour any of the above risked violent and humiliating public retribution. (Mao took a different view in private. Despite his public praise for traditional Chinese medicine, he personally insisted on being treated by a doctor trained in Western medicine.)

Mao actively applied his Great Wall mentality to the internal as well as the external regulation of Chinese society. If the Great Wall was, originally, the most grandiose expression of one of the most ancient and defining impulses in Chinese culture – to encircle houses, temples, villages with walls – Mao scaled this imperially super-sized vision back down in order to divide and rule his country. Instead of bricks and mortar, however, he used political puritanism and class struggle to create partitions among the Chinese. Initially, to win widespread support, the Communist Party adopted a conciliatory approach to the majority of the Chinese population who had not actively supported them before 1949. As it consolidated power, however, it began to turn not just on its most obvious class enemies – oppressive landlords and senior members of the Nationalist establishment – but also on smaller-scale transgressors of Communist orthodoxy: minor businessmen, literary critics who thought that writers needed to be subjective, novelists who expressed a guilty fondness for Western books, listeners who found state radio stations boring.

From the early 1950s, wave upon wave of mass political campaigns were unleashed upon China, each one expanding the definition of political incorrectness into ever more minor crimes. In 1957, a year after Mao had encouraged Chinese to produce criticisms of Communist government, he persecuted and imprisoned more than half a million of those who spoke up as 'Rightists'. Any hope for free expression in the People's Republic – at least during Mao's lifetime – was permanently destroyed. In a political culture that specialized in rooting out heterodoxy through hysterically violent public denunciations and forced confessions, where Chinese were pressurized, for their own safety, to inform on their neighbours and colleagues, to report on chance comments overheard out of open windows, merely having – much less expressing – critical thoughts became hazardous. In the late 1960s, a young Chinese called Wei Jingsheng – who would later fight Mao's totalitarian wall with a Democracy Wall – watched how Mao tore China apart, leaving its people poor, weak and starving, how 'he put people into imaginary interest groups, and set them to struggle against each other so that they lost touch with reality and could no longer see where their true interests lay'.[25] One of the rightists condemned in 1957 succinctly summarized the society that Maoist class struggle had produced: 'Since 1952, campaign has succeeded campaign, each one leaving behind a Great Wall in its wake, a wall which estranges one man from another.'[26]

It was no coincidence that during the Cultural Revolution – the political apogee of Maoist dictatorship – a public campaign was initiated to rehabilitate the First Emperor of Qin, the traditional arch-villain of Chinese history and builder of the first imperial border wall. Thanks to a whirlwind makeover by party historians, the First Emperor underwent a dizzying transformation during the early 1970s from tyrannical philistine to modernizing visionary. The First Emperor's wall, an article in the *People's Daily*, the official national organ of the Communist Party, celebrated, was built 'in order to prevent the harassing attacks of the slave-owning Xiongnu and to consolidate the feudal state based on centralisation of power. This accorded with the interests of the people.'[27] As the First Emperor's stock rose, that of his enemies fell. The year 1975 saw the publication of a book-length denunciation in high Cultural Revolution style of Meng Jiangnu, the legendary weeper at the Qin wall, entitled *Meng Jiangnu was a Pro-Confucian, Anti-Legalist Great Poisonous Weed.*[28] Considering the derelict or dynamited condition of much of the wall during these years, it is hard to think of a more instructive example of Mao's Janus-faced attitude to the past: of his deeply Chinese regard for harnessing history to serve the present (imagine a vaguely equivalent situation in 1980s Britain: Prime Minister Thatcher prodding *The Times* to praise Hadrian and his wall to support her opposition to the European Union); and of his ruthless disregard for any part of that history that did not serve his own totalitarian worldview.

CONCLUSION

The Great Wall, the Great Mall
and the Great Firewall

In a photograph of 23 October 1972, the American president Richard Nixon stands on the Badaling Great Wall, thronged by a slightly distracted-looking Maoist diplomatic entourage. The excursion took place during Nixon's eight-day visit to the People's Republic, a sojourn spent basking in the full glow of Communist hospitality: meetings with Mao, banquets, toasts and serenades by the People's Liberation Army band, which exceptionally departed from its usual repertoire of socialist classics to regale the president with an old American favourite, 'Home, Home on the Range'. In the photograph, the wall is ingratiatingly looking its picturesque best for the leader of the capitalist world: winding over snow dusted mountains under a clear blue sky, cleared of messy, extraneous humanity in honour of the presidential visiting party. (Security, presumably, was lurking both Chinese- and Mongol-style in the watchtowers and greenery at the side of the wall.) Captured staring fixedly at some out-of-shot feature, the sides of his mouth pulled back into an appreciative grin, the president obliged Communist journalists by mumbling into his fur collar an appropriately overawed platitude: 'This is a great wall and it had to be built by a great people.'[1]

That same year, a thirty-one-year-old boiler serviceman called Huang Xiang from Guizhou, in southern China, far out of sight of Sino-American diplomatic high jinks, expressed his own view of the Great

323

Wall in rather different terms. In his poem 'Confessions of the Great Wall', he allowed it to speak wearily for itself:

Under the hazily grey, low-hanging clouds
I have stood through the ages
My arteries have hardened
My legs have numbed
My supports will collapse, my balance will go
Ageing, decrepit, I will fall down and die

…

I am old
My younger sons and grandsons dislike me,
As they would dislike an obstreperous grandfather
When they see me, they immediately turn away
They do not wish to look upon my blackish-green skin
Upon my gaping, cavernous mouth

…

They dart hate-filled glances at me
As if I am a mummy out of its sarcophagus

…

They say that I lie
That I've been deceiving them for centuries

…

They don't want to use me as a yardstick
To measure the unity and will of their race

…

To them, I am as repellent as a snake
Because I am coiled, ruthlessly, over their mental landscape
Gnawing away at their souls, generation after generation

They want to overturn me, demolish me

…

CONCLUSION

I divide the land into infinite small pieces
Into endless narrow, suffocating little courtyards
I am stretched out amidst the people
Dividing this group from that group
Making them guard, at all times, against each other
Never able to see their neighbours' faces
Or even hear their conversation
They want to overturn me, demolish me
Because my vast body is blocking their view
Separating them from the big wide world outside their own courtyards

...

Because every stone of me, every square of mud
weightily recalls the human past
day and night narrating the tragedies of yesterday
I remind them
Of the subjugation and enclosure of countless generations past
Of the fear and hatred of ages
Of the struggles of those dark centuries, the sacrifices and suffering
Of the cacophonous divisions and disharmony
Of the furious history of human conflict
They want to overturn me, demolish me
For the sake of those ancestors of theirs who died within these mental
    walls
In order, for the first time, to leave to their sons and grandsons the legacy
    of science and democracy

...

They are pushing away my trembling, crumbling, blackened corpse
Ripping off my shroud of tradition: its worship of the past, its medioc-
    rity, narrow-mindedness, conservatism

...

Those places that were so distant in the past
Are now very near

My ramparts are disappearing from the earth's surface

Falling down within human minds

I am going   I have died

A generation of sons and grandsons are carrying me into the museum

…[2]

By 1972, the Great Wall itself was a defensive fossil, but Nixon's visit and Huang Xiang's poem showed that the isolationist worldview that had built it over the millennia was still very much alive. Practically every moment of Nixon's trip to China was captured on camera and beamed back on to American televisions, precisely because it represented a sensational breakthrough: the reopening of diplomatic relations between China and one of the leaders of the Western world after a twenty-year hiatus. As an American, Nixon focused on attacking the face of the Great Wall mentality visible to him: the struggle to exclude foreigners from China. As a young Chinese growing up under Mao, Huang Xiang saw the Great Wall mentality from the inside: the impulse to lock the Chinese in, both away from foreigners and away from each other.

Nixon did not hesitate to tell the Maoist leadership everything they wanted and hoped to hear about their national mascot, the Great Wall, doing so in the interests of trade and Cold War realpolitik. His response to the wall was perfectly in step with official views: it was there to act as a tool of totalitarian tourist diplomacy, to function as a no-historical-questions-asked symbol of the greatness of China over past and future millennia. Yet despite his acquiescence in monumental Communist propaganda, Nixon's visit at least opened a chink in Mao's Bamboo Curtain. Six years later, with Mao two years dead, his former comrade-in-arms Deng Xiaoping – twice purged under Mao for his liberal views on the economy – assumed power and widened Nixon's chink into a fully Open Door. Soon foreign companies were swarming to invest and set up in China, taking advantage of Deng's generous tax breaks. The brightest young Chinese started to win scholarships abroad; those who stayed behind began bringing the foreign back home: bell-bottom trousers, long hair, pop music, Kafka.

To an extent, Nixon risked his presidential credibility in his overture to Communist China. In attacking Maoist China's internal Great Wall mentality, Huang Xiang was risking his livelihood, freedom and perhaps even his life (political prisoners in Maoist China had a habit of dying in prison or labour camp). In 1972, merely to write poetry was perilously individualist and anti-proletarian; to write poetry that criticized the political system, as Huang Xiang did, was almost suicidally risky, but entirely typical of his record of courageous rebellion against the straitjacket of Mao's China. Already tarred by his family background – his father, a Nationalist general, had been shot in a camp outside Beijing in 1951 – the young Huang continually made life under Communism difficult for himself by refusing to bow his head and meekly accept the tedious, regulated life handed to him by the dictatorship of the proletariat. At the age of eighteen, he fled his dull factory job in south China for the empty plains and mountains of Qinghai in the north-west. He fell in love without first applying to an administrative department for a permit. Not only did he write poetry – both for the purposes of self-expression and political protest – but also sometimes chose to declaim it at busy public intersections. None of this fitted with the destiny that socialism had marked out for him and, as a result, Huang spent some five years of his early adult life under Mao in prison labour camps – *laogai,* the Communist Chinese version of the Soviet gulag – existing in excrement-smeared cells alongside hardened criminals.

By 1978, however, Mao was dead, the extreme leftist ideologues who had kept his Cultural Revolution running had been arrested and the pragmatic reformist Deng Xiaoping was poised to take power from the faceless Maoist puppets left in control of government. That year, restive Chinese were fighting the Communist Great Wall mentality with another wall: a grey, nondescript, low wall in central Beijing on which, one mid-

November weekend, a motor mechanic pasted a poster which accused Chairman Mao of being 'mistaken'. A couple of days later, several further posters had joined the first, one of which identified the Maoist regime as a 'feudal, fascist dictatorship', run by 'executioners and murderers whose hands are stained with the blood of the people'. By the end of the week, the wall had become a gathering place for thousands of political discontents, gathered to read the pink, yellow, green and white paper patchwork of political opinions that covered its surface. On 5 December, a young electrician called Wei Jingsheng added a poster which demanded a 'fifth modernization' alongside the four post-Mao Communist modernizations (in agriculture, science, technology and national defence) championed by Deng Xiaoping: democracy. Determined to testify to his commitment to free, open speech, he then did something even more unconventional: he signed it. Soon, visitors to Democracy Wall, as it became known, were no longer reading in silence but making speeches, speaking frankly to foreign journalists, distributing samizdat journals, founding societies and discussion groups, and marching to Tiananmen, where impromptu mass meetings took place. 'This Wall,' someone shouted, 'is the base which supports democracy in China.'[3]

In Tiananmen Square, after 24 November, marchers would have been greeted by another impromptu poster display on a fence opposite Mao's mausoleum: a ninety-four-panel exhibition of Huang Xiang's anti-Maoist hymns to freedom and democracy – including his denunciation of the Great Wall. Huang and his friends had travelled thousands of kilometres from Guiyang to the capital, where, buckets of flour paste and rolls of posters in hand, they targeted not only Tiananmen but also the ideological nerve centre of the People's Republic by flyposting a lane next to the offices of the *People's Daily*. The alleyway was almost instantly choked with readers. By December, walls in cities up and down the country were being put to similarly democratic uses, while petitioners from all over China flocked to the capital to present their stories of persecution and poverty.

At the time, Democracy Wall activists had high hopes for Deng Xiaoping, who in 1978 had ousted the dusty old Maoists in the Politburo by mobilizing anti-Cultural Revolution opinion across national newspapers. Until February 1979, Deng profitably rode the wave of discontent manifested most publicly and radically in the Democracy Wall, winning himself national popularity as an opponent of Maoist extremism, even declaring to a Canadian journalist that Democracy Wall was 'good'.[4] As ordinary Chinese wonderingly eyed liberal political models abroad, Deng's openness to the outside world seemed promising. During a week-long visit to the United States in late January 1979, Deng tried on a ten-gallon hat for a Texas rodeo, met the Harlem Globetrotters and had a turn on a space shuttle simulator at Houston.

By the time that Deng returned from the headquarters of global capitalism, however, in February 1979, the anti-Maoism of the Democracy Wall had outlived its usefulness for him. Deng was not a democrat, as wall activists hopefully miscalculated, but a pragmatic authoritarian. His primary concern was national stability, the key to which, he believed, was not democracy but capitalist-style economic prosperity. While his enthusiasm for economic growth made him hate the extreme leftism of the Cultural Revolution and argue for wealth-generating foreign trade and investment, he was also a Communist who never seriously entertained the idea that economic reforms should be managed by anything other than the one-party state. 'You cannot succeed,' he later commented, 'without recourse to methods of dictatorship.'[5] In March 1979, he bowed to conservative opinion among the leadership, making it clear that in Deng's China openness was not considered an absolute good in itself, that 'some utterances are not in the interest of stability and unity'.[6]

[C]ertain bad elements have raised sundry demands ... They have provoked or tricked some of the masses into raiding Party and government organisations ... they have raised such sensational slogans as 'Oppose hunger' and 'Give us human rights,' ... deliberately trying to get foreigners to give worldwide publicity to their words and deeds. There is a so-called China Human Rights Group which has gone so far as to put up big-character posters requesting the President of the United States to 'show concern' for human rights in China. Can we permit such an open call for intervention in China's internal affairs?[7]

The gatekeepers in Deng's Great Wall were immeasurably more permissive than those under Mao; but they assuredly still had work to do. Unlike Mao, Deng could countenance allowing the Chinese people a degree of economic freedom; politically, however, he was cast in the same authoritarian mould as his predecessor. The rub, of course, was that demands for other kinds of liberalization – political, social, cultural – tended to creep in on the back of economic relaxation. Deng's great difficulty, and the reason why the first ten years of his reign see-sawed wildly between control and détente, lay in protecting economic openness while rejecting anything that did not fit with his 'spiritual socialist civilization'. Four years later, during one of his handful of major anti-Western ideological crackdowns, the Anti-Spiritual Pollution campaign, he ruefully spelled out his misgivings about openness: 'If you unlatch the window, it's hard to stop the flies and mosquitoes rushing in.'

In October 1979, the electrician Wei Jingsheng suffered the full weight of the clampdown on Democracy Wall, sentenced to fifteen years in jail, many of them spent in solitary confinement. Deng Xiaoping, some say, wanted him shot; only the threat of adverse international publicity held him back. Huang escaped relatively lightly, with another eighteen months in labour camp. New official regulations formally prohibited 'slogans, posters, books, magazines, photographs and other materials which oppose socialism, the dictatorship of the proletariat, the leadership of the Communist Party, Marxism-Leninism, and Mao Zedong Thought'.[8] Towards the middle of December 1979, after the Beijing city authorities banned any further displays on Democracy Wall, female comrades from the city's sanitation department scrubbed the posters away.[9]

~

Ten years passed, ten good years for the Great Wall. In September 1984, a year after the Anti-Spiritual Pollution campaign cracked down on over-Westernized ideological looseness – a broad, vague concept that included pornography, commercialism, imagistic poetry and Western hairstyles – Deng Xiaoping moved on to his next national campaign: 'Love China, Restore Our Great Wall'. Over the next five or so years, tens of millions of *yuan* were poured into wall works: another 2,500-odd feet of wall around Badaling were smartened up, a second pass in the Ming wall near Beijing buffed to showcase standards. That same autumn of 1984, the wall was wreathed not only in restorative scaffolding but also in roseate socialist pageantry. In the 'Song of the Chinese Revolution', a musical extravaganza celebrating thirty-five years of the People's Republic, the Great Wall rose up out of the mist as a backdrop to an all-singing, all-dancing outflow of patriotic gush.[10] In 1988, the wall even starred in its own television documentary, acclaimed as an expression of 'mankind's vast creativity', of 'the Chinese people's extraordinary intelligence and untiring spirit of self-strengthening'.[11] The Great Wall was one of the largest beneficiaries of the Communist Party's new, pro-traditional cultural policy, one designed to fill the ideological blank left by abandoning Maoist iconoclasm. After years of Confucius-bashing, the sage swung back in fashion, becoming the subject of party-sponsored conferences, workshops and new research institutes. Party planners looked to the fat GDPs of the Four Asian Dragons and started to think that Confucianism – if wedded to capitalism – might have something in it after all. Naturally, its new Communist friends were at the same time not unmindful that Confucianism had for millennia been usefully employed in propping up dictatorship. Democracy Wall, meanwhile, was demolished, replaced by a cathedral to Deng's market reforms: a vast Bank of China.

For the country at large, however, change was more uneven. At the top, there was Deng Xiaoping, the pro-market Communist authoritarian, locked in constant battle with conservative supporters of the old-style socialist command economy. To China's billion-plus population, economic liberalization seemed a mixed blessing, bringing opportunities only to those daring or powerful enough to grasp them confidently – entrepreneurs or savvy officials able to put political connections to profitable use in business. To those still relying on the iron rice bowl (the Communist promise of a secure but unimaginatively remunerated job for life), however, the shift towards a market economy meant both soaring prices that made a mockery of their pay packets, and increasing job insecurity, as state businesses began to broach the Maoist taboos of efficiency and competitiveness.

By 1988, Deng Xiaoping's version of the Great Wall mentality had most of urban China in an ideological head spin: while China's door remained open at all times to foreign investment, every few years its windows slammed shut in the face of foreign 'flies and mosquitoes' (in particular, talk of political freedom). But the inconsistencies of Deng's market socialism would not, perhaps, have jarred so painfully if it had been delivering unarguably improved living standards, a clear sense of material progress. Discontent intensified when, at the Thirteenth Party Congress at the end of 1987, the party general secretary and Deng's second-in-command crushingly informed the nation that, after almost forty years of political and economic blood, sweat and toil, the People's Republic of China was still, remedially, only in the 'primary stage' of socialism. To China's city-dwellers, this primary stage had little to recommend it: in the first three months of 1988, urban vegetable prices rose by almost 50 per cent; pork, eggs and sugar were rationed after bouts of panic buying. In the interests of cutting production costs, state-owned enterprises started to lay off workers, 400,000 in one city in the first half of 1988 alone; beggary, strikes and crime (both economic and violent) were all on the increase. In the midst of these economic setbacks, the party's reputation was tarnished further by popular perceptions that it was turning into an enormous racket, that well-connected officials – buying, selling, embezzling – were the only real winners in China's turn

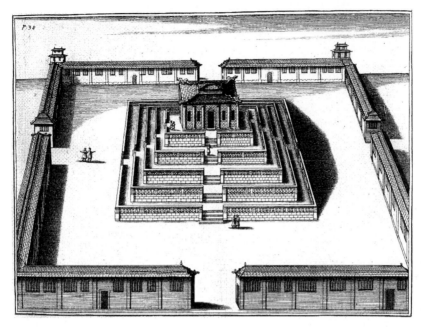

An impression, taken from a late seventeenth-century Jesuit account, of the imperial Chinese throne, set within multiple walls

Parish's sketch of Lord Macartney's audience with the Chinese emperor Qianlong at Jehol.

A nineteenth-century German cartoon of imperialist Western armies gathering to storm the Chinese giant, sheltering behind the Great Wall.

An early twentieth-century view of the loess hills – into which cave dwellings were carved – of northwest China where Mao and the Communists made their headquarters during the mid-1930s.

Chinese soldiers marching along the Great Wall in early 1937.

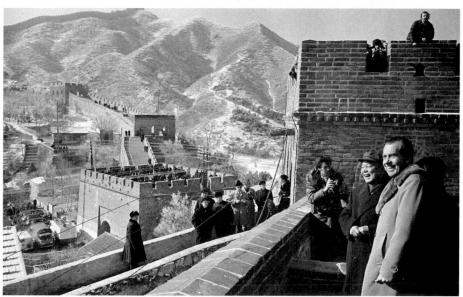

Standing next to the Chinese Vice Premier, Richard Nixon appreciatively surveys the restored Great Wall at Badaling in February 1972.

A stretch of the Ming wall near Beijing undergoing Communist restoration.

towards market socialism. In the minds of the majority of urban Chinese, the Communist Party's Open Door didn't seem to be letting in anything particularly beneficial to them. The result was not nostalgia for the economic and political puritanism of Maoism, but an overwhelming desire to be allowed to control the door themselves.

In June 1988, as discontented mutterings grew in volume in cities up and down the country, a six-part historical documentary was aired on national television. The series electrified the country. Tens, perhaps hundreds of millions of those lucky enough to have access to a television – in the late 1980s, such luxury consumer goods were in short supply and bore inflated price tags – gathered round sets on the six evenings that it was broadcast. Abridged in national newspapers with circulations of several millions, the script of the series also went on to sell more than 700,000 copies in book form. A year later, in the crackdown following the 1989 demonstrations at Tiananmen, its principal author, a self-assured young reportage writer and broadcaster called Su Xiaokang, was identified as a black hand in fermenting the 'counter-revolutionary turmoil' of that spring and had to be smuggled out of the country to Europe.

The series was called *River Elegy* and its broad purpose was straightforward enough: to blame China's troubled present on its landlocked historical geography, and on its failure to embrace maritime exploration and open to the outside world. *River Elegy* mourned the tyranny of the Yellow River, whose changing, flooding, silt-ridden course exhausted the energies and ingenuity of the Chinese, making them obsessed with protecting their own land above all other concerns. The massive, collective challenge of managing river and land forced the Chinese to turn to tight, authoritarian forms of political organization focused inwards on domestic, agrarian concerns. As a result, they had repeatedly failed to look outward, to expand overseas, to broaden their horizons and break with thousands of years of feudal dictatorship. The single monument most expressive of China's political failings, intoned the narrator of *River Elegy*, was the

Great Wall, built to close China's only open frontier, its one border not decisively sealed off by mountains or ocean.

After the First Emperor of Qin built the Great Wall, 'it became possible to resist the attacks of herding peoples from the outside, while at the same time producing a sort of cohesive force on the inside, forcing the people within the walls towards the nucleus of power. Thus whoever built the Great Wall would then possess the land, the territory, and the people within it.'[12] But while it strengthened despotism, *River Elegy* went on, the wall was never effective as a defence:

By the time that Genghis Khan's fierce horsemen had swept down like a tide, not even natural barriers like the Yellow River and the Yangtze, let alone the Great Wall, could stop them ... And the Chinese people, despite their high level of civilisation, were also powerless to resist that fate ... How many tragicomedies of history have been played out before the backdrop of the Great Wall![13]

To the makers of *River Elegy,* the latest of these tragicomedies was the worship of the wall by contemporary Chinese:

People pride themselves on the fact that it is the only feat of human engineering visible to astronauts on the moon. People even wish to use it as a symbol of China's strength. But if the Great Wall could speak, it would very frankly tell its Chinese grandchildren that it is a great and tragic gravestone forged by historical destiny ... it can only represent an isolationist, conservative and incompetent defence and a cowardly lack of aggression ... Alas, O Great Wall, why do we still want to praise you?[14]

River Elegy's devastating case against the Great Wall – this 'act of failure and retreat' – was visually reinforced by images of the scarred and pitted, monotonously yellow-brown ruins of the wall, set among the deserts of the north.[15] The antidote to the stifling earth-based palette of Chinese history was the fresh blue 'progressive tide' of the ocean, 'washing away the accumulated sediment of feudalism' with trade, openness, progress, freedom, capitalist wealth, science and democracy.[16] 'Can we not hear the grand melody of human destiny?' asked the documentary, underlining its point with jauntily synthesized harpsichord music, cheery sailors and images of paradisaical white, palm-fringed beaches.[17]

Although the programme made few direct references to China's uncomfortable present, no educated Chinese watching the programme would have failed to grasp the underlying allegorical purpose of marshalling this case against the Great Wall and the Yellow River: to enable the documentary's makers to criticize the current government and its decade-long vacillation between economic liberalization and political repression. No one would have mistaken criticism of the First Emperor of Qin and his earthen wall for anything but an attack on Mao and his closed socialist system; or praise of the clear, azure ocean for anything but advocacy of openness to the political values of the liberal democratic West. 'We are right now moving from opacity to transparency,' the documentary prophesied optimistically. 'This stretch of dirt-yellow land cannot teach us the true spirit of science. The unruly Yellow River cannot teach us a true democratic consciousness ... Only when the sea-breeze of "blueness" finally turns to rain and once again moistens this stretch of parched yellow soil, only then will this awesome vitality ... be able to bring new life to the vast yellow soil plateau.'[18]

Viewed now, *River Elegy* sounds a little pompous, a little overblown, a little too in love with its own allegory and certainly rather naïve about the West. (In 1980s China, even educated people viewed episodes of *Dallas* as authoritative, documentary sources on contemporary America.) But even today there is much that still seems remarkable about the programme. In a socialist culture that has no interest in encouraging people to think critically or creatively about their past, that wants people to fix hopeful eyes on their tomorrows rather than questioning eyes on their yesterdays, the documentary's willingness to engage with history – despite its factual distortions committed in the interests of polemic – and its eagerness to attack totems of Chinese nationalism such as the Great Wall are still refreshing. A casual comparative flick through China's

Communist-controlled TV channels in the early third millennium –
where sappy pop shows rub shoulders with soap operas preaching kitsch
socialist morality – makes *River Elegy* seem part of another, appealingly
serious cultural world.

When students began taking to the streets in spring 1989, it was easy to
make the link between their demands for increased freedom of expression and transparency in government, and *River Elegy*, the television sen-
sation of the previous year. The documentary's concluding instalment
hailed China's intellectuals as the saviours of the nation: 'They hold in
their hands the weapon to destroy ignorance and superstition … It is they
who can channel the "blue" sweetwater spring of science and democracy
into our yellow earth!'[19] After the students eagerly rose up to shoulder the
lofty historical destiny that *River Elegy* marked out for them, Su Xiaokang
rushed to take part in the protests, stalking Tiananmen Square swathed in
a paper sash identifying him as author of *River Elegy*, addressing the students through a megaphone. 'Very nice,' his more cautious wife snapped
when he returned home, 'you got your moment of glory. All videotaped
by Security.'[20]

At ten p.m. on 4 June 1989, eighteen days after Deng Xiaoping had
rushed the visiting Soviet leader Mikhail Gorbachev away from the
embarrassing demonstrations in Tiananmen to enjoy the fresh spring air
of a trip to the Badaling Great Wall, the Communist leadership ordered
People's Liberation Army troops assembled on the outskirts of the capital to clear the square. Half an hour later, when non-violent crowds
blocked the army's path a few kilometres west of Tiananmen, soldiers
began shooting civilians. Only days later did the guns finally fall silent.
Within a week after the crackdown, the government had issued a 'most-
wanted' list, naming student leaders, human rights activists, members of
independent think tanks and Su Xiaokang, maker of *River Elegy*. Along
with Chai Ling and Wu'er Kaixi, two of the best-known student leaders,
Su was one of the lucky ones who managed to escape, reaching America
via Hong Kong and Paris.

When it failed to get its hands on Su, the government consoled itself by clawing at his televisual brainchild. On 11 September 1989, a group of history professors were assembled in the capital to denounce *River Elegy* and its anti-Yellow River, anti-Great Wall, pro-Western message as 'counter-revolutionary incendiarism', accusing it of 'tricking and deceiving people's hearts', of leading 'public opinion into the political turmoil that broke out everywhere this year and which evolved into counter-revolutionary rebellion in the capital', and of an intolerably 'rash and frivolous attitude towards national heroes, patriots and revolutionary leaders'.[21]

While events in Eastern Europe were leading up to the raising of the Iron Curtain, China's rulers reviewed the experiences of the last ten years in the wake of the Beijing massacre. Returning to total isolationism was not an option. For better or for worse, China under Deng Xiaoping was now committed to some degree of openness: increasing foreign investment and trade was one of the great economic success stories of the 1980s. Even culturally, no one seriously wanted to turn the clock back to Maoism. The government's cultural bureaucrats would have been hard pressed to argue that the literature of the 1980s, stimulated by reading of Western classics newly available once again in translation, was inferior to that produced under Mao, when political controls had so stifled creativity that, between 1949 and 1966, an embarrassing average of only eight novels were published each year in the People's Republic. The government's principal concern remained unchanged from the late 1970s: to embrace the economic fruits of openness to keep the populace contented and stable, while repelling the destabilizing, anti-totalitarian flies and mosquitoes of media freedom and democracy; in other words, to continue closely monitoring China's border transactions.

~

Another ten years passed; another ten good years for the Great Wall. The Berlin Wall might have fallen, but China's remained the country's number-one tourist attraction and national mascot. Festivities organized in Beijing for the 1997 handover of Hong Kong featured a theatrical Great Wall reconstruction made out of glistening Chinese bodies.[22] The symbolism – the Chinese People equalling the Great Wall equalling the Motherland, tucking Hong Kong back inside after 100 years in the outside world – could not have been more obvious.

While the Chinese who had witnessed the crackdown of 1989 did not privately forget, the government made clear that it was in no one's best interests publicly to bear it much in mind. As a result, by 1998, many Chinese students had little idea of what their predecessors had demanded a decade earlier; much less of what had happened in 1978. The catchphrase on many lips in the 1990s was *wang qian kan:* look towards the future, which, in Chinese, neatly punned the word for 'future' on that for 'money'. For the government, the tactic seemed to pay off. Against all apparent certainties in the spring of 1989, three years later the Chinese followed Deng Xiaoping's 1992 directive towards 'faster, better, deeper' economic growth and market reforms. The official media insisted that markets could be socialist, while Deng maintained that 'foreign-funded enterprises ... are good for socialism'.[23]

For the time being, the Chinese accepted what the party publicly allowed past its own Great Wall; while opaque, one-party government continued its grip on the mass media, civilians outwardly focused their energies on earning and consuming. In the early 1980s they were satisfied with bicycles, wristwatches and televisions. By the end of the millennium, they were thinking altogether bigger: cars, houses and foreign holidays. And in 2004, they started thinking bigger still, when a Chinese computer company tried to buy up a branch of the American multinational IBM. Malls as much as walls became the defining, venerated monuments of post-1989 China. Ever the historical survivor, the Great Wall merged seamlessly with China's burgeoning consumer landscape, adopted as trademark for a diverse array of goods and services: logically enough, for a gated-compound housing development; less logically, for a brand of wine, a make of tyres and a credit card.

Yet underneath China's quiescent exterior, its relations with the outside world have been transformed by a quiet but radical assault on its borders: an assault no longer made by nomadic horsemen, but by information and technology, and one in which China's most significant frontiers are no longer earth-based, but virtual.

The first whiff of change came on 20 September 1987, when one man, a Chinese professor of computing, with his own slogan – 'Go beyond the Great Wall, March toward the World' – sent China's first email. For seven years, no one took much notice, until Al Gore's 1994 speech on 'Building the Information Superhighway' finally broke into Chinese consciousness. That year, the first Chinese network was set up; the first public Internet service followed in 1995. Over the next eight years, the number of Chinese Internet users more or less tripled annually, growing from 40,000 to 59.1 million.[24] By the start of 2005, it was estimated that it had topped the 100-million mark.

As with most inventions and innovations that have seeped into China from abroad, the government has been anxious to control and define the Internet's uses. The Internet, according to official decree, is there as a development tool, to spur economic growth by facilitating business communications and investment. While recognizing in 2000 that the Internet 'has played an important role in the world's economic growth', Deng's successor, Jiang Zemin, hoped to 'strengthen the administration of healthy information' on the web, to supervise, as ever, the traffic through his Great Wall.[25]

No great powers of clairvoyance would have been necessary in the 1990s to forecast that matters virtual would not prove as wholesomely cut-and-dried as the government wanted, that the Internet in China would become, in many different hands, a potential means of bringing down the Great Wall mentality and a vehicle for what, by Chinese standards, resembles wildly free expression: for non-official news sources, for democracy activists, for civil and legal organizations, for religious cults, football obsessives and sex-mad urbanites. The US would no doubt like to claim that it predicted all in a 1995 Pentagon report that forecast the Internet would present a 'strategic threat to authoritarian regimes'. Laying down a challenge to Beijing, Bill Clinton in 2000 told journalists that the Chinese government would find a web crackdown as slippery as 'trying to nail Jell-O to the wall'. As then presidential candidate George W. Bush commented in 1999, already harping on his now trademark preoccupation, if the Internet were to take hold in China, 'freedom's genie will be out of the bottle.'[26] Between the late 1990s, when the political freedom of most regional newspapers was limited to shuffling the order of the photographs of the leadership printed in the national *People's Daily,* and 2005, when TV soaps are still only a few notches more psychologically complex than socialist realism, Chinese cyberspace has offered people a much-needed media forum for letting their hair down.

Ever since the Internet took off in China, however, the government has been trying valiantly to combat its dangerous potential for information decontrol and for liberalizing expression. At the outset, this was achieved by old-fashioned Communist truculence: wrapping Internet access up in so much bureaucratic red tape that the majority of aspiring netizens would give up and stick with the *People's Daily* or its local equivalent. In 1996, aspiring Internet users had to fill out a Police File Report Form in triplicate for the local Public Security Bureau, sign a Net Access Responsibility Pledge not to read or transmit material that 'endangers the state, obstructs public safety, or is obscene or pornographic' and provide the Internet Service Provider (ISP) with almost every piece of personal information imaginable, short of unusual birthmarks.[27]

By the end of the millennium, when ISPs started to unravel the red tape around getting wired, the government had upped the technological ante in its efforts to police the Internet. The Communist Party realized that if it were to meet Clinton's challenge of 'nailing Jell-O to the wall', it would first of all need a wall against which to work. Between 1996 and 1997, a new department at the Public Security Bureau devoted to infringing Internet liberties set about constructing the 'Great Firewall of China': a blissful marriage of Chinese tradition with cutting-edge technology. A sprinkling of servers guarding the five gateways at which the Chinese Internet met that of the outside world, the Firewall was programmed to block sensitive sites from abroad – foreign newspapers, pro-Tibetan or Taiwanese independence organizations, religious cults, *Playboy* and so on – from a list updated fortnightly. Five years later, the Firewall had been further armed with 'packet sniffers', software able to detect officially problematic words and phrases in individual web pages and emails from a list that has included 'Falun Gong', 'freedom', 'fuck', 'sex' and 'Jiang Zemin'.[28] One whiff of 'sex', for example, and the packet-sniffer would have the relevant terminal frozen. In 2002, the government blocked Google entirely, because its practice of caching every website that it indexed gave Chinese web users a way of accessing banned pages. Although, after public outcry and an appeal from Google, the government repealed the ban, it continues, more quietly and selectively, to censor Google's caches with packet-sniffers.

The ultimate deterrent to subversive use of the Internet is, of course, the law, or what passes for it in the People's Republic. Reporters without Borders, the Internet freedom organization, estimated that by 2004 sixty-one cyber dissidents were imprisoned in China. In 2003, Liu Di, a psychology student, became an international cause célèbre, detained in a Beijing prison for a year without being charged for protesting in chatrooms about the imprisonment of political dissidents.

Just as there were in the bricks-and-earth Great Wall, however, there are holes in the Firewall. In China itself, the Firewall is also known as the Net Wall, which provides a good sense of the porous nature of its coverage. Enforcement of blocks on banned websites has always been patchy at best: not all the gateways in the Firewall have been equally diligent in carrying out Communist will. Alternatively, like Altan Khan, determined surfers can simply go round the wall, using proxy servers in foreign countries instead of the official gateways to the worldwide web. Frustrated

Chinese users of Google in 2004 accessed the search engine's results by using ElgooG: a mirror image version of the original site originally built as a computer-nerd joke. Linguistically challenged government filters failed to recognize that Chinese users who were able to type English backwards could access banned sites such as Swen CBB (BBC News). In any case, there are simply too many new websites constantly springing up for the government to censor them all.

Another revolutionary feature of the Chinese Internet lies in its ability to bring down walls not just between China and the rest of the world but within China itself. In the last few years, the Internet has played a major role in throwing open China's closed system of government to public scrutiny: exposing police malfeasance (such as the case of a young man who died in police custody in Guangzhou) and official cover-ups (the Aids epidemic in Henan province generated by a blood-selling corruption scandal), and helping mobilize anti-government action (some of the biggest public protests since 1989 have been coordinated by the banned religious sect Falun Gong, whose adherents have rallied around the organizing posts of email and the Internet). The major development on the Chinese Internet in 2003 was the blog boom: in the space of about a year, the number of Chinese bloggers grew from 2,000 to 160,000, a number of whom are journalists who write into their blogs stories and information too sensitive to be published in more old-fashioned mass media. Two features of blogs work in their favour as mechanisms for distributing sensitive information. First of all, there are too many of them for official censors to control, and too many possible outlets for the government to prevent a determined blogger from writing. Secondly, blogs have a semi-private quality – information can be made available to registered users only – which official censors seem to find less threatening than entirely public forums such as bulletin boards and chatrooms.[29] In October 2004, blogs started to realize their subversive potential when a group of farmers in the north-west used a blog to protest the confiscation of their land by the government; instead of stonewalling their critics, local officials felt compelled to respond via their own blog.[30]

But this kind of use of the Internet is still the exception rather than the rule, and direct government censorship is not the only reason. Overt, official measures to censor Chinese cyberspace fill in just half the picture; the other half is self-censorship by users and administrators. The Chinese Internet is, perfectly logically, too big and amorphous for any government to control it directly from the top down. Recognizing this, in its fight against unregulated expression, the government makes use of an equally amorphous force, and one that props it up in power: uncertainty. Mao's obsession with ideological orthodoxy created a punitive political culture in which the fear of surveillance by fellow Chinese and the terror of denunciation in mass meetings led individuals either to confess voluntarily to increasingly insignificant or even imaginary crimes, or to exercise such vigorous self-censorship that they erred far on the side of caution, never risking remotely sensitive or suspicious political behaviour. Living in China today is, assuredly, no longer the political minefield that it was under Mao, but two strands of his legacy survive in everyday political culture: a sense, sometimes vague, sometimes palpable, of being constantly under scrutiny in public transactions, and an uncertainty about where the lines are drawn in public freedom of expression.[31] This is not a problem in the private sphere, where Chinese can say anything they like to people they trust, but it severely restricts freedom of operation in a public and easily accessed medium such as the Internet. The government makes its general stance clear by creating a culture of fear – censoring sites, making arrests, closing Internet cafés. The jangling nerves of administrators and users do the rest. 'The way we prefer to control things is through a decentralised responsibility system,' one of the architects of the Great Firewall commented in 1997. '[T]he user, the ISP, and China Telecom are all held responsible for the information users gain access to. People are used to being wary, and the general sense that you are under surveillance acts as a disincentive. The key to controlling the Net in China is in managing people, and this is a process that begins the moment you purchase a modem.'[32] In contemporary China, where profit margins are as much a concern as political orthodoxy, for most Internet café owners the financial costs of allowing sensitive sites to be surfed and thereby risking closure by security forces are not trivial. In 2003, on the pretext of tightening health and safety standards, the government closed half the country's 200,000 Internet cafés; surveillance software was installed in those permitted to survive the cull, making it possible to track individual users' surfing habits.

Internet use is plagued by a fear of surveillance: a chatroom or BBS board may be, and often is, monitored by vigilantes of political orthodoxy. China abounds with population in need of occupation; to substantial numbers (30,000 according to one recent estimate), censoring the Internet is as good a job as any. While some web users write extremely courageous things, the dissident enterprise is thus shrouded in risk and uncertainty. The case of Liu Di – imprisoned in a cell alongside a convicted murderer for a year without being charged, without knowing who informed on her – is typical.

The net result is that many web users tend to play safe in cyberspace. The vast majority of bloggers – themselves a mainly urban minority within China's unwired rural majority – make use of the Internet to wallow in 'personal stuff': love life, shopping trips, what they had for dinner at the weekend. It is no coincidence that the blog that launched the medium in China was a 2003 sex diary by a Guangzhou fashion editor called Mu Zimei: 'I have a job that keeps me busy,' she wrote, 'and in my spare time I have a very humanistic hobby – making love.'[33] By November that year, 160,000 people had visited her site; 6,000 new readers joined their ranks every day. Fifteen years ago, this kind of frankness about sex would have been hounded as spiritual pollution. Now, however, while not exactly Politburo bedtime reading, book-length tales of torrid sex orgies are fairly run-of-the-mill, and carrying on about sex in public is seen by the government as a relatively harmless spin-off of economic liberalization. Although not quite the 'spiritual socialist civilization' that the party has been trying to build since the early 1980s, it at least represents a way for the Chinese to let off steam without mentioning the dread words 'political transparency' or 'democracy'.

Another politically safe way to let off steam on the Chinese Internet is to worship at the shrine of the state religion that is holding capitalist-Communist China together: angry, anti-foreign nationalism. For almost as long as an Internet community has existed in China, it has been periodically galvanized into nationalistic hysteria around topics and incidents seen as infringing Chinese national dignity: Taiwan's democratic elections, the NATO bombing of the embassy in Belgrade, Japan's refusal to apologize for atrocities committed in the Second World War. (To give some sense of the levels of fury: some cyber nationalists have advocated nuclear war against both Japan and the US.[34]) Although, after 1989, the state is wary of any flare-ups of mass sentiment, it tolerates expressions of angry nationalism because they give China's increasingly affluent but apparently irate young urban men an outlet for their rage, draw attention away from the past and present failings of the Communist Party and coincide with certain state goals: opposing Taiwanese independence, criticizing the US's interference in East Asia and combating Japan's claim to the Diaoyu Islands. So far, Communist authority has been the main winner in cyber nationalism: anti-foreign sentiment blurs into state-defined patriotism, as Internet patriots denounce democracy activists living in exile abroad as the running dogs of foreigners.[35] In China, even the hacking community – almost anywhere else in the world a bunch of individualistic, anti-social nerds – is passionately patriotic. Since 1997, Chinese hackers have waged virtual war on nations accused of insulting China: in spring 2001, after an American spyplane collided with a Chinese jet fighter in China's airspace, hackers splotched images of the Chinese flag across the White House history webpage and scrawled 'Beat down imperialism of American!' across the US National Business Center site. Revealingly, when one successful hacker became jaded with sabotaging US cyberspace and turned his attention to domestic government sites –

covering local government homepages with obscene pictures and changing the leadership's greeting message to 'We are a Bunch of Hogs' – he
was arrested within forty-eight hours.[36]

Genghis Khan's centuries-old aphorism seems to hold true now as
never before: the strength of walls depends on those who defend them.
In the tight ideological nexus that is still the People's Republic, the majority of Internet users have been, wittingly or not, for the time being
coopted as border guards. In this instance, however, unlike almost every
other wall-building dynasty, the Communist government has tried to
guarantee its guards' loyalty by ensuring they are better fed and paid than
almost any other social group in the empire.

Chinese dissidents insist on seeing in the Internet the seeds of destruction for China's resilient autocratic tradition – the final frontier for the
Great Wall mentality. At present, however, it seems just as plausible that
Chinese regulation of the web will become another episode in the
millennia-long history of Chinese wall-building, a history in which the
rulers of Communist China have proved themselves just as good as – if
not better than – any of their imperial predecessors at building, maintaining, restoring and guarding walls.

This is not to insist that the Firewall, with its associated cordoning
measures, will in the end prove any less porous than the most solid of
pre-modern China's frontier lines; or that its present guards will necessarily hold to its authoritarian architects any more staunchly than did many
of the unfortunates banished to wall service across the centuries on
China's desolate northern borders. In the spring of 2005, anti-Japanese
demonstrations broke out across China's major cities, a protest movement that began life converging with state-sponsored goals of anti-
foreign nationalism, that has been fanned and organized by Internet
activists and whose angry violence is, in part, an expression of the deep
latent tensions within Chinese society resulting from the limited possibilities for public political expression.

At present, important aspects of these demonstrations remain opaque:

the extent to which they were organized or influenced by the political centre, and to which they spiralled out of official control and into the hands of grass-roots organizations. Certainly, the former conclusion was suggested by tight police supervision of initial protests, by the government's provision of buses to take students back to campus once Public Security informed them they had 'vented their anger' long enough, by Beijing's flat refusal of Japan's demand for a public apology. But as the protests spread to a third weekend, a newly uneasy note crept into the authorities' pre-emptive announcements: 'Express your passion in an orderly manner,' the police instructed would-be demonstrators on the Internet, warning that all street protests must be approved by the authorities and ordering well-known grass-roots campaigners to stay at home.[37] After the events of spring 1989, the Chinese Communist Party does not feel it can afford to allow nationwide public protest to crescendo too far beyond its own orchestration, no doubt mindful of the fact that large-scale demonstrations in support of a leading liberal politician in the mid-1980s grew out of anti-Japanese demonstrations. Recent protests against Japan happened also to coincide with anti-government rallies by grass-roots interest groups: with thousands of army veterans protesting in the capital for higher pensions, with machete-armed villagers in south-east China fighting back a thousand-strong force of riot police. A few days later, a major government newspaper denounced the anti-Japanese demonstrations as an 'evil plot' with 'ulterior motives' to bring down the Communist Party – a sure indication that a protest movement which started out roughly coinciding with official policy had quickly moved into the far more subversive realm of civil, non-official activism.[38] Could Internet-shaped public opinion and anger be warming up, eventually, to join with contemporary China's many discontents and break past the limits set down by the Great Firewall?

What seems safer to predict is that, whether or not China's most recent wall to see active service crumbles, and with it the regime it protects, the political and cultural worldview that Chinese wall-building has long expressed will, in some form or other, survive; that the now familiar oscillation of policy – between offence and defence, between openness and isolationism, between hunger for foreign exotica and delusions of self-sufficiency – over which millennia of arguments about frontier walls have presided will continue.

It is probably fair to say that, in surviving through and out of the twentieth century, the enduring Chinese love of walls – the embodiment of the imperial, Sinocentric attitude to the outside world – has passed its greatest test and proved its ability to transcend almost any geopolitical circumstance. By emerging as China's pre-eminent national monument while the country struggled to slot, for the first time in its history, into a modern system of international relations beyond its own dictation of terms, by adapting itself to the globalized world and its new, virtual flows of information, the idea of the frontier wall has proved its distinctive, universal appeal to Chinese through the ages. The bizarre cocktail of cultural and political forces currently at work in contemporary China – where powerful yearnings for international 'face' (Nobel Prizes, a Beijing Olympics, entry to the World Trade Organization), for foreign goods and study abroad coexist with periodic eruptions of anti-foreign feeling and with anger against an America seen as seeking to contain a rising China – is, perhaps, only another, albeit more extreme, version of the pull between enclosure and openness that has been asserting itself since, at the very least, King Wuling of the state of Zhao began his court debate about the virtues of the nomadic tunic.

It is, admittedly, a version whose most obvious contradictions and schizophrenia are accentuated by the accelerating processes of globalization, by China's increased and enforced exposure to international influences and by the rise of narrower, more tightly defined and legislated modern expressions of national identity. But we see this same tension between the foreign and the Chinese reappear again and again across the millennia, too often for its contemporary manifestations to be mistaken for a new phenomenon: in the near-simultaneous adoption of barbarian cavalry and wall-building as military strategies during the Warring States period; in the Han opening of the Silk Road, walled and superintended up to the edge of the Taklamakan by towers and ramparts of reeds and clay; in the Northern Wei's shrinking from their ancestors' nomadism into walled Chinese cities behind border walls; in the Sui Emperor Yang's expressions of delight at the tents, mutton and wine of the steppe, even as he dispatched a million Chinese to wall off his yellow plains from the Turkish barbarians; in the volte-face from the adventurous treasure ships of the early Ming to the thousands of kilometres of mud- and brick-walled frontier built by the time the dynasty fell in 1644.

The internationalism and isolationism that have often converged around Chinese wall-building recall also the doubled-edged way in which walls have functioned across the millennia of Chinese history, and still do today in the case of Israel's 'defensive' fence: not only to protect (sometimes oppressively so) those peoples ruled by the wall-builders but also – depending on the distance of a wall from those it supposedly defends – to prop up a strategy of imperialist expansion, to garrison and superintend foreign neighbours whose way of life differs threateningly from that of the wall-builders.

If, then, we sidestep the stridently nationalistic purposes to which some of present day China's more propagandistic commentators have put the wall, if we don't allow its controversy-ridden and often inglorious past to be obscured by the contemporary bombast of the Communist tourist industry, some of the multipurpose, seemingly contradictory claims currently made for the frontier wall begin, finally, to seem a little more reasonable. Although it is still stretching a point to argue that China's border walls defined a single, unified China while simultaneously nurturing multicultural internationalism, it is possible to say that these two contradictory impulses have often coexisted, or closely alternated, throughout Chinese history, weaving in and out of the rise, fall and rise again of wall-building. And the persistent reappearance of walls along the Chinese frontier – despite their liability to bankrupt their builders, to foster and exacerbate internal discontent, to encourage Chinese rulers to abandon the kinds of diplomatic compromise that have historically been far more effective at keeping the peace than haughty, myopic isolationism, to fail as defences when (inevitably) confronted by a mobile, determined, battle-hardened enemy, to fall down – has made them a constant across Chinese history, an almost unthinking, undeniable cultural habit that China's rulers, and some of its people, seem unable and certainly unwilling to kick.

In the century to come, when Chinese nationalism and internationalism promise to become key geopolitical forces in the world, understanding China's millennia-old vacillation between openness and enclosure, and its confidence in its ability to attract and civilize foreign acolytes while continuing to regulate what it allows inside its own frontiers, will become increasingly important to maintaining perspective on China's approach to both domestic and global affairs. This book has tried to provide a history of the Chinese worldview, to reveal its successes and failures, to explain an attitude to the outside world that can seem (and, indeed, often is) puzzling, contradictory and strident, and that shows no sign of evanescing in the face of globalization, the Internet and America's world crusade for freedom and democracy. Even if, over the next decades, the People's Republic were straightforwardly to transform itself into a democracy along the open, Western, liberal or George W. Bush model (a proposition that in itself looks simplistically far-fetched), the Chinese empire has too much history and too much historical awareness to abandon its millennia-old behavioural tics, to lose faith in either its own cultural and political uniqueness, or the need to maintain lines of exclusion and rigorous border controls, physical or psychological, through which to monitor its inevitable droves of visitors, whether they be admiring bearers of tribute, hopeful traders or green-eyed aggressors. China will, it seems, always have its Great Walls.

Principal Characters

(Dates given are AD unless otherwise stated)

ABAOJI (d. 926): Founder of the Khitan Liao dynasty who began adapting his tribe to Chinese forms of government – murdering his critics along the way – and building walls in north-east China.

AGUDA (d. 1123): Founder of the Jurchen Jin dynasty who, after refusing to dance for the Liao emperor, drove the Liao out of north China.

ALTAN KHAN (1507–82): Mongol leader who unified the steppe tribes, terrorized north China and briefly besieged Beijing in the middle decades of the sixteenth century.

AN LUSHAN (700?–757): The Sogdian general and court favourite who launched a highly damaging rebellion against the Tang in 755.

SIR JOHN BARROW (1764–1848): Comptroller on the 1793 Macartney mission to China; later founder of the Royal Geographical Society; admirer of the Great Wall.

CAO CAO (155–200): Poet and former Han general who in 196, by placing the fugitive last Han emperor under permanent palace arrest and founding his own kingdom in the north, brought an end to the Han dynasty.

CEN SHEN (715–70): Aspiring but failed poet-civil servant, now best known for his 'frontier verse' set amidst the far north-west borders of Tang China.

CHEN DUXIU (1880–1942): Important theorist and activist in the May Fourth Movement, and a founding member and leader of the Chinese Communist Party until 1927.

CHIANG KAI-SHEK (1887–1975): Protégé of Sun Yat-sen, leader of the Nationalist Party, instigator of the White Terror against the Chinese Communists and President of the Nationalist regime in Taiwan from 1949 to 1975.

THE CHONGZHEN EMPEROR (1611–44): The last emperor of the Ming, who committed suicide north of the Forbidden City as rebels entered Beijing.

CONFUCIUS (551–479 BC): China's pre-eminent philosopher, who developed the theory of a harmonious political system based around the correct performance of ritual and on the analogy of family relationships.

DENG XIAOPING (1904–97): Twice purged under Mao, the Communist leader who oversaw the liberalizing of the economy after 1976 and ordered the crackdown of 1989.

DORGON (d. 1650): Manchu prince who became Qing regent in 1643 and led the Manchu troops through Shanhaiguan and on to Beijing, where he took possession of the Forbidden City.

DUOJI (r. 609–19): Unruly Turkish khaghan, son of Ran'gan, who in 615 besieged Emperor Yang of the Sui for thirty-six days at Yanmenguan in Shanxi.

ESEN (d. 1455): The Mongol leader who united the steppe tribes and humiliated the Ming army in 1449 at Tumu. He was assassinated after his failure to extract a large ransom from the Chinese court for the emperor captured at Tumu.

ERZHU RONG (d. 530): The north-western tribal leader who marched on Northern Wei Luoyang in 528 and massacred its courtiers.

EMPRESS FENG (d. 490): Empress dowager of the Northern Wei who bore a significant grudge against tribal Xianbi custom and encouraged Chinese-style agriculture.

FUSU (d. 210 BC): Eldest son of the First Emperor of Qin, banished to the northern frontier for protesting the harshness of his father's rule, where he was persuaded to commit suicide by a forged communication from the First Emperor.

GAO LÜ: Chinese official serving Emperor Xiaowen of the Northern Wei and a strong advocate of wall-building.

GAOZU (HAN) (r. 202–195 BC): Bom Lin Bang, founding emperor of the Han dynasty who was humiliated in battle by Maodun and who prematurely repaired frontier walls in the 190s BC.

GAOZU (TANG) (566–635): The Duke of Tang, Li Yuan, who rose up against the Sui dynasty in 618 to proclaim himself first emperor of the Tang.

GENGHIS KHAN (1176?–1227): Unifier of the tribes of the Mongolian steppe and founder of the Mongol empire.

THE HONGWU EMPEROR (1328–98): Born Zhu Yuanzhang, the paranoiac founding Ming emperor who expelled the Mongol Yuan dynasty from China.

HUANG XIANG (1941–): Dissident Chinese poet, author of 'Confessions of the Great Wall'.

HUHAI (r. 210–207 BC): Cruel and extravagant second Emperor of Qin who was driven to madness and suicide by his eunuch tutor Zhao Gao.

HUO QUBING (141?–117 BC): Emperor Wu's favourite horseback general, responsible for some of the most important Han victories against the Xiongnu in Mongolia.

THE JIAJING EMPEROR (1507–67): Born Zhu Houcong, the obstinate, ritually pedantic emperor whose intransigence towards the Mongols led to the building of the sixteenth-century border wall.

JIA YI (201–160 BC): Confucian scholar-official and author of the famous moralizing essay 'The Faults of Qin' who criticized the Qin dynasty for relying on 'walls of metal'.

JIANG ZEMIN (1926–): President of the People's Republic of China from 1989 to 2003; genuinely held supreme power only after the death of Deng Xiaoping in 1997.

KABUL (began ruling 1140?): Great-grandfather of Genghis Khan who offended the Jin court by tweaking the emperor's beard.

THE KANGXI EMPEROR (1654–1722): The second Qing emperor, first of the succession of three vigorous Qing rulers who oversaw a massive expansion of China's frontiers and population. Educated in the Chinese classics, patron of Ferdinand Verbiest and a keen hunter, he was given, legendarily, to travelling through Great Wall passes in mufti to test the fastness of his empire's border controls.

KHUBILAI KHAN (1214–94): Mongol emperor who oversaw the final conquest of all China; builder of the lavish palace in Beijing described by Marco Polo.

LI BO (701–62): Probably the most famous of the Tang poets, a drunken, duelling, romantic wanderer said to have drowned after leaping, drunk, into a river to embrace the reflection of the moon.

LI SHIMIN: See Taizong (Tang).

LI YUAN: See Gaozu (Tang).

LI ZICHENG (1605?–45): Rebel leader who drove the last Ming emperor to suicide, took the capital and then quickly lost it again to the Manchu Qing dynasty.

LIU BANG: See Gaozu (Han).

LORD MACARTNEY (1737–1806): Leader of the abortive 1792–3 British trade mission dispatched to China by George III; deeply impressed by the Great Wall.

MAO ZEDONG (1893–1976): Leader of the Communist Party from 1935 to 1976, founder of the People's Republic of China, architect of the Cultural Revolution and amateur poet; enthusiastic about the idea of the Great Wall if not the reality.

MAODUN (r. 209–174 BC): Founder of the great Xiongnu empire; who usurped the leadership of the tribe by ordering his followers to murder his father.

MARTINO MARTINI (1614–61): Italian Jesuit and cartographer acclaimed as the father of Chinese geography in Europe; author of the influential 1655 map that portrayed the Great Wall as a thick, uniformly crenellated line across north China.

MENG JIANGNU (d. 214–210 BC?): The legendary devoted wife who wept at the First Emperor of Qin's Long Wall when she discovered her husband had died on wall service.

MENG TIAN (d. 210): Trusted general of Qin Shihuangdi who cleared the nomads from the Yellow River area and built the Long Wall.

NURHACI (1559–1626): Founder of the Manchu empire who declared war on the Ming dynasty in 1619 and began the conquest of north-east China.

MARCO POLO (1254–1324): Venetian traveller who allegedly spent the years 1271–95 in China, in the service of Khubilai Khan.

THE QIANLONG EMPEROR (1711–99): After Kangxi and Yongzheng, the last of the vigorous Qing emperors who oversaw China's 'Prosperous Age' and a doubling of the population. A great collector of Chinese art and calligraphy, he claimed to have written 42,000 poems.

QIN SHIHUANGDI (259–210 BC): The First Emperor of Qin, responsible for unifying China and building the first Long Wall in the north.

RAN'GAN (r. 599–609): Turkish khaghan who submitted to the Sui dynasty and asked for his tribe to be fitted out in Chinese clothes.

MATTEO RICCI (1552–1610): Polyglot scholar and first Jesuit priest to be permitted to settle in Beijing; called the frontier wall 'tremendous'.

ADAM SCHALL (1591–1666): German Jesuit and astronomer to the Chinese emperor, persecuted by xenophobic Confucians.

SHANG YANG (d. 338 BC): Prime minister of Qin responsible for implementing Legalist reforms between 356 and 348 BC, he was torn to pieces by chariots for falling foul of the heir to the throne.

SHETU (r. 581–87): Grandson of Tumen and *bête noire* of Emperor Wen of the Sui until civil war among the Turks forced him to acclaim the Sui emperor as a 'purifying influence' in order to seek an alliance with China.

SIMA QIAN (c. 145–86 BC): Author of the canonical history *The Records of the Grand Historian (Shiji)*; castrated on orders of Emperor Wu for protesting an imperial decision.

SIR GEORGE STAUNTON (1737–1801): Second-in-command to Lord Macartney on the 1792–1793 trade mission to China.

SIR THOMAS STAUNTON (1781–1859): Chinese-speaking son of Sir George Staunton who charmed the Qianlong emperor in 1793 and argued in Parliament in favour of the Opium War in 1840.

SIR MARK AUREL STEIN (1862–1943): Archaeologist-explorer who dug the Han wall out of the desert of north-west China and removed thousands of ancient manuscripts to the West from the caves near Dunhuang.

SU XIAOKANG (1949–): Reportage writer and co-author of the controversial 1988 television series *River Elegy*; fled into exile after the Tiananmen crackdown of 1989.

SUN YAT-SEN (also Sun Zhongshan) (1866–1925): 'Father of the Chinese revolution', first president of the Republic of China and engineer of the first United Front between the Communist and Nationalist parties; one of modern China's earliest prominent admirers of the Great Wall.

TAIZONG (Tang) (599–649): Born Li Shimin, son of the first Tang emperor Gaozu, who murdered two of his brothers in 626 to succeed to the throne and later became 'Heavenly Khaghan' of the steppe.

THE TIANSHUN EMPEROR (1428–57): The feckless young emperor captured at Tumu by Esen.

TOUMAN (d. 209 BC?): Xiongnu leader shot dead by the followers of his son Maodun a few years after he himself had tried to arrange for Maodun to be killed.

TUMEN (d. 553): Khaghan who, in revenge for a snub by another tribe, transformed the Turks into the pre-eminent power on the steppe.

TUOBA GUI (r. 386–409): Founder of the Northern Wei dynasty; phenomenally successful conqueror of land and livestock.

FERDINAND VERBIEST (1623–88): Multi-talented Jesuit priest who became the Kangxi emperor's director of astronomy and deviser of mechanical garden ornaments, and who, on safari in Manchuria, proclaimed the Great Wall 'prodigious'.

WAN SITONG (1638–1702): Early Qing literatus and son of an old Ming loyalist; appointed by the Qing dynasty to assist in the writing of the standard *Ming History*; wrote poetry mocking the Great Wall.

WANG CHANGLING (698?–757): An acclaimed Tang poet, renowned for his command of the quatrain form.

WANG YUE (1426–99): The soldier official who fought with nomad-style chutzpah to drive the Mongols out of the Ordos in the 1470s.

WANG ZHEN (d. 1449): The glory- and valuables-obsessed eunuch who encouraged the Tianshun emperor to undertake the disastrous Tumu campaign.

WEI JINGSHENG (1951–): Former electrician and Chinese dissident imprisoned in 1979 for asking, in a Democracy Wall poster, for the 'Fifth Modernization' – democracy.

WEI QING (160?–106? BC): Along with Huo Qubing, one of the great generals fighting in the service of Emperor Wu, responsible for encircling and driving back the Xiongnu around 120 BC.

EMPEROR WEN OF THE SUI (550?–604): Born Yang Jian, irascible founder of the Sui dynasty in 581, reunifier of China and builder of Long Walls.

EMPEROR WU OF THE HAN (r. 140–87 BC): The 'martial emperor' who, following decades of consolidation by his predecessors, expanded and walled the northern frontiers of the Han empire.

WU SANGUI (1612–78): General stationed in the north-east who allied with the Manchus and allowed them to pass through Shanhaiguan on their path to conquering China.

WU XIANG (d. 1644): Father of Wu Sangui, executed by Li Zicheng for Wu Sangui's failure to respond to his letter.

(EMPRESS) WU ZETIAN (625?–705): Former concubine of the Tang emperor Gaozong, she was the only woman in imperial Chinese history to found her own dynasty. Allegedly sprouted new eyebrows at the age of seventy after consuming aphrodisiacs.

KING WULING (325–299 BC): King of the state of Zhao who introduced cavalry reforms to his armies in 307 BC.

XIAOWEN (r. 466–99): Emperor of the Northern Wei responsible for moving the capital to Luoyang.

XIELI (r. 620–34): Turkish khaghan who fought and lost against Xuanzong of the Tang and spent his last few years a mournful captive in the Tang capital, Chang'an.

XU DA (1332–85): One of Zhu Yuanzhang's linchpin generals, entrusted with the job of building up defensive forts in the years following 1368.

XUANZONG (685–762): Tang emperor who presided over the golden years of the Tang, but whose reign ended amid the catastrophic upheavals resulting from the An Lushan rebellion.

YAN SONG (1480–1565): Pragmatic grand secretary in office during Altan Khan's devastating raid on Beijing.

EMPEROR YANG OF THE SUI (569–617): Born Yang Guang, son of Yang Jian, Emperor Wen of the Sui; ruled 604 to 617. Builder of Long Walls and the Grand Canal, his extravagance, lechery and general immorality are blamed for the fall of the Sui dynasty.

YANG GUANG (569–617): See Emperor Yang of the Sui.

YANG GUIFEI (d. 756): Legendarily beautiful and tragic concubine of the Tang emperor Xuangzong, strangled by the emperor's guards, who blamed her for the collapse of the empire.

YANG JIAN: See Emperor Wen of the Sui.

YANG XUANZHI (500?–555?): Civil servant and author of 'Record of the Monasteries of Luoyang', a eulogy to fallen Northern Wei Luoyang.

YELLOW EMPEROR (ascended the throne 2698 BC?): Legendary founding ruler of the Chinese empire.

THE YONGLE EMPEROR (1360–1424): Born Zhu Di, son of the founding Ming emperor; usurped the throne in 1403, moved the capital from Nanjing to Beijing and sponsored the maritime expeditions directed by Zheng He.

THE YONGZHENG EMPEROR (1678–1755): Reigning after Kangxi and before Qianlong, the second of the three most successful Qing rulers; acceding to the throne under confused circumstances, he was accused by contemporaries of forging his father's will and even hastening the death of the old emperor Kangxi with a bowl of poisoned ginseng soup.

YU (c. 2000 BC): Legendary sage ruler, renowned for controlling the flood waters.

YU ZIJUN (1429–89): Conscientious official who petitioned for and oversaw the first major wall-building programme during the Ming.

YUAN SHIKAI (1859–1916): Qing general who sided with the rebels in the 1911 revolution and to whom Sun Yat-sen resigned the presidency of the Republic in 1913. He declared himself emperor in 1916, causing the revolt of China's provinces.

ZHANG JUZHENG (1525–82): The grand secretary who brokered peace with Altan Khan by compelling him to swear allegiance to the Ming court in return for border markets.

ZHANG QIAN (c. 160–110 BC): Envoy and general in the service of Emperor Wu who escaped back to China from Xiongnu captivity and encouraged the emperor's expansionist schemes in the north-west.

ZHANG XUELIANG (1901–2001): Former Manchurian warlord and Nationalist general who arrested a nightshirted Chiang Kai-shek in the 1936 Xi'an Incident in order to force him to abandon the civil war with the Communists.

ZHAO GAO (d. 207 BC): Eunuch tutor to Huhai, son of the First Emperor of Qin, responsible for driving his former charge to madness. Stabbed to death by third Qin emperor.

ZHU DI: See the Yongle emperor.

ZHU HOUCONG: See the Jiajing emperor.

ZHU YUANZHANG: See the Hongwu emperor.

Chronology of Dynasties

(Dates given are AD unless otherwise stated)

Shang *c.*1700–1025 BC

Western Zhou 1025–771 BC

Eastern Zhou 771–256 BC

Qin 221–206 BC

Former Han 202 BC–8

Interregnum of Wang Mang 9–23

Later Han 25–220

Period of the Three Kingdoms 220–80

Western Jin 265–316

PERIOD OF DISUNITY

Southern China

Eastern Jin 317–430

(Liu-) Song 420–79

Southern Qi 479–502

Liang 502–57

Chen 557–89

Northern China

Period of the Sixteen Kingdoms 317–439

Northern Wei 386–534

Eastern Wei 534–50

Western Wei 535–57

Northern Qi 550–77
Northern Zhou 557–81

Sui 581–618
Tang 618–907
Period of the Five Dynasties and Ten Kingdoms 907–60
Liao 947–1115
Northern Song 960–1127
Jin 1115–1234
Southern Song 1127–1279
Yuan 1260–1368
Ming 1368–1644
Qing 1644–1911

Significant Dates in Chinese History and Wall-building

(Dates given are AD unless otherwise stated)

c. 8000 BC:	Beginning of farming in north China.
c. 1384–1025 BC:	Inscriptions on Shang oracle bones provide earliest versions of Chinese characters.
c. 1045–1025 BC:	The Zhou destroys the Shang.
c. 1000 BC:	Development of horse-riding in western Asia.
c. 1000–900 BC:	Earliest religious hymns of the canonical *Classic of Poetry (Shijing).*
c. 900–800 BC:	First raids into China by northern tribes.
841 BC:	Beginning of dated history.
771 BC:	Zhou forced by barbarian invasions to abandon their western capital.
656 BC:	Chu builds the first state wall.
551–479 BC:	Lifetime of Confucius.
c. 481–221 BC:	Warring States period.
c. 356–348 BC:	Legalist reforms of Shang Yang in the state of Qin.
338 BC:	Execution of Shang Yang.
307 BC:	The state of Zhao adopts nomadic-style cavalry.
c. 300 BC:	Beginning of construction of border walls against foreign 'barbarians' by northern states. Death of the Daoist philosopher Zhuang Zhou, author of the *Zhuangzi.*
256 BC:	Qin destroys the house of Zhou.
246 BC:	Accession of King Zheng, the future First Emperor of Qin.
230–221 BC:	Qin conquers the states of Han, Zhao, Wei, Chu, Yan and Qi.
221 BC:	Foundation of the Qin empire.

220 BC: Beginning of imperial road-building programme.

215–214 BC: The First Emperor of Qin dispatches his general, Meng Tian, north to fight the Xiongnu and build a Long Wall.

212 BC: Building of the imperial palaces.

210 BC: Death of the First Emperor. Succession of his son Huhai.

209 BC: Beginning of popular rebellions against the Qin.

c. 209 BC: Rise of Maodun, leader of the Xiongnu.

207 BC: Death of the second emperor.

206 BC: Fall of the Qin dynasty.

202 BC: After several years of civil war, foundation of the Han dynasty.

201–200 BC: Humiliation of first Han emperor at Pingcheng at the hands of Maodun and the Xiongnu.

166 BC: First appearance in sources of signal codes on northern frontier.

141 BC: Accession of Emperor Wu.

c. 139–135 BC: Zhang Qian departs for Central Asia.

126 BC: Zhang Qian returns to China.

121–102 BC: Han expansion into and wall-building in Mongolia and up to the Jade Gate.

87 BC: death of Emperor Wu.

c. 60 BC: Xiongnu begin to decline in power.

9–23: Interregnum of Wang Mang.

25: Re-establishment of the Han after period of civil war.

50: Xiongnu leader forced to kowtow to Chinese.

89: Destruction of northern Xiongnu by Chinese.

140s–80s: Rise of Xianbi.

184: Rebellion of the Yellow Turbans.

190: Rise to pre-eminence of the warlord Cao Cao.

220: Official end of the Han dynasty.

221: Founding of Shu-Han empire in Sichuan.

222: Founding of Wu empire and start of the Three Kingdoms period.

265: Jin dynasty founded.

280: Jin dynasty nominally reunites China.

281: Jin dynasty begins building walls.

304: Foundation of first Xiongnu state in north China.

310: Flight of Chinese aristocracy to the south.

311: Sacking of Chinese capital Luoyang by Xiongnu armies.

317: Founding of the Eastern Jin in Nanjing.

386: Foundation of the Northern Wei.

410–39: Period of conquest of north China by Northern Wei.

423: Building of first, 'outer' Northern Wei wall.

446: Building of second, 'inner' Northern Wei wall.

494: Northern Wei decide to move capital south to Luoyang.

525–7: Rebellions and mutinies on the northern frontier of the Northern Wei.

528: Erzhu Rong marches on Luoyang and massacres its officials.

534: Founding of Eastern Wei empire.

538: Northern Wei Luoyang demolished.

550: Foundation of Northern Qi dynasty.

552: Turks established as pre-eminent power on the steppe.

552–64: Northern Qi build walls across north China.

557: Foundation of Northern Zhou empire at Chang'an and Chen empire at Nanjing.

577: Northern Zhou invades Qi and unifies north China.

581: Yang Jian founds Sui dynasty.

581–7: Yang Jian raises Long Walls in north China.

589: Yang Jian destroys the Chen dynasty and reunites China.

604: Yang Jian dies and Yang Guang succeeds as second Sui emperor.

605: Completion of the Grand Canal.

607–8: Yang Guang undertakes his processional tours north and orders the building of his wall.

612–14: Yang Guang's ill-fated Korea campaigns.

617: Li Yuan rises up in rebellion against the Sui.

618: Assassination of Yang Guang. Li Yuan founds the Tang dynasty.

626: Li Shimin murders his brothers, 'persuades' his father, Li Yuan, to abdicate and becomes emperor Taizong.

630: Leader of the Eastern Turks submits to the Tang and remaining Turkish leaders request Taizong to assume the title 'Heavenly Khaghan'.

640–49: Extension of Tang authority as far west as Kucha, in the middle of the Taklamakan desert.

684: Usurpation of Empress Wu.

712: Accession of the emperor Xuanzong.

755–63: Rebellion of An Lushan.

762: Death of the poet Li Bo.

770: Death of the poet Cen Shen.

790: The Tang lose control of land west of the Jade Gate.

907: Traditional date for the end of the Tang dynasty. The Chinese empire divides into independent kingdoms. Abaoji, the founder of the Khitan Liao dynasty, takes power over the Khitans.

908: Liao begin to build walls in Manchuria.

960: Foundation of the Song dynasty.

1115: The Jurchen establish the Jin empire in Manchuria.

1125: The Jin defeat and expel the Liao from north China.

1127: North China falls to the Jin. The Song dynasty pushed down to a capital further south, at Hangzhou. Start of the Southern Song.

1162: Birth of Genghis Khan.

1166–1201: The Jin build walls in Manchuria and Mongolia.

1194: The Yellow River changes course.

1206: Genghis Khan acclaimed as supreme leader of the Mongolian tribes.

1211: Genghis Khan launches his first assault on the Jin empire.

1215: Massacre by the Mongols of the Jin capital on the site of Beijing.

1234: End of the Jin dynasty.

1260: Accession of Khubilai Khan.

1271–95: Possible dates of Marco Polo's travels in China.

1279: Death of the last Song emperor. All China under Mongol rule.

1294: Death of Khubilai Khan.

1330s–1350s: Plague rages through China.

1351: First mention of the Red Turban rebels.

1368: Foundation of the Ming dynasty by Zhu Yuanzhang, Red Turban rebel leader. Expulsion of the Mongols from China.

1368–97: Zhu Yuanzhang establishes forts and garrisons along the border and deep into Mongolia.

1402: Zhu Di usurps throne and proclaims himself the Yongle emperor.

1403–30: Abandonment of Zhu Yuanzhang's garrisons in Mongolia.

1405–33: Maritime expeditions to South-East Asia and the east coast of Africa.

1421: Official inauguration of the Ming capital at Beijing.

1429: First mention of the old Qin term 'Long Wall' in the Ming *Veritable Records*.

1430s: Esen reunites the tribes of Mongolia.

1448: After his tribute mission is rebuffed at Beijing, Esen mobilizes his forces against areas north of Beijing.

1449: Chinese emperor is captured by Esen at Tumu after disastrous defeat by the Mongols.

1450: Esen returns captured emperor to Beijing.

1470s: After a successful military campaign by Wang Yue, Yu Zijun oversees the building of walls in the Ordos.

1489: Death of Yu Zijun, after falling foul of eunuch politics at court.

1500: Regular trade with Mongols cut off.

1507: Birth of Zhu Houcong, future emperor of China, and Altan Khan, future ruler of the Mongolian steppe.

1522: Accession to throne of Zhu Houcong as the Jiajing emperor.

1541–7: Altan Khan's petitions to bring tribute refused by Chinese court. Heavy raiding results.

1540s: Construction of double line of defences to north-west of Beijing.

1550: Altan Khan rides round the eastern end of Ming walls and besieges Beijing. Jiajing executes his minister of war.

1551–2: Jiajing briefly permits trading markets with Mongols to reopen.

c. 1557: The Portuguese establish a trading presence on Macao.

1560s–1570s: Construction of walls and towers to the north-east of Beijing.

1570s: Earth forts around Datong begin to be bricked.

1601: The Jesuit Matteo Ricci reaches Beijing.

1616: Nurhaci proclaims the Later Jin dynasty. Posthumous publication in Europe of Matteo Ricci's journal.

1618: The first north-eastern Chinese garrison, Fushun, surrenders to the Manchus.

1619: Nurhaci formally declares war on the Ming dynasty.

1621: Nurhaci takes Shenyang and Liaoyang.

1627: Beginning of the popular revolts of the closing years of the Ming.

1629: The Manchus advance as far as Beijing, then fall back for lack of cannons.

1635: The Manchus change their dynastic name to Qing.

1644: The rebel Li Zicheng takes Beijing. The last Ming emperor hangs himself. Wu Sangui surrenders to the Manchus and defeats Li Zicheng at Shanhaiguan. The Manchus enter Beijing and found the Qing empire in China.

1659: The Jesuit Ferdinand Verbiest arrives in Macao.

1661: The Kangxi emperor comes to the throne.

1668: Chinese barred from Manchuria.

1669: Verbiest appointed director of the Bureau of Astronomy in Beijing.

1673: Wu Sangui rebels against the Qing.

1683: The Qing occupy Taiwan.

1697–1759: Qing conquest of Outer Mongolia, Dzungaria, the Ili valley and the Tarim basin.

1719: Publication of Daniel Defoe's *The Farther Adventures of Robinson Crusoe*.

1735: The Qianlong emperor comes to the throne.

1735–8: Jean Baptiste Du Halde's history and descriptions of China published in Europe.

1748: Commodore George Anson publishes his travelogue of an abortive stay in China of 1743.

1792–3: George III dispatches trade mission, led by Lord Macartney, to China.

1816: East India Company begins to develop opium trade to China.

1839–42: First Opium War.

1842: The Treaty of Nanjing cedes Hong Kong to Britain and opens five ports to opium imports.

1850–64: The Taiping Rebellion leaves millions dead.

1856–8: Second Opium War.

1858: The Treaty of Tianjin legalizes the opium trade.

1860: Anglo-French forces sack Beijing and the Summer Palace.

1861: George Fleming sets off from Tianjin into Manchuria.

1860s–1890s: China attempts to modernize its armies and navies with Western knowledge.

1893: *The Century Illustrated Monthly Magazine* makes the first claim that the Great Wall is visible from space.

1894–5: The first Sino-Japanese War. China cedes Taiwan to Japan.

1898: The pro-foreign, modernizing 'Hundred Days' Reform' is bloodily suppressed by Qing conservatives.

1900: Boxer rebels occupy Beijing and lay siege to the embassies.

1901: The foreign allied powers demand 450 million silver dollars as the Boxer indemnity.

1905: Abolition of the Confucian examination system.

1911: The republican revolution brings down the Qing dynasty.

1912: Sun Yat-sen returns to China to become first president of the new Republic.

1913: Sun Yat-sen resigns in favour of former Qing general Yuan Shikai.

1914: Yuan Shikai dissolves parliament.

1915: The Japanese issue their 'Twenty-one Demands' to Yuan Shikai.

1916: Yuan Shikai declares himself emperor. After China's provinces declare independence from Beijing in protest, Yuan dies. Start of the warlord period.

1917–19: Sun Yat-sen works on his *Plan for National Reconstruction* and comes out in favour of the Great Wall.

1919: The Treaty of Versailles grants Germany's former possessions in China to Japan. The May Fourth protest movement breaks out.

1921: Founding of the Chinese Communist Party in Shanghai. Sun Yat-sen forms a Nationalist Party government in Canton.

1923: After winning the promise of support from the Soviet Union, the Nationalist Party enters into a United Front with the Chinese Communist Party.

1925: Death of Sun Yat-sen.

1926: Launch of the Northern Expedition against warlords.

1927: The White Terror - Chiang Kai-shek crushes the Communist revolution in Shanghai and begins a nationwide purge of the Communists.

1929: Establishment of the Jiangxi Soviet.

1930–34: Chiang Kai-shek launches his encirclement campaigns to destroy the Communists in Jiangxi.

1931–2: The Japanese establish an independent state (Manchukuo) in Manchuria.

1933: The Japanese attack and take Shanhaiguan and the province of Jehol. Chinese and Japanese delegations sign the Tanggu treaty, stipulating a demilitarized zone south of the Great Wall.

1934: 80,000 Communist troops break out of Chiang's encirclement of Jiangxi on the Long March to Shaanxi.

1935: Mao Zedong established as leader of the Communist Party; composes the line 'If we fail to reach the Great Wall we are not true men.'

1936: Chiang Kai-shek taken prisoner at Xi'an until he agrees to re-establish United Front against Japanese invasion.

1937: After the Marco Polo Bridge incident, war between China and Japan formally declared. Up to 300,000 Chinese civilians are massacred in the Rape of Nanjing.

1945: Japanese defeat in the Second World War.

1949: Communist victory in the civil war. The Nationalist government flees to Taiwan. Mao Zedong proclaims the People's Republic of China.

1950: The People's Liberation Army marches into Tibet.

1951: Campaign to suppress counter-revolutionaries.

1956–7: Brief period of political openness during the Hundred Flowers campaign.

1957: The Anti-Rightist Campaign cracks down on criticism of the government.

1957–8: The Great Leap Forward – Mao's utopian plan for China to catch up with the industrial West within a few years and achieve Communism.

1959–61: Famine, resulting from the utopian policies of the Great Leap Forward, causes the deaths of an estimated 30 million Chinese.

1966: Mao launches the Cultural Revolution.

1971: The Republic of China (Taiwan) expelled from the United Nations and replaced by the People's Republic of China (the mainland government).

1972: Nixon visits China.

1975: Death of Chiang Kai-shek in Taiwan.

1976: Mao's death brings Cultural Revolution policies to an end.

1978: Deng Xiaoping established as Mao's successor. Start of Democracy Wall movement.

1979: Deng Xiaoping visits US. Cracks down on Democracy Wall protests. Wei Jingsheng sentenced to fifteen years in prison.

1983: The Anti-Spiritual Pollution campaign targets corrupting influences from the West.

1984: Deng Xiaoping launches his 'Love Our Country, Restore our Great Wall' campaign.

1986: Student demonstrations.

1987: Campaign against bourgeois liberalization. China's first email is sent.

1988: Broadcast of *River Elegy*.

1989: Pro-democracy demonstrations violently suppressed by the People's Liberation Army. Jiang Zemin takes over presidency of the People's Republic of China but Deng Xiaoping continues to hold supreme power.

1992: While on his 'Southern Tour', Deng Xiaoping calls for faster market reforms in the Chinese economy.

1994: China's first Internet network set up.

1996–7: The building of the 'Great Firewall of China'.

1997: Deng Xiaoping dies and Jiang Zemin succeeds to position of supreme power. Hong Kong returns to Mainland China.

1999: Major anti-American protests follow the NATO bombing of the Chinese embassy in Belgrade. The Chinese government bans Falun Gong.

2001: The collision between an American spyplane and a Chinese jet fighter in China's airspace generates a major diplomatic incident between China and the US and national outrage in China.

2002: The Chinese government temporarily blocks Google.

2002–3: Jiang Zemin begins power handover to his successor, Hu Jintao.

2003: Mu Zimei's sex diary helps launch the blog boom in China.

2005: Anti-Japanese demonstrations break out in cities across China.

NOTES

Introduction: Who Made the Great Wall of China?

1 J. L. Cranmer-Byng (ed.), *An Embassy to China Being the Journal Kept by Lord Macartney during his Embassy to the Emperor Ch'ien-lung, 1793–94* (London: Longmans, 1962), p. 10.

2 Alain Peyrefitte, *The Collision of Two Civilisations: The British Expedition to China in 1792–4,* trans. Jon Rothschild (London: Harvill, 1993), p. 275.

3 Ibid., p. 150.

4 Ibid., p. 291.

5 Cranmer-Byng, *An Embassy,* pp. 103–4.

6 Peyrefitte, *The Collision,* p. 76.

7 Ibid., p. 13.

8 Ibid., p. 210.

9 Cranmer-Byng, *An Embassy,* p. 84.

10 Peyrefitte, *The Collision,* p. 207.

11 Ibid., p. 88.

12 Sir John Barrow, *Travels in China* (London: T. Cadell and W. Davies, 1806), pp. 107, 11 respectively.

13 Ibid., pp. 214–17.

14 Ibid., pp. 224, 315, 204.

15 Ibid., p. 333.

16 Cranmer-Byng, *An Embassy,* pp. 111–12.

17 Barrow, *Travels,* pp. 334–45.

18 See folio edition of Sir George Leonard Staunton, *An authentic account of an embassy from the King of Great Britain to the Emperor of China* ... (London: G. Nicol, 1798).

19 Cranmer-Byng, *An Embassy,* p. 112.

20 Ibid.

21 Peyrefitte, *The Collision,* p. xxxi.

22 Ibid., p. 526.

23 William Edgar Geil, *The Great Wall of China* (New York: Sturgis & Walton Company, 1909), p. 44; Arthur Waldron, *The Great Wall of China: From History to Myth* (Cambridge: Cambridge University Press, 1992), p. 3.

24 See illustration ibid., p. 213.

25 Peyrefitte, *The Collision,* p. 185.

26 Joseph Needham, *Science and Civilisation in China* (Cambridge: Cambridge University Press, 1954–) IV.3 (1975), p. 47.

27 Quoted in Waldron, *The Great Wall,* p. 225.

28 See, for example, http://www.chinadaily.com.cn/english/livechina/2004-01/14/content_298858.htm.

29 My thanks to Simon Franklin for this reference.

30 Cranmer-Byng, *An Embassy,* p. 113.

31 *Changcheng baike quanshu* (Encyclopedia of the Great Wall) (Jilin: Jilin People's Publishing House, 1994), pp. 7–8.

32 CNN, 'Great Wall myth excised from textbooks', 12 March 2004, http://www.cnn.com/2004/WORLD/asiapcf/03/12/china.great.wall.myth.ap/index.html.

33 Quotations all drawn from the conference papers collected in *Changcheng guoji xueshu yantaohui lunwenji* (Proceedings of the International Academic Symposium on the Great Wall) (Jilin: Jilin renmin chubanshe, 1995), pp. 341, 343, 349, 8 respectively.

34 Ibid., p. 8.

35 Luo Zhewen et al., *The Great Wall* (London: Michael Joseph Ltd, 1981), p. 67.

36 Michael Loewe, *Everyday Life in Early Imperial China* (New York: Harper & Row, 1970), p. 133.

37 Ian Buruma, *Bad Elements: Chinese Rebels from Los Angeles to Beijing* (London: Weidenfeld and Nicolson, 2002), pp. xv–xxiii.

Chapter 1: Why Walls?

1 Joseph Needham, *Science and Civilisation in China* (Cambridge: Cambridge University Press, 1954–) IV.3 (1975), pp. 42–3.

2 See discussions ibid. and Kwang-chih Chang, *Shang Civilisation* (New Haven and London: Yale University Press, 1980).

3 See discussion in Suisheng Zhao, *A Nation-State by Construction: Dynamics of Modern Chinese Nationalism* (Stanford: Stanford University Press, 1994).

4 Ibid., p. 45.

5 W. M. de Bary, *Sources of Chinese Tradition,* Vol. I (New York: Columbia University Press, 1999), p. 6.

6 Valerie Hansen, *The Open Empire: A History of China to 1600* (New York: Norton, 2000), p. 27.

7 Ibid., p. 31.

8 See general discussion in Needham, *Science,* IV.3, pp. 38–57.

9 George B. Cressey, 'The Ordos Desert of Inner Mongolia', in *Denison University Bulletin,* 28.8 (1933), p. 180.

10 Ibid., pp. 176–9.

11 Ibid., p. 181.

12 Ibid., p. 190.

13 Translation slightly adapted from James Legge, *The Chinese Classics,* Vol. IV, *The She King* (Hong Kong: Lane, Crawford and Co., 1871), p. 281.

14 Translation adapted from ibid., pp. 282–3.

15 Translation adapted from ibid., pp. 258–61.

16 Quoted in Nicola Di Cosmo, *Ancient China and Its Enemies: The Rise of Nomadic Powers in East Asian History* (Cambridge: Cambridge University Press, 2002), p. 93; Jaroslav Prusek, *Chinese Statelets and the Northern Barbarians in the Period 1400–300 BC* (New York: Humanities Press, 1971), p. 228.

17 From the *Han shu,* quoted in Arthur Waldron, *The Great Wall of China: From History to Myth* (Cambridge: Cambridge University Press, 1992), p. 35; Burton Watson (trans.), *Records of the Grand Historian of China,* Vol. II (New York and London: Columbia University Press, 1961), p. 169.

18 Di Cosmo, *Ancient China,* pp. 98–9.

19 Dennis Sinor, 'The Inner Asian Warriors', *Journal of the American Oriental Society,* 101.2 (1981), pp. 134, 139.

20 Waldron, *The Great Wall,* p. 34.

21 Sechin Jagchid and Van Jay Symons, *Peace, War and Trade along the Great Wall: Nomadic–Chinese Interaction through Two Millennia* (Bloomington: Indiana University Press, 1989), p. 24.

22 Prusek, *Chinese Statelets,* p. 86.

23 Hansen, *The Open Empire,* p. 34.

24 Translation slightly adapted from Legge, *The Chinese Classics,* Vol. IV, *The She King,* p. 263.

25 Prusek, *Chinese Statelets,* p. 191.

26 Ibid., p. 91.

27 J. I. Crump (trans.), *Chan-kuo ts'e* (University of Michigan: Center for Chinese Studies, 1996), pp. 289–98.

28 Watson (trans.), *Records,* Vol. II, p. 159.

29 Ibid.

30 Ibid.

31 Di Cosmo, *Ancient China,* p. 143.

32 For more details, see the very useful account ibid., pp. 138–52.

33 See discussion ibid.

Chapter 2: The Long Wall

1 Sima Qian, *The Grand Scribe's Records,* Vol. I, ed. William H. Nienhauser Jr (Bloomington: Indiana University Press, 1994–), p. 131.

2 Both quoted in Denis Twitchett and Michael Loewe (eds.), *The Cambridge History of China Volume 1: The Ch'in and Han Empires, 220 BC through AD 220* (Cambridge: Cambridge University Press, 1986), pp. 31–2.

3 Translation after Sima, *The Grand Scribe's Records,* Vol. I, p. 155; Valerie Hansen, *The Open Empire: A History of China to 1600* (New York: Norton, 2000), p. 105.

4 Sima, *The Grand Scribe's Records,* Vol. I, pp. 147–8.

5 J. I. Crump (trans.), *Chan-kuo ts'e* (University of Michigan: Center for Chinese Studies, 1996), p. 81.

6 Hansen, *The Open Empire,* p. 101.

7 Crump (trans.), *Chan-kuo ts'e,* p. 81.

8 Quoted in Twitchett and Loewe (eds.), *The Cambridge History of China Volume 1,* p. 56.

9 Derk Bodde (trans.), *Statesman, Patriot, and General in Ancient China: Three Shih*

Chi Biographies of the Ch'in Dynasty (255–206 BC) (New Haven: American Oriental Society, 1940), p. 54.

10 Hansen, *The Open Empire,* p. 104.

11 William Edgar Geil, *The Great Wall of China* (New York: Sturgis & Walton Company, 1909), p. 4.

12 See illustration in Arthur Waldron, *The Great Wall of China: From History to Myth* (Cambridge: Cambridge University Press, 1992), p. 213.

13 Quoted ibid., p. 15.

14 *Zhongguo changcheng yiji diaocha baogao ji* (Collected reports on surveys of the Great Wall of China) (Beijing: Wenwu, 1981), p. 35.

15 *Changcheng guoji xueshu yantaohui lunwenji* (Proceedings of the International Academic Symposium on the Great Wall) (Jilin: Jilin renmin chubanshe, 1995), p. 243; *Zhongguo changcheng yiji diaocha,* pp. 35–67.

16 See, for example, the photograph in Daniel Schwartz, *The Great Wall of China* (London: Thames and Hudson, 1990), p. 159.

17 *Changcheng guoji,* p. 255.

18 Burton Watson (trans.), *Records of the Grand Historian of China,* Vol. II (New York and London: Columbia University Press, 1961), p. 160.

19 Two good collections of Great Wall legends are *Zhongguo changcheng gushi* (Stories about the Great Wall of China) (Beijing: Yanshan, 1987) and Song Mengyin and Dong Kan (eds.), *Wanli changcheng chuanshuo* (Legends of the Great Wall) (Hebei: Hebei shaonian ertong, 1990).

20 Sima, *The Grand Scribe's Records,* Vol. 1, p. 145.

21 Ibid., p. 146.

22 Liu Qingde et al., *Zhongguo lidai changcheng shi lu* (Poetry of the Great Wall of China through the ages) (Hebei: Hebei meishu chubanshe, 1991), p. 3.

23 Sima, *The Grand Scribe's Records,* Vol. VII, p. 366.

24 Ibid.

25 Translation adapted from Sechin Jagchid and Van Jay Symons, *Peace, War and Trade along the Great Wall: Nomadic–Chinese Interaction through Two Millennia* (Bloomington: Indiana University Press, 1989), pp. 56–7.

26 Quoted in Twitchett and Loewe (eds.), *The Cambridge History of China Volume 1,* p. 83.

27 Watson (trans.), *Records,* Vol. II, p. 160.

28 Quoted in Twitchett and Loewe (eds.), *The Cambridge History of China Volume 1,* p. 85.

29 Quoted in Waldron, *The Great Wall*, p. 195.

Chapter 3: Han Walls: *Plus ça change*

1 Burton Watson (trans.), *Records of the Grand Historian of China*, Vol. II (New York and London: Columbia University Press, 1961), p. 161.

2 Ibid.

3 Quoted in Sechin Jagchid and Van Jay Symons, *Peace, War and Trade along the Great Wall: Nomadic–Chinese Interaction through Two Millennia* (Bloomington: Indiana University Press, 1989), p. 25.

4 Watson (trans.), *Records*, Vol. I, p. 96.

5 Thomas J. Barfield, *The Perilous Frontier: Nomadic Empires and China* (Oxford: Basil Blackwell, 1989), p. 35.

6 Quoted in Denis Twitchett and Michael Loewe (eds.), *The Cambridge History of China Volume 1: The Ch'in and Han Empires, 220 BC through AD 220* (Cambridge: Cambridge University Press, 1986), p. 387.

7 Watson (trans.), *Records*, Vol. II, p. 167.

8 Quoted in Twitchett and Loewe (eds.), *The Cambridge History of China Volume 1*, p. 387.

9 Translation adapted from Watson (trans.), *Records*, Vol. II, p. 176.

10 Translation adapted from Arthur Waldron, *The Great Wall of China: From History to Myth* (Cambridge: Cambridge University Press, 1992), p. 41.

11 Quoted in Twitchett and Loewe (eds.), *The Cambridge History of China Volume 1*, p. 160.

12 Burton Watson (trans.), *Records of the Grand Historian Han Dynasty II* (rev. edn) (Hong Kong and New York: Renditions and Columbia University Press, 1993), pp. 164, 172, 237.

13 Watson (trans.), *Records*, Vol. II, pp. 178–9.

14 *Zhongguo changcheng yiji diaocha baogao ji* (Collected reports on surveys of the Great Wall of China) (Beijing: Wenwu, 1981), p. 36.

15 Ibid., pp. 25–33.

16 See Ann Birrell's excellent translation *The Classic of Mountains and Seas* (London: Penguin, 1999).

17 A. F. P. Hulsewe and Michael Loewe, *China in Central Asia: The Early Stage, 125 BC–AD 23* (Leiden: Brill, 1979), pp. 110–11.

18 Watson (trans.), *Records of the Grand Historian Han Dynasty II*, p. 236.

19 Hulsewe and Loewe, *China in Central Asia*, p. 211.

20 Watson (trans.), *Records of the Grand Historian Han Dynasty II*, p. 237.

21 Michael Loewe, *Everyday Life in Early Imperial China* (New York: Harper & Row, 1970), pp. 128–36.

22 Annabel Walker, *Aurel Stein: Pioneer of the Silk Road* (London: John Murray, 1995), p. 161.

23 Marco Polo, *The Travels,* trans. R. E. Latham (Harmondsworth: Penguin, 1980), p. 84.

24 Walker, *Aurel Stein*, p. 153.

25 Peter Hopkirk, *Foreign Devils on the Silk Road: The Search for the Lost Treasures of Central Asia* (Oxford: Oxford University Press, 1984), p. 12.

26 See account ibid.

27 M. Aurel Stein, *Ruins of Desert Cathay: Personal Narrative of Explorations in Central Asia and Westernmost China,* Vol. I (New York: Dover Publications, 1987), p. 539.

28 Quoted in Jeannette Mirsky's excellent biography, *Sir Aurel Stein: Archaeological Explorer* (Chicago: University of Chicago Press, 1977), p. 253.

29 See Stein, *Ruins,* Vol. I, pp. 538–45.

30 Ibid.

31 Mirsky, *Sir Aurel Stein,* pp. 260–63.

32 Ibid., p. 260.

33 Ibid., p. 263.

34 Stein, *Ruins,* Vol. II, pp. 135, 141–2.

35 Mirsky, *Sir Aurel Stein,* p. 262.

36 M. Aurel Stein, *Serindia,* Vol. II (Oxford: Clarendon Press, 1921), pp. 762–3.

37 Stein, *Ruins,* Vol. II, pp. 63–4.

38 Figures from *Changcheng guoji xueshu yantaohui lunwenji* (Proceedings of the International Academic Symposium on the Great Wall) (Jilin: Jilin renmin chubanshe, 1995), p. 105.

39 Liu Qingde et al., *Zhongguo lidai changcheng shi lu* (Poetry of the Great Wall of China through the ages) (Hebei: Hebei meishu chubanshe, 1991), p. 9.

40 Rafe de Crespigny, *Northern Frontier: The Policies and Strategy of the Later Han Empire* (Canberra: Australian National University, 1984), p. 245.

41 Stein, *Serindia,* Vol. II, p. 692.

42 Liu et al., *Zhongguo lidai,* p. 7.

43 Ibid., p. 8.

44 De Crespigny, *Northern Frontier,* p. 423.

45 Stein, *Ruins,* Vol. II, p. 104.

46 Barfield, *The Perilous Frontier,* p. 56.

47 Ibid., p. 57.

48 Watson (trans.), *Records,* Vol. II, p. 228.

49 Ibid., p. 186.

50 My own translation; original printed in Stephen Owen, *The Great Age of Chinese Poetry: The High T'ang* (New Haven: Yale University Press, 1981), p. 70.

51 Hans Bielenstein, *The Restoration of the Han Dynasty,* Vol. III, *Bulletin of the Museum of Far Eastern Antiquities,* 39 (1967), p. 111.

Chapter 4: Shifting Frontiers and Decadent Barbarians

1 See W. J. F. Jenner's wonderful account of Northern Wei Luoyang and translation of Yang Xuanzhi's 'Record' in *Memories of Loyang: Yang Hsüan-chih and the Lost Capital (493–534)* (Oxford: Clarendon Press, 1981).

2 Quoted in Thomas J. Barfield, *The Perilous Frontier: Nomadic Empires and China* (Oxford: Basil Blackwell, 1989), p. 87.

3 Ibid.

4 Ibid., p. 86.

5 Jacques Gernet, *A History of Chinese Civilization,* trans. J. R. Foster (Cambridge: Cambridge University Press, 1990), pp. 182–5.

6 *Changcheng baike quanshu* (Encyclopedia of the Great Wall) (Jilin: Jilin People's Publishing House, 1994), p. 79.

7 Barfield, *The Perilous Frontier,* p. 115.

8 Ibid., p. 111.

9 Jenner, *Memories,* p. 20.

10 Quoted ibid., p. 21.

11 Ibid.

12 Ibid., p. 219.

13 *Changcheng guoji xueshu yantaohui lunwenji* (Proceedings of the International Academic Symposium on the Great Wall) (Jilin: Jilin renmin chubanshe, 1995), p. 134.

14 Ibid., p. 135.

15 Translation adapted from René Grousset, *The Empire of the Steppes: A History of Central Asia,* trans. Naomi Watford (New Jersey: Rutgers University Press, 1970), p. 63.

16 *Nanqi shu* (History of the Southern Qi) (Beijing: Zhonghua shuju, 1972), p. 985.

17 *Changcheng guoji*, p. 137.

18 Quoted in Denis Twitchett (ed.), *The Cambridge History of China Volume 3: Sui and T'ang China, 589–906, Part I* (Cambridge: Cambridge University Press, 1979), p. 50.

19 Arthur F. Wright, *The Sui Dynasty* (New York: Knopf, 1978), p. 35.

20 Jenner, *Memories,* p. 215.

21 Ibid., pp. 201–2.

22 *Wei shu* (History of the Wei) (Beijing: Zhonghua shuju, 1974), 54.1201–2. Translation influenced by Arthur Waldron, *The Great Wall of China: From History to Myth* (Cambridge: Cambridge University Press, 1992), pp. 44–5.

23 See discussion in *Changcheng guoji*, pp. 134–42, and *Zhongguo changcheng yiji diaocha baogao ji* (Collected reports on surveys of the Great Wall of China) (Beijing: Wenwu, 1981), pp. 6–20.

24 *Wei shu*, 41.927–8.

25 Quoted in Jenner, *Memories,* pp. 38–9.

26 Quoted in Jonathan Fryer, *The Great Wall of China* (London: New English Library, 1975), p. 108.

27 Jenner, *Memories,* p. 224.

28 Ibid., pp. 68–9.

29 Ibid., p. 235.

30 Ibid., pp. 70–71.

31 Ibid., p. 153.

32 See ibid., pp. 74–102.

Chapter 5: China Reunited

1 Denis Twitchett and Michael Loewe (eds.), *The Cambridge History of China Volume 1: The Ch'in and Han Empires, 220 BC through AD 220* (Cambridge: Cambridge University Press, 1986), p. 357.

2 Thomas J. Barfield, *The Perilous Frontier: Nomadic Empires and China* (Oxford: Basil Blackwell, 1989), p. 132.

3 Ibid.

4 Edward H. Parker, 'The Early Turks', *China Review,* 24 (1899–1900), p. 120.

5 *Changcheng baike quanshu* (Encyclopedia of the Great Wall) (Jilin: Jilin People's Publishing House, 1994), p. 96.

6 Ibid., pp. 81–2.

7 Hu Ji, *Sui Yangdi xinzhuan* (New biography of Emperor Yang of the Sui) (Shanghai: Shanghai renmin chubanshe, 1995), pp. 36–7.

8 Ibid., p. 128.

9 Translation adapted from Denis Twitchett (ed.), *The Cambridge History of China Volume 3: Sui and T'ang China, 589–906, Part I* (Cambridge: Cambridge University Press, 1979), p. 62.

10 Arthur F. Wright, *The Sui Dynasty* (New York: Knopf, 1978), p. 67.

11 Translation adapted from Edward H. Parker, 'The Early Turks', *China Review,* 25 (1900–1901), p. 2.

12 *Changcheng baike quanshu,* pp. 82–3.

13 Parker, 'The Early Turks', 25, p. 2.

14 Quoted in Twitchett (ed.), *The Cambridge History of China Volume 3,* p. 108.

15 Parker, 'The Early Turks', 25, p. 3.

16 Ibid., p. 5.

17 *Changcheng baike quanshu,* p. 83. For references to Sui walls in the dynastic sources, see also Arthur Waldron, *The Great Wall of China: From History to Myth* (Cambridge: Cambridge University Press, 1992), p. 235, ns. 147–51.

18 Hu, *Sui Yangdi,* p. 43.

19 Ibid.

20 Ibid., p. 50.

21 Twitchett (ed.), *The Cambridge History of China Volume 3,* p. 137.

22 Parker, 'The Early Turks', 25, p. 72.

23 Hu, *Sui Yangdi,* pp. 129–30.

24 Ibid., pp. 131–2.

25 *Zhongguo changcheng yiji diaocha baogao ji* (Collected reports on surveys of the Great Wall of China) (Beijing: Wenwu, 1981), pp. 129–30.

26 Harry Franck, *Wandering in China* (London: T. Fisher Unwin Ltd, 1924), p. 113.

27 Liu Qingde et al., *Zhongguo lidai changcheng shi lu* (Poetry of the Great Wall of

China through the ages) (Hebei: Hebei meishu chubanshe, 1991), pp. 62–3.

28 Arthur F. Wright, 'Sui Yang-ti: Personality and Stereotype', in *The Confucian Persuasion,* ed. Arthur F. Wright (Stanford: Stanford University Press, 1960), p. 57.

29 See Liu et al., *Zhongguo lidai,* pp. 59–65.

30 Parker, 'The Early Turks', 25, p. 73.

31 Hu, *Sui Yangdi,* pp. 198–202.

32 Ibid., pp. 220–28.

33 Wright, 'Sui Yang-ti', p. 67.

34 See ibid.

Chapter 6: Without Walls: The Chinese Frontiers Expand

1 Adapted from translation in Denis Twitchett (ed.), *The Cambridge History of China Volume 3: Sui and T'ang China, 589–906, Part I* (Cambridge: Cambridge University Press, 1979), p. 156.

2 Edward H. Parker, 'The Early Turks', *China Review,* 25 (1900–1901), pp. 164, 237.

3 Ibid., pp. 166–7, 239.

4 Ibid., p. 239.

5 Ibid., p. 240.

6 Ibid., p. 169.

7 Charles Hartman, *Han Yu and the T'ang Search for Unity* (Princeton: Princeton University Press, 1986), pp. 119–20.

8 Quoted in Twitchett (ed.), *The Cambridge History Volume 3,* p. 223.

9 René Grousset, *The Empire of the Steppes: A History of Central Asia,* trans. Naomi Watford (New Jersey: Rutgers University Press, 1970), p. 95.

10 *Xin tangshu* (Beijing: Zhonghua shuju, 1975), 93.3818–19.

11 Quoted in Edward H. Schafer, *The Golden Peaches of Samarkand* (Berkeley: University of California Press, 1963), p. 16.

12 Qu Shuiyuan and Zhu Jincheng (eds.), *Li Bo ji jiaozhu* ('The annotated collected Li Bo) (Shanghai: Shanghai guji chubanshe, 1980), p. 252.

13 See the wonderful account of the Tang love for foreign exotica in Schafer, *The Golden Peaches.*

14 Twitchett (ed.), *The Cambridge History of China Volume 3,* p. 317.

15 Jacques Gernet, *A History of Chinese Civilization,* trans. J. R. Foster (Cambridge: Cambridge University Press, 1990), p. 294.

16 For more details, see Edwin G. Pulleyblank, *The Background of the Rebellion of An Lu-shan* (Oxford: Oxford University Press, 1966).

17 See Ichisada Miyazaki, *China's Examination Hell: The Civil Service Examinations of Imperial China,* trans. Conrad Shirokauer (New Haven: Yale University Press, 1981).

18 For an excellent critical account of high Tang poetics, see Stephen Owen, *The Great Age of Chinese Poetry: The High T'ang* (New Haven: Yale University Press, 1981).

19 Arthur Waley, 'A Chinese Poet in Central Asia', in *The Secret History of the Mongols* (London: George Allen and Unwin, 1963), pp. 30–46.

20 Chen Tiemin and Hou Zhongyi (eds.), *Cen Shen ji jiaozhu* (The annotated collected Cen Shen) (Shanghai: Shanghai guji chubanshe, 1981), p. 145.

21 Ibid., p. 66.

22 Ibid., p. 77.

23 This analytical point is made by Marie Chan in 'The Frontier Poems of Ts'en Shen', *Journal of the American Oriental Society,* 98.4 (1978), p. 424. The translations are my own, taken from *Quan Tang shi* (The complete Tang poetry) (Beijing: Zhonghua shuju, 1960), pp. 2849, 1700 respectively.

24 Chen and Hou (eds.), *Cen Shen,* p. 148.

25 Ibid., pp. 169–70.

26 Liu Qingde et al., *Zhongguo lidai changcheng shi lu* (Poetry of the Great Wall of China through the ages) (Hebei: Hebei meishu chubanshe, 1991), p. 155.

27 Ibid., p. 154.

28 Ibid., p. 119.

29 Ibid., p. 126.

30 Qu and Zhu (eds.), *Li Bo,* p. 1711.

Chapter 7: The Return of the Barbarians

1 For details of the entire debate, see Hok-lam Chan, *Legitimation in Imperial China: Discussions under the Jurchen-Chin Dynasty (1115–1234)* (Seattle: University of Washington Press, 1984).

2 Thomas J. Barfield, *The Perilous Frontier: Nomadic Empires and China* (Oxford: Basil Blackwell, 1989), p. 202.

3 Ibid., p. 171.

4 Valerie Hansen, *The Open Empire: A History of China to 1600* (New York: Norton, 2000), p. 303; Herbert Franke and Denis Twitchett (eds.), *The Cambridge History of China Volume 6: Alien Regimes and Border States, 907–1368* (Cambridge: Cambridge University Press, 1994), p. 92.

5 *Zhongguo changcheng yiji diaocha baogao ji* (Collected reports on surveys of the Great Wall of China) (Beijing: Wenwu, 1981), pp. 130–31.

6 *Changcheng guoji xueshu yantaohui lunwenji* (Proceedings of the International Academic Symposium on the Great Wall) (Jilin: Jilin renmin chubanshe, 1995), pp. 154–8.

7 Li Chih-Ch'ang, *The Travels of an Alchemist,* trans. Arthur Waley (London: Routledge, 1931), p. 63.

8 *Zhongguo changcheng yiji diaocha,* pp. 77–83. See also photographs in Daniel Schwartz, *The Great Wall of China* (London: Thames and Hudson, 1990).

9 Ibid., pp. 130–1.

10 Ibid.

11 John Man, *Genghis Khan: Life, Death and Resurrection* (London: Bantam, 2004), pp. 55–62.

12 Ibid., p. 103.

13 Ibid., p. 134.

14 *Changcheng guoji,* p. 155.

15 Man, *Genghis Khan,* p. 135.

16 Li, *The Travels,* pp. 62–3.

17 Leo de Hartog, *Genghis Khan: Conqueror of the World* (London: Tauris, 1989), pp. 64–5.

18 Quoted in Barfield, *The Perilous Frontier,* p. 200.

19 Quoted in Michel Hoang, *Genghis Khan* (London: Saki, 1990), p. 184.

20 Marco Polo, *The Travels,* trans. R. E. Latham (Harmondsworth: Penguin, 1980), pp. 124–6.

21 Ibid., pp. 128–9.

22 Hansen, *The Open Empire,* p. 366.

Chapter 8: A Case of Open and Shut: The Early Ming Frontier

1 See Susan Naquin, *Peking: Temples and City Life* (Berkeley: University of California Press, 2000), for a detailed analysis of Ming and Qing Beijing.

2 *Changcheng baike quanshu* (Encyclopedia of the Great Wall) (Jilin: Jilin People's Publishing House, 1994), p. 758.

3 Hua Xiazi, *Ming changcheng kaoshi* (An investigation into the Ming Great Wall) (Qinhuangdao: Dang'an chubanshe, 1988), p. 134.

4 Quoted in Edward L. Farmer, *Early Ming Government: The Evolution of Dual Capitals* (Cambridge, Mass.: Harvard University Press, 1976), pp. 37–8.

5 See Arthur Waldron, *The Great Wall of China: From History to Myth* (Cambridge: Cambridge University Press, 1992), pp. 72–81, for an excellent account of early Ming frontier strategy.

6 Hafiz-i Abru, *A Persian Embassy to China,* trans. K. M. Maitra (New York: Paragon Book Reprint Corp., 1970), pp. 16, 24, 65.

7 Henry Serruys, 'Sino-Mongol Relations during the Ming, III. Trade Relations: The Horse Fairs (1499–1600)', *Mélanges Chinois et Bouddhiques,* 18 (1975), p. 21.

8 Translation adapted from Frederick W. Mote, 'The T'u-mu Incident of 1449', in *Chinese Ways in Warfare,* ed. Frank A. Kierman Jr and John K. Fairbank (Cambridge, Mass.: Harvard University Press, 1974), p. 255.

9 Translation from original printed in James Legge, *The Chinese Classics,* Vol. IV, *The She King* (Hong Kong: Lane, Crawford and Co., 1871), p. 561.

10 The following account of the Ming campaign is based on the information in Frederick Mote's excellent article 'The T'umu Incident'.

11 Ibid., p. 255.

12 Ibid., p. 256.

13 Ibid., p. 258.

14 Translation adapted from ibid., p. 261.

15 Ibid., p. 262.

16 Ibid., p. 266.

17 Ibid., p. 268.

18 Quoted in Frederick W. Mote and Denis Twitchett (eds.), *The Cambridge History of China Volume 7: The Ming Dynasty, 1368–1644, Part I* (Cambridge: Cambridge University Press, 1988), pp. 371–2.

19 Quoted in Mote, 'The T'umu Incident', pp. 368–9.

20 Quoted in Thomas J. Barfield, *The Perilous Frontier: Nomadic Empires and China* (Oxford: Basil Blackwell, 1989), p. 242.

21 See Waldron's account in *The Great Wall*, pp. 91–107.

22 Ibid., p. 79.

23 See L. Carrington Goodrich (ed.), *Dictionary of Ming Biography, 1368–1644* (New York: Columbia University Press, 1976), pp. 155–9.

24 *Ming shi* (History of the Ming) (Beijing: Zhonghua shuju, 1974), 178.4737.

25 Mote and Twitchett (eds.), *The Cambridge History of China Volume 7*, p. 401.

26 *Ming shi*, 178.4736.

27 Henry Serruys, 'Towers in the Northern Frontier Defenses of the Ming', *Ming Studies*, 14 (Spring 1982), p. 35.

28 *Ming shi*, 178.4738.

29 Quoted in Waldron, *The Great Wall*, p. 117.

Chapter 9: The Wall Goes Up

1 Quoted in Arthur Waldron, *The Great Wall of China: From History to Myth* (Cambridge: Cambridge University Press, 1992), p. 123.

2 Henry Serruys, 'Sino-Mongol Relations during the Ming, II. The Tribute System and Diplomatic Missions (1400–1600)', *Mélanges Chinois et Bouddhiques*, 14 (1969), p. 38.

3 Quoted in Sechin Jagchid and Van Jay Symons, *Peace, War and Trade along the Great Wall: Nomadic–Chinese Interaction through Two Millennia* (Bloomington: Indiana University Press, 1989), p. 197.

4 Quoted ibid., p. 87.

5 Serruys, 'Sino-Mongol Relations during the Ming, II', p. 37.

6 Quoted in Waldron, *The Great Wall*, p. 154.

7 *Zhongguo changcheng yiji diaocha baogao ji* (Collected reports on surveys of the Great Wall of China) (Beijing: Wenwu, 1981), pp. 102–5.

8 Frederick W. Mote and Denis Twitchett (eds.), *The Cambridge History of China Volume 7: The Ming Dynasty, 1368–1644, Part I* (Cambridge: Cambridge University Press, 1988), p. 475.

9 Quoted in Frederick W. Mote and Denis Twitchett (eds.), *The Cambridge History of China Volume 8: The Ming Dynasty, 1368–1644, Part II* (Cambridge: Cambridge University Press, 1998), p. 66.

10 Jagchid and Symons, *Peace, War and Trade,* p. 94.

11 Waldron, *The Great Wall,* p. 176; Jagchid and Symons, *Peace, War and Trade,* pp. 94–6.

12 Serruys, 'Sino-Mongol Relations during the Ming, II', p. 58.

13 See ibid., p. 60, and Jagchid and Symons, *Peace, War and Trade,* p. 93.

14 Waldron, *The Great Wall,* p. 161.

15 Ibid., p. 152.

16 Ibid., p. 163.

17 See *Zhongguo changcheng yiji diaocha,* pp. 93–100, 106–17, for detailed surveys of Jiayuguan and Shanhaiguan.

18 Examples drawn from *Zhongguo changcheng gushi* (Stories about the Great Wall of China) (Beijing: Yanshan, 1987) and Song Mengyin and Dong Kan (eds.), *Wanli changcheng chuanshuo* (Legends of the Great Wall) (Hebei: Hebei shaonian ertong, 1990).

19 See table in Waldron, *The Great Wall,* p. 152.

20 Luo Zhewen et al., *The Great Wall* (London: Michael Joseph Ltd, 1981), pp. 128–39.

21 Henry Serruys, 'Towers in the Northern Frontier Defenses of the Ming', *Ming Studies,* 14 (Spring 1982), pp. 28–30.

22 Ibid., pp. 19–20.

23 Ibid., p. 21.

24 For these and further details, see Serruys's excellent survey in ibid.

25 Ibid., p. 58.

26 Waldron, *The Great Wall,* p. 164.

27 Quoted in Jagchid and Symons, *Peace, War and Trade,* p. 106.

28 Serruys, 'Sino-Mongol Relations during the Ming, II', p. 590.

29 Quoted in Jagchid and Symons, *Peace, War and Trade,* p. 104.

Chapter 10: The Great Fall of China

1 Hua Xiazi, *Ming changcheng kaoshi* (An investigation into the Ming Great Wall) (Qinhuangdao: Dang'an chubanshe, 1988), p. 86.

2 Frederic Wakeman Jr, 'The Shun Interregnum of 1644', in *From Ming to Qing: Conquest, Region, and Continuity in Seventeenth-Century China,* ed. Jonathan D. Spence and John E. Wills (New Haven: Yale University Press, 1979), p. 45.

3 See Willard J. Peterson (ed.), *The Cambridge History of China Volume 9, Part One: The Ch'ing Empire to 1800* (Cambridge: Cambridge University Press, 2002), pp. 9–72, for details of the formative years of the Qing state in Manchuria.

4 Wakeman, 'The Shun Interregnum', p. 44.

5 Frederic Wakeman Jr, *The Great Enterprise: The Manchu Reconstruction of Imperial Order in Seventeenth-Century China,* Vol. I (Berkeley: University of California Press, 1985), p. 13.

6 Ibid., p. 238.

7 Frederick W. Mote and Denis Twitchett (eds.), *The Cambridge History of China Volume 7: The Ming Dynasty, 1368–1644, Part I* (Cambridge: Cambridge University Press, 1988), p. 637.

8 Quoted in Jacques Gernet, *A History of Chinese Civilization,* trans. J. R. Foster (Cambridge: Cambridge University Press, 1990), p. 431.

9 Wakeman, 'The Shun Interregnum', p. 45.

10 Wakeman, *The Great Enterprise,* pp. 59–60.

11 Henry Serruys, 'Towers in the Northern Frontier Defenses of the Ming', *Ming Studies,* 14 (Spring 1982), p. 31.

12 Ibid., p. 24.

13 Ibid., p. 45.

14 Ibid., p. 22.

15 Ibid., p. 43.

16 Ibid., p. 48.

17 Translation adapted from ibid., p. 51.

18 Ibid., p. 24.

19 Ibid., p. 25.

20 Ibid., p. 61.

21 Ibid., p. 47.

22 Ibid., p. 38.

23 Ibid., p. 45.

24 Wakeman, *The Great Enterprise,* p. 63.

25 Ibid., pp. 171–90.

26 Ibid., p. 224.

27 Ibid., p. 235.

28 Quoted in ibid., p. 259.

29 Ibid., p. 246.

30 Quoted in ibid., p. 260.

31 Ibid., pp. 260–62.

32 Quoted in ibid., p. 265.

33 Ibid., p. 266.

34 See discussion in, for example, Angela Hsu, 'Wu San-kuei in 1644: A Reappraisal', in *Journal of Asian Studies*, 34.2 (February 1975), pp. 443–53.

35 Wakeman, *The Great Enterprise*, p. 291.

36 Quoted in ibid., p. 291.

37 Quoted in ibid., p. 139.

38 Quoted in ibid., p. 147.

39 Wakeman, 'The Shun Interregnum', p. 70.

40 Wakeman, *The Great Enterprise*, pp. 300–301.

41 Translation adapted from ibid., p. 309.

42 Ibid., p. 310.

43 Translation adapted from ibid., p. 311.

44 Translation adapted from ibid., p. 310.

45 Quoted in ibid., p. 314.

46 Translation adapted from ibid., p. 315.

47 Translation adapted from Wakeman, 'The Shun Interregnum', p. 74.

48 Wakeman, *The Great Enterprise*, p. 318.

49 See Wang Su, 'Qian nian chunqiu lun changcheng' (Discussions of the Great Wall across millennia), *Zhongguo qingnian bao*, 14 August 1988, p. 6.

50 J. L. Cranmer-Byng (ed.), *An Embassy to China Being the Journal Kept by Lord Macartney during his Embassy to the Emperor Ch'ien-lung, 1793–94* (London: Longmans, 1962), p. 113.

51 Wan Sitong, *Xin yuefu ci* (New folk ballads), in *Congshu jicheng xubian,* Vol. 28 (Shanghai: Shanghai shudian chubanshe, 1994), p. 255.

Chapter 11: How Barbarians Made the Great Wall

1 Jean Baptiste Du Halde, *A Description of the Empire of China…* (London: Edward Cave, 1738–41), Vol. II, p. 270.

2 Jonathan D. Spence, *Emperor of China: Self-portrait of Kang Hsi* (New York: Knopf, 1974), pp. xiv–xv.

3 Quoted in Du Halde, *A Description*, Vol. II, p. 271, and Arthur Waldron, *The*

Great Wall of China: From History to Myth (Cambridge: Cambridge University Press, 1992), p. 206.

4 Martino Martini, *Novus Atlas Sinensis* (Amsterdam: Joan Blaeu, 1655). The translation of Martini's text is taken from Athanasius Kircher, SJ, *China monumentis qua sacris qua profanis, Illustrata,* trans. Charles D. Van Tuyl (Oklahoma: Indian University Press, Bacone College, 1987), p. 207.

5 Ibid., p. 207.

6 Waldron, *The Great Wall,* p. 204.

7 Ruth I. Meserve, 'The Inhospitable Land of the Barbarian', *Journal of Asian History,* 16 (1982), pp. 76–7.

8 See discussion in Waldron, *The Great Wall,* pp. 204–5.

9 Du Halde, *A Description,* Vol. I, p. 22.

10 George H. Dunne, *Generation of Giants: The Story of the Jesuits in China in the Last Decades of the Ming Dynasty* (London: Burns and Oates, 1962), p. 16.

11 Ibid., p. 17.

12 Matteo Ricci, *China in the Sixteenth Century: The Journals of Matthew Ricci: 1583–1610,* trans. Louis J. Gallagher, SJ (New York: Random House, 1953), p. 26.

13 Ibid., p. 59.

14 Jonathan Spence, *The Chan's Great Continent: China in Western Minds* (London: Penguin, 2000), p. 33.

15 Ricci, *China,* p. 10; Alexandre de Rhodes, *Divers voyages de la Chine et autres royaumes de l'Orient* (Paris: Christophe Iournel, 1681), p. 46; Verbiest, quoted in Du Halde, *A Description,* Vol. II, p. 271; Philippe Avril, *Travels into divers Parts of Europe and Asia* (London: Tim. Goodwin, 1693), p. 144; Du Halde, *A Description,* Vol. I, p. 20.

16 Louis D. Le Comte, *Memoirs and Observations* ... (London: Benj. Tooke, 1698), p. 74.

17 Du Halde, *A Description,* Vol. I, pp. 20–22.

18 Ibid.

19 John E. N. Hearsey, *Voltaire* (London: Constable, 1976), p. 10.

20 Quoted in Ian Buruma, *Voltaire's Coconuts: or Anglomania in Europe* (London: Phoenix, 2000), p. 31.

21 Voltaire, *Philosophical Dictionary,* Vol. I, trans. Peter Gay (New York: Basic Books, 1962), p. 169.

22 Voltaire, *An Essay on Universal History,* Vol. I, trans. Thomas Mugent (Edinburgh: William Creech, 1782), p. 13.

23 Voltaire, *Dictionnaire Philosophique* (Paris: Garnier frères, 1954), p. 481.

24 Quoted in A. Owen Aldridge, 'Voltaire and the Cult of China', *Tamkang Review*, 2.2–3.1 (1971–2), p. 29.

25 Hearsey, *Voltaire*, p. 291.

26 Voltaire, *Lettres chinoises, indiennes et tartares* (Paris: [s.n.], 1776), p. 60.

27 Ibid., pp. 58–9.

28 Ibid., p. 54.

29 Voltaire, *Dictionnaire Philosophique,* Vol. I (Amsterdam: Marc-Michel Rey, 1789), p. 334.

30 See Buruma, *Voltaire's Coconuts,* pp. 20–51, for a highly entertaining account of Voltaire's English encounters.

31 Quoted in Spence, *The Chan's Great Continent,* pp. 55, 54, 55, 54 respectively.

32 For more details, see ibid., pp. 66–71.

33 Daniel Defoe, *The Farther Adventures of Robinson Crusoe* (London: Constable & Co., 1925), pp. 280–81.

34 See Linda Colley, *Captives: Britain, Empire and the World 1600–1850* (London: Jonathan Cape, 2002).

35 J. H. Dunne, *From Calcutta to Pekin* (London: S. Low, 1861), p. 128.

36 John K. Fairbank (ed.), *The Cambridge History of China Volume 10: Late Ch'ing, 1800–1911, Part 1* (Cambridge: Cambridge University Press, 1978), p. 176.

37 Ibid., p. 192.

38 Quoted in Susan Schoenbauer Thurin, *Victorian Travellers and the Opening of China* (Ohio: Ohio University Press, 1999), pp. 1–2.

39 George Fleming, *Travels on Horseback in Mantchu Tartary* (London: Hurst and Blackett, 1863), pp. 16, 17, 130.

40 Ibid., pp. 29, 26 respectively.

41 Ibid., p. 224.

42 Ibid., pp. 227–9.

43 Ibid., p. 255.

44 Ibid., pp. 228–9.

45 Ibid., p. 181.

46 Ibid., p. 287.

47 Ibid., pp. 322–3.

48 Ibid., pp. 324–8.

49 Ibid., pp. 332–3.

50 Ibid., p. 346.

51 Ibid., pp. 355, 367.

52 Ibid., pp. 368–.

53 Quoted in Rosemary Bailey, *The Man Who Married a Mountain: A Journey through the French Pyrenees* (London: Bantam Books, 2005), p. 175.

54 Fleming, *Travels*, p. 342.

55 Ibid., p. 340.

56 'The Great Wall of China', *Once a Week*, 7 June 1862, p. 672.

57 Adam Warwick, 'A Thousand Miles along the Great Wall of China', *National Geographic Magazine*, 43.2 (February 1923), p. 113.

58 Sir John Francis Davis, *Sketches of China* (London: C. Knight & Co., 1841), pp. 3–4.

59 Frits Holm, *My Nestorian Adventure in China* (London: Hutchinson & Co., 1924), p. 53.

60 Luigi Barzini, *Pekin to Paris: An Account of Prince Borghese's Journey across Two Continents in a Motor-car* (London: E. Grant Richard, 1907), pp. 96–7.

61 Ibid., p. 109.

62 Victor Murdock, *China, the Mysterious and Marvellous* (New York: Chicago, 1920), p. 291.

63 William John Gill, *River of Golden Sand* (London: Murray, 1883), pp. 22–3.

64 Roy Chapman Andrews, *Across Mongolian Plains* (London: D. Appleton & Co., 1921), p. 20.

65 Fleming, *Travels*, p. 318.

66 Ibid., pp. 367–.

Chapter 12: Translating the Great Wall into Chinese

1 Quoted in Jonathan Spence, *The Search for Modern China* (New York: Norton, 1999), pp. 303–4.

2 Teng Ssu-yü and John K. Fairbank (eds.), *China's Response to the West: A Documentary Survey, 1839–1923* (Cambridge, Mass.: Harvard University Press, 1954), pp. 240, 243.

3 Marie-Claire Bergère, *Sun Yat-sen*, trans. Janet Lloyd (Stanford: Stanford University Press, 1998), p. 282.

4 Sun Zhongshan, *Jianguo fanglüe* (Plan for national reconstruction)

(Zhengzhou: Zhongzhou guji chubanshe, 1998), pp. 90–91.

5 Quoted in C. Martin Wilbur, *Frustrated Patriot* (New York: Columbia University Press, 1976), p. 144.

6 Bergère, *Sun Yat-sen,* pp. 358–9.

7 Ibid., p. 372.

8 Edgar Snow, *Red Star over China* (Harmondsworth: Penguin, 1972), p. 68.

9 Quoted in Mark Selden, *China in Revolution: The Yenan Way Revisited* (New York: M. E. Sharpe, 1995), p. 4.

10 For a recent, radical revision of Maoist mythologies of the Long March, see Jung Chang and Jon Halliday, *Mao: The Unknown Story* (London: Jonathan Cape, 2005).

11 Chen Guoliang (ed.), *Mao Zedong shici baishou yizhu* (One hundred annotated poems by Mao Zedong) (Beijing: Beijing chubanshe, 1997), p. 84.

12 See figures in Charles H. Shepherd, *The Case against Japan* (London: Jarrolds, 1939), p. 131.

13 Wenjing, 'Guochi congji ti wu yue' (A May of accumulated national humiliation), *Qiantu,* 1.5 (1 May 1933), p. 3.

14 Junshi kexueyuan junshi lishi yanjiubu, *Zhong guo kang ri zhan zheng shi* (History of the Sino-Japanese War), Vol. 1 (Beijing: Jiefangjun chubanshe, 1991), p. 268.

15 *Changcheng baike quanshu* (Encyclopedia of the Great Wall) (Jilin: Jilin People's Publishing House, 1994), p. 901.

16 Parks M. Coble, *Facing Japan: Chinese Politics and Japanese Imperialism, 1931–37* (Cambridge, Mass.: Council on East Asian Studies, Harvard University, 1991), p. 102.

17 Ibid., pp. 98–9.

18 Ibid., pp. 115–16.

19 Chen (ed.), *Mao Zedong,* pp. 88–9.

20 Quoted in Philip Short, *Mao: A Life* (London: John Murray, 2004), p. 345.

21 In 'Selections from Mao Zedong's Writings on Foreign Relations', www.southcn.com/nflr/ldzb/mzdsx/200312160860.htm.

22 The original Chinese version can be accessed at list.mp3.baidu.com/song/0/82/8253_somp3.htm.

23 www.marxistsorg/reference/archive/mao/selected-works/volume-2/mswv2_10.htm.

24 www.marxistsorg/reference/archive/mao/selected-works/volume-9/mswv9_27.htm.

25 Quoted in Roger Garside, *Coming Alive: China after Mao* (London: Andre Deutsch, 1981), p. 276.

26 Ibid., p. 292.

27 Li Yu-ning (ed.), *The Politics of Historiography: The First Emperor of China* (New York: International Arts and Sciences Press, 1975), p. 163.

28 Guixian jiaoyuju (Guangxi: Guangxi renmin chubanshe, 1975).

Conclusion: The Great Wall, the Great Mall and the Great Firewall

1 See photograph in, for example, Arthur Waldron, *The Great Wall of China. From History to Myth* (Cambridge: Cambridge University Press, 1992), p. 223.

2 Huang Xiang, *Kuangyin bu zui de shouxing* (The form of the beast drinks hard without getting drunk) (New York: Tianxia huaren chubanshe, 1998), pp. 21–4.

3 Roger Garside, *Coming Alive: China after Mao* (London: Andre Deutsch, 1981), p. 226.

4 Ian Buruma, *Bad Elements: Chinese Rebels from Los Angeles to Beijing* (London: Weidenfeld and Nicolson, 2002), p. 100.

5 Roderick MacFarquhar (ed.), *The Politics of China Second Edition: The Eras of Mao and Deng* (Cambridge: Cambridge University Press, 1997), p. 398.

6 Quoted in 'Four Modernizations – Factbites', www.factbites.com/topics/Four-Modernizations.

7 MacFarquhar (ed.), *The Politics,* p. 324.

8 Garside, *Coming Alive,* p. 257.

9 Ibid., p. 262.

10 Waldron, *The Great Wall,* pp. 1, 222–5.

11 Quoted in Su Xiaokang and Wang Luxiang, *Deathsong of the River: A Reader's Guide to the Chinese TV Series* Heshang, trans. Richard W. Bodman and Pin P. Wan (Ithaca: East Asia Program, Cornell University, 1991), p. 12.

12 Ibid., p. 124.

13 Ibid., pp. 126–7.

14 Ibid., p. 130.

15 Ibid., p. 127.

16 Ibid., p. 216.

17 Ibid., p. 204.

18 Ibid., pp. 212–13.

19 Ibid., p. 218.

20 Su Xiaokang, *A Memoir of Misfortune* (New York: Knopf, 2001), p. 20.

21 Ibid., p. 21; Su and Wang, *Deathsong,* pp. 313–14, 325.

22 Buruma, *Bad Elements,* p. xvii.

23 Joe Studwell, *The China Dream: The Elusive Quest for the Greatest Untapped Market on Earth* (London: Profile Books, 2002), p. 56.

24 Jack Linchuan Qiu, 'The Internet in China: Data and Issues' (paper obtained from author), pp. 1–2. My account of the development of the Internet in China is substantially indebted to Jack Linchuan Qiu's wonderfully informative research on the subject.

25 'News Brief', at ojr.usc.edu/content/ojc/brief.cfm?request=1532.

26 Joshua Kurlantzick, 'Dictatorship.com: The Web Won't Topple Tyranny', *New Republic,* 230.12 (4 May 2004).

27 Geremie R. Barmé and Sang Ye, 'The Great Firewall of China', *Wired* 5.06 (June 1997), http://www.wired.com/wired/5.06/china_pr.html.

28 Edward Young, 'The Internet: Beyond the Great Firewall', *China Economic Quarterly* (11 November 2002); Xiao Qiang, 'Words You Never See in Chinese Cyberspace', http://chinadigitaltimes.net/2004/08/the_words_you_n.php (30 August 2004).

29 Xiao Qiang, 'The "Blog" Revolution Sweeps across China', *New Scientist* (24 November 2004), http://www.newscientist.com/article.ns?id=dn6707&print=true.

30 Xiao Qiang, 'Chinese Workers Blog for Protest', http://chinadigitalnews.net/2004/12/chinese_workers.php (20 December 2004).

31 See Perry Link's brilliant essay 'The Anaconda in the Chandelier', *New York Review of Books* (11 April 2002), pp. 67–70.

32 Barmé and Sang Ye, 'The Great Firewall'.

33 Quoted in Xiao Qiang, 'The "Blog" Revolution'.

34 Jack Linchuan Qiu, 'Chinese Nationalism on the Net: An Odd Myth with Normalcy', paper presented at NCA Annual Convention, Atlanta, 1–4 November 2001, p. 13.

35 Qiu, 'Chinese Nationalism', p. 12.

36 Jack Linchuan Qiu, 'Chinese Hackerism in Retrospect: The Legend of a New

Revolutionary Army', *MFC Insight* (17 September 2002), p. 6.

37 Joseph Kahn, 'Chinese Authorities Warn against New Protests', *International Herald Tribune* (16 April 2005),
http://www.iht.com/articles/2005/04/15/news/china.html.

38 Joseph Kahn, 'State-run Chinese Paper Lashes Anti-Japanese Protests as "Evil Plot"', *New York Times* (27 April 2005),
http://www.nytimes.com/2005/04/27/international/asia/27china.html?oref
=login.

SELECTED BIBLIOGRAPHY

GENERAL WORKS ON THE GREAT WALL

Assuredly the best modern historical work on the Great Wall of China in English is *The Great Wall* by Arthur Waldron, whose meticulous dismantling of the myth of the wall blazed a trail in wall scholarship. Luo Zhewen et al., *The Great Wall* contains very useful information and images, while Daniel Schwartz has produced a striking collection of photographs ranging across the length of frontier walls.

Changcheng baike quanshu (Encyclopedia of the Great Wall) (Jilin: Jilin People's Publishing House, 1994)

Changcheng guoji xueshu yantaohui lunwenji (Proceedings of the International Academic Symposium on the Great Wall) (Jilin: Jilin renmin chubanshe, 1995)

Fryer, Jonathan, *The Great Wall of China* (London: New English Library, 1975)

Geil, William Edgar, *The Great Wall of China* (New York: Sturgis & Walton Company, 1909)

Liu Qingde et al., *Zhongguo lidai changcheng shi lu* (Poetry of the Great Wall of China through the ages) (Hebei: Hebei meishu chubanshe, 1991)

Luo Zhewen et al., *The Great Wall* (London: Michael Joseph Ltd, 1981)

Schwartz, Daniel, *The Great Wall of China* (London: Thames and Hudson, 1990)

Song Mengyin and Dong Kan (eds.), *Wanli changcheng chuanshuo* (Legends of the Great Wall) (Hebei: Hebei shaonian ertong, 1990)

Waldron, Arthur, *The Great Wall of China: From History to Myth* (Cambridge: Cambridge University Press, 1992)

Zhongguo changcheng gushi (Stories about the Great Wall of China) (Beijing: Yanshan, 1987)

Zhongguo changcheng yiji diaocha baogao ji (Collected reports on surveys of the Great Wall of China) (Beijing: Wenwu, 1981)

GENERAL WORKS ON CHINESE HISTORY AND GEOGRAPHY

For any single dynastic period in Chinese history, the essays in the relevant volume of *The Cambridge History of China* (listed in the dynasty-by-dynasty section below) provide a tremendously informative survey of the period in question, as well as an extremely helpful introduction to the primary and secondary sources. For more general histories, Gernet, Hansen, Mote and Spence are all very useful, while Needham's monumental work provides a remarkable guide to the history of science in China.

Blunden, Caroline, and Elvin, Mark, *Cultural Atlas of China* (Oxford: Equinox, 1983)

Cressey, George B., *China's Geographic Foundations: A Survey of the Land and Its People* (New York: McGraw-Hill Book Company, Inc., 1934)

– 'The Ordos Desert of Inner Mongolia', in *Denison University Bulletin,* 28.8 (1933), pp. 155–248

De Bary, W. M., and Bloom, Irene, *Sources of Chinese Tradition,* 2 vols. (New York: Columbia University Press, 1999–2000)

Gernet, Jacques, *A History of Chinese Civilization,* trans. J. R. Foster (Cambridge: Cambridge University Press, 1990)

Hansen, Valerie, *The Open Empire: A History of China to 1600* (New York: Norton, 2000)

Needham, Joseph, *Science and Civilisation in China* (Cambridge: Cambridge University Press, 1954 –)

Spence, Jonathan, *The Search for Modern China* (New York: Norton, 1999)

Zhongguo lishi ditu ji (Collected Chinese historical atlases) (Shanghai: Ditu chuban-she, 1982–7)

RELATIONS BETWEEN CHINA AND THE STEPPE

Barfield, Thomas J., *The Perilous Frontier: Nomadic Empires and China* (Oxford: Basil Blackwell, 1989)

Grousset, René, *The Empire of the Steppes: A History of Central Asia,* trans. Naomi Watford (New Jersey: Rutgers University Press, 1970)

Jagchid, Sechid, and Symons, Van Jay, *Peace, War and Trade along the Great Wall: Nomadic–Chinese Interaction through Two Millennia* (Bloomington: Indiana University Press, 1989)

Lattimore, Owen, *Inner Asian Frontiers of China* (New York: American Geographical Society, 1940)

– *Studies in Frontier History: Collected Papers 1928–1958* (London: Oxford University Press, 1962)

Sinor, Dennis, 'The Inner Asian Warriors', *Journal of the American Oriental Society,* 101.2 (1981), pp. 133–44

Sinor, Dennis (ed.), *The Cambridge History of Early Inner Asia* (Cambridge: Cambridge University Press, 1990)

HISTORY BY DYNASTY

The Shang, Zhou and Warring States Period

Birrell, Anne (trans.), *The Classic of Mountains and Seas* (London: Penguin, 1999)

Chang, Kwang-chih, *Shang Civilisation* (New Haven: Yale University Press, 1980)

Crump, J. I. (trans.), *Chan-kuo ts'e* (University of Michigan: Center for Chinese Studies, 1996)

Di Cosmo, Nicola, *Ancient China and Its Enemies: The Rise of Nomadic Powers in East Asian History* (Cambridge: Cambridge University Press, 2002)

Legge, James, *The Chinese Classics* (Hong Kong: Lane, Crawford and Co., 1871)

Prusek, Jaroslav, *Chinese Statelets and the Northern Barbarians in the Period 1400–300 BC* (New York: Humanities Press, 1971)

The Qin, Han and Northern Wei

Bielenstein, Hans, *The Restoration of the Han Dynasty,* 4 vols., *Bulletin of the Museum of Far Eastern Antiquities,* 26, 31, 39, 51 (1954, 1959, 1967, 1979)

Bodde, Derk (trans.), *Statesman, Patriot, and General in Ancient China: Three Shih Chi Biographies of the Ch'in Dynasty (255–206 BC),* (New Haven: American Oriental Society, 1940)

De Crespigny, Rafe, *Northern Frontier: The Policies and Strategy of the Later Han Empire* (Canberra: Australian National University, 1984)

Hopkirk, Peter, *Foreign Devils on the Silk Road: The Search for the Lost Treasures of Central Asia* (Oxford: Oxford University Press, 1984)

Hulsewe, A. F. P., and Loewe, Michael, *China in Central Asia: The Early Stage, 125 BC–AD 23* (Leiden: Brill, 1979)

Jenner, W. J. F., *Memories of Loyang: Yang Hsüan-chih and the Lost Capital (493–534)* (Oxford: Clarendon Press, 1981)

Loewe, Michael, *Records of Han Administration*, 2 vols. (Cambridge: University of Cambridge Oriental Publications, 1967)

– *Everyday Life in Early Imperial China* (New York: Harper & Row, 1970)

– 'The Campaigns of Han Wu-ti', in *Chinese Ways in Warfare,* ed. Frank A. Kierman Jr and John K. Fairbank (Cambridge, Mass.: Harvard University Press, 1974) pp. 67–122

Mirsky, Jeannette. *Sir Aurel Stein: Archaeological Explorer* (Chicago: University of Chicago Press, 1977)

Sima Qian, *The Grand Scribe's Records,* ed. William H. Nienhauser Jr (Bloomington: Indiana University Press, 1994–)

Stein, M. Aurel, *Serindia* (Oxford: Clarendon Press, 1921)

– *Ruins of Desert Cathay: Personal Narrative of Explorations in Central Asia and Westernmost China,* 2 vols. (New York: Dover Publications, 1987)

Twitchett, Denis, and Loewe, Michael (eds.), *The Cambridge History of China Volume 1: The Ch'in and Han Empires, 220 BC through AD 220* (Cambridge: Cambridge University Press, 1986)

Walker, Annabel, *Aurel Stein: Pioneer of the Silk Road* (London: John Murray, 1995)

Watson, Burton (trans.), *Records of the Grand Historian of China,* 2 vols. (New York: Columbia University Press, 1961)

– *Records of the Grand Historian: Han Dynasty II* (rev. edn) (Hong Kong and New York: Renditions and Columbia University Press, 1993)

The Sui and Tang

Chan, Marie, 'The Frontier Poems of Ts'en Shen', *Journal of the American Oriental Society,* 98.4 (1978), pp. 421–37

Chen Tiemin and Hou Zhongyi (eds.), *Cen Shen ji jiaozhu* (Shanghai: Shanghai guji chubanshe, 1981)

Hartman, Charles, *Han Yu and the T'ang Search for Unity* (Princeton: Princeton University Press, 1986)

Hinton, David (trans.), *The Selected Poems of Li Po* (London: Anvil, 1996)

Hu Ji, *Sui Yangdi xinzhuan* (Shanghai: Shanghai renmin chubanshe, 1995)

Owen, Stephen, *The Great Age of Chinese Poetry: The High T'ang* (New Haven: Yale University Press, 1981)

Parker, Edward H., 'The Early Turks', *China Review*, 24 (1899–1900), pp. 120–227

– 'The Early Turks', *China Review*, 25 (1900–1901), pp. 1–270

Pulleyblank, Edwin G., *The Background of the Rebellion of An Lu-shan* (Oxford: Oxford University Press, 1966)

Schafer, Edward H., *The Golden Peaches of Samarkand* (Berkeley: University of California Press, 1963)

Twitchett, Denis (ed.), *The Cambridge History of China Volume 3: Sui and T'ang China, 589–906, Part I* (Cambridge: Cambridge University Press, 1979)

Waley, Arthur, 'A Chinese Poet in Central Asia', in *The Secret History of the Mongols* (London: George Allen and Unwin, 1963), pp. 30–46

Wright, Arthur F., *The Sui Dynasty* (New York: Knopf, 1978)

– 'Sui Yang-ti: Personality and Stereotype', in *The Confucian Persuasion* (Stanford: Stanford University Press, 1960), pp. 47–76

Liao, Jin and the Mongol Yuan

Chan, Hok-lam, *Legitimation in Imperial China: Discussions under the Jurchen-Chin Dynasty (1115–1234)* (Seattle: University of Washington Press, 1984)

De Hartog, Leo, *Genghis Khan: Conqueror of the World* (London: Tauris, 1989)

Franke, Herbert, and Twitchett, Denis (eds.), *The Cambridge History of China Volume 6: Alien Regimes and Border States, 907–1368* (Cambridge: Cambridge University Press, 1994)

Hoang, Michel, *Genghis Khan* (London: Saki, 1990)

Li Chih-Ch'ang, *The Travels of an Alchemist,* trans. Arthur Waley (London: Routledge, 1931)

Man, John, *Genghis Khan: Life, Death and Resurrection* (London: Bantam, 2004)

Martin, H. Desmond, *The Rise of Chingis Khan and His Conquest of North China* (Baltimore: Johns Hopkins University Press, 1950)

Rossabi, Morris, *Khubilai Khan: His Life and Times* (Berkeley: University of California Press, 1988)

The Ming and Rise of the Qing

Hafiz-i Abru, *A Persian Embassy in China,* trans. K. M. Maitra (New York: Paragon Book Reprint Corp., 1970)

Dreyer, Edmund L., *Early Ming China: A Political History 1355–1435* (Stanford:

Stanford University Press, 1982)

Farmer, Edward L., *Early Ming Government: The Evolution of Dual Capitals* (Cambridge, Mass.: Harvard University Press, 1976)

Goodrich, L. Carrington (ed.), *Dictionary of Ming Biography, 1368–1644* (New York: Columbia University Press, 1976)

Hsu, Angela, 'Wu San-kuei in 1644: A Reappraisal', *Journal of Asian Studies,* 34.2 (February 1975), pp. 443–53

Hua Xiazi, *Ming changcheng kaoshi* (An investigation into the Ming Great Wall) (Qinhuangdao: Dang'an chubanshe, 1988)

Levathes, Louise, *When China Ruled the Seas* (New York: Simon & Schuster, 1994)

Mote, Frederick W., 'The T'u-mu Incident of 1449', in *Chinese Ways in Warfare,* ed. Frank A. Kierman Jr and John K. Fairbank (Cambridge, Mass.: Harvard University Press, 1974), pp. 243–72

Mote, Frederick W., and Twitchett, Denis (eds.), *The Cambridge History of China Volume 7: The Ming Dynasty, 1368–1644, Part I* (Cambridge: Cambridge University Press, 1988)

– *The Cambridge History of China Volume 7: The Ming Dynasty, 1368–1644, Part II* (Cambridge: Cambridge University Press, 1998)

Naquin, Susan, *Peking: Temples and City Life* (Berkeley: University of California Press, 2000)

Rossabi, Morris, *China and Inner Asia from 1368 to the Present Day* (New York: Pica Press, 1975)

Serruys, Henry, *The Mongols and Ming China: Customs and History* (London: Variorum Reprints, 1987)

– 'Chinese in Southern Mongolia during the Sixteenth Century', *Monumenta Serica* 18 (1959), pp. 1–95

– 'Sino-Mongol Relations during the Ming, II. The Tribute System and Diplomatic Missions (1400–1600)', *Mélanges Chinois et Bouddhiques,* 14 (1969)

– 'Sino-Mongol Relations during the Ming, III. Trade Relations: The Horse Fairs (1499–1600)', *Mélanges Chinois et Bouddhiques,* 18 (1975)

– 'Towers in the Northern Frontier Defenses of the Ming', *Ming Studies,* 14 (Spring 1982), pp. 8–76

Spence, Jonathan D., and Wills, John E. (eds.), *From Ming to Qing: Conquest, Region, and Continuity in Seventeenth-Century China* (New Haven: Yale University Press, 1979)

Tsai, Henry Shih-shan, *The Eunuchs of the Ming Dynasty* (Albany, New York: State University of New York, 1996)

Wakeman Jr, Frederic, *The Great Enterprise: The Manchu Reconstruction of Imperial Order in Seventeenth-Century China*, 2 vols. (Berkeley: University of California Press, 1985)

– 'The Shun Interregnum of 1644', in *From Ming to Qing*, ed. Spence and Wills, pp. 41–87

The Qing

Fairbank, John K. (ed.), *The Cambridge History of China Volume 10, Part One: Late Ch'ing 1800–1911* (Cambridge: Cambridge University Press, 1978)

Fairbank, John K., and Kwang-Ching Liu (eds.), *The Cambridge History of China Volume 11, Part Two: Late Ch'ing 1800–1911* (Cambridge: Cambridge University Press, 1980)

Kuhn, Philip A., *Soulstealers: The Chinese Sorcery Scare of 1768* (Cambridge, Mass.: Harvard University Press, 1990)

Peterson, Willard J. (ed.), *The Cambridge History of China Volume 9, Part One: The Ch'ing Empire to 1800* (Cambridge: Cambridge University Press, 2002)

Spence, Jonathan D., *Emperor of China: Self-Portrait of Kang-Hsi* (New York: Knopf, 1974)

The Twentieth Century to the Present Day

Bergère, Marie-Claire, *Sun Yat-sen*, trans. Janet Lloyd (Stanford: Stanford University Press, 1998)

Buruma, Ian, *Bad Elements: Chinese Rebels from Los Angeles to Beijing* (London: Weidenfeld and Nicolson, 2002)

The Cambridge History of China Volumes 12–15 (Cambridge: Cambridge University Press, 1983–)

Chang, Jung and Halliday, Jon, *Mao: The Unknown Story* (London: Jonathen Cape, 2005)

Coble, Parks M., *Facing Japan: Chinese Politics and Japanese Imperialism, 1931–37* (Cambridge, Mass.: Council on East Asian Studies, Harvard University, 1991)

Garside, Roger, *Coming Alive: China after Mao* (London: André Deutsch, 1981)

Junshi kexueyuan junshi lishi yanjiubu, *Zhong guo kang ri zhan zheng shi*, 2 vols. (Beijing: Jiefangjun chubanshe, 1991–4)

Li Yu-ning (ed.), *The Politics of Historiography: The First Emperor of China* (New York: International Arts and Sciences Press, 1975)

MacFarquhar, Roderick (ed.), *The Politics of China Second Edition: The Eras of Mao and Deng* (Cambridge: Cambridge University Press, 1997)

Salisbury, Harrison. *The Long March: The Untold Story* (New York: Harper and

Row, 1985)

Schwarcz, Vera, *The Chinese Enlightenment: Intellectuals and the Legacy of the May Fourth Movement of 1919* (Berkeley: California University Press, 1986)

Selden, Mark, *China in Revolution: The Yenan Way Revisited* (New York: M. E. Sharpe, 1995)

Short, Philip, *Mao: A Life* (London: John Murray, 2004)

Snow, Edgar, *Red Star over China* (Harmondsworth: Penguin, 1972)

Studwell, Joe, *The China Dream: The Elusive Quest for the Greatest Untapped Market on Earth* (London: Profile Books, 2002)

Su Xiaokang and Wang Luxiang, Deathsong of the River: *A Reader's Guide to the Chinese TV Series* Heshang, trans. Richard W. Bodman and Pin P. Wan (Ihaca: East Asia Program, Cornell University, 1991)

Teng Ssu-yü and Fairbank, John K. (eds.), *China's Response to the West: A Documentary Survey, 1839–1923* (Cambridge, Mass.: Harvard University Press, 1954)

U.S. Military Intelligence Reports: China 1911–41 (Frederick, MD: University Publications of America, 1983)

Van de Ven, Hans J., *War and Nationalism in China 1925–1945* (London: RoutledgeCurzon, 2003)

Wilbur, C. Martin, *Frustrated Patriot* (New York: Columbia University Press, 1976)

Zha Jianying, *China Pop: How Soap Operas, Tabloids and Bestseller are Transforming a Culture* (New York: The New Press, 1995)

Zhao, Suisheng, *A Nation-State by Construction: Dynamics of Modern Chinese Nationalism* (Stanford: Stanford University Press, 1994)

THE INTERNET AND THE GREAT FIREWALL OF CHINA

Barmé, Geremie R., and Sang Ye, 'The Great Firewall of China', *Wired,* 5.06 (June 1997), http://www.wired.com/wired/5.06/china_pr.html http://chinadigitaltimes.net

Kurlantzick, Joshua, 'Dictatorship.com: The Web Won't Topple Tyranny', *New Republic,* 230.12 (4 May 2004)

Qiu, Jack Linchuan, 'The Internet in China: Data and Issues', paper obtained from author

– 'Chinese Nationalism on the Net: An Odd Myth with Normalcy', paper presented at NCA Annual Convention, Atlanta, 1–4 November 2001

– 'Chinese Hackerism in Retrospect: The Legend of a New Revolutionary Army', *MFC Insight* (17 September 2002)

Xiao Qiang, 'Words You Never See in Chinese Cyberspace', http://chinadigitaltimes.net/2004/08/the_words_you_n.php (30 August 2004)

Young, Edward, 'The Internet: Beyond the Great Firewall', *China Economic Quarterly* (11 November 2002)

WESTERN IMPRESSIONS OF CHINA
AND ITS WALLS

There is a vast amount of primary material in this subject area; the titles mentioned below are a tiny selection of the travelogues and accounts that I found useful. As for secondary works, the most wide-ranging and elegant writer on Western impressions of China is undoubtedly Jonathan Spence; see also Alain Peyrefitte's eloquent account of the 1793 Macartney mission to China.

Aldridge, A. Owen, 'Voltaire and the Cult of China', *Tamkang Review*, 2.2–3.1 (1971–2), pp. 25–49

Andrews, Roy Chapman, *Across Mongolian Plains* (London: D. Appleton & Co., 1921)

Avril, Philippe, *Travels into divers Parts of Europe and Asia* (London: Tim. Goodwin, 1693)

Barrow, Sir John, *Travels in China* (London: T. Cadell and W. Davies, 1806)

Barzini, Luigi, *Pekin to Paris: An account of Prince Borghese's journey across two continents in a motor-car* (London: E. Grant Richard, 1907)

Cameron, Nigel, *Barbarians and Mandarins: Thirteen Centuries of Western Travellers in China* (Hong Kong and Oxford: Oxford University Press, 1989)

Cranmer-Byng, J. L. (ed.), *An Embassy to China Being the Journal Kept by Lord Macartney During his Embassy to the Emperor Ch'ien-lung, 1793–94* (London: Longmans, 1962)

De Rhodes, Alexandre, *Divers voyages de la Chine et autres royaumes de l'Orient* (Paris: Christophe Iournel, 1681)

Du Halde, Jean Baptiste, *A Description of the Empire of China...*, 2 vols. (London: Edward Cave, 1738–41)

Dunne, George H., *Generation of Giants: The Story of the Jesuits in China in the Last Decades of the Ming Dynasty* (London: Burns and Oates, 1962)

Fleming, George, *Travels on Horseback in Mantchu Tartary: being a summer ride beyond the great wall of China* (London: Hurst and Blackett, 1863)

Geil, William Edgar, *The Great Wall of China* (New York: Sturgis and Walton Company, 1909)

Guy, Basil, 'The French Image of China before and after Voltaire', *Studies on Voltaire and the Eighteenth Century*, 21 (1963)

Hayes, L. N., *The Great Wall of China* (Shanghai: Kelly and Walsh, 1929)

Hearsey, John E. N., *Voltaire* (London: Constable, 1976)

Kircher, Athanasius, SJ, *China monumenti qua sacris qua profanis, Illustrata,* trans. Charles D. Van Tuyl (Oklahoma: Indian University Press, Bacone College, 1987)

Le Comte, Louis D., *Memoirs and Observations* ... (London: Benj. Tooke, 1698)

Martini, Martino, *Novus Atlas Sinensis* (Amsterdam: Joan Blaeu, 1655)

Murdock, Victor, *China, the Mysterious and Marvellous* (New York: Chicago, 1920)

Peyrefitte, Alain, *The Collision of Two Civilisations: The British Expedition to China in 1792–4,* trans. Jon Rothschild (London: Harvill, 1993)

Polo, Marco, *The Travels,* trans. R. E. Latham (Harmondsworth: Penguin, 1980)

Ricci, Matteo, *China in the Sixteenth Century: The Journals of Matthew Ricci: 1583–1610,* trans. Louis J. Gallagher, SJ (New York: Random House, 1953)

Spence, Jonathan, *The China Helpers: Western Advisers in China 1620–1960* (London: Bodley Head, 1969)

– *The Chan's Great Continent: China in Western Minds* (London: Allen Lane, Penguin, 1999)

Staunton, Sir George Leonard, *An authentic account of an embassy from the King of Great Britain to the Emperor of China* ... (London: G. Nicol, 1798)

Thurin, Susan Schoenbauer, *Victorian Travellers and the Opening of China* (Ohio: Ohio University Press, 1999)

Voltaire, *Lettres chinoises, indiennes et tartares* (Paris: [s.n.], 1776)

– *An essay on universal history,* trans. Thomas Mugent (Edinburgh: William Creech, 1782)

– *Dictionnaire Philosophique* (Amsterdam: Marc-Michel Rey, 1789)

– *Dictionnaire Philosophique* (Paris: Garnier frères, 1954)

– *Philosophical Dictionary,* 2 vols., trans. Peter Gay (New York: Basic Books, 1962)

Warwick, Adam, 'A Thousand Miles along the Great Wall of China', *National Geographic Magazine,* 43.2 (February 1923), pp. 113–43

INDEX

Ma, Shun 199
Macartney, Lord 2–10, 12, 55, 258–9, 285
Macmillan's Magazine 293
Macao 2, 4, 262, 269, 279
Manchuria/Manchus 17, 18, 31–2, 101–2,
    103, 119, 160–61, 164, 229, 231–2, 234,
    241–2, 246, 247–50, 253–7, 258, 300
'Mandate of Heaven' 118, 148, 160, 233
Mao, Yenshou 89
Mao, Zedong 11, 31, 53, 149, 202, 308–9,
    311, 313, 314–16, 318, 319–22, 326–7,
    335, 343
Maodun 66–9, 96, 98, 99
Martini, Martino 266
May Fourth Movement 197–8, 301, 302–3,
    304
Meng, Jiangnu 322
*Meng Jiangnu was a pro-Confucian, Anti-Legalist
    Great Poisonous Weed* 322
Meng, Tian 53–4, 59, 61–2, 64, 67, 137
Ming dynasty 15, 17, 31, 55–6, 76, 102, 148,
    181–209, 210–31, 233, 236–41, 243–51,
    257, 259–60
    wall-building 107, 166, 179, 180, 184,
    188–90, 201, 205, 206–9, 214–16,
    219–22, 223–6, 227–30, 232, 259–60,
    265
Mongolia/Mongols 14–17, 26, 31–2, 37, 39,
    42, 43, 64, 66–74, 119, 160, 170–76,
    178, 184–6, 187–92, 196–8, 199–208,
    210–19, 230, 243, 244, 246
Mu, Zimei 344
Murong, Jun (emperor) 102

Nan, Zhong 110
National Geographic 292
national identity 30–31, 48–9
Nationalist Party 305–9, 313–16, 321
Natural History of Religion (Hume) 278
Needham, Joseph 11
Nixon, Richard 11, 323, 326–7
Nurhaci 231, 234, 242, 310

Once a Week 293
opium 9, 285, 287
    wars 5, 9–10, 283–4, 286–7, 297
Ordos 33–4, 41, 58–9, 64, 67, 71, 91, 97,
    126, 200, 202–6

Parish, Henry William 8
Pelliot, Paul 77
People's Daily 322, 328, 340
Philosphical Dictionary (Voltaire) 274, 276–7
Plan for National Reconstruction 300–303
poetry, frontier 150–57
Polo, Marco 76, 176–7
Puyi (emperor) 310

Qi dynasty 41, 53–4, 99, 120
    wall-building 120–21
Qiang 72
Qianlong (emperor) 1–3, 5–6, 258, 264, 271,
    276, 285
Qin dynasty 38, 41–6, 47, 49–65, 67, 68, 83,
    135–7, 160
    wall-building 47–65, 67–8, 100, 136, 273
Qin Shihuang (emperor) 45, 47, 49, 51–63,
    118, 137, 292, 302, 322, 334–5
    see also First Emperor
Qing dynasty 17, 138, 148, 257–60, 262–4,
    276, 283–6

Ran'gan 129–30, 134
Reporters Without Borders 341
republicanism 299–37
revolution 299–300, 303–13
    cultural 320–22, 327, 329
Ricci, Matteo 237, 271, 272–3
Ripley, Robert 10, 55
River Elegy (Su) 333–6, 337
road-building 55
Robinson Crusoe (Defoe) 281
Rong 31, 38, 39, 50
Rong, Erzhu 115–16
Rouran 104–5, 115, 119
Russell, Henry 289

Schall, Adam 262, 263, 271
Science and Civilisation in China (Needham) 11
script 29–31, 35
Shang dynasty 29–30, 31, 36, 37, 193
Shang, Yang 52–3
Shetu 124–6
Shizu (emperor) 105–7
Shu-han 99
Shun dynasty 233, 252
Silk Road 74–81, 142–3